ANTHROPOLOGY
92/93

Fifteenth Edition

Editor

Elvio Angeloni
Pasadena City College

Elvio Angeloni received his B.A. from UCLA in 1963, his
M.A. in anthropology from UCLA in 1965, and his M.A. in
communication arts from Loyola Marymount University in
1976. He has produced several films, including "Little
Warrior," winner of the Cinemedia VI Best Bicentennial
Theme, and "Broken Bottles," shown on PBS. He most
recently served as an academic advisor on the instructional
television series, "Faces of Culture."

Annual Editions
A Library of Information from the Public Press

Cover illustration by Mike Eagle

The Dushkin Publishing Group, Inc.
Sluice Dock, Guilford, Connecticut 06437

The Annual Editions Series

Annual Editions is a series of over 55 volumes designed to provide the reader with convenient, low-cost access to a wide range of current, carefully selected articles from some of the most important magazines, newspapers, and journals published today. Annual Editions are updated on an annual basis through a continuous monitoring of over 300 periodical sources. All Annual Editions have a number of features designed to make them particularly useful, including topic guides, annotated tables of contents, unit overviews, and indexes. For the teacher using Annual Editions in the classroom, an Instructor's Resource Guide with test questions is available for each volume.

VOLUMES AVAILABLE

Africa
Aging
American Government
American History, Pre-Civil War
American History, Post-Civil War
Anthropology
Biology
Business and Management
Business Ethics
Canadian Politics
China
Comparative Politics
Computers in Education
Computers in Business
Computers in Society
Criminal Justice
Drugs, Society, and Behavior
Early Childhood Education
Economics
Educating Exceptional Children
Education
Educational Psychology
Environment
Geography
Global Issues
Health
Human Development
Human Resources
Human Sexuality
International Business
Japan
Latin America

Life Management
Macroeconomics
Management
Marketing
Marriage and Family
Microeconomics
Middle East and the Islamic World
Money and Banking
Nutrition
Personal Growth and Behavior
Physical Anthropology
Psychology
Public Administration
Race and Ethnic Relations
Social Problems
Sociology
Soviet Union (Commonwealth of Independent States and Central Europe)
State and Local Government
Third World
Urban Society
Violence and Terrorism
Western Civilization, Pre-Reformation
Western Civilization, Post-Reformation
Western Europe
World History, Pre-Modern
World History, Modern
World Politics

Library of Congress Cataloging in Publication Data
Main entry under title: Annual editions: Anthropology. 1992/93.
    1. Anthropology—Periodicals. I. Angeloni, Elvio, *comp.* II. Title: Anthropology.
301.2   74–84595   ISBN 1–56134–079–0
GN 325.A53

Fifteenth Edition

Manufactured by The Banta Company, Harrisonburg, Virginia 22801

To the Reader

In publishing ANNUAL EDITIONS we recognize the enormous role played by the magazines, newspapers, and journals of the *public press* in providing current, first-rate educational information in a broad spectrum of interest areas. Within the articles, the best scientists, practitioners, researchers, and commentators draw issues into new perspective as accepted theories and viewpoints are called into account by new events, recent discoveries change old facts, and fresh debate breaks out over important controversies.

Many of the articles resulting from this enormous editorial effort are appropriate for students, researchers, and professionals seeking accurate, current material to help bridge the gap between principles and theories and the real world. These articles, however, become more useful for study when those of lasting value are carefully *collected, organized, indexed,* and *reproduced* in a *low-cost format*, which provides easy and permanent access when the material is needed. That is the role played by *Annual Editions*. Under the direction of each volume's *Editor*, who is an expert in the subject area, and with the guidance of an *Advisory Board*, we seek each year to provide in each *ANNUAL EDITION* a current, well-balanced, carefully selected collection of the best of the public press for your study and enjoyment. We think you'll find this volume useful, and we hope you'll take a moment to let us know what you think.

The fifteenth edition of *Annual Editions: Anthropology* contains a variety of articles on contemporary issues in social and cultural anthropology. In contrast to the broad range of topics and minimum depth typical of standard textbooks, this anthology provides an opportunity to read firsthand accounts by anthropologists of their own research. By allowing scholars to speak for themselves about the issues on which they are expert, we are better able to understand the kinds of questions anthropologists ask, the ways in which they ask them, and how they go about searching for answers. Where there is disagreement among anthropologists, this format allows readers to draw their own conclusions.

Given the very broad scope of anthropology—in time, space, and subject matter—the present collection of highly readable articles has been selected according to certain criteria. The articles have been chosen from both professional and nonprofessional publications for the purpose of supplementing the standard cultural anthropology textbook that is used in introductory courses. Some of the articles are considered classics in the field, while others have been selected for their timely relevance.

Included in this volume are a number of features designed to make it useful for students, researchers, and professionals in the field of anthropology. While the articles are arranged along the lines of broadly unifying themes, the *topic guide* can be used to establish specific reading assignments tailored to the needs of a particular course of study. Other useful features include the *table of contents abstracts*, which summarize each article and present key concepts in bold italics, and a comprehensive *index*. In addition, each unit is preceded by an overview that provides a background for informed reading of the articles, emphasizes critical issues, and presents *challenge questions*.

Annual Editions: Anthropology 92/93 will continue to be updated annually. Those involved in producing this volume wish to make the next one as useful and effective as possible. Your criticism and advice is welcomed. Please fill out the article rating form on the last page of the book and let us know your opinions. Any anthology can be improved. This continues to be—annually.

Elvio Angeloni
Editor

Contents

Unit 1

Anthropological Perspectives

Five selections examine the role of anthropologists in studying different cultures. The innate problems in developing productive relationships between anthropologists and exotic cultures are considered by reviewing a number of fieldwork experiences.

The concepts in bold italics are developed in the article. For further expansion please refer to the Topic Guide and the Index.

Unit 2

Culture and Communication

Four selections discuss communication as an element of culture. Ingrained social and cultural values have a tremendous effect on an individual's perception or interpretation of both verbal and nonverbal communication.

Unit 3

The Organization of Society and Culture

Seven selections discuss the influence of the environment and culture on the organization of the social structure of groups.

The concepts in bold italics are developed in the article. For further expansion please refer to the Topic Guide and the Index.

Unit 4

Other Families, Other Ways

Four selections examine some of the influences on the family structure of different cultures. The strength of the family unit is affected by both economic and social pressures.

The concepts in bold italics are developed in the article. For further expansion please refer to the Topic Guide and the Index.

Unit 5

Sex Roles and Statuses

Five selections discuss some of the sex roles prescribed by the social, economic, and political forces of a culture.

The concepts in bold italics are developed in the article. For further expansion please refer to the Topic Guide and the Index.

Unit 6

Religion, Belief, and Ritual

Eight selections examine the role of ritual, religion, and belief in a culture. The need to develop a religion is universal among societies.

The concepts in bold italics are developed in the article. For further expansion please refer to the Topic Guide and the Index.

Unit 7

Sociocultural Change: The Impact of the West

Twelve articles examine the influence that the developed world has had on primitive cultures. Exposure to the industrial West often has disastrous effects on the delicate balance of a primitive society.

The concepts in bold italics are developed in the article. For further expansion please refer to the Topic Guide and the Index.

The concepts in bold italics are developed in the article. For further expansion please refer to the Topic Guide and the Index.

Topic Guide

This topic guide suggests how the selections in this book relate to topics of traditional concern to students and professionals involved with the study of anthropology. It can be very useful in locating articles that relate to each other for reading and research. The guide is arranged alphabetically according to topic. Articles may, of course, treat topics that do not appear in the topic guide. In turn, entries in the topic guide do not necessarily constitute a comprehensive listing of all the contents of each selection.

TOPIC AREA	TREATED IN:	TOPIC AREA	TREATED IN:
Acculturation	15. Symbolism of the Turban 36. Growing Up as a Fore 37. Transformation of the Kalahari !Kung 38. Has Success Spoiled the Sherpas? 39. Trouble in Paradise 42. Bicultural Conflict 43. Inuit Youth in a Changing World 44. Back on the Land	Cultural Relativity and Ethnocentrism	1. Doing Fieldwork Among the Yąnomamö 4. Eating Christmas in the Kalahari 5. Are the Horrors of Cannibalism Fact or Fiction? 33. Body Ritual Among the Nacirema 42. Bicultural Conflict
Aggression and Violence	5. Are the Horrors of Cannibalism Fact or Fiction? 16. Gauging the Winds of War 23. Global War Against Women 30. Dark Side of the Shaman 31. The Real Vampire 32. Rituals of Death 34. Death and Taxes 40. Dark Dreams About the White Man 41. Amazon Tragedy 42. Bicultural Conflict	Culture Shock	1. Doing Fieldwork Among the Yąnomamö 39. Trouble in Paradise 41. Amazon Tragedy 42. Bicultural Conflict 43. Inuit Youth in a Changing World
Cannibalism	5. Are the Horrors of Cannibalism Fact or Fiction?	Ecology and Society	10. Blood in Their Veins 13. Mystique of the Masai 14. Life Without Chiefs 16. Gauging the Winds of War 18. When Brothers Share a Wife 21. Society and Sex Roles 35. Why Can't People Feed Themselves? 37. Transformation of the Kalahari !Kung 39. Trouble in Paradise 41. Amazon Tragedy 43. Inuit Youth in a Changing World 44. Back on the Land 45. Easter Island
Children and Child Care	17. Memories of a !Kung Girlhood 19. Young Traders of Northern Nigeria 20. Child Care in China 27. Mbuti Pygmies 42. Bicultural Conflict 43. Inuit Youth in a Changing World		
Cooperation, Sharing, and Altruism	4. Eating Christmas in the Kalahari 10. Blood in Their Veins 20. Child Care in China 37. Transformation of the Kalahari !Kung 43. Inuit Youth in a Changing World	Economic and Political Systems	2. Doctor, Lawyer, Indian Chief 11. Trading With the Eskimos 13. Mystique of the Masai 14. Life Without Chiefs 18. When Brothers Share a Wife 19. Young Traders of Northern Nigeria 21. Society and Sex Roles 34. Death and Taxes 35. Why Can't People Feed Themselves? 37. Transformation of the Kalahari !Kung 45. Easter Island
Cross-Cultural Experience	1. Doing Fieldwork Among the Yąnomamö 2. Doctor, Lawyer, Indian Chief 3. Amazon Journey 4. Eating Christmas in the Kalahari 38. Has Success Spoiled the Sherpas? 39. Trouble in Paradise 40. Dark Dreams About the White Man 42. Bicultural Conflict 43. Inuit Youth in a Changing World	Ethnographic Fieldwork	1. Doing Fieldwork Among the Yąnomamö 2. Doctor, Lawyer, Indian Chief 3. Amazon Journey 4. Eating Christmas in the Kalahari 5. Are the Horrors of Cannibalism Fact or Fiction?
Cultural Diversity	6. Mother Tongue 7. World's Language 42. Bicultural Conflict 43. Inuit Youth in a Changing World	Health and Welfare	23. Global War Against Women 33. Body Ritual Among the Nacirema 35. Why Can't People Feed Themselves? 41. Amazon Tragedy 43. Inuit Youth in a Changing World
Cultural Identity	13. Mystique of the Masai 15. Symbolism of the Turban 38. Has Success Spoiled the Sherpas? 39. Trouble in Paradise 42. Bicultural Conflict 43. Inuit Youth in a Changing World		

TOPIC AREA	TREATED IN:	TOPIC AREA	TREATED IN:
Hunter-Collectors	10. Blood in Their Veins 11. Trading With the Eskimos 14. Life Without Chiefs 17. Memories of a !Kung Girlhood 27. Mbuti Pygmies 37. Transformation of the Kalahari !Kung 39. Trouble in Paradise 43. Inuit Youth in a Changing World 44. Back on the Land	**Social, Cultural, and Industrial Change**	11. Trading With the Eskimos 12. The Yanomamis 15. Symbolism of the Turban 22. Matter of Honor 25. Primitive Prescription for Equality 26. Psychotherapy in Africa 34. Death and Taxes 35. Why Can't People Feed Themselves? 36. Growing Up as a Fore 37. Transformation of the Kalahari !Kung 38. Has Success Spoiled the Sherpas? 39. Trouble in Paradise 40. Dark Dreams About the White Man 42. Bicultural Conflict 43. Inuit Youth in a Changing World 44. Back on the Land 45. Easter Island
Language	6. Mother Tongue 7. World's Language 8. Language, Appearance, and Reality 42. Bicultural Conflict		
Magic	29. Secrets of Haiti's Living Dead 30. Dark Side of the Shaman 31. The Real Vampire 33. Body Ritual Among the Nacirema	**Social Equality**	14. Life Without Chiefs 23. Global War Against Women 24. Blaming the Victim 25. Primitive Prescription for Equality 27. Mbuti Pygmies
Marriage, Kinship, and Family Systems	17. Memories of a !Kung Girlhood 18. When Brothers Share a Wife 19. Young Traders of Northern Nigeria 20. Child Care in China 21. Society and Sex Roles 22. Matter of Honor 23. Global War Against Women 25. Primitive Prescription for Equality 37. Transformation of the Kalahari !Kung 42. Bicultural Conflict	**Social Relationships**	1. Doing Fieldwork Among the Yanomamö 2. Doctor, Lawyer, Indian Chief 4. Eating Christmas in the Kalahari 9. Who's Interrupting? 15. Symbolism of the Turban 20. Child Care in China 23. Global War Against Women 24. Blaming the Victim 25. Primitive Prescription for Equality 27. Mbuti Pygmies 29. Secrets of Haiti's Living Dead 37. Transformation of the Kalahari !Kung 43. Inuit Youth in a Changing World
Medicine and Healing	26. Psychotherapy in Africa 30. Dark Side of the Shaman 33. Body Ritual Among the Nacirema		
Participant Observation	1. Doing Fieldwork Among the Yanomamö 2. Doctor, Lawyer, Indian Chief 3. Amazon Journey 4. Eating Christmas in the Kalahari	**Trade**	11. Trading With the Eskimos 34. Death and Taxes
Patriarchy	21. Society and Sex Roles 22. Matter of Honor 24. Blaming the Victim 25. Primitive Prescription for Equality	**Values**	4. Eating Christmas in the Kalahari 9. Who's Interrupting? 17. Memories of a !Kung Girlhood 20. Child Care in China 27. Mbuti Pygmies 33. Body Ritual Among the Nacirema 36. Growing Up as a Fore 38. Has Success Spoiled the Sherpas? 39. Trouble in Paradise 42. Bicultural Conflict 43. Inuit Youth in a Changing World 44. Back on the Land
Poverty	35. Why Can't People Feed Themselves? 43. Inuit Youth in a Changing World		
Rituals	15. Symbolism of the Turban 26. Psychotherapy in Africa 27. Mbuti Pygmies 28. Initiation of a Maasai Warrior 29. Secrets of Haiti's Living Dead 30. Dark Side of the Shaman 32. Rituals of Death 33. Body Ritual Among the Nacirema		
Sex Roles/Sexuality	9. Who's Interrupting? 17. Memories of a !Kung Girlhood 18. When Brothers Share a Wife 21. Society and Sex Roles 22. Matter of Honor 23. Global War Against Women 24. Blaming the Victim 42. Bicultural Conflict		

Anthropological Perspectives

For at least a century the goals of anthropology have been to describe societies and cultures throughout the world and to compare the differences and similarities between them. Anthropologists study in a variety of settings and situations, ranging from small hamlets and villages to neighborhoods and corporate offices of major urban centers throughout the world. They study hunters and gatherers, peasants, farmers, labor leaders, politicians, and bureaucrats. They examine religious life in Latin America as well as revolutionary movements.

Wherever practicable, anthropologists take on the role of the "participant observer," for it is through active involvement in the lifeways of the people that they hope to gain an insider's perspective without sacrificing the objectivity of the trained scientist. Sometimes the conditions for achieving such a goal may seem to form an almost insurmountable barrier, but anthropologists' persistence, adaptability, and imagination may be employed to overcome the odds against them.

The diversity of focus in anthropology means that it is earmarked less by its particular subject matter than by its perspective. Although the discipline relates to both the biological and social sciences, anthropologists also know that the boundaries drawn between such disciplines are highly artificial. For example, although it may be possible to examine only the social organization of a family unit or the organization of political power in a nation state, in reality, it is impossible to separate the biological from the social from the economic from the political. The explanatory perspective of anthropology, as the articles in this section exemplify, is to seek out interrelationships among all these factors.

Most of the articles in this section illustrate varying degrees of difficulty an anthropologist may encounter in taking on the role of the participant observer. Napoleon Chagnon's "Doing Fieldwork Among the Yąnomamö" shows, for instance, the hardships imposed by certain physical conditions, the unwillingness of the people to provide needed information, and the vast differences in values and attitudes that must be bridged by the anthropologist just to get along. While Richard Kurin ("Doctor, Lawyer, Indian Chief"), Richard Lee ("Eating Christmas in the Kalahari"), and D. Werner ("Amazon Journey") apparently had fewer problems with the physical conditions and the personalities of the people they were studying, they were not completely accepted by the communities until they found ways to participate as equals in the socio-economic exchange systems.

Since the way in which fieldwork is conducted may have a great deal to do with conclusions reached, and since anthropologists are their own toughest critics, controversy over objectivity has frequently arisen. Witness, for example, Gina Kolata's calling into question historical and anthropological reports of cannibalism ("Are the Horrors of Cannibalism Fact or Fiction?"). Much is at stake in these discussions, since the purpose of anthropology is not only to describe and explain, but to develop a special vision of the world in which cultural alternatives (past, present, and future) can be measured against one another and used as a guide for human action.

Looking Ahead: Challenge Questions

What is culture shock?

How can anthropologists who become personally involved with a community through participant observation maintain their objectivity as scientists?

In what ways do the results of fieldwork depend on the kinds of questions asked?

How does cross-cultural experience help us to understand ourselves?

In what sense is sharing intrinsic to egalitarianism?

How is it that a phenomenon such as cannibalism can be elevated from myth to fact without concrete evidence?

How can we avoid the pitfalls of cultural relativity and ethnocentrism in dealing with what we think of as harmful practices in other cultures?

Doing Fieldwork among the Yąnomamö

Napoleon A. Chagnon

VIGNETTE

The Yąnomamö[1] are thinly scattered over a vast and verdant Tropical Forest, living in small villages that are separated by many miles of unoccupied land. They have no writing, but they have a rich and complex language. Their clothing is more decorative than protective: well-dressed men sport nothing more than a few cotton strings around their wrists, ankles, and waists. They tie the foreskin of their penises to the waistring. Women dress about the same. Much of their daily life revolves around gardening, hunting, collecting wild foods, collecting firewood, fetching water, visiting with each other, gossiping, and making the few material possessions they own: baskets, hammocks, bows, arrows, and colorful pigments with which they paint their bodies. Life is relatively easy in the sense that they can 'earn a living' with about three hours' work per day. Most of what they eat they cultivate in their gardens, and most of that is plantains—a kind of cooking banana that is usually eaten green, either roasted on the coals or boiled in pots. Their meat comes from a large variety of game animals, hunted daily by the men. It is usually roasted on coals or smoked, and is always well done. Their villages are round and open—and very public. One can hear, see, and smell almost everything that goes on anywhere in the village. Privacy is rare, but sexual discreetness is possible in the garden or at night while others sleep. The villages can be as small as 40 or 50 people or as large as 300 people, but in all cases there are many more children and babies than there are adults. This is true of most primitive populations and of our own demographic past. Life expectancy is short.

The Yąnomamö fall into the category of Tropical Forest Indians called 'foot people'. They avoid large rivers and live in interfluvial plains of the major rivers. They have neighbors to the north, Carib-speaking Ye'kwana, who are true 'river people': they make elegant, large dugout canoes and travel extensively along the major waterways. For the Yąnomamö, a large stream is an obstacle and can only be crossed in the dry season. Thus, they have traditionally avoided larger rivers and, because of this, contact with outsiders who usually come by river.

They enjoy taking trips when the jungle abounds with seasonally ripe wild fruits and vegetables. Then, the large village—the *shabono*—is abandoned for a few weeks and everyone camps out a day or so away from the village and garden. On these trips, they make temporary huts from poles, vines, and leaves, each family making a separate hut.

Two major seasons dominate their annual cycle: the wet season, which inundates the low-lying jungle making travel difficult, and the dry season—the time of visiting other villages to feast, trade, and politic with allies. The dry season is also the time when raiders can travel and strike silently at their unsuspecting enemies. The Yąnomamö are still conducting intervillage warfare, a phenomenon that affects all aspects of their social organization, settlement pattern, and daily routines. It is not simply 'ritualistic' war: at least one-fourth of all adult males die violently.

Social life is organized around those same principles utilized by all tribesmen: kinship relationships, descent from ancestors, marriage exchanges between kinship/descent groups, and the transient charisma of distinguished headmen who attempt to keep order in the village and whose responsibility it is to determine the village's relationships with those in other villages. Their positions are largely the result of kinship and marriage patterns—they come from the largest kinship groups within the village. They can, by their personal wit, wisdom, and charisma, become autocrats but most of them are largely "greaters" among equals. They, too, must clear gardens, plant crops, collect wild foods, and hunt. They are simultaneously peacemakers and valiant warriors. Peacemaking often requires the threat or actual use of force, and most headmen have an acquired reputation for being *waiteri*: fierce.

The social dynamics within villages are involved with giving and receiving marriageable girls. Marriages are arranged by older kin, usually men, who are brothers, uncles, and the father. It is a political process, for girls are promised in marriage while they are young, and the men who do this attempt to create alliances with other men via marriage exchanges. There is a shortage of women due in part to a sex-ratio imbalance in the younger age categories, but also complicated by the fact that some men have multiple wives. Most fighting within the village stems from sexual affairs or failure to deliver a promised woman—or out-and-out seizure of a married woman by some other man. This can lead to internal fighting and conflict of such an intensity that villages split up and fission, each group then becoming a new village and, often, enemies to each other.

But their conflicts are not blind, uncontrolled violence. They have a series of graded forms of violence that ranges from chest-pounding and club-fighting duels to out-and-out shooting to kill. This gives them a good deal of flexibility in settling disputes without immediate resort to killing. In addition, they have developed patterns of alliance and friendship that serve to limit violence—trading and feasting with others in order to become friends. These alliances can, and often do, result in intervillage exchanges of marriageable women, which leads to additional amity between villages. No good thing lasts forever, and most alliances crumble. Old friends become hostile and, occasionally, treacherous. Each village must therefore be keenly aware that its neighbors are fickle and must behave accordingly. The thin line between friendship and animosity must be traversed by the village leaders, whose political acumen and strategies are both admirable and complex.

Each village, then, is a replica of all others in a broad sense. But each village is part of a larger political, demographic, and ecological process and it is difficult to attempt to understand the village without knowing something of the larger forces that affect it.

COLLECTING THE DATA IN THE FIELD

I spent 41 months with the Yąnomamö, during which time I acquired some proficiency in their language and, up to a point, submerged myself in their culture and way of life.[2] The thing that impressed me most was the importance of aggression in their culture. I had the opportunity to witness a good many incidents that expressed individual vindictiveness on the one hand and collective bellicosity on the other hand. These ranged in seriousness from the ordinary incidents of wife beating and chest pounding to dueling and organized raids by parties that set out with the intention of ambushing and killing men from enemy villages. One of the villages discussed in the chapters that follow was raided approximately twenty-five times during my first 15 months of fieldwork—six times by the group among whom I was living.

The fact that the Yąnomamö live in a chronic state of warfare is reflected in their mythology, ceremonies, settlement pattern, political behavior, and marriage practices. Accordingly, I have organized this case study in such a way that students can appreciate the effects of warfare on Yąnomamö culture in general and on their social organization and political relationships in particular.

I collected the data under somewhat trying circumstances, some of which I will describe to give the student a rough idea of what is generally meant when anthropologists speak of "culture shock" and "fieldwork." It should be borne in mind, however, that each field situation is in many respects unique, so that the problems I encountered do not necessarily exhaust the range of possible problems other anthropologists have confronted in other areas. There are a few problems, however, that seem to be nearly universal among anthropological fieldworkers, particularly those having to do with eating, bathing, sleeping, lack of privacy, loneliness, or discovering that primitive man is not always as noble as you originally thought—or you yourself not as culturally or emotionally 'flexible' as you assumed.

This is not to state that primitive man everywhere is unpleasant. By way of contrast, I have also done limited fieldwork among the Yąnomamö's northern neighbors, the Carib-speaking Ye'kwana Indians. This group was very pleasant and charming, all of them anxious to help me and honor bound to show any visitor the numerous courtesies of their system of etiquette. In short, they approached the image of primitive man that I had conjured up, and it was sheer pleasure to work with them. Other anthropologists have also noted sharp contrasts in the people they study from one field situation to another. One of the most startling examples of this is in the work of Colin Turnbull, who first studied the Ituri Pygmies (1965, 1983) and found them delightful, but then studied the Ik (1972) of the desolate outcroppings of the Kenya/Uganda/Sudan border region, a people he had difficulty coping with intellectually, emotionally, and physically. While it is possible that the anthropologist's reactions to a particular people are personal and idiosyncratic, it nevertheless remains that there *are* enormous differences between whole peoples, differences that affect the anthropologist in often dramatic ways.

Hence, what I say about some of my experiences is probably equally true of the experiences of many other fieldworkers. I think I could have profited by reading about the pitfalls and field problems of my teachers; at least I might have been able to avoid some of the more stupid errors I made. In this regard there is a growing body of excellent descriptive work on field research. Students who plan to make a career in anthropology should consult these works, which cover a wide range of field situations in the ethnographic present.[3]

The First Day: The Longest One My first day in the field illustrated to me what my teachers meant when they spoke of "culture shock." I had traveled in a small, aluminum rowboat propelled by a large outboard motor for two and a half days. This took me from the territorial capital, a small town on the Orinoco River, deep into Yąnomamö country. On the morning of the third day we reached a small mission settlement, the field "headquarters" of a group of Americans who were working in two Yąnomamö villages. The missionaries had come out of these villages to hold their annual conference on the progress of their mission work and were conducting their meetings when I arrived. We picked up a passenger at the mission station, James P. Barker, the first non-Yąnomamö to make a sustained, permanent contact with the tribe (in 1950). He had just returned from a year's furlough in the United States, where I had earlier visited him before leaving for Venezuela. He agreed to accompany me to the village I had selected for my base of operations to introduce me to the Indians. This village was also his own home base, but he had no been there for over a year and did not plan to join me for another three months. Mr. Barker had been living with this particular group about five years.

We arrived at the village, Bisaasi-teri, about 2:00 P.M. and docked the boat along the muddy bank at the terminus of the path used by the Indians to fetch their drinking water. It was hot and muggy, and my clothing was soaked with perspiration. It clung uncomfortably to my body, as it did thereafter for the remainder of the work. The small biting gnats were out in astronomical numbers, for it was the beginning of the dry season. My face and hands were swollen from the venom of their numerous stings. In just a few moments I was to meet my first Yąnomamö, my first primitive man. What would he be like? I had visions of entering the village and seeing 125 social facts running about calling each other kinship terms and sharing food, each waiting and anxious to have me collect his genealogy. I would wear them out in turn. Would they like me? This was important to me; I wanted them to be so fond of me that they would adopt me into their kinship system and way of life. I had heard that successful anthropologists always get adopted by their people. I had learned during my seven years of anthropological training at the University of Michigan that kinship was equivalent to society in primitive tribes and that it was a moral way of life, "moral" being something "good" and "desirable." I was determined to work my way into their moral system of kinship and become a member of their society—to be 'accepted' by them.

How Did They Accept You? My heart began to pound as we approached the village and heard the buzz of activity within the circular compound. Mr. Barker commented that he was anxious to see if any changes had taken place while he was away and wondered how many of them had died during his absence. I felt into my back pocket to make sure that my notebook was still there and felt personally more secure when I touched it.

The entrance to the village was covered over with brush and dry palm leaves. We pushed them aside to expose the low opening to the village. The excitement of meeting my first Yąnomamö was almost unbearable as I duck-waddled through the low passage into the village clearing.

I looked up and gasped when I saw a dozen burly, naked, sweaty, hideous men staring at us down the shafts of their drawn arrows! Immense wads of green tobacco were stuck between their lower teeth and lips making them look even more hideous, and strands of dark-green slime dripped or hung from their nostrils—strands so long that they clung to their pectoral muscles or drizzled down their chins. We arrived at the village while the men were blowing a hallucinogenic drug up their noses. One of the side effects of the drug is a runny nose. The mucus is always saturated with the green powder and they usually let it run freely from their nostrils. My next discovery was that there were a dozen or so vicious, underfed dogs snapping at my legs, circling me as if I were to be their next meal. I just stood there holding my notebook, helpless and pathetic. Then the stench of the decaying vegetation and filth hit me and I almost got sick. I was horrified. What kind of welcome was this for the person who came here to live with you and learn your way of life, to become friends with you? They put their weapons down when they recognized Barker and returned to their chanting, keeping a nervous eye on the village entrances.

We had arrived just after a serious fight. Seven women had been abducted the day before by a neighboring group, and the local men and their guests had just that morning recovered

five of them in a brutal club fight that nearly ended in a shooting war. The abductors, angry because they had lost five of their seven new captives, vowed to raid the Bisaasi-teri. When we arrived and entered the village unexpectedly, the Indians feared that we were the raiders. On several occasions during the next two hours the men in the village jumped to their feet, armed themselves, and waited nervously for the noise outside the village to be identified. My enthusiasm for collecting ethnographic facts diminished in proportion to the number of times such an alarm was raised. In fact, I was relieved when Barker suggested that we sleep across the river for the evening. It would be safer over there.

As we walked down the path to the boat, I pondered the wisdom of having decided to spend a year and a half with this tribe before I had even seen what they were like. I am not ashamed to admit that had there been a diplomatic way out, I would have ended my fieldwork then and there. I did not look forward to the next day—and months—when I would be left alone with the Indians; I did not speak a word of their language, and they were decidedly different from what I had imagined them to be. The whole situation was depressing, and I wondered why I ever decided to switch from physics and engineering in the first place. I had not eaten all day, I was soaking wet from perspiration, the gnats were biting me, and I was covered with red pigment, the result of a dozen or so complete examinations I had been given by as many pushy Yąnomamö men. These examinations capped an otherwise grim day. The men would blow their noses into their hands, flick as much of the mucus off that would separate in a snap of the wrist, wipe the residue into their hair, and then carefully examine my face, arms, legs, hair, and the contents of my pockets. I asked Barker how to say, "Your hands are dirty"; my comments were met by the Indians in the following way: They would 'clean' their hands by spitting a quantity of slimy tobacco juice into them, rub them together, grin, and then proceed with the examination.

Mr. Barker and I crossed the river

and slung our hammocks. When he pulled his hammock out of a rubber bag, a heavy, disagreeable odor of mildewed cotton came with it. "Even the missionaries are filthy," I thought to myself. Within two weeks, everything I owned smelled the same way, and I lived with that odor for the remainder of the fieldwork. My own habits of personal cleanliness declined to such levels that I didn't even mind being examined by the Yąnomamö, as I was not much cleaner than they were after I had adjusted to the circumstances. It is difficult to blow your nose gracefully when you are stark naked and the invention of handkerchiefs is millenia away.

Life in the Jungle: Oatmeal, Peanut Butter, and Bugs It isn't easy to plop down in the Amazon Basin for a year and get immediately into the anthropological swing of things. You have been told about horrible diseases, snakes, jaguars, quicksand, and getting lost. Some of the dangers are real, but your imagination makes them more real and threatening than many of them really are. What my teachers never bothered to tell me about, however, was the mundane, nonexciting and trivial stuff—like eating, defecating, sleeping, or keeping clean. These turned out to be the bane of my existence during the first several months of field research. I set up my household in Barker's abandoned mud hut, a few yards from the village of Bisaasi-teri, and immediately set to work building my own mud/thatch hut with the help of the Yąnomamö. Meanwhile, I had to eat and try to do my 'field research'. I soon discovered that it was an enormously time-consuming task to maintain my own body in the manner to which it had grown accustomed in the relatively antiseptic environment of the northern United States. Either I would be relatively well fed and relatively comfortable in a fresh change of clothes and do very little fieldwork, or I could do considerably more fieldwork and be less well fed and less comfortable.

It is appalling how complicated it can be to make oatmeal in the jungle. First, I had to make two trips to the river to haul the water. Next, I had to prime my kerosene stove with alcohol to get it burning, a tricky procedure when you are trying to mix powdered milk and fill a coffee pot at the same time: the alcohol prime always burned out before I could turn the kerosene on, and I would have to start all over. Or, I would turn the kerosene on, optimistically hoping that the element was still hot enough to vaporize the fuel, and start a small fire in my palm-thatched hut as the liquid kerosene squirted all over the table and walls and then ignited. Many amused Yąnomamö onlookers quickly learned the English phrase "Oh, Shit!" . . . and, once they discovered that the phrase offended and irritated the missionaries, they used it as often as they could in their presence. I usually had to start over with the alcohol. Then I had to boil the oatmeal and pick the bugs out of it. All my supplies, of course, were carefully stored in rat-proof, moisture-proof, and insect-proof containers, not one of which ever served its purposed adequately. Just taking things out of the multiplicity of containers and repacking them afterward was a minor project in itself. By the time I had hauled the water to cook with, unpacked my food, prepared the oatmeal, milk, and coffee, heated water for dishes, washed and dried the dishes, repacked the food in the containers, stored the containers in locked trunks, and cleaned up my mess, the ceremony of preparing breakfast had brought me almost up to lunch time!

Eating three meals a day was simply out of the question. I solved the problem by eating a single meal that could be prepared in a single container, or, at most, in two containers, washed my dishes only when there were no clean ones left, using cold river water, and wore each change of clothing at least a week—to cut down on my laundry problem—a courageous undertaking in the tropics. I reeked like a jockstrap that had been left to mildew in the bottom of some dark gym locker. I also became less concerned about sharing my provisions with the rats, insects, Yąnomamö, and the elements, thereby eliminating the need for my complicated storage process. I was able to last most of the day on *café con leche*, heavily sugared espresso coffee diluted about five to one with hot milk. I would prepare this in the evening and store it in a large thermos. Frequently, my single meal was no more complicated than a can of sardines and a package of soggy crackers. But at least two or three times a week I would do something 'special' and sophisticated, like make a batch of oatmeal or boil rice and add a can of tuna fish or tomato paste to it. I even saved time by devising a water system that obviated the trips to the river. I had a few sheets of tin roofing brought in and made a rain water trap; I caught the water on the tin surface, funneled it into an empty gasoline drum, and then ran a plastic hose from the drum to my hut. When the drum was exhausted in the dry season, I would get a few Yąnomamö boys to fill it with buckets of water from the river, 'paying' them with crackers, of which they grew all too fond all too soon.

I ate much less when I traveled with the Yąnomamö to visit other villages. Most of the time my travel diet consisted of roasted or boiled green plantains (cooking bananas) that I obtained from the Yąnomamö, but I always carried a few cans of sardines with me in case I got lost or stayed away longer than I had planned. I found peanut butter and crackers a very nourishing 'trail' meal, and a simple one to prepare. It was nutritious and portable, and only one tool was required to make the meal: a hunting knife that could be cleaned by wiping the blade on a convenient leaf. More importantly, it was one of the few foods the Yąnomamö would let me eat in relative peace. It looked suspiciously like animal feces to them, an impression I encouraged.

I referred to the peanut butter as the feces of babies or 'cattle'. They found this disgusting and repugnant. They did not know what 'cattle' were, but were increasingly aware that I ate several canned products of such an animal. Tin cans were thought of as containers made of 'machete skins', but how the cows got inside was always a mystery to them. I went out of my way to describe my foods in such a way as to make them sound unpalatable to them, for it gave me some peace of mind while I ate: they wouldn't beg for a share of something that was too horrible to contemplate. Fieldworkers develop strange defense mechanisms and strategies, and this was one of my own forms of adaptation to the fieldwork. On another occasion I was eating a can of frankfurters and growing very weary of the demands from one of the onlookers for a share in my meal. When he finally asked what I was eating, I replied: "Beef." He then asked: "Shaki![4] What part of the animal are you eating?" To which I replied, "Guess." He muttered a contemptuous epithet, but stopped asking for a share. He got back at me later, as we shall see.

Meals were a problem in a way that had nothing to do with the inconvenience of preparing them. Food sharing is important to the Yąnomamö in context of displaying friendship. "I am hungry!" is almost a form of greeting with them. I could not possibly have brought enough food with me to feed the entire village, yet they seemed to overlook this logistic fact as they begged for my food. What became fixed in their minds was the fact that I did not share my food with whomsoever was present—usually a small crowd—at each and every meal. Nor could I easily enter their system of reciprocity with respect to food: every time one of them 'gave' me something 'freely', he would dog me for months to 'pay him back', not necessarily with food but with knives, fishhooks, axes, and so on. Thus, if I accepted a plantain from someone in a different village while I was on a visit, he would most likely visit me in the future and demand a machete as payment for the time that he 'fed' me. I usually reacted to these kinds of demands by giving a banana, the customary reciprocity in their culture—food for food—but this would be a disappointment for the individual who had nursed visions of that single plantain growing into a machete over time. Many years after beginning my fieldwork I was approached by one of the prominent men who demanded a machete for a piece of meat he claimed he had given me five or six years earlier.

Despite the fact that most of them knew I would not share my food with them at their request, some of them always showed up at my hut during mealtime. I gradually resigned myself to this and learned to ignore their persistent demands while I ate. Some of them would get angry because I failed to give in, but most of them accepted it as just a peculiarity of the subhuman foreigner who had come to live among them. If or when I did accede to a request for a share of my food, my hut quickly filled with Yąnomamö, each demanding their share of the food that I had just given to one of them. Their begging for food was not provoked by hunger, but by a desire to try something new and to attempt to establish a coercive relationship in which I would accede to a demand. If one received something, all others would immediately have to test the system to see if they, too, could coerce me.

A few of them went out of their way to make my meals downright unpleasant—to spite me for not sharing, especially if it was a food that they had tried before and liked, or a food that was part of their own cuisine. For example, I was eating a cracker with peanut butter and honey one day. The Yąnomamö will do almost anything for honey, one of the most prized delicacies in their own diet. One of my cynical onlookers—the fellow who had earlier watched me eating frankfurters—immediately recognized the honey and knew that I would not share the tiny precious bottle. It would be futile to even ask. Instead, he glared at me and queried icily, "Shaki! What kind of animal semen are you pouring onto your food and eating?" His question had the desired effect and my meal ended.

Finally, there was the problem of being lonely and separated from your own kind, especially your family. I tried to overcome this by seeking personal friendships among the Yąnomamö. This usually complicated the matter because all my 'friends' simply used my confidence to gain privileged access to my hut and my cache of steel tools and trade goods—and looted me when I wasn't looking. I would be bitterly disappointed that my erstwhile friend thought no more of me than to finesse our personal relationship exclusively with the intention of getting at my locked up possessions, and my depression would hit new

lows every time I discovered this. The loss of the possessions bothered me much less than the shock that I was, as far as most of them were concerned, nothing more than a source of desirable items. No holds were barred in relieving me of these, since I was considered something subhuman, a non-Yąnomamö.

The hardest thing to learn to live with was the incessant, passioned, and often aggressive demands they would make. It would become so unbearable at times that I would have to lock myself in my hut periodically just to escape from it. Privacy is one of our culture's most satisfying achievements, one you never think about until you suddenly have none. It is like not appreciating how good your left thumb feels until someone hits it with a hammer. But I did not want privacy for its own sake; rather, I simply had to get away from the begging. Day and night for the entire time I lived with the Yąnomamö I was plagued by such demands as: "Give me a knife, I am poor!"; "If you don't take me with you on your next trip to Widokaiya-teri, I'll chop a hole in your canoe!"; "Take us hunting up the Mavaca River with your shotgun or we won't help you!"; "Give me some matches so I can trade with the Reyaboböwei-teri, and be quick about it or I'll hit you!"; "Share your food with me, or I'll burn your hut!"; "Give me a flashlight so I can hunt at night!" "Give me all your medicine, I itch all over!"; "Give me an ax or I'll break into your hut when you are away and steal all of them!" And so I was bombarded by such demands day after day, month after month, until I could not bear to see a Yąnomamö at times.

It was not as difficult to become calloused to the incessant begging as it was to ignore the sense of urgency, the impassioned tone of voice and whining, or the intimidation and aggression with which many of the demands were made. It was likewise difficult to adjust to the fact that the Yąnomamö refused to accept "No" for an answer until or unless it seethed with passion and intimidation—which it did after a few months. So persistent and characteristic is the begging that the early 'semi-official' maps made by the Venezuelan

Malaria Control Service (*Malarialogia*) designated the site of their first permanent field station, next to the village of Bisaasi-teri, as *Yababuhii*; "Gimme." I had to become like the Yąnomamö to be able to get along with them on their terms: somewhat sly, aggressive, intimidating, and pushy.

It became indelibly clear to me shortly after I arrived there that had I failed to adjust in this fashion I would have lost six months of supplies to them in a single day or would have spent most of my time ferrying them around in my canoe or taking them on long hunting trips. As it was, I did spend a considerable amount of time doing these things and did succumb often to their outrageous demands for axes and machetes, at least at first, for things changed as I became more fluent in their language and learned how to defend myself socially as well verbally: I was learning the Yąnomamö equivalent of a left jab to the jawbone. More importantly, had I failed to demonstrate that I could not be pushed around beyond a certain point, I would have been the subject of far more ridicule, theft, and practical jokes than was the actual case. In short, I had to acquire a certain proficiency in their style of interpersonal politics and to learn how to imply subtly that certain potentially undesirable, but unspecified, consequences might follow if they did such and such to me. They do this to each other incessantly in order to establish precisely the point at which they cannot goad or intimidate an individual any further without precipitating some kind of retaliation. As soon as I realized this and gradually acquired the self-confidence to adopt this strategy, it became clear that much of the intimidation was calculated to determine my flash point or my 'last ditch' position—and I got along much better with them. Indeed, I even regained some lost ground. It was sort of like a political, interpersonal game that everyone had to play, but one in which each individual sooner or later had to give evidence that his bluffs and implied threats could be backed up with a sanction. I suspect that the frequency of wife beating is a component in this syndrome, since men can display their *waiteri* (ferocity) and

'show' others that they are capable of great violence. Beating a wife with a club is one way of displaying ferocity, one that does not expose the man to much danger—unless the wife has concerned, aggressive brothers in the village who will come to her aid. Apparently the important thing in wife beating is that the man has displayed his presumed potential for violence and the intended message is that other men ought to treat him with circumspection, caution, and even deference.

After six months, the level of Yąnomamö demand was tolerable in the village I used for my base of operations. We had adjusted somewhat to each other and knew what to expect with regard to demands for food, trade goods and favors. Had I elected to remain in just one Yąnomamö village for the entire duration of my first 15 months of fieldwork the experience would have been far more enjoyable than it actually was. However, as I began to understand the social and political dynamics of this village, it became patently obvious that I would have to travel to many other villages to determine the demographic bases and political histories that lay behind what I could understand in the village of Bisaasi-teri. I began making regular trips to some dozen neighboring Yąnomamö villages as my language fluency improved. I collected local genealogies there, or rechecked and cross-checked those I had collected elsewhere. Hence, the intensity of begging was relatively constant and relatively high for the duration of my fieldwork, for I had to establish my personal flashpoint position in each village I visited and revisited.

For the most part, my own 'fierceness' took the form of shouting back at the Yąnomamö as loudly and as passionately as they shouted at me, especially at first, when I did not know much of the language. As I became more fluent and learned more about their political tactics, I became more sophisticated in the art of bluffing and brinksmanship. For example, I paid one young man a machete (then worth about $2.50) to cut a palm tree and help me make boards from the wood. I used these to fashion a flooring in the bottom of my dugout

canoe to keep my possessions out of the water that always seeped into the canoe and sloshed around. That after noon I was working with one of my informants in the village. The long-awaited mission supply boat arrived and most of the Yą nomamö ran out of the village to see the supplies and try to beg items from the crew. I continued to work in the village for another hour or so and went down to the river to visit with the men on the supply boat. When I reached the river I noticed, with anger and frustration, that the Yąnomamö had chopped up all my new floor boards to use them as crude paddles to get their own canoes across the river to the supply boat.[5] I knew that if I ignored this abuse I would have invited the Yąnomamö to take even greater liberties with my possessions in the future. I got into my canoe, crossed the river, and docked amidst their flimsy, leaky craft. I shouted loudly to them, attracting their attention: they were somewhat sheep-faced, but all had mischievous grins on their impish faces. A few of them came down to the canoe, where I proceeded with a spirited lecture that revealed my anger at their audacity and license: I explained that I had just that morning paid one of them a machete for bringing me the palmwood, how hard I had worked to shape each board and place it in the canoe, how carefully and painstakingly I had tied each one in with vines, how much I perspired, how many gnat bites I had suffered, and so on. Then, with exaggerated drama and finality, I withdrew my hunting knife as their grins disappeared and cut each one of their canoes loose and set it into the strong current of the Orinoco River where it was immediately swept up and carried downstream. I left without looking back and huffed over to the other side of the river to resume my work.

They managed to borrow another canoe and, after some effort, recovered their dugouts. Later, the headman of the village told me, with an approving chuckle, that I had done the correct thing. Everyone in the village, except, of course, the culprits, supported and defended my actions—and my status increased as a consequence.

Whenever I defended myself in such

ways I got along much better with the Yąnomamö and gradually acquired the respect of many of them. A good deal of their demeanor toward me was directed with the forethought of establishing the point at which I would draw the line and react defensively. Many of them, years later, reminisced about the early days of my fieldwork when I was timid and *mobode* ("stupid") and a little afraid of them, those golden days when it was easy to bully me into giving my goods away for almost nothing.

Theft was the most persistent situation that required some sort of defensive action. I simply could not keep everything I owned locked in trunks, and the Yąnomamö came into my hut and left at will. I eventually developed a very effective strategy for recovering almost all the stolen items: I would simply ask a child who took the item and then I would confiscate that person's hammock when he was not around, giving a spirited lecture to all who could hear on the antisociality of thievery as I stalked off in a faked rage with the thief's hammock slung over my shoulder. Nobody ever attempted to stop me from doing this, and almost all of them told me that my technique for recovering my possessions was ingenious. By nightfall the thief would appear at my hut with the stolen item or send it over with someone else to make an exchange to recover his hammock. He would be heckled by his covillagers for having got caught and for being embarrassed into returning my item for his hammock. The explanation was usually, "I just borrowed your ax! I wouldn't think of stealing it!"

Collecting Yąnomamö Genealogies and Reproductive Histories My purpose for living among the Yąnomamö was to systematically collect certain kinds of information on genealogy, reproduction, marriage practices, kinship, settlement pattern, migrations, and politics. Much of the fundamental data was genealogical—who was the parent of whom, tracing these connections as far back in time as Yąnomamö knowledge and memory permitted. Since 'primitive' society is largely organized by kinship relationships, figuring out the social organization of the Yąnomamö es-

sentially meant collecting extensive data on genealogies, marriage, and reproduction. This turned out to be a staggering and very frustrating problem. I could not have deliberately picked a more difficult tribe to work with in this regard. They have very stringent name taboos and eschew mentioning the names of prominent living people as well as all deceased friends and relatives. They attempt to name people in such a way that when the person dies and they can no longer use his or her name, the loss of the word in their language is not inconvenient. Hence, they name people for specific and minute parts of things, such as "toenail of sloth," "whisker of howler monkey," and so on, thereby being able to retain the words "toenail" or "whisker" but somewhat handicapped in referring to these anatomical parts of sloths and monkeys respectively. The taboo is maintained even for the living, for one mark of prestige is the courtesy others show you by not using your name publicly. This is particularly true for men, who are much more competitive for status than women in this culture, and it is fascinating to watch boys grow into young men, demanding to be called either by a kinship term in public, or by a teknonymous reference such as 'brother of Himotoma'. The more effective they are at getting others to avoid using their names, the more public acknowledgement there is that they are of high esteem. Helena Valero, a Brazilian woman who was captured as a child by a Yąnomamö raiding party, was married for many years to a Yąnomamö headman before she discovered what his name was (Biocca, 1970). The sanctions behind the taboo are more complex than just this, for they involve a combination of fear, respect, admiration, political deference, and honor.

I tried to use kinship terms alone to collect genealogies at first, but Yanomamö kinship terms, like the kinship terms in all systems, are ambiguous at some point because the include so many possible relatives (as the term "uncle" does in our own kinship system). Again, their system of kin classification merges many relatives that we 'separate' by using different terms: they

call both their actual father and their father's brother by a single term, whereas we call one "father" and the other "uncle." I was forced, therefore, to resort to personal names to collect unambiguous genealogies or 'pedigrees'. They quickly grasped what I was up to and that I was determined to learn everyone's 'true name', which amounted to an invasion of their system of prestige and etiquette, if not a flagrant violation of it. They reacted to this in a brilliant but devastating manner: They invented false names for everybody in the village and systematically learned them, freely revealing to me the 'true' identities of everyone. I smugly thought I had cracked the system and enthusiastically constructed elaborate genealogies over a period of some five months. They enjoyed watching me learn their names and kinship relationships. I naively assumed that I would get the 'truth' to each question and the best information by working in public. This set the stage for converting my serious project into an amusing hoax of the grandest proportions. Each 'informant' would try to outdo his peers by inventing a name even more preposterous or ridiculous than what I had been given by someone earlier, the explanations for discrepancies being "Well, he has two names and this is the other one." They even fabricated devilishly improbable genealogical relationships, such as someone being married to his grandmother, or worse yet, to his mother-in-law, a grotesque and horrifying prospect to the Yąnomamö. I would collect the desired names and relationships by having my informant whisper the name of the person softly into my ear, noting that he or she was the parent of such and such or the child of such and such, and so on. Everyone who was observing my work would then insist that I repeat the name aloud, roaring in hysterical laughter as I clumsily pronounced the name, sometimes laughing until tears streamed down their faces. The 'named' person would usually react with annoyance and hiss some untranslatable epithet at me, which served to reassure me that I had the 'true' name. I conscientiously checked and rechecked the names and relationships with multiple informants, pleased to see the inconsistencies disappear as my genealogy sheets filled with those desirable little triangles and circles, thousands of them.

My anthropological bubble was burst when I visited a village about 12 hours' walk to the southwest of Bisaasi-teri. I was chatting with the local headman of this village and happened to casually drop the name of the wife of the Bisaasi-teri headman. A stunned silence followed, and then a villagewide roar of uncontrollable laughter, choking, gasping, and howling followed. It seems that the Bisaasi-teri headman was married to a woman named "hairy cunt." It also seems that the Bisaasi-teri headman was called "long dong" and his brother "eagle shit." The Bisaasi-teri headman had a son called "asshole" and a daughter called "fart breath." And so on. Blood welled up to my temples as I realized that I had nothing but nonsense to show for my five months' of dedicated genealogical effort, and I had to throw away almost all the information I had collected on this the most basic set of data I had come there to get. I understood at that point why the Bisaasi-teri laughed so hard when they made me repeat the names of their covillagers, and why the 'named' person would react with anger and annoyance as I pronounced his 'name' aloud.

I was forced to change research strategy—to make an understatement of a serious situation. The first thing I did was to begin working in private with my informants to eliminate the horseplay and distraction that attended public sessions. Once I did this, my informants, who did not know what others were telling me, began to agree with each other and I managed to begin learning the 'real' names, starting first with children and gradually moving to adult women and then, cautiously, adult men, a sequence that reflected the relative degree of intransigence at revealing names of people. As I built up a core of accurate genealogies and relationships—a core that all independent informants had verified repetitiously—I could 'test' any new informant by soliciting his or her opinion and knowledge about these 'core' people whose names and relationships I was confident were accurate. I

was, in this fashion, able to immediately weed out the mischievous informants who persisted in trying to deceive me. Still, I had great difficulty getting the names of dead kinsmen, the only accurate way to extend genealogies back in time. Even my best informants continued to falsify names of the deceased, especially closely related deceased. The falsifications at this point were not serious and turned out to be readily corrected as my interviewing methods improved. Most of the deceptions were of the sort where the informant would give me the name of a living man as the father of some child whose actual father was dead, a response that enabled the informant to avoid using the name of a deceased kinsman or friend.

The quality of a genealogy depends in part on the number of generations it embraces, and the name taboo prevented me from making any substantial progress in learning about the deceased ancestors of the present population. Without this information, I could not, for example, document marriage patterns and interfamilial alliances through time. I had to rely on older informants for this information, but these were the most reluctant informants of all for this data. As I became more proficient in the language and more skilled at detecting fabrications, my informants became better at deception. One of them was particularly cunning and persuasive, following a sort of Mark Twain policy that the most effective lie is a sincere lie. He specialized in making a ceremony out of false names for dead ancestors. He would look around nervously to make sure nobody was listening outside my hut, enjoin me never to mention the name again, become very anxious and spooky, and grab me by the head to whisper a secret name into my ear. I was always elated after a session with him, because I managed to add several generations of ancestors for particular members of the village. Others steadfastly refused to give me such information. To show my gratitude, I paid him quadruple the rate that I had been paying the others. When word got around that I had increased the pay for genealogical and demographic information volunteers be-

gan pouring into my hut to 'work' for me, assuring me of their changed ways and keen desire to divest themselves of the 'truth'.

Enter Rerebawä; Inmarried Tough Guy I discovered that the old man was lying quite by accident. A club fight broke out in the village one day, the result of a dispute over the possession of a woman. She had been promised to a young man in the village, a man named Rerebawä, who was particularly aggressive. He had married into Bisaasi-teri and was doing his 'bride service'—a period of several years during which he had to provide game for his wife's father and mother, provide them with wild foods he might collect, help them in certain gardening and other tasks. Rerebawä had already been given one of the daughters in marriage and was promised her younger sister as his second wife. He was enraged when the younger sister, then about 16 years old, began having an affair with another young man in the village, Bäkotawä, making no attempt to conceal it. Rerebawä challenged Bäkotawä to a club fight. He swaggered boisterously out to the duel with his 10-foot-club, a roof-pole he had cut from the house on the spur of the moment, as is the usual procedure. He hurled insult after insult at both Bäkotawä and his father, trying to goad them into a fight. His insults were bitter and nasty. They tolerated them for a few moments but grew enraged. They came out of their hammocks and ripped out roof-poles, now returning the insults verbally, and rushed to the village clearing. Rerebawä continued to insult them, goading them into striking him on the head with their equally long clubs. Had either of them struck his head—which he held out conspicuously for them to swing at—he would then have the right to take his turn on their heads with his club. His opponents were intimidated by his fury, and simply backed down, refusing to strike him, and the fight ended. He had outbluffed them. All three returned pompously to their respective hammocks, exchanging nasty insults as they departed. But Rerebawä had won the showdown and thereafter swaggered around the village, insulting the two men behind their backs at every opportunity. He was genuinely angry with them, to the point of calling the older man by the name of his long-deceased father. I quickly seized on this incident as an opportunity to collect an accurate genealogy and pumped Rerebawä about this adversary's ancestors. Rerebawä had been particularly 'pushy' with me up to this point, but we soon became warm friends and staunch allies: we were both 'outsiders' in Bisaasi-teri and, although he was a Yanomamö, he nevertheless had to put up with some considerable amount of pointed teasing and scorn from the locals, as all inmarried "sons-in-law" must. He gave me the information I requested of his adversary's deceased ancestors, almost with devilish glee. I asked about dead ancestors of other people in the village and got prompt, unequivocal answers: he was angry with everyone in the village. When I compared his answers to those of the old man, it was obvious that one of them was lying. I then challenged his answers. He explained, in a sort of "you damned fool, don't you know better?" tone of voice that everyone in the village knew the old man was lying to me and gloating over it when I was out of earshot. The names the old man had given to me were names of dead ancestors of the members of a village so far away that he thought I would never have occasion to check them out authoritatively. As it turned out, Rerebawä knew most of the people in that distant village and recognized the names given by the old man.

I then went over the complete genealogical records with Rerebawä, genealogies I had presumed to be close to their final form. I had to revise them all because of the numerous lies and falsifications they contained, much of it provided by the sly old man. Once again, after months of work, I had to recheck everything with Rerebawä's aid. Only the living members of the nuclear families turned out to be accurate; the deceased ancestors were mostly fabrications.

Discouraging as it was to have to recheck everything all over again, it was a major turning point in my fieldwork. Thereafter, I began taking advantage of local arguments and animosities in selecting my informants, and used more extensively informants who had married into the village in the recent past. I also began traveling more regularly to other villages at this time to check on genealogies, seeking out villages whose members were on strained terms with the people about whom I wanted information. I would then return to my base in the village of Bisaasi-teri and check with local informants the accuracy of the new information. If the informants displayed annoyance when I mentioned the new names that I had acquired from informants in distant villages, I was almost certain that the information was accurate. I had to be careful, though, and scrupulously select my local informants in such a way that I would not be inquiring about *their* closely related kin. Thus, for each of my local informants, I had to make lists of names of certain deceased people that I dared not mention in their presence. But despite this precaution, I would occasionally hit a new name that would put my informant into a rage, or into a surly mood, such as that of a dead brother or sister whose existence had not been indicated to me by other informants. This usually terminated my day's work with that informant, for he or she would be too touchy or upset to continue any further, and I would be reluctant to take a chance on accidentally discovering another dead close kinsman soon after discovering the first.

These were always unpleasant experiences, and occasionally dangerous as well, depending on the temperament of my informant. On one occasion I was planning to visit a village that had been raided recently by one of their enemies. A woman, whose name I had on my census list for that village, had been killed by the raiders. Killing women is considered to be bad form in Yanomamö warfare, but this woman was deliberately killed for revenge. The raiders were unable to bushwhack someone who stepped out of the village at dawn to urinate, so they shot a volley of arrows over the roof into the village and beat a hasty retreat. Unfortunately, one of the arrows struck and killed a woman, an accident. For that reason, her village's raiders *deliberately* sought out and killed a woman in retaliation—whose name was on my list. My reason for going to the village was to update my census data on a name-by-name basis and estimate the ages of all the residents. I knew I had the name of the dead woman in my list, but nobody would dare to utter her name so I could remove it. I knew that I would be in very serious trouble if I got to the village and said her name aloud, and I desperately wanted to remove it from my list. I called on one of my regular and usually cooperative informants and asked him to tell me the woman's name. He refused adamantly, explaining that she was a close relative—and was angry that I even raised the topic with him. I then asked him if he would let me whisper the names of *all* the women of that village in his ear, and he would simply have to nod when I hit the right name. We had been 'friends' for some time, and I thought I was able to predict his reaction, and thought that our friendship was good enough to use this procedure. He agreed to the procedure, and I began whispering the names of the women, one by one. We were alone in my hut so that nobody would know what we were doing and nobody could hear us. I read the names softly, continuing to the next when his response was a negative. When I ultimately hit the dead woman's name, he flew out of his chair, enraged and trembling violently, his arm raised to strike me: "You son-of-a-bitch!" he screamed. "If you say her name in my presence again, I'll kill you in an instant!" I sat there, bewildered, shocked, and confused. And frightened, as much because of his reaction, but also because I could imagine what might happen to me should I unknowingly visit a village to check genealogy accuracy without knowing that someone had just died there or had been shot by raiders since my last visit. I reflected on the several articles I had read as a graduate student that explained the "genealogical method," but could not recall anything about its being a potentially hazardous technique. My furious informant left my hut, never again to be invited back to be an informant. I had other similar experiences in different villages, but I was always fortunate in that the dead person had been dead for some time, or was not very closely related to the individual into whose ear I whispered the forbidden name. I was cautioned to desist from saying any more names lest I get people 'angry'.

Kąobawä: The Bisaasi-teri Headman Volunteers to Help Me I had been working on the genealogies for nearly a year when another individual came to my aid. It was Kąobawä, the headman of Upper Bisaasi-teri. The village of Bisaasi-teri was split into two components, each with its own garden and own circular house. Both were in sight of each other. However, the intensity and frequency of internal bickering and argumentation was so high that they decided to split into two separate groups, but would remain close to each other for protection in case they were raided. One group was downstream from the other; I refer to that group as the "Lower" Bisaasi-teri and call Kąobawä's group "Upper" (upstream) Bisaasi-teri, a convenience they themselves adopted after separating from each other. I spent most of my time with the members of Kąobawä's group, some 200 people when I first arrived there. I did not have much contact with Kąobawä during the early months of my work—he was a somewhat retiring, quiet man, and among the Yąnomamö, the outsider has little time to notice the rare quiet ones when most everyone else is in the front row, pushing and demanding attention. He showed up at my hut one day after all the others had left. He had come to volunteer to help me with the genealogies. He was "poor," he explained, and needed a machete. He would work only on the condition that I did not ask him about his own parents and other very close kinsmen who had died. He also added that he would not lie to me as the others had done in the past.

This was perhaps the single most important event in my first year and a half of field research, for out of this incidental meeting evolved a very warm friendship, and what followed from it was a wealth of accurate information on the political history of Kąobawä's village and related villages, highly detailed genealogical information, and hundreds of valuable insights into the Yąnomamö way of like, Kąobawä's familiarity with his group's history and his candidness were remarkable. His knowledge of details was almost encyclopedic, his memory almost photographic. More than that, he was enthusiastic about making sure I learned the truth, and he encouraged me, indeed, demanded that I learn all details I might otherwise have ignored. If there were subtle details he could not recite on the spot, he would advise me to wait until he could check things out with someone else in the village. He would often do this clandestinely, giving me a report the next day, telling me who revealed the new information and whether or not he thought they were in a position to know it. Between Kąobawä and Rerebawä, I made enormous gains in information and understanding toward the end of my first field trip and became lifelong friends with both. And both men knew that I had to get his genealogy from the other one. It was one of those understandings we all had and none of us could mention.

Once again I went over the genealogies with Kąobawä to recheck them, a considerable task by this time: they included about two thousand names, representing several generations of individuals from four different villages. Rerebawä's information was very accurate, and Kąobawä's contribution enabled me to trace the genealogies further back in time. Thus, after nearly a year of intensive effort on genealogies, Yąnomamö demographic patterns and social organization began to make a good deal of sense to me. Only at this point did the patterns through time begin to emerge in the data, and I could begin to understand how kinship groups took form, exchanged women in marriage over several generations, and only then did the fissioning of larger villages into small ones emerge as a chronic and important feature of Yąnomamö social, political, demographic, economic, and ecological adaptation. At this point I was able to begin formulating more sophisticated questions, for there was now a pattern to work from and one to flesh out. Without the help of Rerebawä

and Kacaobawä it would have taken much longer to make sense of the plethora of details I had collected from not only them, but dozens of other informants as well. . . .

Kąobawä was about 40 years old when I first came to his village in 1964. I say "about 40" because the Yąnomamö numeration system has only three numbers: one, two, and more-than-two. It is hard to give accurate ages or dates for events when the informants have no means in their language to reveal such detail. Kąobawä is the headman of his village, meaning that he has somewhat more responsibility in political dealings with other Yąnomamö groups, and very little control over those who live in his group except when the village is being raided by enemies. . . . Most of the time men like Kąobawä are like the North American Indian 'chief' whose authority was characterized in the following fashion: "One word from the chief, and each man does as he pleases." There are different 'styles' of political leadership among the Yąnomamö. Some leaders are mild, quiet, inconspicuous most of the time, but intensely competent. They act parsimoniously, but when they do, people listen and conform. Other men are more tyrannical, despotic, pushy, flamboyant, and unpleasant to all around them. They shout orders frequently, are prone to beat their wives, or pick on weaker men. Some are very violent. I have met headmen who run the entire spectrum between these polar types, for I have visited some 60 Yąnomamö villages. Kąobawä stands at the mild, quietly competent end of the spectrum. He has had six wives thus far—and temporary affairs with as many more, at least one of which resulted in a child that is publicly acknowledged as his child. When I first met him he had just two wives: Bahimi and Koamashima. Bahimi had two living children when I first met her; many others had died. She was the older and enduring wife, as much a friend to him as a mate. Their relationship was as close to what we think of as 'love' in our culture as I have seen among the Yąnomamö. His second wife was a girl of about 20 years, Koamashima. She had a new baby boy when I first met her, her first child. There was speculation that Kạobawä was planning to give Koamashima to one of his younger brothers who had no wife; he occasionally allows his younger brother to have sex with Koamashima, but only if he asks in advance. Kạobawä gave another wife to one of his other brothers because she was *beshi* ("horny"). In fact, this earlier wife had been married to two other men, both of whom discarded her because of her infidelity. Kạobawä had one daughter by her. However, the girl is being raised by Kạobawä's brother, but acknowledged to be Kạobawä's child.

Bahimi, his oldest wife, is about five years younger than he. She is his cross-cousin—his mother's brother's daughter. Ideally, all Yạnomamö men should marry a cross-cousin, as we shall discuss in a later chapter. Bahimi was pregnant when I began my fieldwork, but she destroyed the infant when it was born—a boy in this case—explaining tearfully that she had no choice. The new baby would have competed for milk with Ariwari, her youngest child, who was still nursing. Rather than expose Ariwari to the dangers and uncertainty of an early weaning, she chose to terminate the newborn instead. By Yạnomamö standards, this has been a very warm, enduring marriage. Kạobawä claims he only beats Bahimi 'once in a while, and only lightly' and she, for her part, never has affairs with other men.

Kạobawä is a quiet, intense, wise, and unobtrusive man. It came as something of a surprise to me when I learned that he was the headman of his village, for he stayed at the sidelines while others would surround me and press their demands on me. He leads more by example than by coercion. He can afford to be this way at his age, for he established his reputation for being forthright and as fierce as the situation required when he was younger, and the other men respect him. He also has five mature brothers or half-brothers in his village, men he can count on for support. He also has several other mature 'brothers' (parallel cousins, whom he must refer to as 'brothers' in his kinship system) in the village who frequently come to

his aid, but not as often as his 'real' brothers do. Kạobawä has also given a number of his sisters to other men in the village and has promised his young (8-year-old) daughter in marriage to a young man who, for that reason, is obliged to help him. In short, his 'natural' or 'kinship' following is large, and with this support, he does not have to display his aggressiveness to remind his peers of his position.

Rerebawä is a very different kind of person. He is much younger—perhaps in his early twenties. He has just one wife, but they have already had three children. He is from a village called Karohi-teri, located about five hours' walk up the Orinoco, slightly inland off to the east of the river itself. Kạobawä's village enjoys amicable relationships with Rerebawä's, and it is for this reason that marriage alliances of the kind represented by Rerebawä's marriage into Kạobawä's village occur between the two groups. Rerebawä told me that he came to Bisaasi-teri because there were no eligible women for him to marry in his own village, a fact that I later was able to document when I did a census of his village and a preliminary analysis of its social organization.[6]

Rerebawä is perhaps more typical than Kạobawä in the sense that he is chronically concerned about his personal reputation for aggressiveness and goes out of his way to be noticed, even if he has to act tough. He gave me a hard time during my early months of fieldwork, intimidating, teasing, and insulting me frequently. He is, however, much braver than the other men his age and is quite prepared to back up his threats with immediate action—as in the club fight incident just described above. Moreover, he is fascinated with political relationships and knows the details of intervillage relationships over a large area of the tribe. In this respect he shows all the attributes of being a headman, although he has too many competent brothers in his own village to expect to easily move into the leadership position there.

He does not intend to stay in Kạobawä's group and refuses to make his own garden—a commitment that would reveal something of an intended long-

term residence. He feels that he has adequately discharged his obligations to his wife's parents by providing them with fresh game for several years. They should let him take his wife and return to his own village with her, but they refuse and try to entice him to remain permanently in Bisaasi-teri to continue to provide them with game when they are old. It is for this reason that they promised to give him their second daughter, their only other child, in marriage. Unfortunately, the girl was opposed to the marriage and ultimately married another man.

Although Rerebawä has displayed his ferocity in many ways, one incident in particular illustrates what his character can be like. Before he left his own village to take his new wife in Bisaasi-teri, he had an affair with the wife of an older brother. When it was discovered, his brother attacked him with a club. Rerebawä responded furiously: he grabbed an ax and drove his brother out of the village after soundly beating him with the blunt side of the single-bit ax. His brother was so intimidated by the thrashing and promise of more to come that he did not return to the village for several days. I visited this village with Kạobawä shortly after this event had taken place; Rerebawä was with me as my guide. He made it a point to introduce me to this man. He approached his hammock, grabbed him by the wrist, and dragged him out on the ground: "This is the brother whose wife I screwed when he wasn't around!" A deadly insult, one that would usually provoke a bloody club fight among more valiant Yạnomamö. The man did nothing. He slunk sheepishly back into his hammock, shamed, but relieved to have Rerebawä release his grip.

Even though Rerebawä is fierce and capable of considerable nastiness, he has a charming, witty side as well. He has a biting sense of humor and can entertain the group for hours with jokes and clever manipulations of his language. And, he is one of few Yạnomamö that I feel I can trust. I recall indelibly my return to Bisaasi-teri after being away a year—the occasion of my second field trip to the Yạnomamö. When I reached Bisaasi-teri, Rerebawä was in his own village visiting his kinsmen. Word reached him that I had returned, and he paddled downstream immediately to see me. He greeted me with an immense bear hug and exclaimed, with tears welling up in his eyes, "Shąki! Why did you stay away so long? Did you not know that my will was so cold while you were gone that I could not at times eat for want of seeing you again?" I, too, felt the same way about him—then, and now.

Of all the Yąnomamö I know, he is the most genuine and the most devoted to his culture's ways and values. I admire him for that, although I cannot say that I subscribe to or endorse some of these values. By contrast, Kąobawä is older and wiser, a polished diplomat. He sees his own culture in a slightly different light and seems to even question aspects of it. Thus, while many of his peers enthusiastically accept the 'explanations' of things given in myths, he occasionally reflects on them—even laughing at some of the more preposterous of them. Probably more of the Yąnomamö are like Rerebawä than like Kąobawä, or at least try to be. . . .

FOOTNOTES

1. The word Yąnomamö is nasalized through its entire length, indicated by the diacritical mark ˙. When this mark appears on any Yąnomamö word, the whole word is nasalized. The vowel 'ö' represents a sound that does not occur in the English language. It is similar to the umlaut 'o' in the German language or the 'oe' equivalent in German, as in the poet Goethe's name. Unfortunately, many presses and typesetters simply eliminate diacritical marks, and this leads to multiple spellings of the word Yąnomamö and multiple mispronunciations. Some anthropologists have chosen to introduce a slightly different spelling of the word Yąnomamö since my work began appearing in print, such as Yąnomami, leading to additional misspellings as diacritics are eliminated by some presses, and to the *incorrect* pronunciation "Yanomameee." Words with a vowel indicated as 'ä' are pronounced as the 'uh' sound in the word 'duck'. Thus, the name Kąobawä would be pronounced "cow-ba-wuh," but entirely nasalized.

2. I spent a total of 41 months among the Yąnomamö between 1964 and 1983. The first edition of this case study was based on the first 15 months I spent among them in Venezuela. By the time the first edition had gotten to press, I had made another field trip of four months' duration and the first edition indicated that the work was based, as it technically was, on 19 months of field research. I have, at the time of this writing, made 10 field trips to the Yąnomamö and plan to return regularly to continue my long-term study.

3. See Spindler (1970) for a detailed discussion of field research by anthropologists who have worked in other cultures.

4. They could not pronounce "Chagnon." It sounded to them like their name for a pesky bee, *shąki,* and that is what they called me: pesky, noisome bee.

5. The Yąnomamö in this region acquired canoes very recently. The missionaries would purchase them from the Ye'kwana Indians to the north for money, and then trade them to the Yąnomamö in exchange for labor, produce, or 'informant' work in translating. It should be emphasized that those Yąnomamö who lived on navigable portions of the Upper Orinoco River moved there from the deep forest in order to have contact with the missionaries and acquire the trade goods the missionaries (and their supply system) brought.

6. In 1980 word reached me from a friend who was doing medical work among the Yąnomamö that Kąobawä's village attacked a village that was a splinter group of Rerebawä's and killed a large number of men. This was confirmed for me in 1982 by an ecologist who was working near that area. What this will do to the relationships between Kąobawä's village and Rerebawä's village in the future is problematic, but their groups are probably on very strained terms now.

Doctor, Lawyer, Indian Chief

*As Punjabi villagers say, "You never really know who a man is
until you know who his grandfather and his ancestors were"*

Richard Kurin

*Richard Kurin is the Deputy Director
of Folklife Programs at the Smithsonian Institution.*

I was full of confidence when—
equipped with a scholarly proposal,
blessings from my advisers, and
generous research grants—I set out
to study village social structure in the
Punjab province of Pakistan. But
after looking for an appropriate
fieldwork site for several weeks without success, I began to think that my
research project would never get off
the ground. Daily I would seek out
villages aboard my puttering motor
scooter, traversing the dusty dirt
roads, footpaths, and irrigation
ditches that crisscross the Punjab.
But I couldn't seem to find a village
amenable to study. The major problem was that the villagers I did approach were baffled by my presence.
They could not understand why anyone would travel ten thousand miles
from home to a foreign country in
order to live in a poor village, interview illiterate peasants, and then
write a book about it. Life, they were
sure, was to be lived, not written
about. Besides, they thought, what of
any importance could they possibly

tell me? Committed as I was to ethnographic research, I readily understood their viewpoint. I was a *babu
log*—literally, a noble; figuratively, a
clerk; and simply, a person of the city.
I rode a motor scooter, wore tight-
fitting clothing, and spoke Urdu, a
language associated with the urban
literary elite. Obviously, I did not
belong, and the villagers simply did
not see me fitting into their society.

The Punjab, a region about the size
of Colorado, straddles the northern
border of India and Pakistan. Parti-
tioned between the two countries in
1947, the Punjab now consists of a
western province, inhabited by Muslims, and an eastern one, populated in
the main by Sikhs and Hindus. As its
name implies—*punj* meaning "five"
and *ab* meaning "rivers"—the region
is endowed with plentiful resources to
support widespread agriculture and a
large rural population. The Punjab
has traditionally supplied grains,
produce, and dairy products to the
peoples of neighboring and considerably more arid states, earning it a
reputation as the breadbasket of
southern Asia.

Given this predilection for agriculture, Punjabis like to emphasize that
they are earthy people, having values
they see as consonant with rural life.
These values include an appreciation
of, and trust in, nature; simplicity and

directness of expression; an awareness of the basic drives and desires
that motivate men (namely, *zan, zar,
zamin*—"women, wealth, land"); a
concern with honor and shame as
abiding principles of social organization; and for Muslims, a deep faith in
Allah and the teachings of his prophet
Mohammad.

Besides being known for its fertile
soils, life-giving rivers, and superla-
tive agriculturists, the Punjab is also
perceived as a zone of transitional
culture, a region that has experienced
repeated invasions of peoples from
western and central Asia into the
Indian subcontinent. Over the last
four thousand years, numerous
groups, among them Scythians, Par-
thians, Huns, Greeks, Moguls, Per-
sians, Afghans, and Turks, have
entered the subcontinent through the
Punjab in search of bountiful land,
riches, or power. Although Punjabis—notably Rajputs, Sikhs, and
Jats—have a reputation for courage
and fortitude on the battlefield, their
primary, self-professed strength has
been their ability to incorporate new,
exogenous elements into their society
with a minimum of conflict. Punjabis
are proud that theirs is a multiethnic
society in which diverse groups have
been largely unified by a common
language and by common customs
and traditions.

Given this background, I had not expected much difficulty in locating a village in which to settle and conduct my research. As an anthropologist, I viewed myself as an "earthy" social scientist who, being concerned with basics, would have a good deal in common with rural Punjabis. True, I might be looked on as an invader of a sort; but I was benevolent, and sensing this, villagers were sure to incorporate me into their society with even greater ease than was the case for the would-be conquering armies that had preceded me. Indeed, they would welcome me with open arms.

I was wrong. The villagers whom I approached attributed my desire to live with them either to neurotic delusions or nefarious ulterior motives. Perhaps, so the arguments went, I was really after women, land, or wealth.

On the day I had decided would be my last in search of a village, I was driving along a road when I saw a farmer running through a rice field and waving me down. I stopped and he climbed on the scooter. Figuring I had nothing to lose, I began to explain why I wanted to live in a village. To my surprise and delight, he was very receptive, and after sharing a pomegranate milkshake at a roadside shop, he invited me to his home. His name was Allah Ditta, which means "God given," and I took this as a sign that I had indeed found my village.

"My" village turned out to be a settlement of about fifteen hundred people, mostly of the Nunari qaum, or "tribe." The Nunaris engage primarily in agriculture (wheat, rice, sugar cane, and cotton), and most families own small plots of land. Members of the Bhatti tribe constitute the largest minority in the village. Although traditionally a warrior tribe, the Bhattis serve in the main as the village artisans and craftsmen.

On my first day in the village I tried explaining in great detail the purposes of my study to the village elders and clan leaders. Despite my efforts, most of the elders were perplexed about why I wanted to live in their village. As a guest, I was entitled to the hospitality traditionally bestowed by Muslim peoples of Asia, and during the first evening I was assigned a place to stay. But I was an enigma, for guests leave, and I wanted to remain. I was also perceived as being strange, for I was both a non-Muslim and a non-Punjabi, a type of person not heretofore encountered by most of the villagers. Although I tried to temper my behavior, there was little I could say or do to dissuade my hosts from the view that I embodied the antithesis of Punjabi values. While I was able to converse in their language, Jatki, a dialect of western Punjabi, I was only able to do so with the ability of a four-year-old. This achievement fell far short of speaking the t'et', or "genuine form," of the villagers. Their idiom is rich with the terminology of agricultural operations and rural life. It is unpretentious, uninflected, and direct, and villagers hold high opinions of those who are good with words, who can speak to a point and be convincing. Needless to say, my infantile babble realized none of these characteristics and evoked no such respect.

Similarly, even though I wore indigenous dress, I was inept at tying my lungi, or pant cloth. The fact that my lungi occasionally fell off and revealed what was underneath gave my neighbors reason to believe that I indeed had no shame and could not control the passions of my nafs, or "libidinous nature."

This image of a doltish, shameless infidel barely capable of caring for himself lasted for the first week of my residence in the village. My inability to distinguish among the five varieties of rice and four varieties of lentil grown in the village illustrated that I knew or cared little about nature and agricultural enterprise. This display of ignorance only served to confirm the general consensus that the mysterious morsels I ate from tin cans labeled "Chef Boy-ar-Dee" were not really food at all. Additionally, I did not oil and henna my hair, shave my armpits, or perform ablutions, thereby convincing some commentators that I was a member of a species of subhuman beings, possessing little in the form of either common or moral sense. That the villagers did not quite grant me the status of a person was reflected by their not according me a proper name. In the Punjab, a person's name is equated with honor and respect and is symbolized by his turban. A man who does not have a name, or whose name is not recognized by his neighbors, is unworthy of respect. For such a man, his turban is said to be either nonexistent or to lie in the dust at the feet of others. To be given a name is to have one's head crowned by a turban, an acknowledgment that one leads a responsible and respectable life. Although I repeatedly introduced myself as "Rashid Karim," a fairly decent Pakistani rendering of Richard Kurin, just about all the villagers insisted on calling me Angrez ("Englishman"), thus denying me full personhood and implicitly refusing to grant me the right to wear a turban.

As I began to pick up the vernacular, to question villagers about their clan and kinship structure and trace out relationships between different families, my image began to change. My drawings of kinship diagrams and preliminary census mappings were looked upon not only with wonder but also suspicion. My neighbors now began to think there might be a method to my madness. And so there was. Now I had become a spy. Of course it took a week for people to figure out whom I was supposedly spying for. Located as they were at a cross-roads of Asia, at a nexus of conflicting geopolitical interests, they had many possibilities to consider. There was a good deal of disagreement on the issue, with the vast majority maintaining that I was either an American, Russian, or Indian spy. A small, but nonetheless vocal, minority held steadfastly to the belief that I was a Chinese spy. I thought it all rather humorous until one day a group confronted me in the main square in front of the nine-by-nine-foot mud hut that I had rented. The leader spoke up and accused me of spying. The remainder of the group grumbled jahsus! jahsus! ("spy! spy!"), and I realized that this ad hoc committee of inquiry had the potential of becoming a mob.

To be sure, the villagers had good reason to be suspicious. For one, the times were tense in Pakistan—a national political crisis gripped the country and the populace had been anxious for months over the uncertainty of elections and effective governmental functions. Second, keenly aware of their history, some of the villagers did not have to go too far to imagine that I was at the vanguard of some invading group that had designs upon their land. Such intrigues, with far greater sophistication, had been played out before by nations seeking to expand their power into the Punjab. That I possessed a gold seal letter (which no one save myself could read) from the University of Chicago to the effect that I was pursuing legitimate studies was not enough to convince the crowd that I was indeed an innocent scholar.

I repeatedly denied the charge, but to no avail. The shouts of *jahsus! jahsus!* prevailed. Confronted with this I had no choice.

"Okay," I said. "I admit it. I am a spy!"

The crowd quieted for my long-awaited confession.

"I am a spy and am here to study this village, so that when my country attacks you we will be prepared. You see, we will not bomb Lahore or Karachi or Islamabad. Why should we waste our bombs on millions of people, on factories, dams, airports, and harbors? No, it is far more advantageous to bomb this strategic small village replete with its mud huts, livestock, Persian wheels, and one light bulb. And when we bomb this village, it is imperative that we know how Allah Ditta is related to Abdullah, and who owns the land near the well, and what your marriage customs are."

Silence hung over the crowd, and then one by one the assemblage began to disperse. My sarcasm had worked. The spy charges were defused. But I was no hero in light of my performance, and so I was once again relegated to the status of a nonperson without an identity in the village.

I remained in limbo for the next week, and although I continued my attempts to collect information about village life, I had my doubts as to whether I would ever be accepted by the villagers. And then, through no effort of my own, there was a breakthrough, this time due to another Allah Ditta, a relative of the village headman and one of my leading accusers during my spying days.

I was sitting on my woven string bed on my porch when Allah Ditta approached, leading his son by the neck. "Oh, *Angrez!*" he yelled, "this worthless son of mine is doing poorly in school. He is supposed to be learning English, but he is failing. He has a good mind, but he's lazy. And his teacher is no help, being more intent upon drinking tea and singing film songs than upon teaching English. Oh son of an Englishman, do you know English?"

"Yes, I know English," I replied, "after all, I am an *Angrez.*"

"Teach him," Allah Ditta blurted out, without any sense of making a tactful request.

And so, I spent the next hour with the boy, reviewing his lessons and correcting his pronunciation and grammar. As I did so, villagers stopped to watch and listen, and by the end of the hour, nearly one hundred people had gathered around, engrossed by this tutoring session. They were stupefied. I was an effective teacher, and I actually seemed to know English. The boy responded well, and the crowd reached a new consensus. I had a brain. And in recognition of this achievement I was given a name—"Ustad Rashid," or Richard the Teacher.

Achieving the status of a teacher was only the beginning of my success. The next morning I awoke to find the village sugar vendor at my door. He had a headache and wanted to know if I could cure him.

"Why do you think I can help you?" I asked.

Bhai Khan answered, "Because you are a *ustad,* you have a great deal of knowledge."

The logic was certainly compelling. If I could teach English, I should be able to cure a headache. I gave him two aspirins.

An hour later, my fame had spread. Bhai Khan had been cured, and he did not hesitate to let others know that it was the *ustad* who had been responsible. By the next day, and in fact for the remainder of my stay, I was to see an average of twenty-five to thirty patients a day. I was asked to cure everything from coughs and colds to typhoid, elephantiasis, and impotency. Upon establishing a flourishing and free medical practice, I received another title, *hakim,* or "physician." I was not yet an anthropologist, but I was on my way.

A few days later I took on yet another role. One of my research interests involved tracing out patterns of land ownership and inheritance. While working on the problem of figuring out who owned what, I was approached by the village watchman. He claimed he had been swindled in a land deal and requested my help. As the accused was not another villager, I agreed to present the watchman's case to the local authorities.

Somehow, my efforts managed to achieve results. The plaintiff's grievance was redressed, and I was given yet another title in the village—*wakil,* or "lawyer." And in the weeks that followed, I was steadily called upon to read, translate, and advise upon various court orders that affected the lives of the villagers.

My roles as teacher, doctor, and lawyer not only provided me with an identity but also facilitated my integration into the economic structure of the community. As my imputed skills offered my neighbors services not readily available in the village, I was drawn into exchange relationships known as *seipi. Seipi* refers to the barter system of goods and services among village farmers, craftsmen, artisans, and other specialists. Every morning Roshan the milkman would deliver fresh milk to my hut. Every other day Hajam Ali the barber would stop by and give me a shave. My next-door neighbor, Nura the cobbler, would repair my sandals when required. Ghulam the horse-cart driver would transport me to town when my motor scooter was in disrepair. The parents of my students would send me sweets and sometimes delicious meals. In return, none of my neighbors asked for direct payment for the specific actions performed. Rather, as they told me, they would call upon me when they had need of my services. And they did. Nura needed cough syrup for his children, the milkman's brother needed a job contact in the city, students wanted to continue their lessons, and so on. Through *seipi* relations, various neighbors gave goods and services to me, and I to them.

Even so, I knew that by Punjabi standards I could never be truly accepted into village life because I was not a member of either the Nunari or Bhatti tribe. As the villagers would say, "You never really know who a man is until you know who his grandfather and his ancestors were." And to know a person's grandfather or ancestors properly, you had to be a member of the same or a closely allied tribe.

The Nunari tribe is composed of a number of groups. The nucleus consists of four clans—Naul, Vadel, Sadan, and More—each named for one of four brothers thought to have originally founded the tribe. Clan members are said to be related to blood ties, also called *pag da sak,* or "ties of the turban." In sharing the turban, members of each clan share the same name. Other clans, unrelated by ties of blood to these four, have become attached to this nucleus through a history of marital relations or of continuous political and economic interdependence. Marital relations, called *gag da sak,* or "ties of the skirt," are conceived of as relations in which alienable turbans (skirts) in the form of women are exchanged with other, non-turban-sharing groups. Similarly, ties of political and economic domination and subordination are thought of as relations in which the turban of the client is given to that of the patron. A major part of my research work was concerned with reconstructing how the four brothers formed the Nunari tribe, how additional clans became associated with

it, and how clan and tribal identity were defined by nomenclature, codes of honor, and the symbols of sharing and exchanging turbans.

To approach these issues I set out to reconstruct the genealogical relationships within the tribe and between the various clans. I elicited genealogies from many of the villagers and questioned older informants about the history of the Nunari tribe. Most knew only bits and pieces of this history, and after several months of interviews and research, I was directed to the tribal genealogists. These people, usually not Nunaris themselves, perform the service of memorizing and then orally relating the history of the tribe and the relationships among its members. The genealogist in the village was an aged and arthritic man named Hedayat, who in his later years was engaged in teaching the Nunari genealogy to his son, who would then carry out the traditional and hereditary duties of his position.

The villagers claimed that Hedayat knew every generation of the Nunari from the present to the founding brothers and even beyond. So I invited Hedayat to my hut and explained my purpose.

"Do you know Allah Ditta son of Rohm?" I asked.

"Yes, of course," he replied.

"Who was Rohm's father?" I continued.

"Shahadat Mohammad," he answered.

"And his father?"

"Hamid."

"And his?"

"Chigatah," he snapped without hesitation.

I was now quite excited, for no one else in the village had been able to recall an ancestor of this generation. My estimate was that Chigatah had been born sometime between 1850 and 1870. But Hedayat went on.

"Chigatah's father was Kamal. And Kamal's father was Nanak. And Nanak's father was Sikhu. And before him was Dargai, and before him Maiy. And before him was Siddiq. And Siddiq's father was Nur. And Nur's Asmat. And Asmat was of Channa.

And Channa of Nau. And Nau of Bhatta. And Bhatta was the son of Koduk."

Hedayat had now recounted sixteen generations of lineal ascendants related through the turban. Koduk was probably born in the sixteenth century. But still Hedayat continued.

"Sigun was the father of Koduk. And Man the father of Sigun. And before Man was his father Maneswar. And Maneswar's father was the founder of the clan, Naul."

This then was a line of the Naul clan of the Nunari tribe, ascending twenty-one generations from the present descendants (Allah Ditta's sons) to the founder, one of four brothers who lived perhaps in the fifteenth century. I asked Hedayat to recite genealogies of the other Nunari clans, and he did, with some blanks here and there, ending with Vadel, More, and Saddan, the other three brothers who formed the tribal nucleus. I then asked the obvious question, "Hedayat, who was the father of these four brothers? Who is the founding ancestor of the Nunari tribe?"

"The father of these brothers was not a Muslim. He was an Indian rajput [chief]. The tribe actually begins with the conversion of the four brothers," Hedayat explained.

"Well then," I replied, "who was this Indian chief?"

He was a famous and noble chief who fought against the Moguls. His name was Raja Kurin, who lived in a massive fort in Kurinnagar, about twenty-seven miles from Delhi."

"What!" I asked, both startled and unsure of what I had heard.

"Raja Kurin is the father of the brothers who make up—"

"But his name! It's the same as mine," I stammered. "Hedayat, my name is Richard Kurin. What a coincidence! Here I am living with your tribe thousands of miles from my home and it turns out that I have the same name as the founder of the tribe! Do you think I might be related to Raja Kurin and the Nunaris?"

Hedayat looked at me, but only for an instant. Redoing his turban, he tilted his head skyward, smiled, and asked, "What is the name of your father?"

I had come a long way. I now had a name that could be recognized and respected, and as I answered Hedayat, I knew that I had finally and irrevocably fit into "my" village. Whether by fortuitous circumstances or by careful manipulation, my neighbors had found a way to take an invading city person intent on studying their life and transform him into one of their own, a full person entitled to wear a turban for participating in, and being identified with, that life. As has gone on for centuries in the region, once again the new and exogenous had been recast into something Punjabi.

Epilogue: There is no positive evidence linking the Nunaris to a historical Raja Kurin, although there are several famous personages identified by that name (also transcribed as Karan and Kurran). Estimated from the genealogy recited by Hedayat, the founding of the tribe by the four brothers appears to have occurred sometime between 440 and 640 years ago, depending on the interval assumed for each generation. On that basis, the most likely candidate for Nunari progenitor (actual or imputed) is Raja Karan, ruler of Anhilvara (Gujerat), who was defeated by the Khilji Ala-ud-Din in 1297 and again in 1307. Although this is slightly earlier than suggested by the genealogical data, such genealogies are often telescoped or otherwise unreliable.

Nevertheless, several aspects of Hedayat's account make this association doubtful. Hedayat clearly identifies Raja Kurin's conquerors as Moguls, whereas the Gujerati Raja Karan was defeated by the Khiljis. Second, Hedayat places the Nunari ancestor's kingdom only twenty-seven miles from Delhi. The Gujerati Raja Karan ruled several kingdoms, none closer than several hundred miles to Delhi.

Other circumstances, however, offer support for this identification of the Nunari ancestor. According to Hedayat, Raja Kurin's father was named Kam Deo. Although the historical figure was the son of Serung Deo, the use of "Deo," a popular title for the rajas of the Vaghela and Solonki dynasties, does seem to place the Nunari founder in the context of medieval Gujerat. Furthermore, Hedayat clearly identifies the saint (pir) said to have initiated the conversion of the Nunaris to Islam. This saint, Mukhdum-i-Jehaniyan, was a contemporary of the historical Raja Karan.

Also of interest, but as yet unexplained, is that several other groups living in Nunari settlement areas specifically claim to be descended from Raja Karan of Gujerat, who is said to have migrated northward into the Punjab after his defeat. Controverting this theory, the available evidence indicates that Raja Karan fled, not toward the Punjab, but rather southward to the Deccan, and that his patriline ended with him. It is his daughter Deval Devi who is remembered: she is the celebrated heroine of "Ashiqa," a famous Urdu poem written by Amir Khusrau in 1316. She was married to Khizr Khan, the son of Karan's conqueror; nothing is known of her progeny.

Amazon Journey

D. Werner

FIRST GLIMPSE

The plane had been flying for two and a half hours over the Amazon valley. During the first half hour I occasionally saw cattle ranches on the ground, but afterwards there was only the quiet green of the forest interrupted now and then by a shimmering stream cutting across what looked from the air like a shag rug. The scenery had lulled me into a dreamy state. But as the tiny plane swooped down over the grassy airstrip, my stomach jumped into my chest. I caught my first glimpse of the Indians I would be studying for the coming year.

Naked children romped playfully among the tall grasses that almost hid them from view. Several women, wearing at most a few beads around their waists or necks, carried nursing infants like shoulder bags in woven straw slings. The men wore either swimming trunks or tiny grass sheaths that tied off their foreskins and made their penises point upwards. One woman held aloft a large black umbrella shading her from the bright sun. A man with a large red wooden disk stretching his perforated lower lip, and a baseball cap skewed to one side on his head, leaned nonchalantly against his shotgun. Somewhat stunned by the whole situation, I could not help thinking that they looked like characters from a Fellini movie.

I had been excited about this trip for more than a year before finally arriving in Brazil to do anthropological fieldwork. Now, as I was finally arriving at my destination, I began to think of all the events that led up to my coming to the middle of the Amazon jungle—years of university classes, papers on South American Indians, and finally, stressful grant applications.

While anxiously wondering if funds would come through, I pestered my friends with incessant talk of the possible adventure. In attempt to assuage my anxieties one friend persuaded me to consult the I Ching to foretell the future. Although magic had never appealed to me before, I felt unexpectedly relieved when the sticks gave me the ideograph for "The Traveler."

Only years later would I understand this reaction. As people do in most societies, I was using magic to relieve anxiety about a subject that was unpredictable, uncontrollable, and important—research funds. But I would have to live a bit more with magic to realize its importance.

The grant was approved only a few weeks before the project was to begin. Together with two other anthropologists going into the field with me, I hectically made the rounds of New York camp-goods stores, and visited a few South Americanists to get practical advice on living in the Amazon. "Take along a lot of freeze-dried turkey tetrazzini," suggested one fish-hating anthropologist who had worked with river-dwelling Indians. "Don't buy serrated knives you can't sharpen," an experienced camper recommended. "And be sure to change dollars into cruzeiros before leaving the . U.S.," warned a South Americanist familiar with the artificial exchange rates in Brazil. Heavy-laden with camp goods and valuable advice, my two companions and I boarded a 747 in the middle of February 1976, destined for Brazil.

Sunny Brasília was a welcome change from the cold New York winter, and a learning experience in itself. Built as a stimulus to development in Brazil's interior, it is one of the world's few planned cities. The climate is perfect—never too hot or cold, and there is not too much rain. The natural savannas that surround the city give a pasturelike look to the area, even though cattle have never grazed on much of the acidic grasses, where not many years ago Indians hunted deer and paca. But the vast majority of Brazilians detest the city. It is just too orderly, there is no action in the streets, and all the buildings look alike.

I once heard a peasant from Manaus complain that the city had copied its architecture from the poor along the Amazon River. "Houses in Brasília are all built on stilts just like our own," he pointed out. The entrance to virtually every apartment complex is an open landing with columns supporting the six floors of living space above. Unlike Amazonian huts, houses in Brasília have basements for cars, and usually five or six bedrooms, including one for the maid. The poor live outside the city or else squat in the rat-infested apartments under construction. The designers neglected to think about them.

I waited more than two months to get permission from the Brazilian Indian Foundation (FUNAI) to go into Indian lands. Worried about bad foreign press, the government had declared off-limits to non-Brazilians all Indian communities within a hundred kilometers of any border, and I wondered if they were planning on a few other restrictions as well. While poring over documents about different Indian groups in the FUNAI library, I met Gustaaf Verswijver, a young Belgian anthropologist who had spent a couple of months among the Mekranoti-Kayapo of southern Pará. He suggested I go with him to the Mekranoti village. This way we could share the expenses of the plane trip. I had been thinking about the Kayapo and Gustaaf's reports about the Indians settled the matter. Like most anthropologists, I felt a little uneasy about "sharing" a group with an anthropological colleague, but my research would be fairly specific so I knew there would be plenty of things for both of us to study. Besides, it would be somewhat comforting to go into a village with someone who had a little experience.

Gustaaf, who seemed to know everybody in FUNAI, helped me get my permission, and told me what to buy for the Indians. Shotgun shells were good, but it was illegal for foreigners to buy any. The Indians also like good-quality machetes—no one would want anything that was shoddy. Everyone liked small, dark blue beads or large white ones, but any other size or color would be rejected, Gustaaf pointed out, adding that a few pots might also be helpful. . . .

From the air the village, even though tiny, looked like a bastion of civilization in the endless jungle. The central plaza was clean and neat, thatched roofs stood out, carefully isolated from the trimmed nearby forest. Only a few papaya trees near the houses interrupted the smooth village clearing. Already we could see some of the Indians rushing out of their houses to look at the airplane above.

As we circled several times while the pilot tested the wind, I grew queasy. Now that there was no way of turning back, the scene below was more fearful. The village looked awfully small. I thought of how I would need to depend on its people for food, shelter, and company for a year. There would be no way to call for help if I needed it. As I watched the naked Indians run to the nearby airstrip to greet us, all of the self-doubts I had avoided up to now rushed uncontrollably into my head. What if they didn't like me? How would I carry out any of the studies I wanted to do if they refused to talk to me? Or worse, they could decide not to feed me, or could even kill me outright as they had done in the not too distant past with those who displeased them.

As the plane taxied to a halt, I tried to gather my senses. When the plane stopped, I sat up straight and watched more attentively as the Indians drew closer to peer in at the goods we had brought. At first I thought some of them were wearing clothes. But then I realized they were simply painted with delicate black stripes that looked strangely like leotards and tights. The black genipap dye came to an end at the sternum, looking like a T-shirt with a low neckline, and the unpainted feet and hands gave the appearance of a cuff. Some of the Indians had shaved the tops of their heads, making them bald on top, and both men and women had plucked out all of their facial hair, including eyebrows and eyelashes.

Gustaaf was the first to step outside. Several women, holding their forearms across their bowed heads, wailed loudly. Seemingly unperturbed by the piercing shrieks, their babies continued suckling contentedly on their mothers' breasts while holding loosely onto the sitting sling hanging from their mothers' shoulders. This keening, I later found out, could mean many different things, including the death of a loved one. But on this occasion the wails were simply welcoming cries for Gustaaf's return. Gustaaf reciprocated with heavy backslaps to some of the men, who shouted loudly to each other, as they passed the news of our arrival in the village. The expansive welcomes made me feel awkward.

The Indians seemed to know exactly what to do. With little hesitation or discussion the young men loaded our heavy goods onto their backs, and marched single file out of the airstrip. Surrounded by curious Indians trying to talk to me in a language I could not understand, I followed the group along the broad grassy path, elegantly lined with tall papaya trees. Within a few minutes we had reached the village plaza.

From the ground the village looked less exotic. The houses had a more lived-in look, and the plaza was not quite as clean as it appeared from the air. The "men's house" in the village center looked even more worn than the other buildings. The walls of split saplings placed vertically side by side let the sun pass through the slats, tracing stripes of light and shadow on the ground from the afternoon sun. There was an opening on each side of the rectangular structure, and men seemed to walk constantly in and out. But I had little time to look around before being shuffled into the house of the FUNAI medical attendant.

We would be spending the night here, Gustaaf informed me. Later, the Indians would prepare us a house of our own. The FUNAI house was like most of the other houses in the village. A thatch roof covered a mud-walled structure with a clay floor. But unlike other Mekranoti houses, the FUNAI dwelling had walls to separate bedrooms, a kitchen, and a pharmacy. It also had windows—really just holes where mud was not thrown into the interstices of the wattled walls, giving the spaces a delicate latticed look. At the moment, the only other outsider in the village was Ronaldo, the FUNAI medical attendant. (Later, other visitors would come and go—two missionaries, other FUNAI personnel and even a Brazilian peasant family—but I would be too busy with the Indians to pay much attention to them.)

Ronaldo asked us for our papers as soon as we arrived. We had landed on

April 30th, a day before our permissions allowed, but no one saw any problem with this. Still, Ronaldo had to start up the rickety gasoline generator located in a separate hut behind his house to give him the electricity needed to send off a radio message telling his superiors of our arrival. A short young man from Belém, Ronaldo had been with Mekranoti for three years. He had worked previously in other Indian villages, and felt secure with the Mekranoti during the many months he'd spent alone with them. Ronaldo seemed please to have us for company, and talked excitedly about everything. . . .

Even as our goods were being unloaded in one of the extra rooms, Indians came by to give us presents of yams, bananas, manioc flour, and papaya. One man mumbled a few words and shoved us some meat through a window before disappearing into the crowd. "It's jaguar," Gustaaf reported. We handed the food to Ronaldo, who gave it to a young Indian to cook. Gustaaf and I hung up our hammocks amidst the curious stares of a roomful of talkative and laughing Indians. Some of the women simply plopped themselves down against the mud walls of the room, their babies lying across their laps. The dirt floor must have been cold against their naked skin, but they seemed not to mind at all. They were not going to miss anything that these curious white men would do. Toddlers waddled back and forth between the women. Older children stopped to stare wide-eyed at the bizarre outsiders, before rushing off again to play. A few of the men also sat along the walls or even in the center or the room. And from the outside less aggressive Indians looked on through the wooden grates of the windows.

Some of the Indians simply sat quietly, observing everything, while others chatted loudly. I understood nothing of what they said, but I would tell they were making jokes at our expense. Sometimes they pointed to us with their noses, or even walked up to touch us, or our clothes, but the laughter seemed good-humored so I really didn't care.

After years of reading anthropological accounts, I had expected this undue attention and was even content with the feeling that everything was going "as planned." The Indians obviously enjoyed our presence, even if only to make jokes about us. Gustaaf laughed at my troubles in setting up a mosquito net around my hammock. But a young Mekranoti, feeling pity for me, eventually took charge of the whole operation and set it up in no time. His helpfulness assured me that my stay would be fine.

Our next order of business, according to Gustaaf, was to take some gifts to Tàkkrorok and Pãxkê, the two main chiefs in the village. I decided to present an ax head to each. To establish a good reputation, Gustaaf also thought it would be wise to give Tàkàkrorok a number of smaller items to redistribute to the rest of the villagers. So, as the Indians crowded around me, I searched through my bags for combs, cups, small knives, rubber sandals, and beads to give away. Unfortunately, the small items I needed were not on top, so I had to unpack everything to get to them. The Indians examined carefully every item I brought out. Gustaaf complained that I should not reveal my trade goods and insisted I be more careful in the future. I was not quite sure why I should hide these articles from the Indians, as everything would eventually end up in their hands anyway. But I reasoned it was best to trust in Gustaaf's judgment since he had already spent time in the village. Eventually I got a collection of presents together, and the two of us headed off for the structure called the *nga* (men's house) in the center of the plaza.

The Indians who had been watching us since our arrival followed behind. The procession we created attracted the attention of the other villagers, and soon we were surrounded by a noisy mob as we all stepped into the darkness inside the men's house. The crowd opened up for Tàkàkrorok to pass through. A tall, lean man with wavy black hair and a large smooth face, Tàkàkrorok looked a lot younger than his sixty-odd years. Unlike most of the other men he did not wear a lip disk, but had only a small hole in his lower lip where he was punctured as a child. Physically, he was not at all what I expected of an Indian chief. I anticipated an ancient man with a pipe in his mouth and a serious demeanor—something like the Indian chiefs from all the cowboy movies I had seen. There were a few men in the crowd who fit this image well. But Tàkàkrorok looked sportier than this. His wry smile verged in impishness, and his gait was fast and determined.

In the dark of the overcrowded men's house, Tàkàkrorok received our gifts and spread them out on a woven straw mat placed on the ground before him. Squatting on the dirt floor behind the mat, he picked up the various articles, and mulled over them in silence. Then, after looking briefly at the people in the crowd, he announced a name and held an item in the air. Returning his glance to the goods on the mat, Tàkàkrorok could not even see the person who picked up the gift from his hand. The other Indians chatted and joked good-humoredly with each other while awaiting Tàkàkrorok's pronouncements.

I thought the whole process took an extraordinarily long time and felt guilty about wasting people's energy on such cheap trinkets. But the Indians themselves seemed pleased with the presents. At least no one complained to us, and most people smiled.

After this spree, we walked over to Pãxkê's hut, behind the first row of village houses and closer to the FUNAI building. A gruff burly man, Pãxkê had none of Tàkàkrorok's elegance. His chin had a large unsightly hole where once he had worn a lip disk. Like several of the men, he had FUNAI surgeons sew the aperture partly shut, but the hole never really closed. Since a few days after his birth, when his lip was first pierced, his mother had been stretching the opening so that it would eventually accommodate a balsa wood disk three or four inches in diameter. A few men still wore the brightly painted red plates that stood tightly against their noses when they smiled, or vibrated threateningly in front when angry. The disks still had an exotic charm about them, but after operation the holes that remained were ugly deformities from which saliva constantly dripped.

The hole in Pãxkê's lower lip looked even more unkempt than usual because of the stray chin hairs he failed to pluck off his broad face. Wearing only a pair of unwashed shorts, Pãxkê smiled as we approached him, somewhat surprised at our visit. He accepted our gifts and then returned quickly to his house with only the fewest of words to Gustaaf, asking how long our visit would be.

There were still some Indians with us when Gustaaf and I returned to the FUNAI building, but the darkening skies sent many people home. Ronaldo was busy helping a young man prepare our dinner. The wind would alternately put out the fire on the makeshift clay stove or fan it into dangerous flames that could burn down the entire village if ever they caught on to the thatch roof. "It's important to get the right kind of wood to burn," Ronaldo informed me. "Otherwise the fire is too irregular and can get out of control."

Our food was simple but good—the jaguar boiled in salted water and served with manioc flour, with canned guava paste for dessert. The meat tasted like a greasy stewing beef or oxtail, and seemed familiar. But the manioc flour was different from any I had tried before. Made by toasting the grated root of the cassava plant, manioc flour is usually finely ground to give it a consistency (and flavor) like sawdust. But the Mekranoti do not bother to remove all of the fibers or to grind the final product into tiny granules. Instead, they simply leave the flour in the form of hard stonelike pellets that are impossible to eat unless soaked in juice or saliva. When I first tried the finely ground Brazilian flour I thought it tasted terrible, but eventually I grew to like it. I was confident I could like the Mekranoti version as well.

I had not minded the crowds during the day, but now I was beginning to get annoyed at all of the stares. The Indians stood against the walls with their arms folded over their chests. They were obviously planning on staring at us all night. Watching everything we did, the young men sometimes commented to each other about our actions, and then laughed. They made no effort to hide the fact that we were the subject of their conversation. I could not help thinking they were mocking our table manners.

Eating, like other body functions, has a personal quality to it, and doing it in front of the Indians made me feel embarrassed. Things might have been different if the Indians ate with us, but they didn't. Occasionally Ronaldo or Gustaaf would talk a bit to one of the onlookers, but I understood nothing that was said. I felt especially awkward when Ronaldo gave a few Indians a piece of guava paste from his plate.

Several of the day's events had made me feel like an eighteenth-century English explorer who had arrived uninvited in one of the crown colonies and ordered the natives to work for him. First, there was the line of Indians carrying our bags on their backs to FUNAI headquarters. Then we made a show of generosity in giving out cheap trinkets. Later we were served by Ronaldo's helper at the table. Now we were giving the Indians crumbs from their masters' table.

Ronaldo and Gustaaf did not seem to notice the class distinctions we were setting up. As with many Brazilians, they were accustomed to maids and found nothing strange in being served by so many Indians. But I was not at all interested in setting myself apart from the people I came to study. I hoped soon to become a more normal part of the community.

The crowd of onlookers began to shrink after nine o'clock and by ten there was no one left. The Mekranoti usually go to bed between eight and nine, a custom I found difficult to accept at first. New York City's nightlife had given me a sleeping schedule quite different from theirs. But the calm of the evening, the lack of electric lights, and the exhaustion I felt after the day's excitement made going to bed at ten seem like a reasonable idea. I had never actually slept in a hammock before, but I knew enough to arrange myself diagonally across the sling in order to make a flatter bed. Since the night was cool I needed a few blankets, both underneath and on top. It took a bit of struggling with the hammock, blankets, and mosquito net to get myself comfortable, but once everything was in order I felt good. Gustaaf blew out the kerosene lamp, and I was left to think through the day's activities. A few bats whizzed past my ear, trying to get as close as possible without touching. But I felt snug and secure wrapped in my blankets and surrounded by the mosquito net.

In the distance I could hear the wistful sound of a flute. The tune was simple and hypnotic. The flute-player trilled slowly the two upper notes, a whole tone apart, and then sensuously touched a third tone, a whole step below, before falling to a mysterious, dark diminished fifth. The music floated gently like a breeze in the cool night air. I imagined the Indians' lives would be as simple and complex as that far-off lilting melody, so enticingly unassuming and yet so hard to capture, or remember.

The music was soothing. Living with the Indians would be good, I felt, as I reflected briefly on the day's events, before falling off into a good night's sleep.

SETTLING IN

Awakened by the sound of giggling voices around me, I opened one eye. At first, I could see only the delicate patterns of light and shadow on the floor as the bright sun filtered through the latticed windows. Gradually I left my dreams behind and realized I was actually living in a far more fantastic place than the one I had been dreaming about. Glancing up from my hammock, I could see several Indians watching me from the windows. Using their noses, they pointed to different things in the room and then laughed to each other. When they saw I was awake they smiled a friendly greeting. I wanted to greet them in return, but had no idea how. I simply smiled back, and gathered my senses while remaining inside the mosquito net.

Surrounded by curious onlookers,

Gustaaf and I got dressed and went off to enjoy a breakfast of leftovers from the previous night. There were fewer Indians watching us, but they made more attempts to communicate. Gustaaf translated. "They want to know what you're going to give them. Just say '*adjym*,' " he advised. "It means 'later.' " I tried the new word a few times but was met with cold stares. The Indians were familiar with the trick and did not approve. Gustaaf warned that I would be plagued with requests throughout my entire stay in the village.

After breakfast Ronaldo had to attend to his medical duties, and Gustaaf went off to make arrangements for our house. This left me alone with the Mekranoti for the first time. Frustrated with their requests for goods, a few Indians tried to talk about other matters. Unfortunately, I could understand nothing else. A fat young woman with a jolly face pointed to objects in the room and slowly pronounced Kayapo words. Thankful for the opportunity to learn Kayapo, I tried to repeat her speech, but encountered laughter after everything I said. On second and third tries the laughter grew more and more intense and I soon realized I would never learn the language like this. The Indians were out for amusement; they cared nothing about my linguistic abilities. Still, the laughter was far preferable to the cold stares I got at breakfast, and I began to feel more at ease with the Indians.

Gustaaf returned shortly afterwards with information about our future lodgings. We would be living in the village's rice granary, near Tàk-àkrorok's house. The structure was smaller than most Mekranoti dwellings, but after years of sharing studio apartments in New York City, it looked large to me. Some of the bachelors gathered saplings that they lashed into the walls to keep out dogs and chickens. Others took a wheelbarrow to the river to bring back mud for the floor. With a latrine in back and a makeshift clay stove, our house would be complete in a few days.

In the meantime, we decided to make some visits to people at home.

Before leaving Brasília I had copied Gustaaf's census data, so I already knew the names of many Mekranoti and even some of their kinsmen, but I could not connect any of the names with faces. Visiting people at home seemed like a good way to meet them in an environment where I would remember them.

The Mekranoti houses were dark, windowless structures up to thirty feet long and fifteen feet wide, with high vaulted ceilings giving a cathedral-like feel to the spacious single room below. Blackened with the thick tar from years of household fires kept burning day and night, the thatched roofs housed myriads of harmless and not-so-harmless arthropods. Giant forest roaches crawled over the beams, and once in a while an eight-inch tarantula fell to the ground. Snakes sometimes made their way into the grassy ceilings, looking for the mice that infested many of the houses and could be heard or seen late at night.

On long cords hanging from the ceiling the Indians stored their bags or baskets of shotgun shells, beads, and prized ceremonial ornaments made of mollusk shells, reeds, and feathers. Usually a bunch of ripening green bananas also hung from the ceiling in the house's corner, along with baskets of cassava roots or grated manioc flour. Sometimes pet macaws or parrots paced back and forth on the house beams or on the high shelves the Indians liked to build along the mud-wattled walls to store their water pots or prized garden fruits like papaya, pineapple, or pumpkin.

When we entered the houses we found people sitting on the floor or on one of the many sleeping platforms built from split saplings and covered with straw mats. The beds were built just high enough off the ground to be out of jumping range of the fleas that infested the mud floors. Usually a single large platform was reserved for mother, father, and young children. Old women sometimes shared one of the hard beds with their unmarried daughters. A few families had Brazilian hammocks stretched across a corner, but these were used mostly

during the day for lounging about. Only the older boys who had to spend the nights in the men's house in the village center slept in hammocks, although a young man would sometimes set up his bedding in his girlfriend's house for a night of sexual adventures.

Between the platforms women tended the small fires used for cooking during the day and for warmth at night. The smoke-filled air made my eyes water, and because the ashes on the floor were overrun with annoying fleas, I learned quickly not to sit, but rather to squat, leaning slightly forward with the weight on the balls of my feet. We received gifts of food everywhere we went. Usually people offered us fresh meat, but sometimes we got partially eaten scraps from the banana leaves people were using as plates when we walked in on them. Apparently having nothing else to give, they seemed embarrassed at their offerings.

I met many new people during those first few days, but because I could speak very little Kayapo, there was little we could talk about. Not remembering anything they said, I was nowhere close to remembering the 285 new faces. But I did remember a few people, like Mrytàmti, the old man who talked so quietly that even if I had spoken Kayapo I would not have understood him. He was sitting alone staring into space when we walked in on him, but greeted us with a gentle, friendly smile and offered us some meat. Mrytàmti fit my image of a tribal leader much better than Tàk-àkrorok. With an ancient, quiet face that appeared full of wisdom, he seemed absolutely sure of everything he said. At night he sometimes gave speeches to the villagers, but he was not, I was told, one of the main leaders. The other people stuck much less well in my memory. I need to talk with them first. It would be months before I could get them all straight, and even then I would never learn all of the children.

Frustrated with both the language and people's names, I resolved to gather some data that required my knowing neither. Although I had no good reason for needing it, I decided to make a map of the village. I could at least occupy my time until I figured out how to handle the more important matters. So using a compass, a ruler, and a measuring tape, I spent the next few days calculating angles, and pacing from the men's house in the village center to each of the twenty-four residences surrounding it. When I had just about finished, Gustaaf asked me how I had been handling the dogs. "Why?" I asked. "Well," he answered, "they usually attack people near the houses. Haven't they bothered you?" Up to that point I had had no trouble, and wondered what he meant. But the next time I went out I found out.

Although the Mekranoti love their dogs, mourning their deaths and threatening people who might inadvertently harm them, they keep the pets half-starved and beat them mercilessly. This makes for good hunting animals, but also creates vicious, psychotic personalities. Whenever one dog begins an attack, the other village curs join in. Sometimes there is nothing to attack at all, but the dogs make a mad rush out of the houses and bark at the air just the same. On my next mapping trip I found myself surrounded by at least twenty snapping and snarling animals. Fortunately, the villagers rushed to my aid, grabbing their dogs and taking them back to the houses. I never figured out how I managed to escape attack during those first few days. Maybe my own naiveté protected me from the beasts at first; then they later picked up on my nervousness. Maybe the Indians simply watched me more closely at first and kept their dogs away from me. In any case, from that day

forward I always carried a stick to protect me while crossing the village. I was bitten only once.

We conversed little during those first few weeks, but the Indians gradually came to recognize me as part of the community, and soon I received a new name from one of the elders. He simply walked by my hut one day and in front of the others declared that I was to be called Beproti. The name was a "good" name, usually awarded only with a special ceremony sponsored by one's parents, but I was given it as an honorary distinction. Since Gustaaf had only a "common" name, the Indians felt obligated to award him a special name as well. He was christened Bepita, and we both became respected members of the community.

I could not help thinking that this bestowal of honors had a great deal to do with all of the goods we brought in. The constant haranguing for presents began to wear on me. Sometimes I felt like a battered vending machine that gives out goods when kicked hard enough. At one point an old woman went into a screaming rampage. She had been giving me food and firewood since I arrived, she complained, but I always refused her requests. Instead, I gave to people who never gave me anything at all.

I was tempted to give everything away at once and trust to people's generosity. But I remembered an anthropologist who lavished all of his trade goods on the Indians as soon as he arrived in their village. Soon afterwards he found himself without food, and was forced to go out hunting every day to fend for himself. Hunting alone,

or with only a child to keep an eye on him, he was able to learn very little. I wanted to avoid that mistake.

True, the village missionaries freed themselves of all their goods as soon as they arrived among the Mekranoti. But they gave only to those who had "earned" the articles during their previous visits. After years of the missionaries' comings and goings, the Indians knew they could count on their benefactors, but I was new in the village and the Mekranoti had no reason to trust me. Also, I needed to interview everyone, and could not play economic favorites like the missionaries who worked with only a few people. I would have to come up with a system of my own.

After several weeks of harassment, I finally hit upon a solution. Whenever anyone brought me anything I wrote it down on a five-by-eight card that I had prepared for that person. Later, when asked for a present, I could look at this card before deciding whether to give or not, and could record my gifts there as well. If people complained about unfairness, I cited examples of what they and others had given me, and what I had given them. The Indians soon caught on to my record-keeping. By the end of my stay they would ask what they could give in order to receive one of my trade items. In a deal, I could trade a large metal pot for two hunks of meat, a load of firewood, and a formal two-hour interview in my hut. The arrangement was more mercantile than I might have wanted, but it worked. Instead of being a vending machine, I became as human as any town storekeeper. . . .

Eating Christmas in the Kalahari

Richard Borshay Lee

Richard Borshay Lee is a full professor of anthropology at the University of Toronto. He has done extensive field-work in southern Africa, is coeditor of Man the Hunter *(1968) and* Kalahari Hunter-Gatherers *(1976), and author of* The !Kung San: Men, Women, and Work in a Foraging Society.

The !Kung Bushmen's knowledge of Christmas is thirdhand. The London Missionary Society brought the holiday to the southern Tswana tribes in the early nineteenth century. Later, native catechists spread the idea far and wide among the Bantu-speaking pastoralists, even in the remotest corners of the Kalahari Desert. The Bushmen's idea of the Christmas story, stripped to its essentials, is "praise the birth of white man's god-chief"; what keeps their interest in the holiday high is the Tswana-Herero custom of slaughtering an ox for his Bushmen neighbors as an annual goodwill gesture. Since the 1930's, part of the Bushmen's annual round of activities has included a December congregation at the cattle posts for trading, marriage brokering, and several days of trance-dance feasting at which the local Tswana headman is host.

As a social anthropologist working with !Kung Bushmen, I found that the Christmas ox custom suited my purposes. I had come to the Kalahari to study the hunting and gathering subsistence economy of the !Kung, and to accomplish this it was essential not to provide them with food, share my own food, or interfere in any way with their food-gathering activities. While liberal handouts of tobacco and medical supplies were appreciated, they were scarcely adequate to erase the glaring disparity in wealth between the anthropologist, who maintained a two-month inventory of canned goods, and the Bushmen, who rarely had a day's supply of food on hand. My approach, while paying off in terms of data, left me open to frequent accusations of stinginess and hard-heartedness. By their lights, I was a miser.

The Christmas ox was to be my way of saying thank you for the cooperation of the past year; and since it was to be our last Christmas in the field, I determined to slaughter the largest, meatiest ox that money could buy, insuring that the feast and trance-dance would be a success.

Through December I kept my eyes open at the wells as the cattle were brought down for watering. Several animals were offered, but none had quite the grossness that I had in mind. Then, ten days before the holiday, a Herero friend led an ox of astonishing size and mass up to our camp. It was solid black, stood five feet high at the shoulder, had a five-foot span of horns, and must have weighed 1,200 pounds on the hoof. Food consumption calculations are my specialty, and I quickly figured that bones and viscera aside, there was enough meat—at least four pounds—for every man, woman, and child of the 150 Bushmen in the vicinity of /ai/ai who were expected at the feast.

Having found the right animal at last, I paid the Herero £20 ($56) and asked him to keep the beast with his herd until Christmas day. The next morning word spread among the people that the big solid black one was the ox chosen by /ontah (my Bushman name; it means, roughly, "whitey") for the Christmas feast. That afternoon I received the first delegation. Ben!a, an outspoken sixty-year-old mother of five, came to the point slowly.

"Where were you planning to eat Christmas?"

"Right here at /ai/ai," I replied.

"Alone or with others?"

"I expect to invite all the people to eat Christmas with me."

"Eat what?"

"I have purchased Yehave's black ox, and I am going to slaughter and cook it."

"That's what we were told at the well but refused to believe it until we heard it from yourself."

"Well, it's the black one," I replied expansively, although wondering what she was driving at.

"Oh, no!" Ben!a groaned, turning to her group. "They were right." Turning back to me she asked, "Do you expect us to eat that bag of bones?"

"Bag of bones! It's the biggest ox at /ai/ai."

"Big, yes, but old. And thin. Everybody knows there's no meat on that old ox. What did you expect us to eat off it, the horns?"

Everybody chuckled at Ben!a's one-liner as they walked away, but all I could manage was a weak grin.

1. ANTHROPOLOGICAL PERSPECTIVES

That evening it was the turn of the young men. They came to sit at our evening fire. /gaugo, about my age, spoke to me man-to-man.

"/ontah, you have always been square with us," he lied. "What has happened to change your heart? That sack of guts and bones of Yehave's will hardly feed one camp, let alone all the Bushmen around /ai/ai." And he proceeded to enumerate the seven camps in the /ai/ai vicinity, family by family. "Perhaps you have forgotten that we are not few, but many. Or are you too blind to tell the difference between a proper cow and an old wreck? That ox is thin to the point of death."

"Look, you guys," I retorted, "that is a beautiful animal, and I'm sure you will eat it with pleasure at Christmas."

"Of course we will eat it; it's food. But it won't fill us up to the point where we will have enough strength to dance. We will eat and go home to bed with stomachs rumbling."

That night as we turned in, I asked my wife, Nancy: "What did you think of the black ox?"

"It looked enormous to me. Why?"

"Well, about eight different people have told me I got gypped; that the ox is nothing but bones."

"What's the angle?" Nancy asked. "Did they have a better one to sell?"

"No, they just said that it was going to be a grim Christmas because there won't be enough meat to go around. Maybe I'll get an independent judge to look at the beast in the morning."

Bright and early, Halingisi, a Tswana cattle owner, appeared at our camp. But before I could ask him to give me his opinion on Yehave's black ox, he gave me the eye signal that indicated a confidential chat. We left the camp and sat down.

"/ontah, I'm surprised at you: you've lived here for three years and still haven't learned anything about cattle."

"But what else can a person do but choose the biggest, strongest animal one can find?" I retorted.

"Look, just because an animal is big doesn't mean that it has plenty of meat on it. The black one was a

beauty when it was younger, but now it is thin to the point of death."

"Well I've already bought it. What can I do at this stage?"

"Bought it already? I thought you were just considering it. Well, you'll have to kill it and serve it, I suppose. But don't expect much of a dance to follow."

My spirits dropped rapidly. I could believe that Ben!a and /gaugo just might be putting me on about the black ox, but Halingisi seemed to be an impartial critic. I went around that day feeling as though I had bought a lemon of a used car.

In the afternoon it was Tomazo's turn. Tomazo is a fine hunter, a top trance performer . . . and one of my most reliable informants. He approached the subject of the Christmas cow as part of my continuing Bushman education.

"My friend, the way it is with us Bushmen," he began, "is that we love meat. And even more than that, we love fat. When we hunt we always search for the fat ones, the ones dripping with layers of white fat: fat that turns into a clear, thick oil in the cooking pot, fat that slides down your gullet, fills your stomach and gives you a roaring diarrhea," he rhapsodized.

"So, feeling as we do," he continued, "it gives us pain to be served such a scrawny thing as Yehave's black ox. It is big, yes, and no doubt its giant bones are good for soup, but fat is what we really crave and so we will eat Christmas this year with a heavy heart."

The prospect of a gloomy Christmas now had me worried, so I asked Tomazo what I could do about it.

"Look for a fat one, a young one . . . smaller, but fat. Fat enough to make us //gom ('evacuate the bowels'), then we will be happy."

My suspicions were aroused when Tomazo said that he happened to know of a young, fat, barren cow that the owner was willing to part with. Was Tomazo working on commission, I wondered? But I dispelled this unworthy thought when we approached the Herero owner of the

cow in question and found that he had decided not to sell.

The scrawny wreck of a Christmas ox now became the talk of the /ai/ai water hole and was the first news told to the outlying groups as they began to come in from the bush for the feast. What finally convinced me that real trouble might be brewing was the visit from u!au, an old conservative with a reputation for fierceness. His nickname meant spear and referred to an incident thirty years ago in which he had speared a man to death. He had an intense manner; fixing me with his eyes, he said in clipped tones:

"I have only just heard about the black ox today, or else I would have come here earlier. /ontah, do you honestly think you can serve meat like that to people and avoid a fight?" He paused, letting the implications sink in. "I don't mean fight you, /ontah; you are a white man. I mean a fight between Bushmen. There are many fierce ones here, and with such a small quantity of meat to distribute, how can you give everybody a fair share? Someone is sure to accuse another of taking too much or hogging all the choice pieces. Then you will see what happens when some go hungry while others eat."

The possibility of at least a serious argument struck me as all too real. I had witnessed the tension that surrounds the distribution of meat from a kudu or gemsbok kill, and had documented many arguments that sprang up from a real or imagined slight in meat distribution. The owners of a kill may spend up to two hours arranging and rearranging the piles of meat under the gaze of a circle of recipients before handing them out. And I also knew that the Christmas feast at /ai/ai would be bringing together groups that had feuded in the past.

Convinced now of the gravity of the situation, I went in earnest to search for a second cow; but all my inquiries failed to turn one up.

The Christmas feast was evidently going to be a disaster, and the incessant complaints about the meagerness of the ox had already taken the fun out of it for me. Moreover, I was getting bored with the wisecracks, and after losing my temper a few times, I resolved to serve the beast anyway. If the meat fell short, the hell with it. In the Bushmen idiom, I announced to all who would listen:

"I am a poor man and blind. If I have chosen one that is too old and too thin, we will eat it anyway and see if there is enough meat there to quiet the rumbling of our stomachs."

On hearing this speech, Ben!a offered me a rare word of comfort. "It's thin," she said philosophically, "but the bones will make a good soup."

At dawn Christmas morning, instinct told me to turn over the butchering and cooking to a friend and take off with Nancy to spend Christmas alone in the bush. But curiosity kept me from retreating. I wanted to see what such a scrawny ox looked like on butchering, and if there *was* going to be a fight, I wanted to catch every word of it. Anthropologists are incurable that way.

The great beast was driven up to our dancing ground, and a shot in the forehead dropped it in its tracks. Then, freshly cut branches were heaped around the fallen carcass to receive the meat. Ten men volunteered to help with the cutting. I asked /gaugo to make the breast bone cut. This cut, which begins the butchering process for most large game, offers easy access for removal of the viscera. But it also allows the hunter to spot-check the amount of fat on the animal. A fat game animal carries a white layer up to an inch thick on the chest, while in a thin one, the knife will quickly cut to bone. All eyes fixed on his hand as /gaugo, dwarfed by the great carcass, knelt to the breast. The first cut opened a pool of solid white in the black skin. The second and third cut widened and deepened the creamy white. Still no bone. It was pure fat; it must have been two inches thick.

"Hey /gau," I burst out, "that ox is loaded with fat. What's this about the ox being too thin to bother eating? Are you out of your mind?"

"Fat?" /gau shot back, "You call that fat? This wreck is thin, sick,

dead!" And he broke out laughing. So did everyone else. They rolled on the ground, paralyzed with laughter. Everybody laughed except me; I was thinking.

I ran back to the tent and burst in just as Nancy was getting up. "Hey, the black ox. It's fat as hell! They were kidding about it being too thin to eat. It was a joke or something. A put-on. Everyone is really delighted with it!"

"Some joke," my wife replied. "It was so funny that you were ready to pack up and leave /ai/ai."

If it had indeed been a joke, it had been an extraordinarily convincing one, and tinged, I thought, with more than a touch of malice as many jokes are. Nevertheless, that it was a joke lifted my spirits considerably, and I returned to the butchering site where the shape of the ox was rapidly disappearing under the axes and knives of the butchers. The atmosphere had become festive. Grinning broadly, their arms covered with blood well past the elbow, men packed chunks of meat into the big cast-iron cooking pots, fifty pounds to the load, and muttered and chuckled all the while about the thinness and worthlessness of the animal and /ontah's poor judgment.

We danced and ate that ox two days and two nights; we cooked and distributed fourteen potfuls of meat and no one went home hungry and no fights broke out.

But the "joke" stayed in my mind. I had a growing feeling that something important had happened in my relationship with the Bushmen and that the clue lay in the meaning of the joke. Several days later, when most of the people had dispersed back to the bush camps, I raised the question with Hakekgose, a Tswana man who had grown up among the !Kung, married a !Kung girl, and who probably knew their culture better than any other non-Bushman.

"With us whites," I began, "Christmas is supposed to be the day of friendship and brotherly love. What I can't figure out is why the Bushmen went to such lengths to criticize and belittle the ox I had bought for the feast. The animal was

perfectly good and their jokes and wisecracks practically ruined the holiday for me."

"So it really did bother you," said Hakekgose. "Well, that's the way they always talk. When I take my rifle and go hunting with them, if I miss, they laugh at me for the rest of the day. But even if I hit and bring one down, it's no better. To them, the kill is always too small or too old or too thin; and as we sit down on the kill site to cook and eat the liver, they keep grumbling, even with their mouths full of meat. They say things like, 'Oh this is awful! What a worthless animal! Whatever made me think that this Tswana rascal could hunt!' "

"Is this the way outsiders are treated?" I asked.

"No, it is their custom; they talk that way to each other too. Go and ask them."

/gaugo had been one of the most enthusiastic in making me feel bad about the merit of the Christmas ox. I sought him out first.

"Why did you tell me the black ox was worthless, when you could see that it was loaded with fat and meat?"

"It is our way," he said smiling. "We always like to fool people about that. Say there is a Bushman who has been hunting. He must not come home and announce like a braggard, 'I have killed a big one in the bush!' He must first sit down in silence until I or someone else comes up to his fire and asks, 'What did you see today?' He replies quietly, 'Ah, I'm no good for hunting. I saw nothing at all [pause] just a little tiny one.' Then I smile to myself," /gaugo continued, "because I know he has killed something big.

"In the morning we make up a party of four or five people to cut up and carry the meat back to the camp. When we arrive at the kill we examine it and cry out, 'You mean to say you have dragged us all the way out here in order to make us cart home your pile of bones? Oh, if I had known it was this thin I wouldn't have come.' Another one pipes up, 'People, to think I gave up a nice day in the shade for this. At home we may be hungry but at least we have nice cool water to drink.' If the horns are big, someone says, 'Did you think that somehow you were going to boil down the horns for soup?'

"To all this you must respond in kind. 'I agree,' you say, 'this one is not worth the effort; let's just cook the liver for strength and leave the rest for the hyenas. It is not too late to hunt today and even a duiker or a steenbok would be better than this mess.'

"Then you set to work nevertheless; butcher the animal, carry the meat back to the camp and everyone eats," /gaugo concluded.

Things were beginning to make sense. Next, I went to Tomazo. He corroborated /gaugo's story of the obligatory insults over a kill and added a few details of his own.

"But," I asked, "why insult a man after he has gone to all that trouble to track and kill an animal and when he is going to share the meat with you so that your children will have something to eat?"

"Arrogance," was his cryptic answer.

"Arrogance?"

"Yes, when a young man kills much meat he comes to think of himself as a chief or a big man, and he thinks of the rest of us as his servants or inferiors. We can't accept this. We refuse one

who boasts, for someday his pride will make him kill somebody. So we always speak of his meat as worthless. This way we cool his heart and make him gentle."

"But why didn't you tell me this before?" I asked Tomazo with some heat.

"Because you never asked me," said Tomazo, echoing the refrain that has come to haunt every field ethnographer.

The pieces now fell into place. I had known for a long time that in situations of social conflict with Bushmen I held all the cards. I was the only source of tobacco in a thousand square miles, and I was not incapable of cutting an individual off for non-cooperation. Though my boycott never lasted longer than a few days, it was an indication of my strength. People resented my presence at the water hole, yet simultaneously dreaded my leaving. In short I was a perfect target for the charge of arrogance and for the Bushmen tactic of enforcing humility.

I had been taught an object lesson by the Bushmen; it had come from an unexpected corner and had hurt me in a vulnerable area. For the big black ox was to be the one totally generous, unstinting act of my year at /ai/ai,

and I was quite unprepared for the reaction I received.

As I read it, their message was this: There are no totally generous acts. All "acts" have an element of calculation. One black ox slaughtered at Christmas does not wipe out a year of careful manipulation of gifts given to serve your own ends. After all, to kill an animal and share the meat with people is really no more than Bushmen do for each other every day and with far less fanfare.

In the end, I had to admire how the Bushmen had played out the farce—collectively straight-faced to the end. Curiously, the episode reminded me of the *Good Soldier Schweik* and his marvelous encounters with authority. Like Schweik, the Bushmen had retained a thorough-going skepticism of good intentions. Was it this independence of spirit, I wondered, that had kept them culturally viable in the face of generations of contact with more powerful societies, both black and white? The thought that the Bushmen were alive and well in the Kalahari was strangely comforting. Perhaps, armed with that independence and with their superb knowledge of their environment, they might yet survive the future.

Are the Horrors of Cannibalism Fact—or Fiction?

Reports about cannibals have been believed throughout the ages, but skeptics argue that most accounts are based on hearsay

Gina Kolata

Gina Kolata, a writer for Science *magazine, last wrote on obesity in the January 1986* Smithsonian.

William Arens, an anthropology professor at the State University of New York at Stony Brook, forgets the student's name now, but he wishes he could give her credit. He was teaching an introductory course in anthropology when the student, a young woman, came to his office and asked why he was spending his time lecturing about kinship relationships and politics and economics. What ever happened to the really interesting topics, she asked, the topics such as witchcraft and cannibalism that made her and others want to take a course in anthropology in the first place?

Arens was struck by her observation. He himself had gone into anthropology wanting to know about strange human practices, but somehow he had been waylaid and ended up studying kinship relationships, a traditional and not particularly exciting field. So he decided to add a lecture or two on cannibalism to his introductory course —who did it, when and why? He assumed cannibalism was well documented and the existence of man-eating societies to be beyond question.

But what he found when he began to prepare a lecture on the subject was something quite different. The evidence, he felt, simply was not there.

No credible observer has ever documented cannibalism as a custom, Arens claims. But, he emphasizes, he is not saying that there is no such thing as cannibalism; there clearly are instances when people ate human flesh in order to survive. Yet this is quite different from cannibal societies in which people purportedly ate other humans as a matter of custom. "I don't think any anthropologist has come up with any good evidence of cannibalistic societies," Arens says. "And if there is no evidence, we can't say that these societies existed. If I'm right, anthropologists are engaged not in a hoax and not in a lie, but in mythmaking. They are retelling what is always assumed to be true."

It is a provocative hypothesis, to say the least, and Arens has infuriated many anthropologists since he published his book *The Man-Eating Myth* in 1979. Thomas Riley of the University of Illinois at Urbana-Champaign, for example, says that since Arens and his supporters reject reports of cannibalism by early explorers, reject more recent reports by anthropologists and reject archaeological evidence, their reasoning "is along the lines of those few historians who would claim the holocaust of World War II never happened."

Others who disagree with Arens are bemused. Robert L. Carneiro of the American Museum of Natural History says that "there is an *overwhelming* body of evidence that cannibalism was

practiced. There must be literally *thousands* of accounts in different societies. There would have to have been the most incredible conspiracy in the history of the world for all this evidence to be fraudulent. The real question is how Arens can sustain the idea that there is no such thing as cannibalism."

But other anthropologists are swayed by Aren's arguments. William Durham of Stanford University remarks, the "interest in cannibalism runs deep. It is just considered the inverse of humanity, unponderable. But although Arens has been challenged, there has been little concrete evidence in response to his charges. I think Arens is largely correct in saying that anthropologists and others have been too quick to suspect cannibalism and too quick to accept it without adequate scrutiny."

"The idea of cannibalism is almost universal"

Fitz John Porter Poole, an anthropologist at the University of California, San Diego, who has actually witnessed a form of ritual cannibalism in New Guinea, says that Arens has done the field of anthropology a service in questioning the cannibalism stories. It is not so important, Poole says, whether there literally are any examples of cannibalism or "whether a given group of people does or does not do it; the holding of ideas about the phenomenon, however, may be almost universal and that fact is very interesting." Moreover, what is important, he says, is that "Arens pointed out, and rightly so, that a great deal of the information that is regarded as historical truth is probably not. Arens is dead right, in at least this regard."

Not only do tales of cannibal societies abound, but virtually every group of people has, at one time or another, been said to be cannibalistic. Although some tribes even now say their neighbors are cannibals, not many seem ready to admit to being cannibals themselves. And although modern anthropologists have written about cannibal societies, they always seem to write without having personally observed the event. Neighboring tribes were their informants, or the tribespeople say they once ate human flesh, but do so no longer. It is a practice they gave up generations ago. "It is a way," says Lyle Steadman of Arizona State University, "of saying how far they've come."

Basically, what Arens and his supporters say is that the old accounts of cannibalism are not credible and that there are few believable modern accounts of cannibalistic societies. Even the popular stories that the mysterious brain infection kuru was recently spread by cannibalism in New Guinea is not credible, these anthropologists insist. Moreover, cannibalism serves as a way to insult people—to say they are less than human—and virtually every group of people has accused its enemies or those it considered inferior of being cannibals. "If you want to say that people are really nasty, you say that they are cannibals," says Erik Trinkaus of the University of New Mexico. Europeans have said that Africans ate human flesh until, of course, they were civilized by the Europeans. But Africans also thought the Europeans were cannibals. The Chinese thought the Koreans were cannibals and the Koreans thought the Chinese were.

Yet we tend to believe only those cannibal tales that apply to societies other than our own, Arens notes. For example, historians dismiss charges by the Romans that early Christians were

cannibals and charges by early Christians that Jews drank human blood. And although the women accused of being witches in Europe sometimes admitted that they were cannibals and even ate their own children, historians do not seriously believe that they did this. But until recently most people accepted without question the notion that Africans, Polynesians and New Guineans are or were cannibals.

Arens himself came across cannibalism charges during his fieldwork in Africa. In 1968, he went to Tanzania to study a rural community. Shortly after he arrived, a neighbor shouted something to him in Swahili. Arens asked for a translation. "My guide was clearly embarrassed, and told me it was nothing of consequence; but after persistent badgering on my part, he admitted that his co-resident wanted to know why he was walking with a *mchinja-chinja*. The obvious next query revealed that the phrase was best translated as 'blood-sucker.'" Arens later learned "bizarre stories about these bloodsuckers." The Africans thought that Westerners would slit the throats of the tribespeople and collect their blood. They would transport the blood by fire engine to a hospital "where it was converted into red capsules. These pills were taken on a regular basis by Europeans who, I was informed, needed these potations to stay alive in Africa. I must admit that it was exactly stories of this type about Africans which I had hoped to collect, but I was disconcerted to find myself a central figure in such a drama. At the time I failed to appreciate the political symbolism of the narrative, which cast colonial Europeans as the consumers of African vitality, and paternally concluded that the Africans were entitled to their ignorance."

Arens was somewhat distressed to find that the Africans still persisted in their belief that Westerners were "blood-suckers" a year and a half later when his fieldwork was complete. He believes the story originated when the British tried to carry out a blood drive during World War II for the African troops fighting overseas. A fire engine was stationed nearby at a small air-

strip. To the Africans, this was sufficient circumstantial evidence for their belief that the Westerners were cannibals. And, says Arens, now that he thinks about it, "similar beliefs about Africans on our part no longer seem so reasonable."

So what kind of stories are there about cannibals? First, there are countless explorers' tales. According to Arens, these stories tend to be told and retold through the centuries until they take on an air of irrefutable truth. But, he says, a look back at the original material is revealing. For example, there are the famous stories of Hans Staden, "an extraordinary fellow who visited the South American coast in the mid-sixteenth century as a common seaman on a Portuguese trading ship." Staden was shipwrecked and captured by the Tupinamba Indians. He later returned to Germany where he published a book entitled *Hans Staden: The True History and Description of a Country of Savages, a Naked and Terrible People, Eaters of Men's Flesh, who Dwell in the New World called America. Being Wholly Unknown in Hesse Both Before and After Christ's Birth Until Two Years Ago, when Hans Staden of Hamberg in Hesse Took Personal Knowledge of Them and Now Presents His Story in Print.* The story is illustrated with woodcuts of the cannibal Indians. . . . Since Staden's narrative is frequently referred to by others "in more abstract discourses on cannibalism," Arens examined it in detail.

He became increasingly suspicious as he studied the evidence. For example, Staden recounts verbatim what the Indians said on the very first day they captured him—how, when and where they would eat him, although it is not clear how he knew the Indian language, or that he took notes, or even that he could read or write. But language barriers seem not to be a problem for the Indians either. In one scene, Staden calls out lines from a Psalm: "Out of the depths I have cried unto thee." The Indians respond: "See how he cries; now he is sorrowful indeed." Arens comments, "One would have to assume that the Indians also had a flair for languages in order to understand and respond to Staden's German so quickly."

Arens also notes that the Indian women were the "worst culprits" in Staden's tales. In the woodcuts, for example, it is the women and children who are actually eating human flesh. This is a common theme in tales of cannibals and occurs again in New Guinea, in the accounts of the transmission of the brain disease kuru. It is a way, say Arens and Steadman, to illustrate the inferiority of women—sort of a subclass of persons who are denigrated by the cannibal epithet.

Travelers who came after Staden confirmed his accounts, frequently with exactly the same dialogue. The Tupinamba vanished after the 16th century, as a result of their contact with Europeans, and so there is no modern information on their traditional culture. Arens concludes, "Although there may be some legitimate reservations about who ate whom, there can be none on the question of who exterminated whom."

But many anthropologists, even those who specialize in South America, still cite the Tupinamba stories and think Arens is wrong to question them. Carneiro of the American Museum of Natural History, for example, is familiar with Arens' arguments, yet says that Arens is dismissing Tupinamba cannibalism. "There were a dozen or more explorers who came after Staden and either observed cannibalism directly as Staden did or heard accounts of it. The stories are so numerous and most are independent. Yet they coincide and agree in their detail," Carneiro says.

William Crocker, a Smithsonian anthropologist, also emphasizes that Hans Staden's account is persuasive evidence that the Tupinamba ate human flesh. "The information about their entire institution of cannibalism, which covers at least a complete annual cycle, is so detailed and complex that it is unlikely that the whole picture was invented." Furthermore, Crocker maintains that Staden *did* know the Tupi

language because several years prior to his capture, Staden was in contact with other Tupi-speaking tribes.

But the Tupinamba are just one of many groups that Arens doubts were cannibals. The stories of African cannibalism are just as suspect as those of the Tupinamba, according to Arens. For example, Herbert Ward, in his 1890 book *Five Years With The Congo Cannibals,* wrote that he was told by the Arabs that many of the Congo natives deserved to be taken as slaves because they were cannibals. Ward said he later visited these natives and noticed their filed teeth—a sure sign, he decided, that they were indeed eaters of human flesh. But he was certain, he wrote, that "white men of upright character" would soon "put an end to this."

Then there is the story of David Livingstone and his would-be rescuer, Sir Henry Morton Stanley. Livingstone, who spent much of his life living with natives of east and central Africa, considered the allegations that a group he knew were cannibals and wrote in 1874, "A Scotch jury would say, Not Proven." Stanley, who set out to find Livingstone, had quite different perceptions of the African natives. As Arens explains, Stanley's own reports "portray him as constantly set upon, in the very same areas traversed peacefully by Livingstone, by the most bellicose and savage people, whom he was forced to dispatch and rout with regularity." At one point, Stanley wrote, he captured three cannibals. Stanley's guides, Arens says, told him that these cannibals "smelled from the odor of human meat." Stanley, however, does not say he saw cannibalism firsthand. Arab slavers told him about it. These slavers, Arens wryly notes, also spread the word that Stanley and his group were cannibals, "which might explain to some extent his often harsh reception during his adventures.

A second source of information on cannibalism is modern anthropologists. But what is missing is a body of real, credible, firsthand accounts of cannibalism, according to Arens. For example, Margaret Mead, one of the first professional anthropologists to do

fieldwork in New Guinea (SMITHSONIAN, April 1983; September 1984), helped fuel the cannibalism literature with her stories of the Mundugumor. She described this tribe in Part Two of her 1935 book called *Sex and Temperament in Three Primitive Societies.* In the ninth chapter, entitled "The Pace of Life in a Cannibal Tribe," Mead wrote in the present tense about cannibalism. But in a footnote, she confessed that she did not actually witness cannibalism among the Mundugumor. The Australian authorities had outlawed it three years before she arrived and she used the present tense, she explained, to refer to the period when the tribespeople were, in fact, cannibals.

The only eyewitness account of New Guinea cannibalism is Poole's report of a group that ate various body parts of their dead relatives as part of a complex ritual. The Bimin-Kuskusmin, according to Poole, classify some body parts as "male" and others as "female." For example, when a man dies, members of his lineage, but not his direct descendants, eat morsels of his bone marrow, which is a male substance, in order to honor him, to ensure the safe passage of his spirit and to recycle his strength among his relatives. His female relatives eat small morsels of his lower belly fat, a female substance, in order to enhance their reproductive power and their ritual power.

Although Poole saw the Bimin-Kuskusmin perform these acts of cannibalism when he lived with them from 1971 until 1974, he stresses that the group by no means considered human flesh to be food. In fact, he says "these people themselves think that [the ritual cannibalism they practice] is anxiety-provoking and nauseating. I was told that some people fake it. They palm the morsels or put them in their mouth and then spit them out or they vomit them."

Poole also emphasizes that Arens' thesis that the cannibalism epithet is the ultimate insult also holds for the Bimin-Kuskusmin. "They had horrifying stories about their neighbors, the Miyanmin and they said that the fact that the Miyanmin treat human flesh as food is a sure sign that they are savages."

There are no eyewitness accounts of Miyanmin cannibalism, but there is the next best thing. George Morren, an anthropologist at Rutgers University who lived with the group in 1968–69, and again in 1980–81, has persuasive indirect evidence that they ate human flesh. According to the Bimin-Kuskusmin and other neighboring tribes, the Miyanmin raided their neighbors and left behind carcasses of people that they killed and, presumably, ate.

During his first visit Morren was interested in the history of warfare among the Miyanmin, so he interviewed tribe members and took down detailed accounts of battles and campaigns. When he interviewed the tribesmen, Morren says, the men told him the entire tribe had been cannibals in the recent past. The accounts were consistent and, says Morren, "some material was particularly detailed and it was possible to cross-check. Some people were witnesses to things that other people did."

In addition, Morren read court records of a trial in 1959 involving more than 30 Miyanmin who were accused of murder in connection with a raid on a neighboring tribe. Sixteen people were killed and eaten. "In pretrial investigations, the accused were very open in saying what they did. They did not know that what they had done was wrong and they didn't believe it was wrong. So they did not know what to censor in their accounts," Morren explains. The Miyanmin told Morren that the flesh of their neighbors was "just meat."

Morren did not directly observe cannibalism because the area was officially pacified when he visited it and the people no longer fought. (A section of Miyanmin territory that was not pacified by the Australian authorities was restricted and Morren was not allowed to go there.) In the area that he went to, Morren says, the "Miyanmin already knew that Westerners disapproved of cannibalism." They implied that these are old ways and that they were joining the modern world in which people don't eat each other.

A number of anthropologists and medical researchers say that, if nothing else, the story of kuru is good evidence of cannibalism in New Guinea. But others dispute it. Kuru is a disease that, from 1957 until 1977, was epidemic among the Fore, a tribe that lived in New Guinea highlands and that was, many believe, transmitted by eating human flesh. The Fore thought that the disease was caused by sorcery. It was rapidly killing them—particularly the women and children of the tribe—by destroying their brains and their ability to move. The word *kuru* means trembling and describes the first symptoms of the disease. Most victims died within a year.

The mystery of kuru fascinated Daniel Carleton Gajdusek of the National Institutes of Health, who later won a Nobel Prize for his work on the disease. It turned out that kuru is caused by a strange organism called a slow virus, and that people can only catch the disease by directly contacting the infected brains of kuru victims. The question is, how did the Fore contact these brains? Gajdusek says it was in the course of funerary rites which involved cannibalism, and published a photograph in *Science* magazine that was widely cited as proving his point.

The *Science* photograph is of a woman who died from kuru and, just below it, is another photograph of some Fore sitting around a campfire eating meat. The caption tells how the Fore prepare and eat human flesh. It says, "All cooking, including that of human flesh from diseased kinsmen, was done in pits with steam made by pouring water over the hot stones, or the flesh was cooked in bamboo cylinders in the hot ashes. Children participated in both the butchery and the handling of the cooked meat, rubbing their soiled hands in their armpits or hair, and elsewhere on their bodies. They rarely or never washed. Infection with the kuru virus was most probably through the cuts and abrasions of the skin, or from nose picking, eye rubbing, or mucosal injury." Most people who saw the pictures and read the caption assumed they were viewing a photograph of cannibalism in action.

Not so, says Gajdusek. He explains that anyone should know that that could not be a picture of cannibals because there are men eating meat and only the women were cannibals. Actually, he says, it is a picture of a pig feast.

Gajdusek disagrees with those who question New Guinea cannibalism and the cannibalism of the Fore in particular. "The whole of Australia from the prime minister on down knows these people are cannibals," he says. "The old people tell of cooking and eating their relatives—they give a complete list of who ate whom and when."

Gajdusek refuses to enter into the cannibalism debate or to show the photographs he has taken of cannibalism to those who doubt the Fore ate human flesh. "The people who know of it [the cannibalism] have not deigned to get into the argument. It's beneath our dignity," he remarks.

Lyle Steadman, however, who has worked with the Hewa people in New Guinea, not only questions Gajdusek's statements that cannibalism is well documented in general in New Guinea but also does not believe that it had anything to do with the transmission of kuru. According to Steadman, "cannibalism is irrelevant to the transmission of kuru." New Guinea natives engage in mortuary rites that could easily allow women and children—but not men—to come in contact with the kuru slow viruses. "Skull handling and the handling of corpses is prevalent," Steadman says. Because the women often handle the skulls, and since the women and children are together, the kuru virus could be transmitted from their hands to the children. It has been suggested, says Steadman, that it is extremely unlikely that you can get kuru by eating the virus—slow viruses are most likely transmitted through mucous membranes by touching them to the eyes, nose or mouth. So cannibalism is not necessary to explain the transmission of kuru. In fact, it would only be indirectly, by touching the brain before they would have eaten it, that the women and children would get kuru.

In addition, says Steadman, "there is no evidence of conventional cannibalism in New Guinea." He does not deny that New Guinea natives often say that other members of other tribes are cannibals, or that they themselves once were cannibals or that some members still are cannibals. But he likens it to the witch hunts in Europe. "People were killed for being witches, and at the trials a lot of women said they were witches and that they ate human babies. That does not mean that they did. The tribe that I lived with told me that some of their members were cannibals, but only after I spent time there and really probed did I learn that they were not."

Finally, there is the argument that even if people aren't cannibals now, they were in prehistoric times, before they may have developed taboos against eating human flesh. It is a difficult argument to make, notes Eric Trinkaus, because you have to show, first, that the bones you find really were part of cannibalism and, second, that you are not looking at an isolated occurrence of survival cannibalism but instead are dealing with a cannibal society. "Most of the damage attributed to cannibalism is just a result of the way fossils break when they roll in riverbeds or when they are damaged by carnivores," Trinkaus argues.

To illustrate the difficulty in interpreting the historical record, Trinkaus tells of a Neanderthal skeleton he studied. "The man had an injured rib—he was struck in the rib—and he died one to three weeks later, probably from a collapsed lung. Here was a clear-cut case. The man was stabbed and he died of the consequences. Another archaeologist then claimed it was the earliest case of human-to-human violence. But it could have been anything—murder, an argument or an accident in which someone stabbed him or an accident in which he stabbed himself. This is the only clear case we have of someone dying violently in the whole Paleolithic era and this is the kind of problem we always have in interpreting the prehistoric record."

Recently, however, an international team of researchers, led by Paola Villa of the University of Colorado, reported that they have evidence of cannibalism among Stone Age people who lived in southeastern France 6,000 years ago. They found a pit in Fontbrégoua Cave containing the bones of six people and they noticed that the bones had distinctive cut marks on them. When Pat Shipman of Johns Hopkins University examined the cut marks, she agreed that the most plausible explanation for them was cannibalism. The human carcasses had been stripped of their meat in the same way that animals' carcasses were stripped. "From the evidence we have, it looks like there wasn't any mental distinction between people and animals," says Shipman. "If that was true—and it's a big if—it says something very interesting. These were people. They were Homo sapiens. They had domestic animals and they made pots. Many tribal people have as words for themselves 'humans,' and for all others, 'non-humans.' " What may have happened, according to Shipman, is that these Stone Age people did not distinguish between those outside their tribe and animals when they sought meat. "It's the ultimate sort of 'us' and 'them,' " Shipman says.

But others remain to be convinced. It is a big step and unjustified, says Trinkaus, to conclude from the remains of six people, who may have been eaten by other humans, that these Stone Age people were a cannibal society. "I would not be surprised if there were survival cannibalism in the Stone Age, but I have not run across any evidence of ritualistic cannibalism," he says. Moreover, it is almost certainly impossible to obtain evidence of ritualistic cannibalism in prehistoric times because we have so few bones to examine. The cannibalism hypothesis "is untestable," Trinkaus argues.

But the current interest in cannibalism among our most distant ancestors may nonetheless be telling us something about ourselves, Trinkaus proposes. In the first half of the 20th century, archaeologists either ignored the cannibalism hypothesis as an explanation for cut marks on human fossils or dismissed it. Then, "starting in the early 1950s, suddenly it was accepted. I think it was the horrors of World War II. The atrocities very much changed people's perceptions of how nasty we are as a species and we projected that back on early history," Trinkaus says. The point is that we will never be able to prove that prehistoric people were or were not cannibals—so the way we interpret the data we have tells us more about us than about them.

Culture and Communication

Anthropologists are interested in all aspects of human behavior and how they interrelate with each other. Language is a form of such behavior (albeit primarily verbal behavior), and therefore worthy of study. It is patterned and passed down from one generation to the next through learning, not instinct.

Since language is learned, it changes easily, and any alterations in a given language may be arbitrary and unpredictable or adaptive in response to new circumstances. In either case, it stands to reason that after two or more groups of people with a common language become isolated from each other, the length of their separation will be reflected in the degree of difference in the way they speak. The commonalities and differences between languages may then be used by anthropologists to reconstruct the prehistoric separations of cultural groups over time. It may even be possible, as "The Mother Tongue" suggests, to reconstruct at least some aspects of the original culture and language of our ancient ancestors.

In keeping with the idea that language is integral to human social interaction, it has long been recognized that human communication through language is by its nature different from the kind of communication found among other animals. Central to this difference is the fact that humans communicate abstractly, with symbols that have meaning independent of the immediate sensory experiences of either the sender or the receiver of messages. Thus, for instance, humans are able to refer to the future and the past instead of just the here and now.

Recent experiments have shown that anthropoid apes can be taught a small portion of Ameslan, the sign language used to overcome hearing and speech disabilities. It must be remembered, however, that their very rudimentary ability has to be tapped by painstaking human effort, and that the degree of difference between apes and humans serves only to emphasize the peculiarly human need for and development of language.

Just as the abstract quality of symbols lifts our thoughts beyond immediate sense perception, it also inhibits our ability to think about and convey the full meaning of our personal experience. No categorical term can do justice to its referents—the variety of forms to which the term refers. The degree to which this is an obstacle to clarity of thought and communication relates to the degree of abstraction in the symbols involved. The word "chair," for instance, would not present much difficulty since it has rather objective referents. Consider the trouble we have, however, in thinking and communicating with words whose referents are not quite so tied to immediate sense perception—words such as "freedom," "democracy," and "justice." At best, the likely result is symbolic confusion: an inability to think or communicate in objectively definable symbols. At its worst, language may be used to purposefully obfuscate, as is shown in the article "Language, Appearance, and Reality," or it may be used for dominance and control, as illustrated in "Who's Interrupting? Issues of Dominance and Control."

A related issue, in "The World's Language" by Bill Bryson, has to do with the fact that languages differ as to what is relatively easy to express within the restrictions of their particular vocabularies. Thus, although a given language may not have enough words to allow one to cope with a new situation or a new field of activity, the typical solution is to invent or borrow words. In this way, it may be said that any language can be used to teach anything.

Taken collectively, therefore, the articles in this section show how symbolic confusion may occur between individuals or groups on a verbal and nonverbal level. They also demonstrate the tremendous potential of recent research to enhance effective communication among all of us.

Looking Ahead: Challenge Questions

What can comparative linguistics tell us about the origins and migrations of our ancient ancestors?

Why is English becoming the most global of languages?

Does language restrict our thought processes?

In what ways is communication difficult in a cross-cultural situation?

How has this section enhanced your ability to communicate more effectively?

How do American men and women differ in their conversational styles?

What is the difference between "high-considerateness" and "high-involvement" conversation?

The Mother Tongue

Linguists are working back from modern speech to re-create the first language of the human race

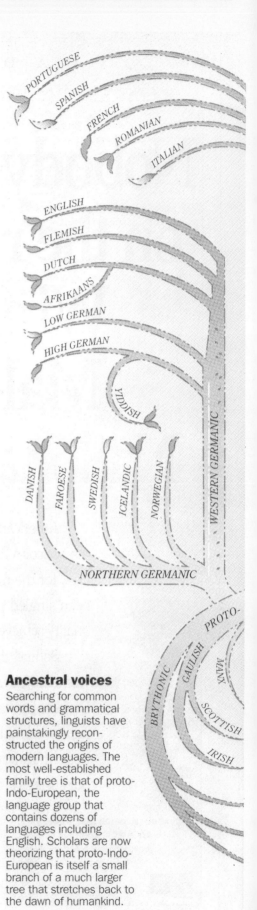

In 1786, Sir William Jones, an Englishman serving the Crown as a judge in India, turned a series of seeming coincidences into an extraordinary discovery about human nature. A scholar of the Orient by training, Jones had embarked on an effort to learn Sanskrit, the language in which many ancient Indian religious and literary texts are written. To his amazement, Jones found that Sanskrit's grammatical forms and vocabulary bore a striking resemblance to those of Greek and Latin, so much so that "no philologer could examine them all three without believing them to have sprung from some common source." As Charles Darwin was to assert almost a century later about the human body, Jones suggested that a fundamental part of the human psyche—language—had a hidden ancestry of its own.

Today, scientists are leading a new revolution in understanding the roots of language. While linguistic pioneer Noam Chomsky and his followers have focused on language as a psychological phenomenon, a small band of renegade scholars is revealing how languages are a product of cultural evolution. Sifting through modern tongues for linguistic "fossils" in the form of common words and grammatical structures, these "linguistic paleoanthropologists," many of whom have worked in obscurity in the Soviet Union, are reconstructing the pathways by which the world's roughly 5,000 languages arose from a handful of ancient "mother" tongues. A few radical linguists have gone even further, claiming they have reconstructed pieces of the mother of them all: The original language spoken at the dawn of the human species.

These linguistic findings are a windfall for archaeologists, anthropologists and other social scientists who are trying to piece together the story of the peopling of the earth. "We've come to realize," says Alexis Manaster Ramer, a researcher at Wayne State University in Detroit, "that a lot of the answers to the big questions lie in something you might call anthro-psycho-socio-linguistics." Language is an integral part of the cultural glue that binds people together and signals their presence. Tracing the evolution of language can reveal how ancient peoples migrated into new lands, for instance, just as reconstructing the vocabularies of lost languages can give researchers clues to what ancient people saw, ate and thought, or how one culture coexisted—or collided—with another. The new linguistic findings also neatly

Ancestral voices

Searching for common words and grammatical structures, linguists have painstakingly reconstructed the origins of modern languages. The most well-established family tree is that of proto-Indo-European, the language group that contains dozens of languages including English. Scholars are now theorizing that proto-Indo-European is itself a small branch of a much larger tree that stretches back to the dawn of humankind.

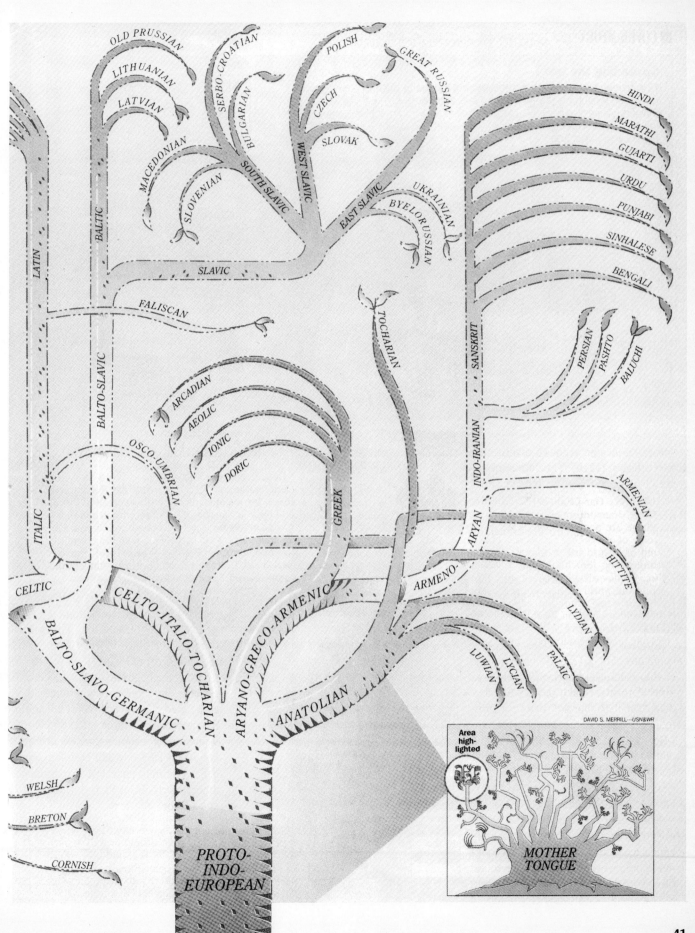

OLD PRUSSIAN
LITHUANIAN
LATVIAN
SERBO-CROATIAN
POLISH
GREAT RUSSIAN
BULGARIAN
CZECH
SLOVAK
MACEDONIAN
SOUTH SLAVIC
WEST SLAVIC
SLOVENIAN
EAST SLAVIC
UKRAINIAN
BYELORUSSIAN
BALTIC
SLAVIC
LATIN
FALISCAN
BALTO-SLAVIC
TOCHARIAN
ARCADIAN
AEOLIC
IONIC
DORIC
OSCO-UMBRIAN
ITALIC
GREEK
SANSKRIT
INDO-IRANIAN
CELTIC
CELTO-ITALO-TOCHARIAN
ARYANO-GRECO-ARMENIC
ARYAN
ARMENO-
BALTO-SLAVO-GERMANIC
ANATOLIAN
WELSH
BRETON
CORNISH
PROTO-INDO-EUROPEAN

HINDI
MARATHI
GUJARTI
URDU
PUNJABI
SINHALESE
BENGALI
PERSIAN
PASHTO
BALUCHI
ARMENIAN
HITTITE
LYDIAN
LUWIAN
LYCIAN
PALAIC

DAVID S. MERRILL---USN&WR

Area high-lighted

MOTHER TONGUE

41

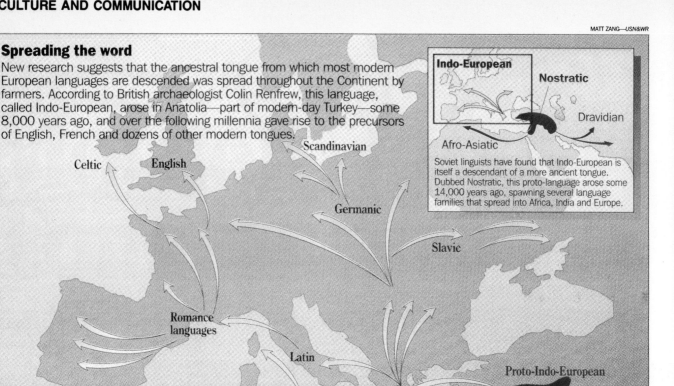

MATT ZANG—USN&WR

Spreading the word

New research suggests that the ancestral tongue from which most modern European languages are descended was spread throughout the Continent by farmers. According to British archaeologist Colin Renfrew, this language, called Indo-European, arose in Anatolia—part of modern-day Turkey—some 8,000 years ago, and over the following millennia gave rise to the precursors of English, French and dozens of other modern tongues.

Indo-European | **Nostratic** | Dravidian | Afro-Asiatic

Soviet linguists have found that Indo-European is itself a descendant of a more ancient tongue. Dubbed Nostratic, this proto-language arose some 14,000 years ago, spawning several language families that spread into Africa, India and Europe.

Celtic · English · Scandinavian · Germanic · Slavic · Romance languages · Latin · Greek · Proto-Indo-European · ANATOLIA

USN&WR—Basic data: *Archaeology and Language* by Colin Renfrew, Cambridge University Press, 1988

dovetail with conclusions drawn from a very different area of evolutionary research. Comparisons of human genes worldwide have produced a "family tree" of the human race whose branches closely mirror the branching of languages proposed by linguists, leading to the startling suggestion that all people—and perhaps all languages—are descended from a tiny population that live in Africa some 200,000 years ago.

English pedigree. The idea that languages are constantly evolving is obvious from looking at English over time: Consider Shakespeare's Elizabethan "Shall I compare thee to a summer's day?"; Chaucer's 14th-century, Middle English "Whan that Aprille with his shourse sote," and the opening line from the eighth-century Old English epic *Beowulf:* "Hwaet! We Gar-Dena, in geardagum."

These dramatic sound changes within a single language are possible only because, with the exception of onomatopoeic words like sizzle, the sound of a word has no direct connection to its meaning, says Merritt Ruhlen, a

LINEAGE OF
A WORD
· · · · · · · · ·
Haku
Proto-World
▪
Hakw
Amerind
▪
Kwa
Dene-Caucasian
▪
Haku
Nostratic
▪
Hakw
Indo-European
▪
Aqua
Latin
▪
Wazzar
Old German
▪
Water
English

scholar in Palo Alto, Calif., who is tracing the relationships among the world's languages. Like coins, words get their value from the community at large, which must agree on what they represent. The word *dog* may mean a furry creature with four legs and a wagging tail, for instance, but *hippopotamus* or *ziglot* would serve just as well, as long as both speaker and listener agreed on its meaning.

Cream in your coffee. These arbitrary associations between sounds and meanings provide the key to reconstructing the linguistic past, says Ruhlen. Because any number of sounds could be associated with a particular meaning, the presence of similar-sounding words with similar meanings in two different languages suggests that both languages had a common ancestor. For instance, diners might order their coffee *au lait, con leche* or *latte,* depending on whether they are in a French, Spanish or Italian restaurant. Using these similar-sounding "daughter" words for milk and a knowledge of how the sounds of words change as languages evolve, linguists could come close to

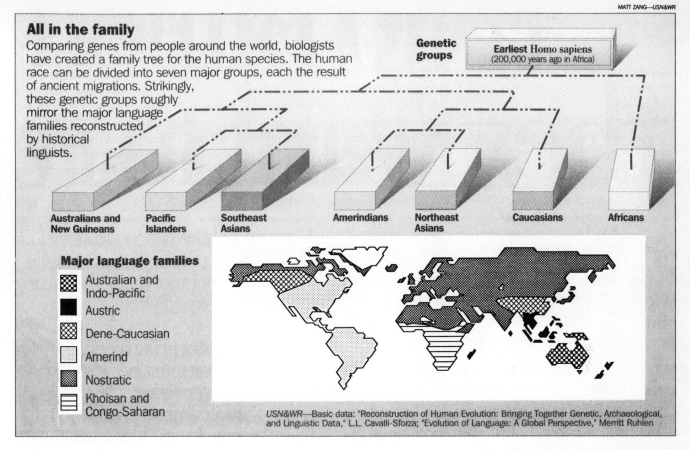

All in the family

Comparing genes from people around the world, biologists have created a family tree for the human species. The human race can be divided into seven major groups, each the result of ancient migrations. Strikingly, these genetic groups roughly mirror the major language families reconstructed by historical linguists.

Genetic groups

Earliest Homo sapiens (200,000 years ago in Africa)

Australians and New Guineans
Pacific Islanders
Southeast Asians
Amerindians
Northeast Asians
Caucasians
Africans

Major language families

- Australian and Indo-Pacific
- Austric
- Dene-Caucasian
- Amerind
- Nostratic
- Khoisan and Congo-Saharan

USN&WR—Basic data: "Reconstruction of Human Evolution: Bringing Together Genetic, Archaeological, and Linguistic Data," L.L. Cavalli-Sforza; "Evolution of Language: A Global Perspective," Merritt Ruhlen

reconstructing the Latin form, *lacte,* even if this mother tongue of Romance languages were unknown.

Similar comparisons among words are what led Jones to suspect that Latin, along with Greek and Sanskrit, had descended from an even more ancient mother tongue. The word for the number three, for instance, is *tres* in Latin, *treis* in Greek and *tryas* in Sanskrit. Over the years, scholars following up on Jones's suggestion have demonstrated that dozens of languages, including English, Swedish, German, Russian, Polish, Hindi, Persian, Welsh and Lithuanian, are all descendants of this same ancient "proto-language." Called Indo-European by linguists, this mother tongue was spoken some 8,000 years ago, before the invention of writing, and is known only by the traces left behind in the vocabularies of its daughter languages.

From these remnants, however, linguists have reconstructed a vast lexicon of proto-Indo-European words, providing clues to the origins of the ancient people who spoke the language when they populated nearly all of Eu-

LINEAGE OF A WORD
··········
Hita
Proto-World
∎
Hit–
Amerind
∎
–ita
Nostratic
∎
Hed
Indo-European
∎
Edmenai
Greek
∎
Edere
Latin
∎
Ezzan
Old German
∎
Eat
English

rope. According to recent work by two Soviet linguists, Thomas Gamkrelidze and Vyacheslav Ivanov, words for domesticated animals such as cows, sheep and dogs as well as plants such as barley, flax and wheat suggest that the people who spoke proto-Indo-European were farmers. Likewise, the prevalence of words evoking mountains and rapidly flowing rivers suggests the Indo-European people originally lived in a hilly terrain.

Using these and other linguistic clues, Soviet researchers have offered new evidence that Indo-European originated in an area known as Anatolia, which is now part of Turkey, and from there spread throughout Europe and the sub-Continent. Linguists had long thought that the Indo-European-proto-language had originated in southern Russia and had been spread throughout Europe by hordes of conquering warriors. But Gamkrelidze, Ivanov and other Soviet scholars cite words in proto-Indo-European that appear to have been borrowed from the languages of Mesopotamia and the Near East, suggesting that the speakers of proto-Indo-European lived in close geographical proximity to these cultures. The proto-Indo-European word for wine, for instance, appears to have its ancient roots in the non-Indo-European Semitic word *wanju* and the Egyptian *wns*.

Farming in Europe. The Soviets' linguistic work has found unexpected support in new research by British archaeologist Colin Renfrew, who, unaware of the linguistic studies, independently determined that the Indo-European homeland was in Anatolia, based on a reassessment of the archaeological evidence. Renfrew suggests that it was farmers, not warriors, who were responsible for the spread of the Indo-European language into Europe. He notes that even if a farmer's off-spring had moved only 10 miles from the family farm to set up farms of their own, the resulting wave of agriculture could have swept throughout Europe from Anatolia in about 1,500 years, carrying the Indo-European language with it. Because farming can support a larger number of people than hunting and gathering, the existing inhabitants of Europe were probably pushed out or adapted to farming on their own, says Renfrew.

While the existence of proto-Indo-European has been accepted among scholars for years, linguists have now begun to trace the lineage of languages back even further. Linguists studying languages from other areas of the world have identified ancestral mother tongues such as Altic, which gave rise to east Asian languages including Japanese and Korean, and Afro-Asiatic, the ancestor of Semitic. Working backward from reconstructions of Indo-European, Altic, Afro-Asiatic and several others, Soviet scholars have found that these ancestral tongues derived from an even more ancient language. Called "Nostratic," meaning "our language," this ancestral tongue was reconstructed independently by Soviet linguists Vladislav Illich-Svitych and Aharon Dolgopolsky during the 1960s, though their work was not translated into English until recently.

To re-create this ancient mother tongue, the Soviet scholars examined words considered by linguists to be the most stable parts of a vocabulary, such as names for body parts, personal pro-

---

FIRST WORDS
Original utterance: Chimps, dolphins and early humans

As historical linguists trace the world's languages back to their earliest sources of diction and syntax, other researchers are taking on the deep mystery of how and when humans started to talk in the first place. In the forthcoming book *Uniquely Human: The Evolution of Speech, Thought and Selfless Behavior* (Harvard University Press, $27.95), linguist Philip Lieberman of Brown University argues that ancient hominids lacked the modern human's elongated vocal tract, which he contends is essential for the wide range of sounds characteristic of language. Fossil evidence suggests that fully developed language may have arisen only with the appearance of anatomically modern humans some 200,000 years ago, and that their sophisticated powers of communication may have been a key to the species' migration around the globe.

But some crude form of language may have existed long before the evolution of language as we know it. Studies of fossil skulls indicate that a part of the brain crucial to language production in modern humans ex-isted in hominids millions of years ago, suggesting that our ancient ancestors may have had at least rudimentary linguistic abilities. In his new book, *Language and Species* (University of Chicago Press, $24.95), linguist Derek Bickerton of the University of Hawaii contends that primitive language may have arisen not so much from the need to communicate as from the mind's effort to grasp the world around it. Vestiges of this language remain with us, he says, in the form of the simple, one and two-word utterances of toddlers and adults who speak to each other in pidgin.

Apes and other intelligent animals may also share this rudimentary form of language. Studies of chimpanzees have shown that animals can communicate with signs or symbols only in a very limited fashion. But just last month, researchers from the University of California at Los Angeles and Emory University's Yerkes Regional Primate Research Center reported that a 5 ½-year-old pygmy chimp named Kanzi spontaneously learned to use grammatical rules similar to those of a 2-year-old child. UCLA psychologist Patricia Marks Greenfield and Yerkes biologist Sue Savage-Rumbaugh found that the order in which Kanzi used symbols was an integral part of their meaning. Recent studies with dolphins and sea lions demonstrate that these creatures can learn to understand word order as well.

Whether the utterances of animals represent true humanlike language abilities remains a matter of intense scientific debate, however. Critics of animal-language studies argue that the animals are only using rote behavior to get food or are responding to unconscious cues from their trainers. "All the evidence suggests that the animals are merely using sophisticated ways to request things," says Columbia University psychologist Herbert Terrace, whose ape research convinced him that animals could not learn to communicate in a humanlike language. Evidence that language may be a uniquely human trait, say some researchers, ultimately lies not in animals' language abilities but in how they use that ability. In animals, language appears to be just one more way to fulfill physical desires; in humans, language reflects not only our earthly needs but our heavenly desires, thoughts and emotions.

nouns and natural objects such as the sun and moon. Analyzing how the sounds for these words changed among Nostratic's various daughter languages, they were able to reconstruct hundreds of words. The Nostratic word for young man, for instance, is *majra,* which evolved into *merio* in Indo-European and thousands of years later became *mari* in French, meaning husband, and *marry* in English.

The reconstructed words of Nostratic vocabulary offer a glimpse of how the people who spoke the language lived, and they suggest a date when the language thrived. The absence of words for domesticated plants suggests the Nostratic speakers were probably hunter-gatherers, says Vitaly Sheveroskin, a former student of Dolgopolsky's who is now at the University of Michigan. Even more intriguing is the word *kuyna,* which can mean either dog or wolf; the "k" evolved into an "h" in Germanic languages, leading to *hound* in English. The ambiguity of meaning in the word suggests that wolves were in the process of becoming domesticated, says Sheveroskin, who notes that the oldest bones of dogs date to 14,000 years ago, giving a time frame when Nostratic was spoken. The speakers of Nostratic were well-traveled: Not only is the lexicon peppered with words that refer to "long journey" but over the next several thousand years, Nostratic split into several major language families as its speakers migrated from the Near East, their suspected homeland, into Europe, Persia and India.

The reconstruction of another such "macrofamily" of languages has given new clues to another mass migration, the original settling of the Americas. Joseph Greenberg, a linguist at Stanford University, recently proposed a controversial theory that all the languages spoken by Native Americans can be grouped into three families that correspond to three waves of migration from Asia into the New World thousands of years ago. The largest, oldest and most controversial group proposed by Greenberg is a macrofamily that he calls Amerind, which is made up of all the languages in South and Central

LINEAGE OF
A WORD
· · · · · · · · · ·
Kuni
Proto-World
▪
Küni
Nostratic
▪
Gwen
Indo-European
▪
Queen
English

America as well as many in North America. The other two language groups are Na-Dene, which includes tongues spoken by Native Americans in the Northwest as well as Navajo and Apache, and Eskimo-Aleut, which contains languages spoken mostly in the Arctic; this group was the last to arrive in the New World.

Scholarly furor. Greenberg's theory has created a furor among linguists, even some of those who champion the deep reconstruction of languages. At a recent conference in Boulder, Colo., linguists attacked Greenberg's admittedly unconventional methodology, in which he compares common-sounding words across many languages rather than attempting to reconstruct the sound shifts that occurred when one tongue diverged from another. Yet Greenberg's defenders cite his track record: A classification of African languages he made 20 years ago created a similar furor among linguists and is now widely accepted.

Greenberg's theory is being given new weight by an upheaval in archaeological thinking about the peopling of the Americas. Archaeologists have long believed that the first migration to the New World occurred some 12,000 years ago—too short a time, some linguists argue, for the hundreds of Indian languages to arise from Greenberg's proposed Amerind mother tongue. But recently, several archaeological sites in

the Americas have been shown to be far older than 12,000 years, suggesting that the first migration to the New World may have occurred much earlier—thus allowing more time for languages to diverge. One site, a rock shelter in Pennsylvania, has been dated at 16,000 years and another site in Chile may date back as far as 33,000 years. New studies that compare changes in the genes of Native Americans suggest that the date of the first migration might stretch back as far as 60,000 years.

Research on American languages is also throwing light on a longstanding linguistic mystery in Europe—as well as testifying to the remarkable wanderlust of ancient humans. Linguists have long wondered about the origins of Basque, a language spoken in the north of Spain that is one of the few non-Indo-European languages on the Continent. Soviet linguists have uncovered evidence that Basque is related to Na-Dene, and that both languages are part of yet another language macrofamily that includes tongues ranging from Chinese to the ancient Mediterranean tongue Etruscan. Called Dene-Caucasian, this ancient language was reconstructed in large part by Soviet linguist Sergei Starostin, another student of Dolgopolsky's. This wide-ranging tongue, spoken on both sides of the Bering Strait and at both ends of the Eurasian land mass, reflects the vast movements of ancient peoples who took their language with them and in some cases, such as Basque, kept it alive despite their being surrounded by other tongues.

The survival of an exotic linguistic island like Basque suggests that language, like genes, can sometimes serve as a marker for a distinct group of people. Historical linguistic studies are generating widespread interest among scientists involved in one of the most exciting new developments in science: Tracing the evolutionary history of human genes. "It's quite clear why you have a correlation between genes and language," says Stanford University geneticist Luigi Cavalli-Sforza, a pioneer in the new genetic techniques. "When the human expansion around the earth took place some 50,000 years ago, it caused a number of separations between groups that didn't communicate again, genetically or linguistically. As the genes become different, the languages become different, too."

Cavalli-Sforza and his colleagues recently examined genetic markers from 42 different indigenous peoples from around the world and used the divergence among the genes to construct a family tree for the entire human race. The tree shows the human diaspora over tens of thousands of years, as a single population split into several large groups and then into the smaller tribes that exist today.

African split. More important, Cavalli-Sforza found that the groupings of the human family based on genetic evidence closely mirrored the language groupings laid out independently by historical linguists. The oldest split occurred between Africans and other world populations, reflecting the migration of Homo sapiens out of Africa. This split is reflected in languages as well: Africa's Khoisan languages, such as that of the !Kung San, which uses a clicking noise denoted by an exclamation point, is only distantly related to other languages in the world. A recent paleoanthropological discovery in the Near East of the oldest fossils of Homo sapiens gives a rough date for when this first split might have occurred: The fossils date back 92,000 years.

Another study that similarly traced the human genetic lineage suggests that all languages may have their roots in a small population that lived some

LINEAGE OF
A WORD
··········
Kujan
Proto-World

▪

Kuyna
Nostratic

▪

Kuon
Indo-European

▪

Hound
English

200,000 years ago. In their famed "Eve" hypothesis, Allan Wilson, Mark Stoneking and Rebecca Cann of the University of California at Berkeley traced genetic material from women around the world and concluded that all humans alive today are descendants of a tiny population of Homo sapiens that lived in Africa.

If the human race did arise from this small group of people, then it is likely they all spoke the same language, contends Sheveroskin. What's more, he says, the same techniques that gave rise to the reconstructions of ancient macrofamilies can also be used to dredge up bits of the original mother tongue of the human race. For example, the Nostratic word for leaf, *lapa,* is similar to *tlapa* in Dene-Caucasian and *dap* in Amerind. And the Amerind word for women, *kuni,* closely resembles the Nostratic word for woman, *küni.* It is from this word that the English word *queen* is derived.

Fleas and in-laws. Sheveroskin and other linguists have reconstructed dozens of words in this original mother tongue, which has been dubbed simply "proto-World." The word for I, for instance, is *ngai; nas* means nose. The linguists have also reconstructed proto-World words referring to body parts, fleas, in-laws and a category of words that referred to pairs of objects—reflecting, perhaps, a culture that before the invention of mathematics counted the world in ones, twos and many. *Niwha* and *hwina* refer simultaneously to life, breath and blood, but, strangely, notes Sheveroskin, there appear to be no words in proto-World that refer to human emotions.

In the end, discovering the roots of language is inexorably tied to the still unresolved task of defining what language is, and this is where the ultimate impact of the new linguistic research may lie. The deep connections between languages demonstrate that far from a mere communication device, language is the palette from which people color their lives and culture. Intimately connected to the human experience, language oils the gears of social interactions and solidifies the ephemera of the mind into literature, history and collective knowledge. It is the calling card of the human race; announcing the presence not only of those alive today but, with its deep roots into the past, the ancient ancestors who came before us.
William F. Allman

The World's Language

Bill Bryson

More than 300 million people in the world speak English and the rest, it sometimes seems, try to. It would be charitable to say that the results are sometimes mixed.

Consider this hearty announcement in a Yugoslavian hotel: "The flattening of underwear with pleasure is the job of the chambermaid. Turn to her straightaway." Or this warning to motorists in Tokyo: "When a passenger of the foot heave in sight, tootle the horn. Trumpet at him melodiously at first, but if he still obstacles your passage, then tootle him with vigor." Or these instructions gracing a packet of convenience food from Italy: "Besmear a backing pan, previously buttered with a good tomato sauce, and, after, dispose the cannelloni, lightly distanced between them in a only couch."

Clearly the writer of *that* message was not about to let a little ignorance of English stand in the way of a good meal. In fact, it would appear that one of the beauties of the English language is that with even the most tenuous grasp you can speak volumes if you show enough enthusiasm—a willingness to tootle with vigor, as it were.

To be fair, English is full of booby traps for the unwary foreigner. Any language where the unassuming word *fly* signifies an annoying insect, a means of travel, and a critical part of a gentleman's apparel is clearly asking to be mangled. Imagine being a foreigner and having to learn that in English one tells *a* lie but *the* truth, that a person

---

The English language is fast becoming a world language

---

who says "I could care less" means the same thing as someone who says "I couldn't care less," that a sign in a store saying ALL ITEMS NOT ON SALE doesn't mean literally what it says (that every item is *not* on sale) but rather that only some of the items are on sale, that when a person says to you, "How do you do?" he will be taken aback if you reply, with impeccable logic, "How do I do what?"

The complexities of the English language are such that even native speakers cannot always communicate effectively, as almost every American learns on his first day in Britain. Indeed, Robert Burchfield, editor of the *Oxford English Dictionary,* created a stir in linguistic circles on both sides of the Atlantic when he announced his belief that American English and English English are drifting apart so rapidly that within 200 years the two nations won't be able to understand each other at all.

That may be. But if the Briton and American of the twenty-second century baffle each other, it seems altogether likely that they won't confuse many others—not, at least, if the rest of the world continues expropriating words and phrases at its present rate. Already Germans talk about *ein Image Problem* and *das Cash-Flow,* Italians program their computers with *il software,* French motorists going away for a *weekend break* pause for *les refueling stops,* Poles watch *telewizja,* Spaniards have a *flirt,* Austrians eat *Big Mäcs,* and the Japanese go on a *pikunikku.* For better or worse, English has become the most global of languages, the lingua franca of business, science, education, politics, and pop music. For the airlines of 157 nations (out of 168 in the world), it is the agreed international language of discourse. In India, there are more than 3,000 newspapers in English. The six member nations of the European Free Trade Association conduct all their business in English, even though not one of them is an English-speaking country. When companies from four European countries—France, Italy, Germany, and Switzerland—formed a joint truck-making venture called Iveco in 1977, they chose English as their working language because, as one of the founders wryly observed, "It puts us all at an equal disadvantage." For the same reasons, when the Swiss company Brown Boveri and the Swedish company ASEA merged in 1988, they decided to make the official company language English, and when Volkswagen set up a factory in Shanghai it found that there were too few Germans who spoke Chinese and too few Chinese who spoke German, so now Volkswagen's German engineers and Chinese managers communicate in a language that is alien to both of them, English. Belgium has two languages, French and Flemish, yet on a recent visit to the country's main airport in Brussels, I counted more than fifty posters and billboards and not one of them was in French or Flemish. They were all in English.

For non-English speakers everywhere, English has become the common tongue. Even in France, the most determinedly non-English-speaking nation in the world, the war against English encroachment has largely been lost. In early 1989, the Pasteur Institute announced that henceforth it would publish its famed international medical review only in English because too few people were reading it in French.

English is, in short, one of the world's great growth industries. "English is just as much big business as the export of manufactured goods," Professor Randolph Quirk of Oxford University has written. "There are problems with what you might call 'after-sales service'; and

'delivery' can be awkward; but at any rate the production lines are trouble free." [*The Observer,* October 26, 1980] Indeed, such is the demand to learn the language that there are now more students of English in China than there are people in the United States.

It is often said that what most immediately sets English apart from other languages is the richness of its vocabulary. *Webster's Third New International Dictionary* lists 450,000 words, and the revised *Oxford English Dictionary* has 615, 000, but that is only part of the total. Technical and scientific terms would add millions more. Altogether, about 200,000 English words are in common use, more than in German (184,000) and far more than in French (a mere 100,000). The richness of the English vocabulary, and the wealth of available synonyms, means that English speakers can often draw shades of distinction unavailable to non-English speakers. The French, for instance, cannot distinguish between house and home, between mind and brain, between man and gentleman, between "I wrote" and "I have written." The Spanish cannot differentiate a chairman from a president, and the Italians have no equivalent of wishful thinking. In Russia there are no native words for efficiency, challenge, engagement ring, have fun, or take care [all cited in *The New York Times,* June 18, 1989]. English, as Charlton Laird has noted, is the only language that has, or needs, books of synonyms like *Roget's Thesaurus.* "Most speakers of other languages are not aware that such books exist." [*The Miracle of Language,* page 54]

On the other hand, other languages have facilities we lack. Both French and German can distinguish between knowledge that results from recognition (respectively *connaître* and *kennen*) and knowledge that results from understanding (*savoir* and *wissen*). Portuguese has words that differentiate between an interior angle and an exterior one. All the Romance languages can distinguish between something that leaks into and something that leaks out of. The Italians even have a word for the mark left on a table by a moist glass

(*culacino*) while the Gaelic speakers of Scotland, not to be outdone, have a word for the itchiness that overcomes the upper lip just before taking a sip of whiskey. (Wouldn't they just?) It's *sgriob.* And we have nothing in English to match the Danish *hygge* (meaning "instantly satisfying and cozy"), the French *sang-froid,* the Russian *glasnost,* or the Spanish *macho,* so we must borrow the term from them or do without the sentiment.

At the same time, some languages have words that we may be pleased to do without. The existence in German of a word like *schadenfreude* (taking delight in the misfortune of others) perhaps tells us as much about Teutonic sensitivity as it does about their neologistic versatility. Much the same could be said about the curious and monumentally unpronounceable Highland Scottish word *sgiomlaireachd,* which means "the habit of dropping in at mealtimes." That surely conveys a world of information about the hazards of Highland life—not to mention the hazards of Highland orthography.

Of course, every language has areas in which it needs, for practical purposes, to be more expressive than others. The Eskimos, as is well known, have fifty words for types of snow—though curiously no word for just plain snow. To them there is crunchy snow, soft snow, fresh snow, and old snow, but no word that just means snow. The Italians, as we might expect, have over 500 names for different types of macaroni. Some of these, when translated, begin to sound distinctly unappetizing, like strozzapreti, which means "strangled priests." Vermicelli means "little worms" and even spaghetti means "little strings." When you learn that muscatel in Italian means "wine with flies in it," you may conclude that the Italians are gastronomically out to lunch, so to speak, but really their names for foodstuffs are no more disgusting than our hot dogs or those old English favorites, toad-in-the hole, spotted dick, and faggots in gravy.

The residents of the Trobriand Islands of Papua New Guinea have a hundred words for yams, while the Maoris of New Zealand have thirty-five words for dung (don't ask me why). Meanwhile, the Arabs are said (a little unbelievably, perhaps) to have 6,000 words for camels and camel equipment. The aborigines of Tasmania have a word for every type of tree, but no word that just means "tree," while the Araucanian Indians of Chile rather more poignantly have a variety of words to distinguish between different degrees of hunger. Even among speakers of the same language, regional and national differences abound. A Londoner has a less comprehensive view of extremes of weather than someone from the Middle West of America. What a Briton calls a blizzard would, in Illinois or Nebraska, be a flurry, and a British heat wave is often a thing of merriment to much of the rest of the world. (I still treasure a London newspaper with the

---

English has a flexibility that sets it apart from other languages

---

A second commonly cited factor in setting English apart from other languages is its flexibility. This is particularly true of word ordering, where English speakers can roam with considerable freedom between passive and active sense. Not only can we say "I kicked the dog," but also "The dog was kicked by me"—a construction that would be impossible in many other languages. Similarly, where the Germans can say just "ich singe" and the French must manage with "je chante," we can say "I sing," "I do sing," or "I am singing." English also has a distinctive capacity to extract maximum work from a word by making it do double duty as both noun and verb. The list of such versatile words is practically endless; *drink, fight, fire, sleep, run, fund, look, act, view, ape, silence, worship, copy, blame, comfort, bend, cut, reach, like, dislike,* and so on. Other languages sometimes show inspired flashes of versatility, as with the German *auf,* which can mean "on," "in," "upon," "at," "toward," "for," "to," and "upward," but these are relative rarities.

At the same time, the endless versatility of English is what makes our rules of grammar so perplexing. Few English-speaking natives, however well educated, can confidently elucidate the difference between, say, a complement and a predicate or distinguish a full infinitive from a bare one. The reason for this is that the rules of English grammar were originally modeled on those of Latin, which in the seventeenth century was considered the purest and most admirable of tongues. That it may be. But it is also quite clearly another language altogether. Imposing Latin rules on English structure is a little like trying to play baseball in ice skates. The two simply don't match. In the sentence "I am swimming," swimming is a present participle. But in the sentence "Swimming is good for you," it is a gerund—even though it means exactly the same thing.

A third—and more contentious—supposed advantage of English is the relative simplicity of its spelling and pronunciation. For all its idiosyncrasies, English is said to have fewer of the awkward consonant clusters and singsong tonal variations that makes other languages so difficult to master. In Cantonese, *hae* means "yes." But, with a fractional change of pitch, it also describes the female pudenda. The resulting scope for confusion can be safely left to the imagination. In other languages it is the orthography, or spelling, that leads to bewilderment. In Welsh, the word for beer is *cwrw*—an impossible combination of letters for any English speaker. But Welsh spellings are as nothing compared with Irish Gaelic, a language in which spelling and pronunciation give the impression of having been devised by separate committees, meeting in separate rooms, while implacably divided over some deep semantic issue. Try pronouncing *geimhreadh,* Gaelic for "winter," and you will probably come up with something like "gem-reed-uh." It is in fact "gyeeryee." *Beaudhchais* ("thank you") is "bekkas" and *O Séaghda* ("Oh-seeg-da?") is simply "O'Shea." Against this, the Welsh pronunciation of *cwrw*—"koo-roo"—begins to look positively self-evident.

In all languages pronunciation is of course largely a matter of familiarity mingled with prejudice. The average English speaker confronted with agglomerations of letters like *tchst, sthm,* and *tchph* would naturally conclude that they were pretty well unpronounceable. Yet we use them every day in the words matchstick, asthma, and *catchphrase.* Here, as in almost every other area of language, natural bias plays an inescapable part in any attempt at evaluation. No one has ever said, "Yes, my language is backward and unexpressive, and could really do with some sharpening up." We tend to regard other people's languages as we regard their cultures—with ill-hidden disdain. In Japanese, the word for foreigner means "stinking of foreign hair." To the Czechs a Hungarian is "a pimple." Germans call cockroaches "Frenchmen," while the French call lice "Spaniards." We in the English-speaking world take French leave, but Italians and Norwegians talk about departing like an Englishman, and Germans talk of running like a Dutchman. Italians call syphilis "the French disease," while both French and Italians call con games "American swindle." Belgian taxi drivers call a poor tipper "un Anglais." To be bored to death in French is "être de Birmingham," literally "to be from Birmingham" (which is actually about right). And in English we have "Dutch courage," "French letters," "Spanish fly," "Mexican carwash" (i.e., leaving your car out in the rain), and many others. Late in the last century these epithets focused on the Irish, and often, it must be said, they were as witty as they were wounding. An Irish buggy was a wheelbarrow. An Irish beauty was a woman with two black eyes. Irish confetti was bricks. An Irish promotion was a demotion. Now almost the only slur against these fine people is to get one's Irish up, and that isn't really taken as an insult.

So objective evidence, even among the authorities, is not always easy to come by. Most books on English imply in one way or another that our language is superior to all others. In *The English Language*, Robert Burchfield writes: "As a source of intellectual power and entertainment the whole range of prose writing in English is probably unequalled anywhere else in the world." I would like to think he's right, but I can't help wondering if Mr. Burchfield would have made the same generous assertion had he been born Russian or German or Chinese. There is no reliable way of measuring the quality or efficiency of any language. Yet there are one or two small ways in which English has a demonstrable edge over other languages. For one thing its pronouns are largely, and mercifully, uninflected. In German, if you wish to say *you,* you must choose between seven words: *du, dich, dir, Sie, Ihnen, ihr,* and *euch.* This can cause immense social anxiety. The composer Richard Strauss and his librettist, Hugo von Hofmannsthal, were partners for twenty-five years and apparently adored each other and yet never quite found the nerve to address each other as anything but the stiff "Sie." In English we avoid these problems by relying on just one form: *you.*

In other languages, questions of familiarity can become even more agonizing. A Korean has to choose between one of six verb suffixes to accord with the status of the person addressed. A speaker of Japanese must equally wend his way through a series of linguistic levels appropriate to the social position of the participants. When he says thank you he must choose between a range of meanings running from the perfunctory *arigato* ("thanks") to the decidedly more humble *makotoni go shinsetsu de gozaimasu,* which means "what you have done or proposed to do is a truly and genuinely kind and generous deed." Above all, English is mercifully free of gender. Anyone who spent much of his or her adolescence miserably trying to remember whether it is "la plume" or "le plume" will appreciate just what a pointless burden masculine and feminine nouns are to any language. In this regard English is a godsend to students

everywhere. Not only have we discarded problems of gender with definite and indefinite articles, we have often discarded the articles themselves. We say in English, "It's time to go to bed," where in most other European languages they say, "It's *the* time to go to *the* bed." We possess countless examples of pithy phrases—"life is short," "between heaven and earth," "to go to work"—which in other languages require articles.

English also has a commendable tendency toward conciseness, in contrast to many languages. German is full of jaw-crunching words like *Wirtschaftstreuhandgesellschaft* (business trust company), *Bundesbahnangestelltenwitwe* (a widow of a federal railway employee), and *Kriegsgefangenanentschädigungsgesetz* (a law pertaining to war reparations), while in Holland

---

English is a very concise language

---

companies commonly have names of forty letters or more, such as Douwe Egberts Koninlijke Tabaksfabriek-Koffiebranderijen-Theehandal Naamloze Vennootschap (literally Douwe Egberts Royal Tobacco Factory-Coffee Roasters-Tea Traders Incorporated; they must use fold-out business cards). English, in happy contrast, favors crisp truncations: IBM, laser, NATO. Against this, however, there is an occasional tendency in English, particularly in academic and political circles, to resort to waffle and jargon. At a conference of sociologists in America in 1977, love was defined as "the cognitive-affective state characterized by intrusive and obsessive fantasizing concerning reciprocity of amorant feelings by the object of the amorance." That is jargon—the practice of never calling a spade a spade when you might instead call it a manual earth-restructuring implement—and it is one of the great curses of modern English.

But perhaps the single most notable

characteristic of English—for better *and* worse—is its deceptive complexity. . . .

. . . English is unique in possessing a synonym for each level of our culture: popular, literary, and scholarly—so that we can, according to our background and cerebral attainments, rise, mount, or ascend a stairway, shrink in fear, terror, or trepidation, and think, ponder, or cogitate upon a problem. This abundance of terms is often cited as a virtue. And yet a critic could equally argue that English is an untidy and acquisitive language, cluttered with a plethora of needless words. After all, do we really need *fictile* as a synonym for *moldable, glabrous* for *hairless, sternutation* for *sneezing?* Jules Feiffer once drew a strip cartoon in which the down-at-heel character observed that first he was called poor, then needy, then deprived, then underprivileged, and then disadvantaged, and concluded that although he still didn't have a dime he sure had acquired a fine vocabulary. There is something in that. A rich vocabulary carries with it a concomitant danger of verbosity, as evidenced by our peculiar affection for redundant phrases, expressions that say the same thing twice: *beck and call, law and order, assault and battery, null and void, safe and sound, first and foremost, trials and tribulations, hem and haw, spick-and-span, kith and kin, dig and delve, hale and hearty, peace and quiet, vim and vigor, pots and pans, cease and desist, rack and ruin, without let or hindrance, to all intents and purposes, various different.*

Despite this bounty of terms, we have a strange—and to foreigners it must seem maddening—tendency to load a single word with a whole galaxy of meanings. *Fine,* for instance, has fourteen definitions as an adjective, six as a noun, and two as an adverb. In the *Oxford English Dictionary* it fills two full pages and takes 5,000 words of description. We can talk about fine art, fine gold, a fine edge, feeling fine, fine hair, and a court fine and mean quite separate things. The condition of having many meanings is known as *polysemy,* and it is very common. *Sound* is another polysemic word. Its vast repertory of meanings can suggest an audible noise, a state of healthiness (sound mind), an outburst (sound off), an inquiry (sound out), a body of water (Puget Sound), or financial stability (sound economy), among many others. And then there's *round*. In the *OED*, *round* alone (that is without variants like *rounded* and *roundup*) takes 7½

pages to define or about 15,000 words of text—about as much as is contained in the first hundred pages of this book. Even when you strip out its obsolete sense, *round* still has twelve uses as an adjective, nineteen as a noun, seven as a transitive verb, five as an intransitive verb, one as an adverb, and two as a proposition. But the polysemic champion must be *set*. Superficially it looks

a wholly unseeming monosyllable, the verbal equivalent of the single-celled organism. Yet it has 58 uses as a noun, 126 as a verb, and 10 as a participial adjective. Its meanings are so various and scattered that it takes the *OED* 60,000 words—the length of a short novel—to discuss them all. A foreigner could be excused for thinking that to know *set* is to know English. . . .

Language, Appearance, and Reality: Doublespeak in 1984

William D. Lutz

William D. Lutz, chair of the Department of English at Rutgers University, is also chair of the National Council of Teachers of English (NCTE) Committee on Public Doublespeak and editor of the Quarterly Review of Doublespeak.

There are at least four kinds of doublespeak. The first kind is the euphemism, a word or phrase that is designed to avoid a harsh or distasteful reality. When a euphemism is used out of sensitivity for the feelings of someone or out of concern for a social or cultural taboo, it is not doublespeak. For example, we express grief that someone has *passed away* because we do not want to say to a grieving person, "I'm sorry your father is dead." The euphemism *passed away* functions here not just to protect the feelings of another person but also to communicate our concern over that person's feelings during a period of mourning.

However, when a euphemism is used to mislead or deceive, it becomes doublespeak. For example, the U.S. State Department decided in 1984 that in its annual reports on the status of human rights in countries around the world it would no longer use the word *killing*. Instead, it uses the phrase *unlawful or arbitrary deprivation of life*. Thus the State Department avoids discussing the embarrassing situation of the government-sanctioned killings in countries that are supported by the United States. This use of language constitutes doublespeak because it is designed to mislead, to cover up the unpleasant. Its real intent is at variance with its apparent intent. It is language designed to alter our perception of reality.

A second kind of doublespeak is jargon, the specialized language of a trade, profession, or similar group. It is the specialized language of doctors, lawyers, engineers, educators, or car mechanics. Jargon can serve an important and useful function. Within a group, jargon allows members of the group to communicate with each other clearly, efficiently, and quickly. Indeed, it is a mark of membership in the group to be able to use and understand the group's jargon. For example, lawyers speak of an *involuntary conversion* of property when discussing the loss or destruction of property through theft, accident, or condemnation. When used by lawyers in a legal situation, such jargon is a legitimate use of language, since all members of the group can be expected to understand the term.

However, when a member of the group uses jargon to communicate with a person outside the group, and uses it knowing that the nonmember does not understand such language, then there is doublespeak. For example, a number of years ago a commercial airliner crashed on takeoff, killing three passengers, injuring twenty-one others, and destroying the airplane, a 727. The insured value of the airplane was greater than its book value, so the airline made a profit of three million dollars on the destroyed airplane. But the airline had two problems: it did not want to talk about one if its airplanes crashing and it had to account for the three million dollars when it issued its annual report to its stockholders. The airline solved these problems by inserting a footnote in its annual report explaining that this three million dollars was due to "the involuntary conversion of a 727." Note that airline officials could thus claim to have explained the crash of the airplane and the subsequent three million dollars in profit. However, since most stockholders in the company, and indeed most of the general public, are not familiar with legal jargon, the use of such jargon constitutes doublespeak.

A third kind of doublespeak is gobbledygook or bureaucratese. Basically, such doublespeak is simply a matter of piling on words, of overwhelming the audience with words, the bigger the better. For example, when Alan Greenspan was chairman of the President's Council of Economic Advisors, he made this statement when testifying before a Senate committee:

It is a tricky problem to find the particular calibration in timing that would be appropriate to stem the acceleration in risk premiums created by falling incomes without prematurely aborting the decline in the inflation-generated risk premiums.

Did Alan Greenspan's audience really understand what he was saying? Did he believe his statement really explained anything? Perhaps there is some meaning beneath all those words, but it would take some time to search it out. This seems to be language that pretends to communicate but does not.

The fourth kind of doublespeak is inflated language. Inflated language designed to make the ordinary seem extraordinary, the common, uncommon; to make everyday things seem impressive; to give an air of importance to people, situations, or things

From *ETC (Et Cetera)*, Winter 1987, pp. 383-391. Excerpt from *The Legacy of Language—A Tribute to Charlton Laird*, edited by Philip C. Boardman. Copyright © University of Nevada Press.

that would not normally be considered important; to make the simple seem complex. With this kind of language, car mechanics become *automotive internists,* elevator operators become members of the *vertical transportation corps,* used cars become not just *pre-owned* but *experienced cars.* When the Pentagon uses the phrase *pre-emptive counterattack* to mean that American forces attacked first, or when it uses the phrase *engage the enemy on all sides* to describe an ambush of American troops, or when it uses the phrase *tactical redeployment* to describe a retreat by American troops, it is using doublespeak. The electronics company that sells the television set with *non-multicolor capability* is also using the doublespeak of inflated language.

Doublespeak is not a new use of language peculiar to the politics or economics of the twentieth century. Thucydides in *The Peloponnesian War* wrote that

revolution thus ran its course from city to city. . . . Words had to change their ordinary meanings and to take those which were now given them. Reckless audacity came to be considered the courage of a loyal ally; prudent hesitation, specious cowardice; moderation was held to be a cloak for unmanliness; ability to see all sides of a question, inaptness to act on any. Frantic violence become the attribute of manliness; cautious plotting, a justifiable means of self-defense. The advocate of extreme measures was always trustworthy; his opponent, a man to be suspected.[1]

Caesar in his account of the Gallic Wars described his brutal conquest as "pacifying" Gaul. Doublespeak has a long history.

Military doublespeak seems always to have been with us. In 1947 the name of the War Department was changed to the more pleasing if misleading *Defense Department.* During the Vietnam War the American public learned that it was an *incursion,* not an invasion; a *protective reaction strike* or a *limited duration protective reaction strike* or *air support,* not bombing; and *incontinent ordinance,* not bombs and artillery shells, fell on civilians. This use of language continued with the invasion of Grenada, which was conducted not by the United States Army, Navy, or Air Force, but by the Caribbean Peace Keeping Forces. Indeed, according to the Pentagon, it was not an invasion of Grenada, but a *predawn, vertical insertion.* And it wasn't that the armed forces lacked intelligence data on Grenada before the invasion, it was just that "we were not micromanaging Grenada intelligencewise until about that time frame." In today's army forces, it's not a shovel but a *combat emplacement evacuator,* not a toothpick but a *wood interdental stimulator,* not a pencil but a portable, handheld communications inscriber, not a bullet hole but a *ballistically induced aperture in the subcutaneous environment.*

Members of the military and politicians are not the only ones who use doublespeak. People in all parts of society use it. Take educators, for example. On some college campuses what was once the Department of Physical Education is now the *Department of Human Kinetics* or the *College of Applied Life Studies.* Home Economics is now the *School of Human Resources and Family Studies.* College campuses no longer have libraries but *learning resource centers.* Those are not desks in the classroom, they are *pupil stations.* Teachers—*classroom managers* who apply an *action plan* to a *knowledge base*—are concerned with the *basic fundamentals,* which are *inexorably linked* to the *education user's* (not student's) *time-on-task.* Students don't take tests; now it is *criterion referencing testing* which measures whether a student has achieved the *operational curricular objectives.* A school system in Pennsylvania uses the following grading system on report cards: "no effort, less than minimal effort, minimal effort, more than minimal effort, less than full effort, full effort, better than full effort, effort increasing, effort decreasing." Some college students in New York come from *economically nonaffluent* families, while the coach at a Southern university wasn't fired, "he just won't be asked to continue in that job." An article in a scholarly journal suggests teaching students three approaches to writing to help them become better writers: "concretization of goals, procedural facilitation, and modeling planning." An article on family relationships entitled "Familial Love and Intertemporal Optimality" observes that "an altruistic utility function promotes intertemporal efficiency. However, altruism creates an externality that implies that satisfying the condition for efficiency, does not insure intertemporal optimality." A research report issued by the U.S. Office of Education contains this sentence: "In other words, feediness is the shared information between toputness, where toputness is at a time just prior to the inputness." Educations contributes more than its share to current doublespeak.

The world of business has produced large amounts of doublespeak. If an airplane crash is one of the worst things that can happen to an airline company, a recall of automobiles because of a safety defect is one of the worst things that can happen to an automobile company. So a few years ago, when one of the three largest car companies in America had to recall two of its models to correct mechanical defects, the company sent a letter to all those who had bought those models. In its letter, the company said that the rear axle bearings of the cars "can deteriorate" and that "continued driving with a failed bearing could result in disengagement of the axle shaft and adversely affect vehicle control." This is the language of nonresponsibility. What are "mechanical deficiencies"—poor design, bad workmanship? If they do, what causes the deterioration? Note that "continued driving" is the subject of the sentence and suggests that it is not the company's poor manufacturing which is at fault but the driver who persists in driving. Note, too, "failed bearing," which implies that the bearing failed, not the company. Finally, "adversely affect vehicle control" means nothing more than that the driver could lose control of the car and get killed.

If we apply Hugh Rank's criteria for examining such language, we quickly discover the doublespeak here. What the car company should be saying to its customers is that the car the company sold them has a serious defect which should be corrected immediately—otherwise the customer runs the risk of being killed. But the reader of the letter must find this message beneath the doublespeak the company has used to disguise the harshness of its message. We will probably never know how many of the customers never brought their cars in for the necessary repairs because they did not think the problem serious enough to warrant the inconvenience involved.

When it come time to fire employees, business has produced more than enough doublespeak to deal with the unpleasant situation. Employees are, of course, never fired. They are *selected out, placed out, non-retained, released, dehired, non-renewed*. A corporation will *eliminate the redundancies in the human resources area*, assign *candidates for derecruitment* to a *mobility pool*, *revitalize the department* by placing executives on *special assignment*, *enhance the efficiency of operations*, *streamline the field sales organization*, or *further rationalize marketing efforts*. The reality behind all this doublespeak is that companies are firing employees, but no one wants the stockholders, public, or competition to know that times are tough and people have to go.

Recently the oil industry has been hard hit by declining sales and a surplus of oil. Because of *reduced demand for product*, which results in *spare refining capacity* and problems in *down-stream operations*, oil companies have been forced to *re-evaluate and consolidate their operations* and take *appropriate cost reduction actions*, in order to *enhance the efficiency of operations*, which has meant the *elimination of marginal outlets*, *accelerating the divestment program*, and the *disposition of low throughput marketing units*. What this doublespeak really means is that oil companies have fired employees, cut back on expenses, and closed gas stations and oil refineries because there's surplus of oil and people are not buying as much gas and oil as in the past.

One corporation faced with declining business sent a memorandum to its employees advising them that the company's "business plans are under revision and now reflect a more moderate approach toward our operating and capital programs." The result of this "more moderate approach" is a "surplus of professional/technical employees." To "assist in alleviating the surplus, selected professional and technical employees" have been "selected to participate" in a "Voluntary Program." Note that individuals were selected to "resign voluntarily." What this memorandum means, of course, is that expenses must be cut because of declining business, so employees will have to be fired.

It is rare to read that the stock market *fell*. Members of the financial community prefer to say that the stock market *retreated, eased, made a technical adjustment* or a *technical correction*, or perhaps that *prices were off due to profit taking*, or *off in light trading*, or *lost ground*. But the stock market never falls, not if stockbrokers have their say. As a side note, it is interesting to observe that the stock market never rises because of a *technical adjustment* or *correction*, nor does it ever *ease* upwards.

The business sections of newspapers, business magazines, corporate reports, and executive speeches are filled with words and phrases such as *marginal rates of substitution, equilibrium price, getting off margin, distribution coalition, non-performing assets*, and *encompassing organizations*. Much of this is jargon or inflated language designed to make the simple seem complex, but there are other examples of business doublespeak that mislead, that are designed to avoid a harsh reality. What should we make of such expressions as *negative deficit* or *revenue excesses* for profit, *invest in* for buy, *price enhancement* or *price adjustment* for price increase, *shortfall* for a mistake in planning or *period of accelerated negative growth* or *negative economic growth* for recession?

Business doublespeak often attempts to give substance to wind, to make ordinary actions seem complex. Executives *operate* in *timeframes* within the *context* of which a *task force* will serve as the proper *conduit* for all the necessary *input* to *program a scenario* that,

within acceptable *parameters*, and with the proper *throughput*, will *generate* the *maximum output* for a *print out* of *zero defect terminal objectives* that will *enhance the bottom line*.

There are instances, however, where doublespeak becomes more than amusing, more than a cause for a weary shake of the head. When the anesthetist turned the wrong knob during a Caesarean delivery and killed the mother and unborn child, the hospital called it a *therapeutic misadventure*. The Pentagon calls the neutron bomb "an efficient nuclear weapon that eliminates an enemy with a minimum degree of damage to friendly territory." The Pentagon also calls expected civilian casualties in a nuclear war *collateral damage*. And it was the Central Intelligence Agency which during the Vietnam War created the phrase *eliminate with extreme prejudice* to replace the more direct verb *kill*.

Identifying doublespeak can at times be difficult. For example, on July 27, 1981, President Ronald Reagan said in a speech televised to the American public: "I will not stand by and see those of you who are dependent on Social Security deprived of the benefits you've worked so hard to earn. You will continue to receive your checks in the full amount due you." This speech had been billed as President Reagan's position on Social Security, a subject of much debate at the time. After the speech, public opinion polls revealed that the great majority of the public believed that President Reagan had affirmed his support for Social Security and that he would not support cuts in benefits. However, five days after the speech, on July 31, 1981, an article in the *Philadelphia Inquirer* quoted White House spokesman David Gergen as saying that President Reagan's words had been "carefully chosen." What President Reagan did mean, according to Gergen, was that he was reserving the right to decide who was "dependent" on those benefits, who had "earned" them, and who, therefore, was "due" them.[2]

The subsequent remarks of David Gergen reveal the real intent of President Reagan as opposed to his apparent intent. Thus Hugh Rank's criteria for analyzing language to determine whether it is doublespeak, when applied in light of David Gergen's remarks, reveal the doublespeak of President Reagan. Here indeed is the insincerity of which Orwell wrote. Here, too, is the gap between the speaker's real and declared aim.

In 1982 the Republican National Committee sponsored a television advertisement which pictured an elderly, folksy postman delivering Social Security checks "with the 7.4% cost-of-living raise that President Reagan promised." The postman then added that "he promised that raise and he kept his promise, in spite of those sticks-in-the-mud who tried to keep him from doing what we elected him to do." The commercial was, in fact, deliberately misleading. The cost-of-living increases had been provided automatically by law since 1975, and President Reagan tried three times to roll them back or delay them but was overruled by congressional opposition. When these discrepancies were pointed out to an official of the Republican National Committee, he called the commercial "inoffensive" and added, "Since when is a commercial supposed to be accurate? Do women really smile when they clean their ovens?"

Again, applying Hugh Rank's criteria to this advertisement reveals the doublespeak in it once we know the facts of past actions by President Reagan. Moreover, the official for the Republican National Committee assumes that all advertisements, whether for political candidates or commercial products, are lies, or in his doublespeak term, *inaccurate*. Thus, the real intent of the advertisement was to mislead while the apparent purpose was to inform the public of President Reagan's position on possible cuts in Social Security benefits. Again there is insincerity, and again there is a gap between the speaker's real and declared aims.

In 1981 Secretary of State Alexander Haig testified before congressional committees about the murder of three American nuns and a Catholic lay worker in El Salvador. The four

women had been raped and shot at close range, and there was clear evidence that the crime had been committed by soldiers of the Salvadoran government. Before the House Foreign Affairs Committee, Secretary Haig said,

I'd like to suggest to you that some of the investigations would lead one to believe that perhaps the vehicle the nuns were riding in may have tried to run a roadblock, or may accidentally have been perceived to have been doing so, and there'd been an exchange of fire and then perhaps those who inflicted the casualties sought to cover it up. And this could have been at a very low level of both competence and motivation in the context of the issue itself. But the facts on this are not clear enough for anyone to draw a definitive conclusion.

The next day, before the Senate Foreign Relations Committee, Secretary Haig claimed that press reports on his previous testimony were inaccurate. When Senator Claiborne Pell asked whether Secretary Haig was suggesting the possibility that "the nuns may have run through a roadblock." Secretary Haig replied, "You mean that they tried to violate . . .? Not at all, no, not at all. My heavens! The dear nuns who raised me in my parochial schooling would forever isolate me from their affections and respect." When Senator Pell asked Secretary Haig, "Did you mean that the nuns were firing at the people, or what did 'exchange of fire' mean?" Secretary Haig replied, "I haven't met any pistol-packing nuns in my day, Senator. What I meant was that if one fellow starts shooting, then the next thing you know they all panic." Thus did the secretary of state of the United States explain official government policy on the murder of four American citizens in a foreign land.

Secretary Haig's testimony implies that the women were in some way responsible for their own fate. By using such vague wording as "would lead one to believe" and "may accidentally have been perceived to have been," he avoids any direct assertion. The use of "inflicted the casualties" not only avoids using the word *kill* but also implies that at the worst the kill-

ings were accidental or justifiable. The result of this testimony is that the secretary of state has become an apologist for murder. This is indeed language in defense of the indefensible; language designed to make lies sound truthful and murder respectable; language designed to give an appearance of solidity to pure wind.

These last three examples of doublespeak should make it clear that doublespeak is not the product of careless language or sloppy thinking. Indeed, most doublespeak is the product of clear thinking and is language carefully designed and constructed to appear to communicate when in fact it does not. It is language designed not to lead but to mislead. It is language designed to distort reality and corrupt the mind. It is not a tax increase but *revenue enhancement* or *tax base broadening,* so how can you complain about higher taxes? It is not acid rain, but *poorly buffered precipitation,* so don't worry about all those dead trees. That is not the Mafia in Atlantic City, New Jersey, those are *members of a career offender cartel,* so don't worry about the influence of organized crime in the city. The judge was not addicted to the pain-killing drug he was taking, it was just that the drug had "established an interrelationship with the body, such that if the drug is removed precipitously, there is a reaction," so don't worry that his decisions might have been influenced by his drug addiction. It's not a Titan II nuclear-armed, intercontinental ballistic missile with a warhead 630 times more powerful than the atomic bomb dropped on Hiroshima, it is just a *very large, potentially disruptive re-entry system,* so don't worry about the threat of nuclear destruction. It is not a neutron bomb but a *radiation enhancement device,* so don't worry about escalating the arms race. It is not an invasion but a *rescue mission,* or a *predawn vertical insertion,* so don't worry about any violations of United States or international law.

Doublespeak has become so common in our everyday lives that we fail to notice it. We do not protest when we are asked to check our packages at the desk "for our convenience" when it is not for our convenience at all but for someone else's convenience. We see advertisements for *genuine imitation leather, virgin vinyl,* or *real counterfeit diamonds* and do not question the language or the supposed quality of the product. We do not speak of slums or ghettos but of the *inner city* or *substandard housing where the disadvantaged* live and thus avoid talking about the poor who have to live in filthy, poorly heated, ramshackle apartments or houses. Patients do not die in the hospital; it is just *negative patient care outcome.*

Doublespeak which calls cab drivers *urban transportation specialists,* elevator operators *members of the vertical transportation corps,* and automobile mechanics *automotive internists* can be considered humorous and relatively harmless. However, doublespeak which calls a fire in a nuclear reactor building *rapid oxidation,* an explosion in a nuclear power plant an *energetic disassembly,* the illegal overthrow of a legitimate administration *destabilizing a government,* and lies *inoperative statements* is language which attempts to avoid responsibility, which attempts to make the bad seem good, the negative appear positive, something unpleasant appear attractive, and which seems to communicate but does not. It is language designed to alter our perception of reality and corrupt our minds. Such language does not provide us with the tools needed to develop and preserve civilization. Such language breeds suspicion, cynicism, distrust, and, ultimately, hostility.

Doublespeak is insidious because it can infect and ultimately destroy the function of language, which is communication between people and social groups. If this corrupting process does occur, it can have serious conse-quences in a country that depends upon an informed electorate to make decisions in selecting candidates for office and deciding issues of public policy. After a while we may really believe that politicians don't lie but only *misspeak,* that illegal acts are merely *inappropriate actions,* that fraud and criminal conspiracy are just *miscertification.* And if we really believe that we understand such language, then the world of *Nineteen Eighty-four* with its control of reality through language is not far away.

The consistent use of doublespeak can have serious and far-reaching consequences beyond the obvious ones. The pervasive use of doublespeak can spread so that doublespeak becomes the coin of the political realm with speakers and listeners convinced that they really understand such language. President Jimmy Carter could call the aborted raid to free the hostages in Tehran in 1980 an "incomplete success" and really believe that he had made a statement that clearly communicated with the American public. So, too, President Ronald Reagan could say in 1985 that "ultimately our security and our hopes for success at the arms reduction talks hinge on the determination that we show here to continue our program to rebuild and refortify our defenses" and really believe that greatly increasing the amount of money spent building new weapons will lead to a reduction in the number of weapons in the world.

The task of English teachers is to teach not just the effective use of language but respect for language as well. Those who use language to conceal or prevent or corrupt thought must be called to account. Only by teaching respect for and love of language can teachers of English instill in students the sense of outrage they should experience when they encounter doublespeak. But before students can experience that outrage, they must first learn to use language effectively, to understand its beauty and power. Only then will we begin to make headway in the fight against doublespeak, for only by using language well will we come to appreciate the perversion inherent in doublespeak.

In his book *The Miracle of Language,* Charlton Laird notes that

language is . . . the most important tool man ever devised. . . . Language is [man's] basic tool. It is the tool more than any other with which he makes his living, makes his home, makes his life. As man becomes more and more a social being, as the world becomes more and more a social community, communication grows ever more imperative. And language is the basis of communication. Language is also the instrument with which we think, and thinking is the rarest and most needed commodity in the world.[3]

In this opinion Laird echoes Orwell's comment that "if thought corrupts language, language can also corrupt thought."[4] Both men have given us a legacy of respect for language, a respect that should prompt us to cry "Enough!" when we encounter doublespeak. The greatest honor we can do Charlton Laird is to continue to have the greatest respect of language in all its manifestations, for, as Laird taught us, language is a miracle.

NOTES AND REFERENCES

1. Thucydides, *The Peloponnesian Way,* 3.82.
2. David Hess, "Reagan's Language on Benefits Confused, Angered Many," *Philadelphia Inquirer,* July 31, 1981, p. 6-A.
3. Charlton Laird, *The Miracle of Language* (New York: Fawcett, Premier Books, 1953), p. 224.
4. Orwell, *The Collected Essays,* 4:137.

Who's Interrupting? Issues of Dominance and Control

Deborah Tannen

Here is a joke that my father likes to tell.

A woman sues her husband for divorce. When the judge asks her why she wants a divorce, she explains that her husband has not spoken to her in two years. The judge asks the husband, "Why haven't you spoken to your wife in two years?" He replies, "I didn't want to interrupt her."

This joke reflects the commonly held stereotype that women talk too much and interrupt men.

In direct contradiction of this stereotype, one of the most widely cited findings to emerge from research on gender and language is that men interrupt women. I have never seen a popular article on the subject that does not cite this finding. It is deeply satisfying because it refutes the misogynistic stereotype that accuses women of talking too much, and it accounts for the experience reported by most women, who feel they are often cut off by men.

Both claims—that men interrupt women and that women interrupt men—reflect and bolster the assumption that an interruption is a hostile act, a kind of conversational bullying. The interrupter is seen as a malevolent aggressor, the interrupted an innocent victim. These assumptions are founded on the premise that interruption is an intrusion, a trampling on someone else's right to the floor, an attempt to dominate.

The accusation of interruption is particularly painful in close relationships, where interrupting carries a load of metamessages—that a partner doesn't care enough, doesn't listen, isn't interested. These complaints strike at the core of such a relationship, since that is where most of us seek, above all, to be valued and to be heard. But your feeling interrupted doesn't always mean that someone set out to interrupt you. And being accused of interrupting when you know you didn't intend to is as frustrating as being cut off before you've made your point.

Because the complaint "You interrupt me" is so common in intimate relationships, and because it raises issues of dominance and control that are fundamental to the politics of gender, the relationship between interruption and dominance bears closer inspection. For this, it will be necessary to look more closely at what creates and constitutes interruption in conversation.

DO MEN INTERRUPT WOMEN?

Researchers who report that men interrupt women come to their conclusion by recording conversation and counting instances of interruption. In identifying interruptions, they do not take into account the substance of the conversations they studied: what was being talked about, speakers' intentions, their reactions to each other, and what effect the "interruption" had on the conversation. Instead mechanical criteria are used to identify interruptions. Experimental researchers who count things need operational criteria for identifying things to count. But ethnographic researchers—those who go out and observe people doing naturally whatever it is the researchers want to understand—are as wary of operational criteria as experimenters are wedded to them. Identifying interruptions by mechanical criteria is a paradigm case of these differences in points of view.

Linguist Adrian Bennett explains that "overlap" is mechanical: Anyone could listen to a conversation, or a tape recording of one, and determine whether or not two voices were going at once. But interruption is inescapably a matter of interpretation regarding individuals' rights and obligations. To determine whether a speaker is violating another speaker's rights, you have to know a lot about both speakers and the situation. For example, what are the speakers saying? How long has each one been talking? What has their past relationship been? How do they feel about being cut off? And, most important, what is the content of the second speaker's comment, relative to the first: Is it a reinforcement, a contradiction, or a change in topic? In other words, what is the second speaker trying to *do*? Apparent support can subtly undercut, and an apparent change of topic can be an indirect means of support—as, for example, when an adolescent boy passes up the opportunity to sympathize with his friend so as not to reinforce the friend's one-down position.

All these and other factors influence whether or not anyone's speaking rights have been violated and, if they have been, how significant the violation is. Sometimes you feel interrupted but you don't mind. At other times, you mind very much. Finally, different speakers have different conversational styles, so a speaker might *feel* interrupted even if the other did not *intend* to interrupt.

Here is an example that was given by Candace West and Don Zimmerman to show a man interrupting a woman. In this case I think the interruption is justified in terms of interactional rights. (The vertical lines show overlap.)

FEMALE:	So uh you really can't bitch when you've got all those on the same day (4.2) but I uh asked my physics professor if I couldn't chan|ge that|
MALE:	|Don't |touch that (1.2)
FEMALE:	What? (pause)
MALE:	I've got everything jus' how I want it in that notebook, you'll screw it up leafin' through it like that.

West and Zimmerman consider this an interruption because the second speaker began while the first speaker was in the middle of a word (*change*). But considering what was being said, the first speaker's rights may not have been violated. Although there are other aspects of this man's talk that make him seem like a conversational bully, interrupting to ask the woman to stop leafing through his notebook does not in itself violate her right to talk. Many people, seeing someone handling their property in a way that was destroying their painstaking organization of it, would feel justified in asking that person to stop immediately, without allowing further damage to be done while waiting for the appropriate syntactic and rhetorical moment to take the floor.

Sociologist Stephen Murray gives an example of what he regards as a prototypical case of interruption—where someone cuts in to talk about a different topic when the first speaker

has not even made a single point. Here is his example:

H:	I think |that
W:	|Do you want some more salad?

This simple exchange shows how complex conversation can be. Many people feel that a host has the right, if not the obligation, to offer food to guests, whether or not anyone is talking. Offering food, like asking to have salt or other condiments passed, takes priority, because if the host waited until no one was talking to offer food, and guests waited until no one was talking to ask for platters beyond their reach, then the better the conversation, the more likely that many guests would go home hungry.

This is not to say that any time is the right time to interrupt to offer food. If a host *habitually* interrupts to offer food *whenever* a partner begins to say something, or interrupts to offer food just when a speaker reaches the climax of a story or the punchline of a joke, it might seem like a violation of rights or the expression of mischievous motives. But the accusation of interrupting cannot be justified on the basis of a single instance like this one.

Conversational style differences muddy the waters. It may be that one person grew up in a home where conversation was constant and all offers of food overlapped ongoing talk, while another grew up in a home where talk was sparse and food was offered only when there was a lull in the conversation. If two such people live together, it is likely that one will overlap to offer food, expecting the other to go on speaking, but the overlapaversant partner will feel interrupted and maybe even refuse to resume talking. Both would be right, because interruption is not a mechanical category. It is a matter of individual habits and expectations.

INTERRUPTION WITHOUT OVERLAP

In these examples, an overlap—two voices talking at once—is not necessarily an interruption, that is, a violation of someone's speaking rights.

There are also instances where speakers do feel that their rights have been infringed on, and may even feel interrupted, when there is no overlap. An example of such an instance appears in Alice Greenwood's analysis of dinner table conversations among her three children (twins Denise and Dennis, twelve, and Stacy, eleven) and their friends. In the following example, Denise and Stacy have performed a verbal routine for the benefit of their brother's dinner guest, Mark, fourteen. This dialogue, which Greenwood calls the Betty routine, is one the sister's often perform together. Before they start, they get Mark's attention: Denise says, "Listen to this. Mark, listen to this." Then Denise and Dennis announce, "It's so funny." But Mark doesn't agree:

DENISE:	[In Betty voice] Excuse me, are you Betty?
	. . .
STACY:	Oh, yes.
DENISE:	[In Betty voice] Betty who?
STACY:	[In Betty voice] Bettybita-bitabittabuttabut— [Dennis, Denise, and Stacy laugh.]
MARK:	Whaaaat? [Dennis, Denise, and Stacy laugh hysterically.]

Although this routine sparks delighted laughter from the three siblings, and on other occasions also sparked laughter among friends, Mark did not laugh and claimed not to get the joke. Denise and Stacy tried to explain it to him:

DENISE:	I said, "Betty who?," like you say "Betty Jones." Then she says, "Bettybitabitabitta—"
→DENNIS:	Did anyone eat from this yet?
MARK:	No. Actually, what I was going to say was can I try that soup? It looks quite good.
DENISE:	Listen, listen, listen, listen.
MARK:	Say it in slow motion, okay?
STACY:	Betty bought a bit of bitter butter and she said, "This butter's bitter. If I put it in my batter, it will make my batter bitter." So Betty bought a bit of better butter to—
→ DENISE:	You never heard that before?
MARK:	No. Never.

DENISE: Mark, seriously?
MARK: Seriously.
DENISE: It's like the famous
       to—|
→ STACY: |tongue twister.
MARK: No. The famous tongue
       twister is
       Peterpiperpicked—|
→ DENISE: |Same
       thing. It's like that. It's like
       that one.
MARK: **You keep interrupting me.**

In this excerpt, Denise and Stacy repeatedly cut each other off, as shown by the arrows and vertical lines, but there is no indication that either resents it. They do seem to mind their brother Dennis's overlapping to ask about the food ("Did anyone eat from this yet?") because he's interrupting their explanation (Denise protests, "Listen, listen, listen, listen"). The girls are supporting each other, talking on the same team.

Most striking is Mark's complaint, "You keep interrupting me." This is intriguing because what Mark was saying when he got interrupted ("No. The famous tongue twister is Peterpiperpicked—") was actually an interruption of the girls' explanation, even though his voice did not overlap theirs. The same is true for the previous time they "interrupted" him: Just as Denise said, "All right. Watch this," Mark began to ask, "Is it as funny as a—" but he didn't get to finish because Dennis laughed and Denise launched the routine, as announced. So Mark's protest seems like a real-life instance of the humorous line "Don't talk while I'm interrupting you."

Mark also took an oppositional stance, even though he was really supporting rather than disagreeing. The girls just said that their tongue twister was *like* the famous tongue twister." If Mark had simply offered "the famous tongue twister" (Peter Piper picked a peck of pickled peppers), then his interruption would have been supportive, furnishing the end of Denise's explanation. Instead, he began by saying "No," as if they had been claiming that theirs *was* the famous tongue twister.

In this conversation, the girls were trying to include Mark in their friendly banter. Greenwood found, in studying her children's conversations with their friends, that the more interruptions a conversation contained, the more comfortable the children felt in it and the more they enjoyed it. But Mark refused to be part of their fun by insisting on his right to hold the floor without interruption. Perhaps his being a few years older was a factor. Perhaps he did not like being cast in the role of audience. Perhaps he felt he was being put down when Denise asked, "You never heard that before? . . . Mark, seriously?" Whatever the reason, Denise, Stacy and Dennis were doing rapport-talk, and Mark wanted to do something more like report-talk. It is not surprising that Denise later told her mother that she didn't like Mark.

Although Denise did "interrupt" Mark to tell him he had the idea ("Same thing. It's like that"), thee is no evidence that she was trying to dominate him. Furthermore, though Denise and Stacy interrupted each other, there is no evidence that they were trying to dominate each other. There is, however, some evidence that Mark might have been trying to dominate Stacy and Denise, for example by refusing to laugh at their jokes and rejecting their explanation of their verbal routine, even though he did not overlap their speech. So it is not the interruption that constitutes dominance but what speakers are trying to do when they talk to each other.

OVERLAP WITHOUT INTERRUPTION

Claiming that an interruption is a sign of dominance assumes that conversation is an activity in which one speaker speaks at a time, but this reflects ideology more than practice. Most Americans *believe* one speaker *ought* to speak at a time, regardless of what they actually do. I have recorded conversations in which many voices were heard at once and it was clear that everyone was having a good time. When I asked people afterward their impressions of the conversation, they told me that they had enjoyed themselves. But when

I played the tape back for them, and they heard that people had been talking all together, they were embarrassed and made comments like "Oh, God, do we really do that?" as if they had been caught with their verbal pants down.

In a book entitled *Conversational Style,* I analyzed two and a half hours of dinner table conversation among six friends. Looking back on the conversation, some of the friends told me they had felt that others had "dominated" the conversation—and when I first listened to the tape, I too thought that it looked that way. But the accused pleaded innocent: They claimed they had not intended to dominate; in fact, they wondered why the others had been so reticent. Only by comparing different parts of the conversation to each other was I able to solve the puzzle.

The inadvertent interruptions—and the impression of domination—came about because the friends had different conversational styles. I call these styles "high considerateness" and "high involvement" because the former gave priority to being considerate of others by not imposing, and the latter gave priority to showing enthusiastic involvement. Some apparent interruptions occurred because high-considerateness speakers expected longer pauses between speaking turns. While they were waiting for the proper pause, the high-involvement speakers got the impression they had nothing to say and filled in to avoid an uncomfortable silence.

Other unintended interruptions resulted when high-involvement speakers chimed in to show support and participation: High-considerateness speakers misinterpreted the choral support as attempts to yank the floor away from them, and they stopped, to avoid what to them would have been a cacophony of two voices at once. Ironically, these interruptions were not only the interpretations of the apparent victims—they were their creations. When high-involvement speakers used exactly the same techniques with each other, the effect was positive rather than negative: Chiming in with speakers didn't stop anybody from talking. It greased the conversational wheels and enlivened spirits.

Here are two examples from my study that illustrate these two contrasting situations, and the different effects of overlap on conversation. The first example shows overlapping that had a positive effect, in a segment of conversation among three high-involvement speakers. The second shows overlapping between high-involvement and high-considerateness speakers that disrupted the conversation. Though gender is not a factor in the overlap patterns in these conversations, understanding how overlap can work—or fail to work—is fundamental to making sense of the relationship between gender and interruption.

SUCCESSFUL COOPERATIVE OVERLAPPING

The first example took place in the context of a discussion about the impact of television on children. Only three of the six friends were talking here, the three high-involvement speakers: Steve (the host), Peter (Steve's brother, who was a guest), and Deborah (the author, who was also a guest). Steve made the statement that television has been bad for children, and I responded by asking whether Steve and Peter had grown up with television. It might not be a coincidence that I, the woman, shifted the focus from an abstract, impersonal statement to a personal one.

STEVE: I think it's basically done damage to children. That what good it's done is outweighed by the damage. |

→ DEB-ORAH: |Did you two grow up with television?

PETER: Very little. We had a TV in the Quonset— |

→ DEB-ORAH: |How old were you when your parents got it? |

→ STEVE: |We had a TV, but we didn't watch it all the time. We were very young. I was four when my parents got a TV. |

→ DEB-ORAH: |You were four?

PETER: I even remember that. |I don't remember /??/

→ STEVE: |I re-

member they got a TV before we moved out of the Quonset huts. In 1954. |

→ PETER: |I remember we got it in the Quonset huts.

DEBORAH: [Chuckle] You lived in Quonset huts? When you were how old?

STEVE: You know my father's dentist said to him, "What's a Quonset hut?" And he said, "God, you must be younger than my children." He was. Younger than both of us.

As indicated by vertical lines and arrows, this conversation includes many overlaps and "latchings"—instances where a second speaker begins speaking without leaving any perceptible pause. Yet the speakers show no evidence of discomfort or annoyance. All three speakers take turns that latch onto or intrude into others' turns. In this conversation, Peter and Steve, who are brothers, operate as a duet, much as Denise and Stacy did in the earlier example.

This example contains a clue to why high-involvement speakers don't mind being overlapped. These speakers yield to an intrusion if they feel like it, but if they don't feel like it, they put off responding, or ignore the intrusion completely. For example, when Peter is saying, "We had a TV in the Quonset [huts]," I interrupt to ask, "How old were you when your parents got it?" Steve doesn't answer my question right away. Instead, he first finishes Peter's statement: "We had a TV, but we didn't watch it all the time." Only then does he turn to answering my question: "We were very young. I was four when my parents got a TV." At another point, Steve ignores my question. I ask, "You lived in Quonset huts? When you were how old?" Without even acknowledging my question, Steve simply offers a vignette about his father that the topic of Quonset huts called to his mind. Part of the reason Steve does not find my questions intrusive is that he does not feel compelled to answer them—exactly the assumption that frees me to toss them out exuberantly. Another reason that the overlaps are cooperative is that they do not change the topic but elaborate on it.

UNSUCCESSFUL COOPERATIVE OVERLAPPING

The success of this brief conversation had nothing to do with whether or not speakers overlapped or interrupted; it was successful because the speakers had similar habits and attitudes about overlapping speech. The next example shows a segment of the same dinner table conversation that was not successful. Peter and I appear again here, but, instead of Steve, we are talking to David, who has a high-considerateness style.

David, an American Sign Language interpreter, is telling us about ASL. As listeners, Peter and I use overlap and latching to ask supportive questions, just as I asked supportive, overlapping questions of Peter and Steve in the previous example. Here too our questions show interest in what the speaker is saying rather than shifting focus. But the effect is very different:

DAVID: So, and this is the one that's Berkeley. This is the Berkeley sign for |Christmas.

→ DEB-ORAH: |Do you figure out those, those, um correspondences? Or do—

DAVID: |/?/| when you learn the signs, does somebody tell you?

DAVID: Oh, you mean|watching it? Like—

→ DEB-ORAH: |'Cause I can imagine knowing that sign, and not figuring out that it had anything to do with the decorations.

DAVID: No. Y-you know that it has to do with the decorations. |

→ DEB-ORAH: |'Cause somebody tells you? Or you figure|it out? |

→ DAVID: |No. |Oh. You, you talking about me?

DEBORAH: Yeah.

DAVID: Or a deaf person? |

→ DEB-ORAH: |You. You.

DAVID: Me? Uh, someone tells me, usually. But a lot of them I can tell. I mean they're obvious. The better I get, the more I can tell. The longer I do it the more I can tell what they're talking about. |Without |knowing

```
             what the
 → DEB-             |Huh  |That's inter-
    ORAH:   esting.
    DAVID:  sign is.|
 → PETER:          |But how do you
            learn a new sign?
    DAVID:  How do I learn a new
            sign?|
    PETER:        |Yeah. I mean suppos-
            ing Victor's talking and all of
            a sudden he uses a sign for
            Thanksgiving, and you've
            never seen it before.
```

All Peter's and my comments are latched or overlapped on David's, as the arrows show. But only two of David's seven comments overlap ours. Furthermore, these two utterances—one that was inaudible (shown by a question mark in slashes) and one in which David said, "No"—are probably both attempts to answer the first parts of my double-barreled questions ("Do you figure out those—those, um, correspondences?" and "'Cause somebody tells you?"). David shows evidence of discomfort in his pauses, hesitations, repetitions, and circumlocutions. When I played the segment back for him, he told me that the fast pace of the conversation in general and the questions in particular had caught him off guard and made him feel borne in upon.

It is difficult for me to regard this conversation in merciless print, because it makes me look overbearing. Yet I recall my goodwill toward David (who remains one of my closest friends) and my puzzlement at the vagueness of his answers. Comparing this effect on David to the effect of my "machine-gun questions" on Steve and Peter, I was relieved to see that "machine-gun questions" had exactly the effect I had intended when used with other high-involvement speakers: They were taken as a show of interest and rapport; they encouraged and reinforced the speaker. But when such questions were used with high-considerateness speakers, they created disruptions and interruptions. It was not the overlapping or fast pacing that created the interruption and discomfort *but the style difference.* Style differences are the very basis of such terms as *fast pacing* and *pausing.* Characteristics such as "fast pacing" are not inherent, but result from the

styles of speakers *relative to each other.* I might add that as a result of doing this research, I learned not to use machine-gun questions or cooperative overlapping with people who don't respond well—a tangible benefit of understanding conversational style.

CULTURAL DIFFERENCES

In my study of dinner table conversation, the three high-involvement speakers were New York City natives of Jewish background. Of the three high-considerateness speakers, two were Catholics from southern California and one was from London, England. Although a sample of three does not prove anything, nearly everyone agrees that many (obviously not all) Jewish New Yorkers, many New Yorkers who are not Jewish, and many Jews who are not from New York have high-involvement styles and are often perceived as interrupting *in conversations with speakers from different backgrounds,* such as the Californians in my study. But many Californians expect shorter pauses than many midwesterners or New Englanders, so in conversations between them, the Californians end up interrupting. Just as I was considered extremely polite when I lived in New York but was sometimes perceived as rude in California, a polite Californian I know was shocked and hurt to find herself accused of rudeness when she moved to Vermont.

The cycle is endless. Linguists Ron and Suzanne Scollon show that midwestern Americans, who may find themselves interrupted in conversations with easterners, become aggressive interrupters when they talk to Athabaskan Indians, who expect much longer pauses. Many Americans find themselves interrupting when they talk to Scandinavians, but Swedes and Norwegians are perceived as interrupting by the longer-pausing Finns, who are themselves divided by regional differences with regard to length of pauses and rate of speaking. As a result, Finns from certain parts of the country are stereotyped as fast talking and pushy, and those from other parts of the country are stereotyped as slow talking and

stupid, according to Finnish linguists Jaakko Lehtonen and Kari Sajavaara.

Anthropologists have written about many cultures in the world where talking together is valued in casual conversation. This seems to be the norm in more parts of the world than the northern European norm of one-speaker-speaks-at-a-time. Karl Reisman coined the term *contrapuntal conversations* to describe the overlapping style he observed in Antigua. Karen Watson borrowed his term to describe Hawaiian children's verbal routines in which they jointly joke and engage in "talk story." Watson explains that for these children, taking a turn is not a matter of individual performance but "partnership in performance." Michael Moerman makes similar observations about Thai conversation. Reiko Hayashi finds far more simultaneous speech among Japanese speakers in casual conversation than among Americans. Jeffrey Shultz, Susan Florio, and Frederick Erickson found that an Italian-American boy who was considered a serious behavior problem at school was simply chiming in as was appropriate and normal in his home. All of these researchers document overlapping speech that is not destructive, not intended to exercise dominance and violate others' rights. Instead, it is cooperative, a means of showing involvement, participation, connection. In short, simultaneous talk can be rapport-talk.

WOMEN AS COOPERATIVE OVERLAPPERS

Paradoxically (in light of the men-interrupt-women research), and most important for our discussion here, another group that has been found to favor conversations in which more than one person speaks at a time is women. Folklorist Susan Kalčik was one of the first to observe women's use of overlapping talk by taping a women's group. In reviewing studies that compared all-male and all-female interaction, linguists Deborah James and Janice Drakich found that, of those reporting differences, the great majority observed more interruptive talk among females.

Linguist Carole Edelsky inadvertently uncovered women's preference for overlapping talk when she set out to determine who talked more at a series of faculty committee meetings. She found that men talked more than women if one person was speaking while the others listened silently, but women talked as much as men during periods when more than one voice was heard at the same time. In other words, women were less likely to participate when the situation felt more like report-talk, more likely to do so when it felt like rapport-talk. Cooperative overlapping framed parts of the meeting as rapport-talk.

Following is an example of women in casual conversation overlapping in a highly cooperative and collaborative way. It comes from a conversation recorded at a kitchen table by linguist Janice Hornyak, who was a party to the conversation. Jan and her mother, Peg, who are from a southern state, were visiting relatives in the North, where Jan got to see snow for the first time. Peg and Marge, who are sisters-in-law, reminisce, for Jan's benefit, about the trials of raising small children in a part of the country where it snows. (Jan's mother raised her older children in the North but moved to the South before Jan was born.)

Peg: The part I didn't like was putting everybody's snow pants and boots|and
→ Marge: |Oh yeah, that was the worst part,
Peg: |and scarves
→ Marge: |and get them all bundled up in boots and everything and they're out for half an hour and then they come in and they're all covered with this snow and they get that *shluck* all over|
→ Peg: |All that wet stuff and
→ Jan: That's why adults don't like snow, huh?
Marge: That's right.
Peg: Throw all the stuff in the dryer and then they'd come in and sit for half|an hour
Marge: |And in a little while they'd want to go back out again.

Peg: Then they want to go back out again.

As in the conversation among Steve, Peter, and myself presented above, all three speakers in this example initiate turns that either latch onto or intrude into other speakers' turns. Like Denise and Stacy and like Steve and Peter in earlier examples, Peg and Marge play a conversational duet: They jointly hold one conversational role, overlapping each other without exhibiting (or reporting) resentment at being interrupted.

Hornyak points out the even more intriguing fact that these speakers often end a comment with the conjunction *and,* creating the appearance of interruption when there is none, as when Peg says, "All that wet stuff and." Hornyak claims that this strategy is used by many speakers in her family, and is satisfying and effective when used with each other. She is criticized, however, for using this same strategy among others, who protest that it confuses them. They may even get the impression that someone who ends a sentence with *and* doesn't know whether or not she is finished.

Why would anyone want to create the impression of interruption when there is none? One reason that speakers from some cultural groups leave little or no pause between turns is that they see silence in friendly conversation as a sign of lack of rapport. Overlapping is a way to keep conversation going without risking silence. I should note, though, that Hornyak and the family members she taped do not speak loudly or quickly or all at once. Their overlaps, though frequent, are brief; ending sentences with *and* is a way to achieve the appearance of interruption when there is minimal overlap.

Though Hornyak feels the strategy of creating the appearance of overlap by ending a sentence with *and* is peculiar to her family, others have commented that they know people who do this. At least one man I spoke to said that his mother (to his father's chagrin) regularly ends her comments with *and uh,* and that *her* mother and all her sisters do it too—but her father and brother don't. This man also considered this a family style. Although it

clearly does run in families, the style seems to result from a combination of gender and culture.

Gender and culture also dovetail in another example of the false appearance of interruption. William Labov and David Fanshel, in a study of a psychotherapy session between a nineteen-year-old patient called Rhoda and a social worker, show that Rhoda never ended a speaking turn by falling silent. Instead, when she had said all she wanted to say, she began to repeat herself. Her repetitions were an invitation to the therapist to begin speaking by interrupting her. Both client and therapist were New Yorkers, Jewish, and women.

CULTURAL EXPLANATIONS: A MIXED BLESSING

The realization that people with similar cultural backgrounds have similar ways of talking often comes as a revelation and a relief to people who thought they had personal quirks or even psychological problems. For example, a Greek-American man I interviewed for a study of indirectness in conversation had been told by friends and lovers throughout his life that there was something wrong with him, because he always beat around the bush instead of coming out and saying what was on his mind. He told me that his parents spoke that way, and I told him that I had found that Greeks often tended to be more indirect than Americans, and Greek-Americans were somewhere in the middle. This man was enormously relieved, saying that my explanation rang a bell. He went on to say:

I see it as either something heroically different or a real impediment. . . . Most of the time I think of it as a problem. And I can't really sort it out from my family and background. . . . I don't know if its' Greek. I just know that it's me. And it feels a little better to know that it's Greek.

Viewing his "family style as an ethnic style relieved this man of the burden of individual pathology otherwise implied by being different from most of the people he communicated with.

But the tendency of people from

similar cultural backgrounds to have habitual ways of speaking that are similar to each other's and different from those of people from other cultural backgrounds, has had unfortunate, even tragic consequences. When people who are identified as culturally different have different conversational styles, their ways of speaking become the basis for negative stereotyping. As I mentioned earlier, anti-Semitism classically attributes loudness, aggressiveness, and "pushiness" to Jewish people—making a leap from ways of speaking to character. For example, in a letter to Henry Miller, Lawrence Durrell described a Jewish fellow writer: "He is undependable, erratic, has bad judgment, loud-mouthed, pushing, vulgar, thoroughly Jewish. . . ."

The perception that Jews (or New Yorkers—the categories are often fused in many people's minds) are loud and pushy simply blames the minority group for the effect of their style *in interaction with others who use a different style.* Anthropologist Thomas Kochman shows that a parallel style difference underlies the stereotyping of "community" blacks as inconsiderate, overbearing, and loud. When members of one group have the power to persecute members of the other, the results of such misjudgments are truly tragic.

If cultural differences are likely to cause misjudgment in personal settings, they are certain to do so in international ones. I would wager that the much-publicized antipathy between Nancy Reagan and Raisa Gorbachev resulted from cultural differences in conversational style. According to Nancy Reagan, "From the moment we met, she talked and talked and *talked*—so much that I could barely get a word in, edgewise or otherwise." I suspect that if anyone asked Raisa Gorbachev, she would say she'd been wondering why her American counterpart never said anything and made her do all the conversational work.

Of course not all Russians or Jews or New Yorkers or blacks are high-involvement speakers. Many use the style in some situations but not others. Some have erased, modified, or never used such styles at all. No group is homogeneous; for example, the high-involvement style I describe is more common among East European than German Jewish speakers. But many Jewish speakers do use some variety of high-involvement style in some situations, as do many Italian, Greek, Spanish, South American, Slavic, Armenian, Arab, African, and Cape Verdean speakers—and members of many other groups I have not mentioned.

A WORD OF CAUTION

The juxtaposition of these two lines of inquiry—gender and interruption on the one hand, and ethnicity as conversational style on the other—poses a crucial and troubling dilemma. If it is theoretically wrongheaded, empirically indefensible, and morally insidious to claim that speakers of particular ethnic groups are pushy, dominating, or inconsiderate because they appear to interrupt in conversations with speakers of different, more "mainstream" ethnic backgrounds, can it be valid to embrace research that "proves" that men dominate women because they appear to interrupt them in conversation? If the researchers who have found men interrupting women in conversation were to "analyze" my audiotapes of conversations among New York Jewish and California Christian speakers, they would no doubt conclude that the New Yorkers "interrupted" and "dominated"—the impression of the Californians present. This was not, however, the intention of the New Yorkers, and—crucially—not the result of their behavior alone. Rather, the pattern of apparent interruption resulted from the *difference* in styles. In short, such "research" would do little more than apply the ethnocentric standards of the majority group to the culturally different behavior of the minority group.

In a parallel way, claims that men dominate women because they interrupt them in conversation accept the assumption that conversation is an enterprise in which only one voice should be heard at a time. This erroneous assumption has significant negative consequences for women. Many women, when they talk among themselves in situations that are casual, friendly, and focused on rapport, use cooperative overlapping: Listeners talk along with speakers to show participation and support. It is this practice, when overheard, that has led men to stereotype women as noisily clucking hens. And women who enjoy such conversations when they have them may later feel embarrassed and guilty, because they accept the one-speaker-at-a-time ethic that is more appropriate to men's "public speaking" conversational style, or report-talk, than it is to women's "private speaking" style, which emphasizes rapport-talk.

Juxtaposing research claiming that men interrupt women with my study of dinner table conversation provides a linguistic parallel but a political contrast. Jews are a minority in the United States, as are blacks and members of the other groups that I mentioned as having high-involvement style. Minorities are at a disadvantage. But in the male-female constellation, it is women who are at a social and cultural disadvantage. This transforms the political consequences of blaming one group for dominating the other.

Most people would agree that women as a class are dominated by men as a class in our culture, as in most if not all cultures of the world. Therefore many would claim that viewing gender differences as cross-cultural communication is copping out, covering up real domination with a cloth of cultural difference. Though I am sympathetic to this view, my conscience tells me that we cannot have it both ways. If we accept the research in one paradigm— the men-interrupt-women one—then we are forced into a position that claims that high-involvement speakers, such as blacks and Jews and, in many circumstances, women, are pushy, aggressive, or inconsiderately or foolishly noisy.

The consequences of such a position are particularly dangerous for American women of ethnic or regional backgrounds that favor high-involvement conversational styles. The United States witnessed a dramatic example of just such consequences when Geraldine Ferraro, a New Yorker of Italian extraction, ran for vice president and was labeled a bitch by Barbara Bush, a woman of more "mainstream" background. The view of high-involvement style as dominance, taken from the men-interrupt-women paradigm, yields the repugnant conclusion that many women (including many of us of African, Caribbean, Mediterranean, South American, Levantine, Arab, and East European backgrounds) are dominating, aggressive, and pushy—qualities that are perceived as far more negative in women than in men.

As a woman who has personally experienced the difficulty many women report in making themselves heard in some interactions with men (especially "public" situations), I am tempted to embrace the studies that men interrupt women: It would allow me to explain my experience in a way that blames others. As a high-involvement-style speaker, however, I am offended by the labeling of a feature of my conversational style as loathsome, based on the standards of those who do not share or understand it. As a Jewish woman raised in New York who is not only offended but frightened by negative stereotyping of New Yorkers and women and Jews, I recoil when scholarly research serves to support the stereotyping of a group of speakers as possessing negative intentions and character. As a linguist and researcher, I know that the workings of conversation are more complex than that. As a human being, I want to understand what is going on.

WHO'S INTERRUPTING?

The key to understanding what is going on, at least in part, is the distinction between rapport-talk and report-talk— the characteristic ways that most women use language to create a community and many men use it to manage contest. As a result, though both women and men complain of being interrupted by each other, the behaviors they are complaining about are different.

In many of the comments I heard from people I interviewed, men felt interrupted by women who overlapped with words of agreement and support and anticipation of how their sentences

and thoughts would end. If a woman supported a man's story by elaborating on a point different from the one he had intended, he felt his right to tell his own story was being violated. He interpreted the intrusion as a struggle for control of the conversation.

For example, a man was telling about some volunteer work he had done as a cashier at a charity flea market. At the end of the day, there had been a shortfall in his cash register, which he had to make up from his own pocket. A woman listening to him kept overlapping his story with comments and expressions of sympathy, elaborating on how unfair it was for him to have to pay when he had been volunteering his time. As a matter of fact, the man had not been telling his experience in order to emphasize the injustice of it, and he felt interrupted and "manipulated" by the woman, whom he saw as trying to take over his story. Her offense was an excess (in his view) of rapport-talk.

This brings me back to my father, and why he might take particular relish in telling the joke about the man who didn't talk to his wife because he didn't want to interrupt her. My father believes that only one person should speak at a time. As a result, he often has a hard time getting the floor in conversations involving my mother, my two sisters, and me, since we overlap and do not leave pauses between our comments. He also feels that once he begins to talk, he should be permitted to continue until he is satisfied that he has explained his ideas completely. My mother and sisters and I feel that in a casual conversation among friends or family, it is acceptable to chime in when you think you know what others are getting at; if you're wrong, they are free to correct you, but if you're right, everyone prefers the show of connection and rapport that comes from being understood without having to spell everything out.

My father's view of this situation surfaced some years ago when he was talking and my mother chimed in. He wistfully sighed and said to my mother, "You have an advantage dear. If I want to say something, I have to wait until

no one else is talking. But you can say what you want whenever you think of it." For her part, my mother can't understand why my father needs special privileges to say something—why doesn't he just jump in like the rest of us? And I can recall feeling as a teenager that listening to my father, who is an attorney, explain something to me was like hearing a summation to the jury.

So both the man and the women in my family feel oppressed, at times, by others' ways of talking—he because he is interrupted and doesn't find the pauses he needs to enter the conversation, and we because he forbids and eschews overlaps and won't just take part like everyone else. The women in the family value overlaps and interruptions as shows of involvement in rapport-talk, and the man in the family values not being imposed on in report-talk. And he approaches casual conversations at home more like report-talk than the women do.

Then what is the source of women's complaints that they are interrupted by men? Just as my sisters, my mother, and I expect my father to toss out brief comments like the rest of us, men who approach conversation as a contest in which everyone competes for the floor might be treating women as equals, expecting them to compete for the floor like everyone else. But women are far less likely to do so, since they do not regard conversations as contests and have little experience in fighting for the right to be heard. Quite the opposite, Elizabeth Aries found that women who talked a lot in discussion groups often invited quieter group members to speak.

UNCOOPERATIVE OVERLAPPING

Whereas women's cooperative overlaps frequently annoy men by seeming to co-opt their topic, men frequently annoy women by usurping or switching the topic. An example of this kind of interruption is portrayed in "You're Ugly, Too," a short story by Lorrie Moore. The heroine of this story, a history professor named Zoë, has had an ultrasound scan to identify a growth in her abdomen. Driving home after the test, she looks at herself in the rearview mirror and recalls a joke:

She thought of the joke abut the guy who visits his doctor and the doctor says, "Well, I'm sorry to say, you've got six weeks to live."

"I want a second opinion," says the guy. . . .

"You want a second opinion? O.K.," says the doctor. "You're ugly, too." She liked that joke. She thought it was terribly, terribly funny.

Later in the story, at a Halloween party, Zoë is talking to a recently divorced man named Earl whom her sister has fixed her up with. Earl asks, "What's your favorite joke?" This is what happens next:

"Uh, my favorite joke is probably— O.K., all right. This guy goes into a doctor's office, and—"

"I think I know this one," interrupted Earl, eagerly. He wanted to tell it himself. "A guy goes into a doctor's office, and the doctor tells him he's got some good news and some bad news—that one, right?"

"I'm not sure," said Zoë. "This might be a different version."

"So, the guy says, 'Give me the bad news first,' and the doctor says, 'O.K. You've got three weeks to live.' And the guy cries, 'Three weeks to live! Doctor, what is the good news?' And the doctor says, 'Did you see that secretary out front? I finally . . . her.' "

Zoë frowned.

"That's not the one you were thinking of?"

"No." There was accusation in her voice. "Mine was different."

"Oh," said Earl. He looked away and then back again. "What kind of history do you teach?"

When Earl interrupts Zoë, it is not to support her joke but to tell her joke for her. To make matters worse, the joke he tells isn't just different; it's offensive. When he finds out that his joke was not the same as hers, he doesn't ask what hers was. Instead, he raises another topic entirely ("What kind of history do you teach?").

Most people would agree that Earl's interruption violated Zoë's speaking rights, because it came as Zoë was about to tell a joke and usurped the role of joke teller. But Zoë yielded quickly

to Earl's bid to tell her joke. As soon as he said "some good news and some bad news," it was obvious that he had a different joke in mind. But instead of answering "No" to his question " . . . that one, right?" Zoë said, "I'm not sure. This might be a different version," supporting his bid and allowing for agreement where there really was disagreement. Someone who viewed conversation as a contest could have taken back the floor at this point, if not before. But Zoë seemed to view conversation as a game requiring each speaker to support the other's words. If they had known each other well enough to argue about this later, Earl might have challenged, "Why didn't you stop me when you saw I was going to tell a different joke, instead of letting me go on and then getting mad?"

Another part of the same story shows that it is not overlap that creates interruption but conversational moves that wrench a topic away from another speaker's course. Zoë feels a pain in her stomach, excuses herself, and disappears into the bathroom. When she returns, Earl asks if she's all right, and she tells him that she has been having medical tests. Rather than asking about her health, Earl gives her some food that was passed around while she was in the bathroom. Chewing, she says, "With my luck it'll be a gallbladder operation." Earl changes the subject: "So your sister's getting married? Tell me, really, what you think about love." Zoë begins to answer:

"All right. I'll tell you what I think about love. Here is a love story. This friend of mine—"

"You've got something on your chin," said Earl, and he reached over to touch it.

Like offering food, taking something off someone's face may take priority over talk, but doing so just as Zoë starts to tell a story seems like a sign of lack of interest in her story, and lack of respect for her right to continue it. Furthermore, this is not an isolated incident, but one in a series. Earl did not follow up Zoë's revelation about her health with questions or support, didn't offer advice, and didn't match

her revelation with a mutual one about himself. Instead, he shifted the conversation to another topic—love—which he might have felt was more appropriate than a gallbladder operation for initiating a romantic involvement. For the same reason, taking something off her chin may have been too good an opportunity for touching her face to pass up. Indeed, many of his moves seem to be attempts to steer the conversation in the direction of flirting.

WHO'S DRIVING?

Interruption, then, has little to do with beginning to make verbal sounds while someone else is speaking, though it does have to do with issues of dominance, control, and showing interest and caring. Women and men feel interrupted by each other because of the differences in what they are trying to accomplish with talk. Men who approach conversation as a contest are likely to expend effort not to support the other's talk but to lead the conversation in another direction, perhaps one in which they can take center stage by telling a story or joke or displaying knowledge. But in doing so, they expect their conversational partners to mount resistance. Women who yield to these efforts do so not because they are weak or insecure or deferential but because they have little experience in deflecting attempts to grab the conversational wheel. They see steering the conversation in a different direction not as a move in a game, but as a violation of the rules of the game.

Being blamed for interrupting when you know you didn't mean to is as frustrating as feeling interrupted. Nothing is more disappointing in a close relationship than being accused of bad ntentions when you know your intenions were good, especially by someone you love who should understand you, if anyone does. Women's effusion of support can be irritating to men who would rather meet with verbal sparring. And a left jab meant in the spirit of sparring can become a knockout if your opponent's fists are not raised to fight.

The Organization of Society and Culture

Human beings do not interact with one another or think about their world in random fashion. Instead, they engage in both structured and recurrent physical and mental activities. In this section, such patterns of behavior and thought—referred to here as the organization of society and culture—may be seen in a number of different contexts, from the hunter-collectors of the Arctic to the cattle-herding Masai of East Africa ("Mystique of the Masai"), to the turban-wearers of Rajasthan ("Symbolism of the Turban").

Of special importance are the ways in which people make a living—in other words, the production, distribution, and consumption of goods and services. It is only by knowing the basic subsistence systems that we can hope to gain insight into the other levels of social and cultural phenomena, for, as anthropologists have found, they are all inextricably bound together.

Noting the various aspects of a sociocultural system in harmonious balance, however, does not imply an anthropological seal of approval. To understand abortion in the manner that it is practiced among the Yanomamö is neither to condone nor condemn it. Nevertheless, the adaptive patterns that have been in existence for a long time, such as many of the patterns of hunters and gatherers, probably owe their existence to their contributions to long-term human survival.

The articles in this section demonstrate that anthropologists are far more interested in problems than they are in place. "The Blood in Their Veins" conveys the hardships of living in the Arctic in such personal terms that the reader cannot help but understand the actions of Inuit (Eskimos) from their viewpoint. In fact, if it were not for the firsthand descriptions such as those provided by Peter Freuchen in "Trading With the Eskimos," the abilities of some people to exploit economic opportunities with such guile would be beyond belief.

Anthropologists, however, are not content with the data derived from individual experience. On the contrary, personal descriptions must become the basis for sound anthropological theory. Otherwise, they remain meaningless, isolated relics of culture in the manner of museum pieces. Thus, "Life Without Chiefs" expresses the constant striving in anthropology to develop a general perspective from particular events by showing how shifts in technology may result in centralization of political power and marked changes in life-style. In a related manner, we can see in "Gauging the Winds of War" how anthropologists grapple with the question of the causes of human conflict.

Articles in this volume offer evidence that anthropologists are not always in agreement, even when they are studying and analyzing the very same cultures. For example, in some ways Napoleon Chagnon's "Doing Fieldwork Among the Yanomamö" (Unit 1) is a direct contradiction of Shelly Kellman's description of the very same people in "The Yanomamis: Portrait of a People in Crisis."

While the articles in this section are to some extent descriptive, they also serve to challenge both academic and commonsense notions about why people behave and think as they do. These clashes of opinion remind us that assumptions are never really safe. Any time anthropologists are kept on their toes, the field as a whole is the better for it.

Looking Ahead: Challenge Questions

What traditional Inuit (Eskimo) practices do you find contrary to values professed in your society, but important to Inuit survival under certain circumstances?

How does Inuit- (Eskimo-)style trading bridge the gap between the modern and the traditional?

What can contemporary hunter-collector societies tell us about the quality of life in the prehistoric past?

In what ways can the Masai be seen as ecological conservationists?

How does the game of waiting in modern society relate to who has the power?

What has been the symbolism of the turban, past and present?

Is human conflict the result of a natural human condition, or is it the result of circumstances?

The Blood in Their Veins

Farley Mowat

Barely visible from Gene Lushman's rickety dock at the mouth of Big River, Anoteelik stroked his kayak to seaward on the heaving brown waters of Hudson Bay. Vanishing, then reappearing on the long, slick swells, the kayak was so distant it might have been nothing more than an idle gull drifting aimlessly on the undulating waters.

I had helped Anoteelik prepare for that journey. Together we had carried the skin-wrapped packages of dress goods, food and tobacco down from Lushman's trading shack. Then the squat, heavy-bodied Eskimo, with his dreadfully scarred face, lashed the cargo to the afterdeck and departed. I watched him until the bright flashing of his double-bladed paddle was only a white flicker against the humped outlines of a group of rocky reefs lying three miles offshore.

This was the third time I had seen Anoteelik make his way out of the estuary to the farthest islet on the sombre rim of the sea but it was the first time I understood the real reason behind his yearly solitary voyage.

Gene Lushman, barrenland trapper and trader, had first drawn my attention to him three years earlier.

"See that old Husky there? Old Ano . . . tough old bugger . . . one of the inland people and queer like all of them. Twenty years now, every spring soon as the ice clears, Ano, he heads off out to the farthest rock, and every year he takes a hundred dollars of my best trade goods along. For why? Well, me son, that crazy old bastard is taking the stuff out there to his dead wife! That's

true, so help me God! He buried her there . . . far out to sea as there was a rock sticking up high enough to hold a grave!

"Father Debrie, he's tried maybe a half dozen times to make the old fellow quit his nonsense. It has a bad influence on the rest of the Huskies— they're supposed to be Christians, you know—but Ano, he just smiles and says: 'Yes, Father,' and every spring he turns in his fox skins to me and I sell him the same bill of goods, and he takes it and dumps it on that rock in the Bay."

It was the waste that bothered and puzzled Gene. Himself the product of a Newfoundland outport, he could not abide the waste . . . a hundred dollars every spring as good as dumped into the sea.

"Crazy old bastard!" he said, shaking his head in bewilderment.

Although he had traded with the Big River people for a good many years, Gene had never really bridged the gap between them and himself. He had learned only enough of their language for trade purposes and while he admired their ability to survive in their harsh land he had little interest in their inner lives, perhaps because he had never been able to stop thinking of them as a "lesser breed." Consequently, he never discovered the reason for Anoteelik's strange behaviour.

During my second year in the country, I became friendly with Itkut, old Anoteelik's son—indeed his only offspring. Itkut was a big, stocky man still in the full vigour of young manhood; a man who laughed a lot and liked making jokes. It was he who gave me my Eskimo name, *Kipmetna*, which translates as "noisy little dog." Itkut and I spent a lot of time together

that summer, including making a long boat trip north to Marble Island after walrus. A few days after our return, old Ano happened into Itkut's tent to find me struggling to learn the language under his son's somewhat less-than-patient guidance. For a while Ano listened to the garbled sounds I was making, then he chuckled. Until that moment the old man, with his hideously disfigured face, had seemed aloof and unapproachable, but now the warmth that lay hidden behind the mass of scar tissue was revealed.

"Itkut gave you a good name," he said smiling. "Indeed, the dog-spirit must live in your tongue. *Ayorama*— it doesn't matter. Let us see if we can drive it out."

With that he took over the task of instructing me, and by the time summer was over we had become friends.

One August night when the ice fog over the Bay was burning coldly in the long light of the late-setting sun, I went to a drum dance at Ano's tent. This was forbidden by the priest at Eskimo Point, who would send the R.C.M.P. constable down to Big River to smash the drums if he heard a dance was being held. The priest was a great believer in an ever-present Devil, and he was convinced the drums were the work of that Devil. In truth, these gatherings were song-feasts at which each man, woman or child took the drum in turn and sang a song. Sometimes it was an ancient song from far out of time, a voice from the shadowy distances of Innuit history; or perhaps it might be a comic song in which the singer made fun of himself. Often it was the story of a spectacular hunting incident; or it might be a song of tragic happenings and of the spirits of the land.

That night Itkut sang a song of the Hunting of Omingmuk, the muskox. As the story unwound, Ano's face came alight with pride—and with love.

Toward dawn people began to drift away and Ano suggested we walk to the shore and have a smoke. Flocks of plover, grey and ephemeral in the half light, fled shrilling before us, and out on the dim wastes of the sea spectral loons yapped at one another.

Ano's face was turned to the sea.

"I know you wonder at me, Kipmetna, yet you look at this torn face of mine and your questions are never heard. You watch as I make my spring journey out to the rock in the sea and your questions remain silent. That is the way also with my People. Tonight, perhaps because Itkut sang well and brought many memories to me from a long time ago, I would tell you a story."

Once there was a woman, and it was she who was my belly and my blood. Now she waits for me in that distant place where the deer are as many as the stars.

She was Kala, and she was of the Sea People, and not of my People who lived far from the sea on the great plains where no trees grow. But I loved her beyond all things in the sea or on the land. Some said I loved her too much, since I could never find the strength to share her, even with my song-cousin, Tanugeak. Most men respected my love and the *angeokok*, Mahuk, said that the sea-mother, Takanaluk Arnaluk, was pleased by the love I had for my wife.

My mother was Kunee and my father was Sagalik. I was born by the shore of Tulemaliguak, Lake of the Great Bones, far west of here, in the years when the camps of the inland people were almost emptied of life by the burning breath of the white man's sickness. My father died of it soon after my birth.

I was born in the late summer months, and Kunee, my mother, was dead before autumn. Then I was taken into the childless tent of Ungyala and his wife Aputna. They

were not young people. Once they had lived very far to the south but their camps too had been stricken by the sickness and they had fled north. They too had been burned by the flame in the lungs, and their sons and daughters had died.

Soon after they took me into their tent, Ungyala and Aputna made ready to flee again, for there were not enough people left in our camps even to bury the dead. So we three went west . . . far off to the west into a land where the Innuit had never lived for fear of the Indians who sometimes came out of the forests into the plains. The deer were plentiful in that place and we lived very well while I grew toward the age of a man and learned to hunt by myself and to drive the long sled over the hard-packed snow.

All the same, it was a lonely land we had come to. There were not even any Indians—perhaps they too, had been burned by the plague. We saw no *inukok*, little stone men set on the hills to tell us that other men of our race had travelled those long, rolling slopes. It was a good land but empty, and we hungered to hear other voices.

In the winter of the year when I became *angeutnak*, almost a man, the blizzards beat upon us for a very long time. Ungyala and I had made good kills of deer in the autumn so we three did not suffer; yet we longed for the coming of spring, the return of the deer and the birds. We yearned for the voices of life, for the voices we heard were of wind and, sometimes I thought, of those spirits who hide in the ground.

In the month when the wolves begin to make love there came a break in the storms. Then I, in the pride of my youth and filled with a hunger I could not yet name, decided to make a journey to the northwest. I said I hoped to kill muskox and bring fresh meat to the camp. Ungyala agreed to my going, though he was not very willing for he was afraid of the lands to the northwest. I took seven dogs and drove the komatik over the snow-hidden hills for three days, and saw no living thing. That land was dead, and my heart was chilled, and only

because I was stubborn and young did I go on.

On the fourth day I came to the lip of a valley, and as I began to descend my lead dog threw up her head. In a moment the dogs were plunging into soft snow, the traces all tangled, and all of them yelling like fiends. I stopped them and walked cautiously forward until I could look down into the flat run of a gulley that lay sheltered by walls of grey stone. There was movement down there. It was *kakwik*, the wolverine, digging with his slashing front claws into the top of what looked like a drift. I ran back to my team and tried to unleash a few of the dogs so they could chase him, but now they were fighting each other; and before I could free them, kakwik was gone, lumbering up the long slope and over the rocks.

I kicked at the dogs, jumped on the sled, and drove headlong into the gulley; but when I slowed past the place where kakwik had dug, my heart went out of the chase.

He had been digging into the top of a buried snowhouse.

Ungyala believed that no men lived to the west and north of our land, yet here was a house. The door tunnel was snowed in and drifts had almost buried the place. I took my snow probe and slid it into a crack between blocks in the roof. It went in so easily I could tell the inside was empty of snow.

I grew cautious and more than a little afraid. The thought came that this might be the home of an *Ino*, a dwarf with knives where his hands should be. Yet the thought that this might instead be the home of true men gave me courage.

With my snowknife I cut a hole in the dome . . . squeezed through it and dropped to the floor. As my eyes grew used to the gloom, I saw that this had been a shelter for men . . . only now it was a tomb for the dead.

There were many bones lying about and even in that dim light I could see that not all had belonged to deer or muskox. One was a skull with black hair hanging down over gleaming white bone where the flesh of the cheeks had been cut away with a knife.

I was about to leap up to the hole in the roof and drag myself out of that terrible place when I saw a shudder of movement under a pile of muskox robes at the back of the sleeping ledge. I was sure something terrible crouched there in the darkness and I raised my snowknife to strike, and fear was a sliver of ice in my belly.

But it was no devil that crawled painfully out from under that pile of rotting hides.

Once, I remember, I found the corpse of a fawn wedged in a deep crevice among some great rocks. It had been missed by the ravens, foxes and wolves and, because it was autumn, the maggots had not eaten the meat. It had dried into a bundle of bones bound around the skin.

The girl who lay helpless before me on the ledge of the snowhouse looked like that fawn. Only her eyes were alive.

Although I was young, and greatly afraid, I knew what I must do. There was a soapstone pot on the floor. I slid the blade of my knife into the flesh of my left arm and let the hot blood flow into the bowl.

Through the space of one day and night I fed the thing I had found with the blood from my veins. Drop by drop was she fed. In between feedings I held her close in my arms under a thick new robe I had fetched from my sled, and slowly the warmth from my body drove the chill from her bones.

Life came back to her but it was nearly three days before she could sit up at my side without aid. Yet she must have had hidden strength somewhere within her for later that day when I came back into the snowhouse after feeding my dogs, all the human bones on the floor, to the last fragment, had vanished. She had found strength, even though death still had his hands on her throat, to bury those things under the hard snow of the floor.

On the fifth day she was able to travel so I brought her back to Ungyala's camp and my parents-by-right took her in and were glad she had come. Neither one made any comment when I told how I had found her and what else I had found in the snowhouse. But later, when Ungyala and I were on a journey away from the camp picking up meat from an autumn cache, he spoke to me thus:

"Anoteelik, my son, this person has eaten the flesh of the dead . . . so much you know. Yet until you too have faced death in the way that he came to this girl, do not judge of her act. She has suffered enough. The spirits of those she has eaten will forgive her . . . the living must forgive her as well."

The girl quickly recovered her youth—she who had seemed beyond age—and as she grew fat she grew comely and often my heart speeded its beat when she was near. She spoke almost no words except to tell us her name was Kala and that her family, who were Sea People, had come inland from the north coast in the fall to hunt muskox.

It was not until the ravens returned that one day when we men were far from camp, she broke into speech to my mother-by-right. Then she told how the family dogs had died of the madness which is carried by foxes and wolves, and how, marooned in the heart of the dark frozen plains, her parents and brother had followed the Snow Walker. She told how she also had waited for death until hunger brought its own madness . . . and she began to eat the flesh of the dead. When she finished her tale she turned from my mother-by-right and cried, "I am unworthy to live!" She would have gone into the night and sought her own end had my mother not caught her and bound her and held her until we returned.

She was calmer by the next day, but she asked that we build her a snowhouse set apart from the camp, and we followed her wish. She lived alone there for many days. Aputna took food to her and talked to her, but we two men never saw her at all.

It was good that spring came so soon after, for spring is the time for forgetting the past. The deer streamed back into our land. The ptarmigan mated and called from the hills, and the male lemmings sought out the females deep in the moss.

The snowhouses softened under the sun and then Kala came back and lived with us in the big skin tent that we built. She seemed to have put out of mind the dark happenings of the winter, and she willingly helped with the work . . . but it was seldom she laughed.

My desire for the girl had become heavy and big during the days she had kept out of sight. It was more than the thrust of my loins; for I had known pity for her, and pity breeds passion in men.

One evening after the snow was all gone, I came and sat by her side on a ridge overlooking our camp where she had gone to watch the deer streaming by. I spoke awkwardly of my love. Kala turned her face from me, but one hand crept to my arm and touched the place where I had thrust the knife into my vein. That night, as we all lay together inside the big tent, she came into my arms and we became husband and wife.

Such was my finding of Kala—a finding that brought me the happiest days of my life, for she was a woman of women. Her sewing was gifted by spirits, and her cooking made even Ungyala grow fat. She could hunt nearly as well as a man. And she was avid for love, as one who has once nearly drowned is avid for air. We four lived a good life all that summer and it seemed as if Kala had brought many good things to our land. The deer were never so fat, the muskox never so many, the trout in the rivers never so large. Even our two bitch dogs, which had been fruitless for over two years, gave birth to big litters and raised eleven fine pups that became the best sled dogs I ever owned. So we believed the girl was forgiven . . . that the spirits wished her to suffer no more.

On a day of the following winter, Ungyala and I were sent out of the snowhouse and we sat and shivered in the lee of some rocks until we heard the voice of my mother-by-right singing birth songs to the Whispering Ones who flame in the sky.

After the birth of Itkut, our son, a restlessness seemed to come over us all. Kala yearned to return to the sea. Aputna was feeling her years, and longed once again to hear the voices and see the faces of people she had known long ago. As for me, I was anxious to visit some trader and buy the things Ungyala had told me about; especially guns, for I thought that hunting with spears, bows and arrows did not let me show what a fine hunter I had become. Only Ungyala thought that perhaps we should stay where we were. He remembered too well that he and Aputna had twice had to flee for their lives when the people in the camps where they were living were struck down by the new kind of dying that came from beyond the borders of the Innuit lands. Yet in his heart he too wished to see people again, so we decided to go.

We had two good teams and two sleds. We drove north and then east, making a broad detour around the now empty camps where I had been born. We saw no sign of living men until we finally came to Big River. There we met two families who spent their summers near Eskimo Point and their winters inland on the edge of the plains. We stayed with them for the rest of that winter, hearing much about the world Ungyala and Aputna had almost forgotten and that Kala and I had never known. In the spring, before the ice softened, we followed Big River down to the coast.

So we took up a new way of life. Every autumn we journeyed in a big canoe, with our dogs running free on the shore, up Big River to a lake near its head where the southbound deer crossed a narrows. Here Ungyala and I speared fat bucks in the water and shot more of them out on the bare, rocky plains with the rifles we had traded for at the coast. By the time the first snows drove the deer out of the land, we would have more than enough meat for the winter, plenty of fat for our lamps, and the best of hides for our clothing and robes.

In the late days of autumn, after the deer had passed and before we began trapping white foxes, there was little to do. Sometimes then I would sit and

think and weigh up the worth of my life. It was good, but I understood that its goodness dwelt mainly in Kala. I loved her for the son she had borne, for the clothes that she made me, for the help that she gave me . . . but it went beyond that. I do not know how to explain it, but Kala held me in her soul. The love she gave me passed far beyond respect for a husband and entered that country of pleasure which we of the People do not often know. Such was our life as the child, Itkut, grew with the years.

Now I must tell how it was when we came to the coast. There we met the first white man we had ever seen. It was he who built the wood house at the mouth of Big River. He seemed a good man in some ways, but he was crazy for women. Before he had lived in the country a year, there were few women who had not spent a night in his house, for it was still our law then that a man might not refuse any gift that lay in his giving if another man asked. Kala never went to the house of the white man, though he asked me for her many times. He put shame upon me, for I was forced to refuse.

In the autumn of our fourth year in the new land, we had gone up the river as usual and made our camp at the lake of the Deer Crossing. Ours was the farthest camp from the sea, for we had come from the inland plains and they held no terrors for us. The coast dwellers did not care to go as far as we went. Our tent was pitched within sight of the ford and from the door we could look to see if the deer had arrived.

The time came when the forerunners of the big herd should have appeared, but the crossing remained empty of life. The darkening lichens on the bank were unmarked by the feet of the deer. The dwarf shrubs began to burn red in the first frosts. Ungyala and I walked many miles over the land, climbing the hills and staring out to the north. We saw none of the usual harbingers of the great herds—no ravens floating black in the pale sky, no wolves drifting white on the dark land.

Although we were worried, nothing was said. Kala and Aputna became

very busy fishing for trout, suckers and char in the river. They caught little, for the autumn run was nearly over, yet they fished night and day. The dogs began to grow hungry and their howling became so loud we had to move them some miles from the camp in case they frightened the deer. Thinking back to those days I wonder if it was hunger alone that made them so distressed. Maybe they already knew what we would not believe could be true.

The morning came when snow blew in the air . . . only a thin mist of fine snow but enough to tell us that winter had come and it had not brought the deer.

But a few days afterwards the deer came. Ungyala and I went out with light hearts but only a few deer had come to the river. These few were so poor and lacking in fat that we knew they were not the forerunners of the great herds but stragglers that lagged behind, being either too weak or too sick to keep up. We knew then that the deer spirit had led the herds southward by some different path.

The next day there were no deer at the crossing and none to be seen anywhere upon the sweep of the plains and we had killed barely enough meat to feed ourselves and the dogs for two months.

The real snows came and we began the winter with hearts that were shaken by misgivings. We thought of abandoning our camp and trying to make our way to the coast but we could not do this until enough snow had fallen to make sled travel possible. So we stayed where we were, hoping we would find some of the solitary winter deer that sometimes remain in the land. Ungyala and I roamed with pack dogs over the country for many long miles. A few hares and ptarmigan fell to our guns, but these were no more than food for our hopes.

Before long we ran out of fat, then there was neither light nor heat in the snowhouse. One day Ungyala and I resolved to travel southeast on a journey to some distant islands of little trees where in times past deer used to winter. We took only one small team of dogs, but even these we could not feed and they soon weakened until after a few days they could go no farther. That night we camped in the lee of some cliffs and it was too cold to sleep so we sat and the old man talked of the days of his youth. He was very weak and his voice almost too low to hear. At last he dozed and I covered him with both our robes; but before the dawn he had ceased to breathe, and so I buried my father-by-right in the snow in a grave I cut with my snowknife.

I turned back, but before I reached the snowhouse I heard women's voices singing the song of the dead. Aputna had seen the death of Ungyala in the eye of her mind, and the two women were mourning.

A little time after the death of Ungyala, I wakened one night to the muted whispering of the women. I lay with my face turned to the wall and listened to what Kala was saying to my mother-by-right.

"My mother, the time is not yet come for you to take your old bones to sleep in the snow. Your rest will come after. Now comes a time when I have need of your help."

I knew then that Aputna had decided to take the way of release, and had been held from it by Kala. I did not understand why my wife had restrained her, for it is the right of the old ones that they be the first to die when starvation comes to a camp. But I had small time to wonder, for Kala moved over beside me and spoke softly in my ear, and she told me what I dreaded to hear—that now I must take the few dogs that were left and make my way eastward, down river, until I found a camp that had meat to spare.

I refused, and I called her a fool, for she knew the other camps could be no better off then we were. Kala had always been a woman of sense yet I could not make her see that such a trip would be useless. I knew, and she knew, I could not hope to find help until I reached the coast camps where people depended more on seal meat than on deer, and such a trip, there

and back with weak dogs, could not take less than a month. It would be better, I told her, if we killed and ate all the dogs, let my mother-by-right go to her rest, and wait where we were, eking out our lives by fishing for what little could be caught through holes in the ice. Then, if it came to the worst, we three, Kala and Itkut and I, would at least lie down for the last time together.

She would not heed what I said and I heard for the first time the hard edge of anger in her voice.

"You *will* go!" she whispered fiercely. "If you do not, I shall myself put the noose of release on your son when you are gone out of the snow-house and so save him from the torments that were mine in a time you remember."

And . . . oh, Kipmetan . . . though I knew she was wrong, I could no longer refuse. No, and I did not, although I should have guessed at that which was hidden deep in her thoughts.

At parting next day only the old woman wept. There were no tears from Kala who knew what she knew, and none from young Itkut who was still too young to know what was afoot.

That was a journey! I walked eight days to the nearest camps of the people, for the dogs were too weak to do more than haul the empty sled along at a crawl. In that first camp I found it was as I had feared. Famine had got there before me. Things were nearly as bad all the way down the river. One by one I killed my dogs to keep me and their remaining brothers and sisters alive, and sometimes I shared a little of that lean, bitter meat with people in the camps that I passed.

I was almost in sight of the sea when I came to the camp of my song-cousin, Tanugeak. He and those with him were in good health for they had been living on the meat and the fat of seals Tanugeak had speared far out on the sea ice. They had none too much, though, for they had been helping feed many people who had already fled east from the inland camps. All the same, Tanugeak

proved his friendship. He gave me four seals and loaned me five of his own strong dogs, together with fish enough to feed them on the long journey home.

My strength was not much, but I began the up-river journey at once and I sang to the dogs as they ran strongly to the west. I had been away from my camp only two weeks, and now I hoped to return there in eight days at the most. So I sang as the sled ran smoothly over the hard river ice.

Two days up river and a few miles north of my track was a lake and by it two camps where I had stopped overnight on my way to the sea. In those camps I had been given soup made of old bones by people who were almost old bones themselves. Now, with much food on my sled, I did not turn off to give them at least a little of my meat and fat. I told myself I could spare neither the time nor the food if I was to save my own family from death . . . but I knew I did wrong. As my sled slipped into the darkening west I felt a foreboding and I almost turned back. If only I had . . . but such thoughts are useless, and they are a weakness in man; for he does what he does, and he must pay what he pays.

I decided to drive all that night, but when darkness came on it brought a blizzard that rose, full blown, right in my face. The thundering wind from the northwest lashed me with piercing arrows of snow until I could not tell where I was, and the dogs would face it no more. At last I made camp, turning the sled on its side and making a hole in a snowbank nearby for myself. I did not unharness the dogs but picketed them in their traces some way from the sled. Then I crawled into my robes, intending only to doze until the wind dropped. But I was more weary than I knew and I was soon so sound asleep that even the roar of the blizzard faded out of my mind.

All unknowing because of the storm, I had made my camp less than a mile upwind from another camp of the people. The surviving dogs of that camp were roaming about, a famished and half-mad pack. As I slept, they winded my load of seal meat.

I heard nothing until the damage was done. Only when the marauders attacked my own dogs did I awake. In my anguish and rage I flung myself on those beasts with only my small knife as a weapon. The dogs turned upon me and, though I killed some, the smell of fresh blood drove the remainder to fury. They tore the deerskin clothes from my body, savaged one arm until I dropped the knife, and slashed my face until the flesh hung down over my chin. They would have killed me if the fight with my own dogs had not drawn them off, leaving me to crawl back to my hole in the snow.

The morning broke clear and calm, as if no wind had ever blown. I could only manage to stand and shuffle about, and I went to the sled, but the meat was all gone. Nothing was left but some shreds of skin and some bones. Two of my own dogs had been killed and the remainder were hurt.

There was nothing to do. I began to look for my rifle in the debris near the sled but before I could find it I heard dogs howl in the distance and when I looked to the west I saw the domes of three snowhouses below the bank of the river. I turned and shuffled toward them.

I remember but little of the days I spent in that camp because my wounds festered and I was often unconscious. Those people were kind and they fed me with food they could ill spare—though in truth it was partly my food, for it was the meat of the dogs who had eaten the seals. Before I could travel again, the sun had begun to grow warm and to rise higher up in the sky. Yet the warmth of the oncoming spring could not thaw the chill in my heart.

I made a light sled for the two dogs I had left and prepared to depart. Those in the camps tried to keep me with them for they said that by now there would be no life in my snow-house that stood by the lake of the deer crossing, and I would only die there myself if I returned before spring brought the deer herds back to the land.

But I did not fear death anymore so I set out. Weak as we were, the dogs and I made the journey home in ten days. We had luck, for we found a deer cache that must have been lost by some hunter in the spring of the previous year. It was a foul mess of hair, bones, and long-rotted meat, but it gave us the strength to continue.

When we came in sight of the lake my belly grew sick and my legs weakened and I could hardly go on; yet when I neared the camp life pounded back through my veins . . . for the snowhouse still stood and snow had recently been dug away from the door!

I shouted until my lungs crackled in the bright, cold air and when none answered, I began to run. I reached the passage and scrambled inside.

Abruptly Anoteelik ceased speaking. He sat staring out over the lightening waters of the Bay . . . out toward the islands that were still no more than grey wraiths on the shifting horizon. Tears were running down his disfigured cheeks . . . running like rain. Then with his head bowed forward over his knees, very quietly he finished the tale.

I was greeted by Aputna, my mother-by-right, and by Itkut. The old woman had shrunk to a miserable rag of a thing that should have been gone long ago; but Itkut seemed strong and his body was firm to the touch when I took him up in my arms.

I looked over his shoulder, and asked, "Where is Kala?" though I knew what the answer would be.

Aputna's reply was no louder than the whisper of wind on the hills.

"What was done . . . was done as she wished. As for me, I will not go away from this place, yet I only did what she said must be done . . . and Itkut still lives . . . Where is Kala? Hold your son close in your arms, love him well for the blood in his veins. Hold him close, oh, my son, for you hold your wife too in your arms."

When the ice left the river, Itkut and I came back down to the coast. Kala was of the Sea People, so I took her bones out to that island which lies far from the shore. While I live I shall take gifts to her spirit each spring . . . in the spring, when the birds make love on the slopes and the does come back to our land, their bellies heavy with fawn.

Trading With the Eskimos

Peter Freuchen

As the Eskimo came into closer contact with the civilized world, their opportunities for trading with white men became more frequent. But trading was a completely foreign idea to Eskimos and they had to learn it from the bottom. European and American people think that anybody can trade; if there is only something to pay with and something to sell, trading seems easy enough! But it was not so with the Eskimos.

Living in the world's most inhospitable country, happy to be able to wrench from it the bare necessities of life, they had never developed any trade. There were of course exchanges, but these were always in the form of gifts. For the Eskimos always feel an obligation, whenever they receive gifts; they want to give *qooyanasat*, i.e., "something to say thank-you with." But this is quite different from payment. The exchange of one thing for another of similar value never occurred to Eskimos.

When Knud Rasmussen and I established our trading post at Thule, the land of the Polar Eskimos was not as yet under Danish rule, and the people there had been trading almost solely with Scottish whalers, the *upernatleet*, as they called them, meaning "those who arrive in spring." The whalers never permitted them to choose what they wanted, and gave to them only sparingly from such stores as they happened not to need for themselves. After all, they didn't want to spoil the Eskimos by teaching them the monetary value of things!

Then, a few years before we came, the great American explorer Robert Peary had come to the place and, as the whole tribe just consisted of some two hundred people, he became a provider of American goods for all of them, giving them guns, tools, and other goods in return for their services on his many expeditions. He did not care much for fur: neither did the natives have much time for trapping when he was using them on his expeditions.

As for Knud and me, we arrived with the backing of a small private capital, and we didn't have many goods. But Knud explained to the Eskimos that if we got a lot of fox skins, we could exchange them in Denmark for more goods that would arrive the next year. The natives could supply quite a number of fox skins, most of them blue foxes, for we usually got only a couple of white ones in about a hundred blue skins. To start in trading with an entirely new tribe is always an experience, and, as our stock was limited, the natives felt sorry for us when we were departing with our goods. They always came as my guests and stayed in my house, and the regular trading was done in the following way:

Each man trades just once, or maybe twice a year. The first time is when the ice has formed and the fall foxes have been caught in sufficient numbers to make a good showing. A man always brings his wife and all his children, as this is a great event for the year. It is dark during the four months from October 19 to February 24, and when the sledge comes out of the darkness all the inhabitants of the village gather around and lots of cere-monies are gone through to show how glad the visitors are to be there and for the inhabitants to tell them how welcome they are. They come into my house, after the dogs are looked after and everything is taken care of, and get something to eat. My boiled meat is followed by tea with sugar, and it is a big feast for everybody. All the villagers come in too, listening, talking, and telling.

We discuss the weather, the hunting in the summer, the dogs, the scandals of different places, and other events. The only matter we don't talk about is foxes. Next day the same thing—eating, dancing, talking—and the next day and the next, until I for my part think that the hospitality has come to an end. Then I just casually ask the man whether he has caught any foxes this year.

"Me, foxes?" He answers. "Nothing doing. One is a poor hunter as far as that goes, but especially for foxes."

"Well," I say, "I'm sorry, because I'd like to have a few foxes just to send home to the white people's country when the ship arrives next summer, and I ought to have a few absolutely first-class ones; and I know that in that case I will have to see you to get the very best grade."

"Oh!" the man yells out. The big, nice white man has made a mistake. "Oh, you don't know how unable I am to catch foxes. And what about it? Even if I had a few skins in my possession, what do you think my awful lazy and dirty wife would do with them? She can't tan skins. In fact she can't do anything."

The wife sits listening, but doesn't protest.

"Well," I remark, "I saw a couple of

bags out on the load which is now on the meat racks, and I thought they contained fox skins."

"Well," the man says, "maybe there's just a couple of fox skins in the bags, but we just use them to wipe the grease off our hands and other dirty things; and anyway, they are full of oil and far below such skins as your eyes should be bothered with looking at."

"Good!" I say. "But just the same I might like to have some of them. What about looking at them tomorrow?"

We arrange that, and the man keeps on for half an hour complaining that tomorrow will be his day of shame and dishonor. "Oh, why couldn't I get a real able wife to work like you, and you" (he points at every woman present). "Now I know that I have seen this place for the last time, because after the laugh that will be made over me tomorrow I will never show up again, even if I am tough enough to survive it, which I doubt."

Next day comes, and after breakfast I again have to encourage the customer to show his merchandise. Groaning and lamenting, he goes for his bags, the wife following him. Now comes the big moment of the year. They bring in a couple of sacks, each containing some fifty blue fox skins, and they have beforehand assured themselves that the whole village is present to witness their triumph. As if they were being dragged to the gallows, they open the sacks and pour the contents out. Now it is my turn. I look at the skins amazed, surprised and beaten.

"Well," I say, "as usual, those are the best skins in the year. I knew they would come from you; and they certainly did. Here is something I will have to mourn about for years, because I am unable to get those foxes."

The man raises his head, interested. "What did you say? Are they too poor for you to accept?"

"Oh no; not at all. Just the opposite. You will have to take every one of your skins back with you because I have nothing to pay with. The trading goods that came out this year were especially bad. We haven't got enough of them and they certainly aren't of a kind that can pay for such skins as yours."

"Pay!" yells the man at the top of his voice. "You don't think that I would show myself low enough to take any pay for those poor skins? I will feel myself happy if you'll accept them. Oh! Pay! My ears must be thick or my mind is turned crazy, because the sound I got in my head made it seem as though it was your intention to pay something for those terrible skins."

This takes some time, but finally I put in a question. "I am unable to pay for the skins but anxious to show my gratitude through my poor gifts. What could you be thinking of wanting in case I should be presumptuous enough to compare my unworthy goods to your valuable furs?

He starts in, talking to himself, trying to remember; but it is impossible for him. "What do I want! What do I want! Oh, I am a man without wishes. I don't know if I want anything."

It is then up to me. "Don't you want a gun?"

"A gun! A gun! Oh, a gun had been in my mind and in my dreams for a long, long time; but I, the man you listen to now, am a terrible hunter. Why should I have a gun?"

"Well, I will give you a gun. You need a knife, too, and you need some tools. And what more?"

Now that the big time is here he doesn't know what he wants. But I have the skins, so I invite the man, his wife, and his children to go into the store and look the things over. They get the key and go down to the store. They go in, closing the door carefully behind them, and spend the best day in the year going through everything. There isn't one gun that isn't taken down and looked over; no kettle but what is unpacked and examined, but packed again and put in its place. All the knives are tested, every pipe sucked at. The scissors are looked over, the needles taken out, and the dry goods, hardware, everything is gone through—soap and what else. They spend the whole day in that store.

Meantime, I get a chance to look these skins over and figure out my prices, and finally, in the evening when the couple comes back, the man has his wishes. He never tells what he wants, but he relates of what fine knives he saw, both those with the white handles and those with the brown, and the small ones with the point. He goes on: "And then I looked at the files. My, what beautiful files! Just what I needed last summer when I gave up my routine laziness and happened to work a little. And I saw out there that you have axes. I guess the big hunters—of course not me, but the real big hunters—they have plenty of use for such axes for chopping up the frozen meat in the wintertime." And he keeps on as if he were sent out to advertise the store to the public. He is interrupted by a sort of yelling or crying from the background. It is his wife, carefully instructed by him, who now breaks in complaining what a bold and fresh husband she has, keeping on asking like a beggar even when it has been proved to everybody that he has nothing to pay with. This, of course, only serves to cause me to protest that his skins are marvelous, unmatched so far, etc.

When the man has been talking for some time, I turn to the wife. "What about you? Aren't you going to trade? Don't you want something?

She blushes and looks for a place to hide. "Me? Certainly not! What should I want? Am I one who deserves anything? Oh, no; I have no wants, no wishes at all. Haven't I been a guest in your splendid house? Haven't I spoiled the fur he brought? Don't talk to me. Why does a big, strong man direct his words to a poor woman and make me ashamed?

"But wasn't there something you would like?"

"I would like to have—oh, I happen to be without wishes; only those people who are worth something should have something."

"Well, but I just want you to take something with you."

And after several more excuses, she tells what she might like to have. A few needles, just to possess them, because she can't sew, and it is only because other women have such things and know how to use them.

And she wanted some scissors, and she wanted thread. Maybe for the children some undershirts would be good, and some for herself; also combs. And "I would like to have a mirror, even though I, of course, will never look at myself in it. But sometimes real women lower themselves to visit me. And a kettle and some cups; maybe a pot. But because I am so bad I will not ask for a sewing box, but I looked at one out there which was good, so I will have something to think about. Of course I don't want it. And then I saw—

But here her husband interrupts. "Wait a moment! I have to go outside and beat my fresh and shameless wife. Oh, I am a poor man at everything, and here you see I can't even educate my wife. Where is my whip? What can I have to lash her with?

The wife keeps on asking, and finally I have to stop her from asking for more. Meanwhile I have figured out how much they can have for each skin and write it down on a piece of paper, sending them out to my clerk, who now is in the store ready to deliver the goods: It pays better and saves me lots of talk and time when I'm not there. They look at the piece of paper I give them as a nun looks at the Holy Bible. Now the clerk has his troubles out there while they are making their choice between the different cups, the different kettles, the guns, and what not.

And now comes the end of the trading, where they show their smartness and prove what fine business people they are.

The man will come running in. "Oh, I'm so sorry; when I told you what my needs were I forgot to ask for tobacco. I'd like to have some tobacco."

"All right." I allow him the tobacco.

A few minutes after he will be back with his purchases.

"Well," he will say, "I saw a knife out there I would like to have instead of this one, though it will ruin my sleep to part with this one, too."

I let him have the knife.

The wife will be there. "There was also some red cloth. My, I would rather have that than some of the things I got, but I'll begin to cry when I have to give them away again."

Then the man comes again. "When I am going out on long bear hunts my thoughts will go back to this hatchet, and I'll be thinking of having had it in my possession, because I'll have to give it back and procure a saw I saw out there. I have the whole time been thinking of a saw, but my tongue refused to pronounce the word."

I let him have the saw. And they keep on. The only way to stop them is to have lunch ready. Big helpings of meat; whaleskin in mighty plates, piles of frozen bear meat, bags of duck eggs frozen hard as stones, but delicious to bite into like apples—all given to make them use their mouths

for everything but asking for more. And the deal is closed.

Next day the departure takes place. The dogs are harnessed up and attached to the sledge. The man and wife are loading and lashing their stuff on the sledge. But sure enough, he comes in at the last moment: "Oh, I forgot matches! Why didn't I mention a saw file! If I had only asked for a little more goods! Enough for a harpoon shaft!"

The smartest man is the man who remembers most. He gets a reputation amongst his countrymen. Of course the perfectly straight-minded man doesn't know about this and doesn't allow for it, but the seasoned trader keeps back four or five fox skins to make up for the forgettings and additional wishes.

When everything is loaded on and the woman and children placed on top of the sledge, the man gives a signal to the dogs to rise up and be alert. Then I come out with a package in my hand, giving the wife some tea and sugar, or whatever else I know she would like. Of course these things have been allowed for, too.

The whip cracks and away they go. They soon disappear in the darkness, coming again late in the spring before the ice breaks and they have to go to the places where there is open water and the summer keeps them from communication with the outside world.

The Yąnomamis:
Portrait of a People in Crisis

Shelly Kellman

It is 1973. The Brazilian government is cutting through the rain forest, the Amazon jungle. The whine of chain saws reverberates through the dense tangle of trees and vines: "the green wall," it has been called. Trees fall 150 feet with a slashing, tearing sound. The animals flee; exotic birds nervously retreat from branch to branch as their nests fall, too, and are crushed. Some species will perish as a result.

And there are people here as well—most of whom have never seen a human being unlike themselves. They emerge into the clearing curious and unafraid, naked and unashamed. They are Yanomami Indians, members of the largest known culturally intact native tribe in the Americas. The highway workers, mostly illiterate peasants recruited from the poorest parts of the country with the promise of good wages for "easy" work, are unprepared for this encounter. They gape and shout in Portuguese: "You people are naked! Are you crazy?"

The tribespeople are not so surprised: ironically, they are friendlier to the light-skinned intruders than they would be to strangers of their own kind. The roadworkers, they think, must be the long-gone "foreigners" who left at the time of Creation. The hero Omam, their legend says, created all people from the foam of the rapids. Sitting on a rock by the river one day, chanting, Omam scooped up handfuls of foam and shaped them into human beings. Those who settled in the surrounding territory became the Yanomami; those who traveled downriver, far away, became the foreigners.

The Yanomami were given the land, the forest, and the animals, and the foreigners other kinds of goods. Someday, the legend said, the foreigners would return, coming up the river in canoes laden with goods for their Yanomami relatives.

And goods these newcomers have in abundance: elaborate cloth coverings for their bodies, knives that gleam unlike any knife ever cut from forest cane, and similarly gleaming cooking pots—much lighter and stronger than the Yanomamis' own clay vessels. Eagerly, the Indians initiate a trade: they offer the workers their harvest of bananas, yams, and manioc. Eventually, they will end up bargaining with their culture and with their very lives.

During the ensuing two years, from 1973 to 1975, hundreds of Yanomamis would die as a result of their friendly curiosity, and the Brazilian government's indifference. The government had known of the Yanomamis' presence in the area, and the locations of their villages, for many years prior to the highway project, and it had seen the devastating effects on many other tribes of sudden, uncontrolled contact with outsiders. Missionaries and anthropologists who had been working in the area since the early 1960s had already submitted five proposals for creating a protected Yanomami reserve or park, as provided by Brazilian law. Yet the government did not prepare the highway workers to meet the indigenous people, nor even screen the workers for health problems. Dysentery, influenza, measles, and the complications of the common cold were fatal to the Yanomami, who had developed no immunities to these ailments. Tuberculosis, malaria, and onchocerciasis ("river blindness," an African import) also swept through the area.

In one river valley, fifty percent of the people fell victim to the highway plagues, and the survivors inhabited a shattered world. Many tribespeople developed a consuming fascination with the road, becoming nomads who hitchhiked from construction site to construction site, begging or trading their labor for food and goods. The remnants of entire villages left their *malocas* (communal houses) to live in roadside shacks, their fields abandoned, their traditional routines of planting, harvesting, and feasting seemingly forgotten. Gone too were a rich mythology and the once-central healing arts of shamanism. In July 1975 Brazilian anthropologist Alcida Ramos observed despairingly in her field diary that the roadside Indians seemed to be a people in shell shock: "None of them," she wrote, "is willing to admit that he/she knows his language enough to teach us. They play deaf, dumb, uninterested . . . They have no basketry, no hammocks of their own; all of them wear something [western]—from rags to real clothes . . . If they stay around here, and if they survive physically, they'll become the most desperate beggars of the whole country!"

Today, the majority of Yanomamis have escaped the fate Ramos predicted, thanks largely to the efforts of anthropologists like him, and missionaries. These groups, with a little cooperation and sometimes active interference from FUNAI (the Brazilian Indian agency), have carried out large-scale vaccination programs, cared for the sick, attracted native people deeper into the forest (away from the road), and have continuously tried to mediate between the Yanomami and the intrusions of resource "development." It is probably due to the efforts of these intervenors that the tribe remains to this day our hemisphere's largest known culturally intact indigenous group, with 20,000 members inhabiting more than 25 million acres in and around the Parima Mountains on the Brazilian-Venezuelan border.

The tribe's future remains nonetheless uncertain: the Yanomamis are caught in a tug-of-war between the call for human rights and cultural diversity, and the relentless push of industry to dig up, process, reshape, commoditize and monetize every cubic inch of the planet. Moreover, the threat to their land is ultimately a threat to the entire world, and a more immediate one than most people realize. According to Britain's Alan Grainger and other "tree experts," the net loss of just 1-2 percent more of the world's tree cover may render the planet unable to reprocess enough oxygen to support human life. "The fate of the [Brazilian] Indians," writes British journalist Norman Lewis "cannot be separated from the fate of the trees." And the fate of the trees is central to the fate of all humanity.

A WANING WAY OF LIFE

In a very real sense, the Yanomami represent the last chance for survival of Brazilian Indians. Since the Europeans landed in 1500, the native population has been reduced from an estimated 6 million to, at most, 240,000 today. Dozens of tribes have been exterminated. The war against them has taken many forms: officially sanctioned slavery (abolished, in 1755) "pacification" carried out by religious orders (which meant befriending Indians and "helping" them to abandon their culture and get in step with "national" norms); the seizure and destruction of Indian lands; military attacks, bombings, and even the use of napalm.

The Yanomami were spared all of this, until recently, because of their remote location, far away from any major tributary of the Amazon. Even the appearance during the 1950s, of rubber tree tappers, nut gatherers, and hunters seeking ocelot, jaguar, and tropical birds in Yanomami lands did not cause significant problems. Yet the missionaries who established outposts at Surucucu in 1963 and Catrimani in 1965 (intending not to "pacify" the Indians but to respect and support their culture) had an uneasy sense that these people's time was running out. "There was a certain feeling that we had been called there," says Father Giovanni Saffirio, who lived among the Yanomami from 1968 to 1978, "although nobody quite knew why."

In 1968, the first epidemic—measles—struck the Yanomami on both sides of the Parima Mountains. While the missionaries were able to save all but one stricken Indian on the Brazilian side, the Venezuelan Yanomami had no health assistance: between 8 and 15 percent of their number died. During this period, a young anthropologist named Napoleon Chagnon was living with the Venezuelan groups; with the publication of his book, *The Fierce People,* the tribe's name became, briefly, a household word throughout the U.S. Focusing on the Yanomamis' inter-village raids, battle preparations, and competitive male rituals (e.g., chest pounding and spear dancing), Chagnon gave them a reputation for violence that other observers would dispute. Chagnon's critics don't quarrel with his descriptions of Yanomami customs, but with the impression he created that fighting is a constant, undertaken for enjoyment. Father Saffirio agrees that the Yanomami are well able to defend themselves; however, he considers the warfare which Chagnon observed to be a direct result of the measles epidemic. "Traditionally, the Yanomami believe that when someone dies suddenly and inexplicably, it's because someone from another, unrelated village has cast a spell on the victim," he explains. "The shaman then determines which village was responsible, and the victim's relatives often retaliate with a raid, in which they might kill, at most, three men." Today, says the priest, most of the Indians understand the biological spread of disease.

Father Saffirio recalls only three raids during his ten-year stay. In striking contrast to Chagnon's portrait, he describes his adopted people as warm and affectionate. The Catrimani mission, where Father Saffirio served, had only two or three nonnative people at a time, so the missioners were immersed in the Yanomamis' way of life.

"The most amazing aspect of Yanomami culture is their togetherness," says Saffirio. "They never feel isolated, as we do; one is never alone with a problem. Anything you need, you can find.

"Of course," he chuckles, "everybody knows *everything* you do. If you leave the house to pee, if a husband and wife are going out to the forest to make love—everybody knows it." He recalls a fun-loving animated people: "They always have *so much* to talk about! They will talk for a week about how 'the Bald One' (their nickname for me) fell down, or about something a child or an animal has done."

Each extended Yanomami family of twenty to eighty people lives in a large communal house, and the smaller, "nuclear" families are apportioned outer sections of the house and separate entrances. Built by the men from poles and woven leaves, the Yanomami houses are comfortable and watertight, but must be abandoned and replaced every four or five years when the cockroach population in the walls and ceilings grows to such proportions that not a scrap of food can be stored overnight. Each *maloca* centers on an open area used for fires, ceremonies, and feasts: almost a monthly event, these feasts (featuring spider monkey as the preferred delicacy) may bring 120 people together under one roof for a week.

Men definitely have the upper hand in this culture. Between the ages of fifteen and forty, they spend most of their time hunting; when they're older, they turn to gardening. Women work in the house, garden, and collect fruit in the forest. Marriages are generally monogamous, though a few men, usually shamans or leaders of the group, may have two or three wives. "This increases the leader's power and status, because it increases his potential kinship ties," says Father Saffirio. "Each marriage gives his group ties with another family or village; and he can have more children, which further increases his relationships, and his share in posterity.

"Children get the best of everything, especially food," Saffirio notes, and both children and the elderly get a great deal of physical affection, although adults are not affectionate with one another in public.

Child-bearing is highly regulated to assure that each child will be well taken care of. Women nurse their babies for two and a half to three years, and the nursing, Saffirio observes, "usually" prevents pregnancy. If a nursing mother should become pregnant, the milk is then considered to be unhealthy, and she will try to abort, using herbal and spiritual remedies. Such attempts usually succeed. Traditionally, the few babies born before they are wanted—or born with no man to take responsibility for them—have been put to death. "Their single question is, Who will be responsible for the child?," according to Father Saffirio. "There is no place in the culture for a child without a father."

This is one of the very few aspects of Yanomami culture that the Catramani missionaries have tried to influence: a family that finds itself with a baby it can't care for may leave the infant at the mission, which later may place the baby with an older couple. "We respect their culture and try not to interfere with it," says Father Saffirio, "but in this case we felt that it's important to try to replace the many people killed in the epidemics."

The soft-spoken, Italian-born priest found the Yanomami culture in no way lacking in comparison to "modern, westernized" ways. He found no cruelty or random violence among the forest people; rather, he was deeply touched by their warmth, their animation and enjoyment of life, and their acceptance of people strange and different from them.

"It was very hard to leave them," admits Saffirio, 42, who is now working towards a Ph.D. in anthropology at the University of Pittsburgh. "If you are trying to help, if you care about them, they know it—and they give it all back. Everyone who really *stays,* and works there awhile, has a hard time leaving the Indians."

THE POLITICAL BATTLE FOR SURVIVAL

Beginning in 1968, the tribe's advocates both outside and inside the Brazilian government began preparing carefully documented reports on the location and condition of the Yanomami, and proposals for their future protection, including the creation of a Yanomami reserve or park. To date there have been twelve such proposals; all but the last two have been tabled or mysteriously "lost" in a labyrinth of governing agencies. The missionaries and anthropologists trying to intervene on the Indians' behalf have dogged the footsteps of officials at every level—local, federal and military—and have encountered contradictory responses and mixed results. A University of Brasilia health team organized by Scottish anthropologist Kenneth I. Taylor, for example, waited nine months for FUNAI funds, then received only a fraction of the promised amount; when FUNAI pulled out, the Yanomami Project went forward on its own, limited resources and achieved at least one clear success. Acting as consultant to a company doing mineral exploration, the team showed that with proper screening, preparation, and supervision, outsiders *could* work in Yanomami territory without harmful effects.

But by this time the trickle of "foreigners" had become a flood. In 1975 government mineral surveyors confirmed that there was gold in that thar' rainforest—as well as diamonds, uranium, and a rich tin ore called cassiterite. The Brazilian government, looking to unbridled resource development as a quick-fix solution to its $60 billion foreign debt, was overjoyed. Surucucu, where most of the minerals—as well as most of the Yanomami (4,500)—are concentrated, looked like a promising prospect for a boom town. The attitudes of local officials were typified in a remark made by the governor of Roraima Territory (where most Yanomami land is located): "An area such as this cannot afford the luxury of having a half dozen Indian tribes obstruct development."

How the People Got the Fire from the IYO

The Yanomami assume a lot of free flow and transmutation between people and animals; people have animal alter-egos; they can become animals, and vice versa. In one myth a Yanomami had become IYO ("*eewoe*"), a big alligatorlike creature who lived on land and had fire. But IYO was selfish with the fire, so everyone else had to eat raw meat. The people noticed that IYO cooked his meat by spitting fire on it, so they tried to make him smile; if he did, they thought, the fire would fall out of his mouth. Finally, the people in bird form (Seis, Kore) did something to make the IYO open his mouth. (There are many versions of what the birds did: let their droppings fall on him, threw dust at him, made him laugh, etc.) The fire fell out of the IYO's mouth, and the people grabbed it up and hid it in the Poronaihi, or cocoa tree (the Yanomami still start fires with the hard wood of a cocoa tree). The IYO was so ashamed of himself that he went to the river and became an alligator (represented by the spirit Caiman). There he has stayed to this day, only showing his eyes, because he is afraid of the Yanomami, and still ashamed.

3. ORGANIZATION OF SOCIETY AND CULTURE

The unsupervised influx of 500 tin prospectors and placer (surface) miners in 1975 had much the same impacts as the highway incursion in 1973. Though placer mining by non-indigenous people is against the law, the Brazilian authorities waited eighteen months—until fighting broke out between Indians and miners—before evacuating the miners. Currently, according to the ARC, at least 1,500 gold prospectors are illegally present in Yanomami territory.

Pressure on the Yanomami and their environment has recently been escalating from many directions: one government bureau has clear-cut part of their territory so that corporate cattle ranching could move in; another agency is encouraging poor peasants to become landowners by "colonizing" the jungle. The usual complement of Brazilian state-owned companies and multinational interests are busily acquiring permits to go in and dig up the minerals. There are plans on government and business drawing boards for dozens of massive hydroelectric plants on the Amazon and its tributaries, gas and oil wells in the jungle, and even a proposal for liquefying most of the remaining 415 billion cubic feet of the Amazon forest for fuel.

If there's any hope for protecting the Yanomamis, as well as their territory, it lies in a dedicated international human rights movement organized by Brazilian native rights advocates in 1979, with the creation of the Commission for the Creation of a Yanomami Park (CCPY). Aided by the Anthropology Resource Center (ARC), the American Anthropological Association, Cultural Survival, Survival International, and the Indian Law Resource Center (CCPY) brought the Yanomamis' plight to the attention of the world community and to human rights forums in the United Nations, the Organization of American States, and the Fourth Russell Tribunal on the Rights of Indians in the Americas (held in Rotterdam, Holland, in November 1980). The effort has been a resounding success: more than 15,000 letters, petitions, and telegrams have been sent to the Brazilian government in support of CCPY's proposal for a Yanomami Park that would include most of the tribe's natural range.

This spring, in mid-March, FUNAI agreed to do just that: it interdicted 17 million acres to be set aside for the Yanomamis, with the federal government having the only right of outside access.

While those who have created and fought for the park are deservedly rejoicing in this victory, they emphasize that the government must go further to make the Yanomami park a reality. "It's an election year in Brazil," ARC's Robin Wright points out. "On several occasions in the past, the government has interdicted Indian areas, but has later revoked them. The most important step has yet to be taken: that of *delimiting* (formally mapping) Yanomami land. It's important now for people to pressure FUNAI to take this step immediately."

If and when a park plan goes into effect, its proponents have no illusions about its vulnerabilities. Under Brazilian law, the tribe's "exclusive use and control" is only of the land's *surface:* the minerals below still belong to the government and can be taken by the authority of the Ministry of Mines and Energy. The National Institute of Forestry Development, the Special Secretariat for the Environment, and other agencies are also typically given certain kinds of rights on reservation lands. All of this external pressure on the Park will theoretically be strictly supervised and regulated by FUNAI, but FUNAI's effectiveness depends both on the commitment of its personnel and on the amount of power and recognition accorded to it by higher levels of officialdom.

"We are aware that there are no guarantees," says Father Saffirio. "But this really is the best we can hope for. At least it gives us some official protection we can work with. Anything stronger has simply never been an option."

Support organizations are hoping that continued international observation and pressure can be exerted to keep Brazil's administration of the reserve in line with the tribe's rights. However, Saffirio's statement points up a tragedy both moral and ecological, which will remain no matter how well the Yanomami Park is administered: that to leave a relatively tiny segment of the vast Amazon basin just as it's been for hundreds of years, in the hands of people who live there, is not, and has never been, an option. There are laws on the books in Brazil, in many other nations, and in international covenants which talk lavishly about preserving cultural diversity and which guarantee autonomy and self-determination to every indigenous people left on earth. Yet any proposal that would make these principles a reality, anywhere, by allowing a people and their habitat to continue as they were before "civilization" discovered them, has been categorically superseded by the demands of development. It seems to be a given that the reshaping of the physical world into money or items having monetary value is always—everywhere—a priority to which all other considerations must bow. There is overwhelming evidence that this policy is damaging—ethically, ecologically, psychologically, spiritually, and in the long run, even economically. Yet those people who don't understand or don't want to see this evidence are still making the decisions about how land is used on our globe. It is up to the rest of us—somehow—to call the current path of "progress" into question before the damage is irreversible.

Mystique of the Masai

*Pastoral as well as warlike, they have persisted in
maintaining their unique way of life*

Ettagale Blauer

*Ettagale Blauer is a New York-based
writer who has studied the Masai culture extensively in numerous trips to
Africa and who specializes in writing
about Africa and jewelry.*

The noble bearing, self-assurance, and
great beauty of the Masai of East Africa have been remarked upon from the
time the first Europeans encountered
them on the plains of what are now
Kenya and Tanzania. (The word 'Masai'
derives from their spoken language,
Maa.) Historically, the Masai have lived
among the wild animals on the rolling
plains of the Rift Valley, one of the most
beautiful parts of Africa. Here, the last
great herds still roam freely across the
plains in their semiannual migrations.

Although the appearance of people
usually marks the decline of the game,
it is precisely the presence of the Masai
that has guaranteed the existence of
these vast herds. Elsewhere in Kenya
and Tanzania, and certainly throughout
the rest of Africa, the herds that once
roamed the lands have been decimated.
But the Masai are not hunters, whom
they call *iltorrobo*—poor men—because
they don't have cattle. The Masai do not
crave animal trophies, they do not value
rhinoceros horns for aphrodisiacs, meat
is not part of their usual diet, and they

don't farm the land, believing it to be
a sacrilege to break the earth. Traditionally, where Masai live, the game is
unmolested.

In contrast to their peaceful and harmonious relationship to the wildlife,
however, the Masai are warlike in relationship to the neighboring tribes, conducting cattle raids where they take
women as well as cattle for their prizes,
and they have been fiercely independent
in resisting the attempts of colonial
governments to change or subdue them.
Although less numerous than the neighboring Kikuyu, the Masai have a strong
feeling of being "chosen" people, and
have been stubborn in maintaining their
tribal identity.

However, that traditional tribal way
of life is threatened by the exploding
populations of Kenya and Tanzania (41
million people), who covet the vast open
spaces of Masai Mara, Masai Amboseli, and the Serengeti Plain. Today, more
than half of the Masai live in Kenya,
with a style of life that requires extensive territory for cattle herds to roam
in search of water and pastureland, and
the freedom to hold ceremonies that
mark the passage from one stage of life
to the next. The Masai's need for land
for their huge herds of cattle is not appreciated by people who value the land
more for agriculture than for pasturage
and for herds of wild animals.

The Masai live in countries that are
attractive to tourists and whose leaders
have embraced the values and life-style
of the Western world. These two facts
make it increasingly difficult for the
Masai to live according to traditional
patterns. The pressure to change in
Kenya comes in part from their proximity to urban centers, especially the
capital city of Nairobi, whose name is
a Masai word meaning cool water.

Still, many Masai live in traditional
homes and dress in wraps of bright cloth
or leather, decorated with beaded jewelry, their cattle nearby. But the essence
of the Masai culture—the creation of
age-sets whose roles in life are clearly
delineated—is under constant attack. In
both Kenya and Tanzania, the governments continually try to "civilize" the
Masai, to stop cattle raiding, and especially to put an end to the *morani*—the
warriors—who are seen as the most disruptive of the age-sets.

TRADITIONAL LIFE

Masai legends trace the culture back
some 300 years, and are recited according to age-groups, allowing fifteen years
for each group. But anthropologists believe they arrived in the region some
1,000 years ago, having migrated from
southern Ethiopia. As a racial group,
they are considered a Nilo-Hamitic mix.

3. ORGANIZATION OF SOCIETY AND CULTURE

Although deep brown in color, their features are not negroid. (Their extensive use of ochre may give their skin the look of American Indians but that is purely cosmetic.)

Traditional Masai people are governed by one guiding principle: that all the cattle on earth are theirs, that they were put there for them by *Ngai,* who is the god of both heaven and earth, existing also in the rains which bring the precious grass to feed the cattle. Any cattle they do not presently own are only temporarily out of their care, and must be recaptured. The Masai do not steal material objects; theft for them is a separate matter from raiding cattle, which is seen as the *return* of cattle to their rightful owners. From this basic belief, an entire culture has grown. The grass that feeds the cattle and the ground on which it grows are sacred; to the Masai, it is sacrilege to break the ground for any reason, whether to grow food or to dig for water, or even to bury the dead.

Cattle provide their sole sustenance: milk and blood to drink, and the meat feast when permitted. Meat eating is restricted to ceremonial occasions, or when it is needed for gaining strength, such as when a woman gives birth or someone is recovering from an illness. When they do eat meat at a ceremony they consume their own oxen, which are sacrificed for a particular reason and in the approved way. Hunting and killing for meat are not Masai activities. It is this total dependence on their cattle, and their disdain for the meat of game animals, that permits them to coexist with the game, and which, in turn, has kept intact the great herds of the Masai Mara and the Serengeti Plain. Their extraordinary diet of milk, blood, and occasionally, meat, keeps them sleek and fit, and Westerners have often noted their physical condition with admiration.

In 1925 Norman Leys wrote, "Physically they are among the handsomest of mankind, with slender bones, narrow hips and shoulders and most beautifully rounded muscles and limbs." That same description holds today. The Masai live on about 1,300 calories a day, as opposed to our consumption of nearly 3,000. They are invariably lean.

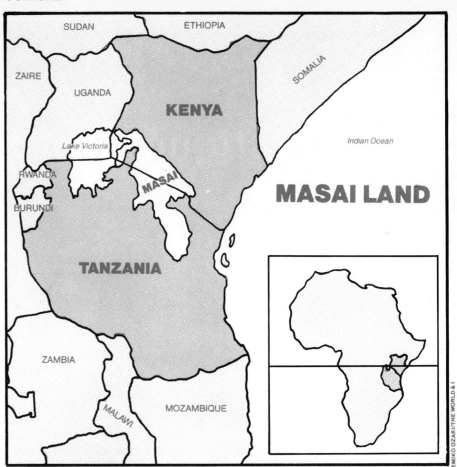

A map of Masai Land. The Masai's traditional territory exists within the two countries of Kenya and Tanzania.

Traditional nomadic life of the Masai, however, was ferocious and warlike in relation to other tribes. The warriors (*morani*) built *manyattas,* a type of shelter, throughout the lands and used each for a few months at a time, then moved to another area when the grazing was used up. As the seasons changed, they would return to those manyattas. They often went out raiding cattle from neighboring tribes whom they terrorized with their great ferocity.

A large part of that aggressiveness is now attributed to drugs; the morani worked themselves into a frenzy as they prepared for a raid, using the leaves and barks of certain trees known to create such moods. A soup was made of fat, water, and the bark of two trees, *il kitosloswa* and *il kiluretti.* From the description, these seem to act as hallucinogens. As early as the 1840s, Europeans understood that the morani's extremely ag- gressive behavior derived from drug use. Drugs were used for endurance and for strength throughout warriorhood. During a meat feast, which could last a month, they took stimulants throughout, raising them to a virtual frenzy. This, combined with the natural excitement attendant to crowd behavior, made them formidable foes.

Having gained this supernatural energy and courage, they were ready to go cattle raiding among other tribes. To capture the cattle, the men of the other tribe had to be killed. Women were never touched in battle, but were taken to Masailand to become Masai wives. The rate of intermarriage was great during these years. Today, intermarriage is less frequent and the result mostly of chance meetings with other people. It is likely that intermarriage has actually prolonged the life of the Masai as a people; many observers from the early

1900s remarked upon the high rate of syphilis among the Masai, attributable to their habit of taking multiple sexual partners. Their birthrate is notably lower than the explosive population growth of the other peoples of Kenya and Tanzania. Still, they have increased from about 25,000 people at the turn of the century to the estimated 300,000-400,000 they are said to number today.

While the ceaseless cycle of their nomadic life has been sharply curtailed, many still cross the border between the two countries as they have for hundreds of years, leading their cattle to water and grazing lands according to the demands of the wet and dry seasons. They are in tune with the animals that migrate from the Serengeti Plain in Tanzania to Masai Mara in Kenya, and back again.

MALE AGE-SETS

The life of a traditional Masai male follows a well-ordered progression through a series of life stages.

Masai children enjoy their early years as coddled and adored love objects. They are raised communally, with great affection. Children are a great blessing in Africa. Among the Masai, with the lack of emphasis on paternity, and with a woman's prestige tied to her children, natural love for children is enhanced by their desirability in the society. Children are also desired because they bring additional cattle to a family, either as bride-price in the case of girls or by raiding in the case of boys.

During their early years, children play and imitate the actions of the elders, a natural school in which they learn the rituals and daily life practices of their people. Learning how to be a Masai is the lifework of every one in the community. Infant mortality in Africa remains high; catastrophic diseases introduced by Europeans, such as smallpox, nearly wiped them out. That memory is alive in their oral traditions; having children is a protection against the loss of the entire culture, which they know from experience could easily happen. Africans believe that you must live to see your face reflected in that of a child; given the high infant mortality rate, the only way to protect that human

chain is by having as many children as possible.

For boys, each stage of life embraces an age-group created at an elaborate ceremony, the highlight of their lives being the elevation to moran. Once initiated, they learn their age-group's specific duties and privileges. Males pass through four stages: childhood, boyhood, warriorhood, and elderhood. Warriors, divided into junior and senior, form one generation, or age-set.

Four major ceremonies mark the passage from one group to another: boys who are going to be circumcised participate in the *Alamal Lenkapaata* ceremony, preparation for circumcision; *Emorata* is followed by initiation into warriorhood—status of moran; the passage from warrior to elderhood is marked by the *Eunoto* ceremony; and total elderhood is confirmed by the *Olngesherr*. All ceremonies have in common ritual head shaving, continual blessings, slaughter of an animal, ceremonial painting of face or body, singing, dancing, and feasting. *Laibons*—spiritual advisers—must be present at all ceremonies, and the entire tribe devotes itself to these preparations.

Circumcision is a rite of passage and more for teenage boys. It determines the role the boy will play throughout his life, as leader or follower. How he conducts himself during circumcision is keenly observed by all; a boy who cries out during the painful operation is branded a coward and shunned for a long time; his mother is disgraced. A boy who is brave, and who had led an exemplary life, becomes the leader of his age-group.

It takes months of work to prepare for these ceremonies so the exact date of such an event is rarely known until the last minute. Westerners, with contacts into the Masai community, often stay ready for weeks, hoping to be on hand when such a ceremony is about to take place. Each such ceremony may well be the last, it is thought.

Before they can be circumcised, boys must prove themselves ready. They tend the cattle—the Masai's only wealth—and guard them from predators whose tracks they learn to recognize. They know their cattle individually, the way

we know people. Each animal has a name and is treated as a personality. When they feel they are ready, the boys approach the junior elders and ask them to open a new circumcision period. If this is approved, they begin a series of rituals, among them the Alamal Lenkapaata, the last step before the formal initiation. The boys must have a laibon, a leader with the power to predict the future, to guide them in their decisions. He creates a name for this new generation. The boys decorate themselves with chalky paint, and spend the night out in the open. The elders sing and celebrate and dance through the night to honor the boys.

An Alamal Lenkapaata held in 1983 was probably the most recent to mark the opening of a new age-set. Ceremonies were held in Ewaso Ngiro, in the Rift Valley. As boys joined into groups and danced, they raised a cloud of dust around themselves. All day long, groups would form and dance, then break apart and later start again.

Under a tree, elders from many areas gathered together and their discussion was very intense. John Galaty, professor of anthropology from McGill University in Montreal, who has studied the Masai extensively, flew in specifically to attend this ceremony. He is fluent in Masai and translated the elders' talk. "We are lucky," they said, "to be able to have this ceremony. The government does not want us to have it. We have to be very careful. The young men have to be warned that there should be no cattle raiding." And there wasn't any.

An ox was slaughtered, for meat eating is a vital element of this ceremony. The boys who were taking part cut off hunks of meat which they cooked over an open fire. Though there was a hut set aside for them, the boys spent little time sleeping. The next day, all the elders gathered to receive gifts of sugar and salt from John Keen, a member of Kenya's parliament, and himself a Masai. (Kenya has many Masai in government, including the Minister of Finance, George Saitoti.) The dancing, the meat eating, all the elements of the ceremony continued for several days. If this had been a wealthy group, they might have kept up the celebration for as long as a month.

Once this ceremony is concluded, the boys are allowed to hold councils and to discuss important matters. They choose one from their own group to be their representative. The Alamal Lenkapaata ceremony includes every boy of suitable age, preparing him for circumcision and then warriorhood. The circumcisions will take place over the next few years, beginning with the older boys in this group. The age difference may be considerable in any age-group since these ceremonies are held infrequently; once a circumcision period ends, though, it may not be opened again for many years.

THE MORAN

The Masai who exemplifies his tribe is the moran. This is the time of life that expresses the essence of the Masai—bravery, willingness to defend their people and their cattle against all threats, confidence to go out on cattle raids to increase their own herds, and ability to stand up to threats even from Europ-

eans, whose superior weapons subdued the Masai but never subjugated them. The Masai moran is the essence of that almost mythical being, the noble savage, a description invented by Europeans but here actually lived out. With his spear, his elaborately braided and reddened hair, his bountiful beaded jewelry, his beautiful body and proud bearing, the moran is the symbol of everything that is attractive about the Masai. When a young man becomes a moran, his entire culture looks upon him with reverence.

The life a moran enjoys as his birthright is centered on cattle raiding, enhancing his appearance, and sex. The need to perform actual work, such as building fences, rescuing a cow that has gone astray, and standing ready to defend their homeland—Masailand—is only occasionally required. Much of his time is devoted to the glorification of his appearance. His body is a living showcase of Masai art.

From the moment a boy undergoes the circumcision ceremony, he looks ahead to the time when he will be a moran. He grows his hair long so it can be braided into myriad tiny plaits, thickened with ochre and fat. The age-mates

spend hours at this, the whole outdoors being their salon. As they work, they chat, always building the bonds between them. Their beaded jewelry is made by their girlfriends. Their bare legs are ever-changing canvases on which they trace patterns, using white chalk and ochre. Though nearly naked, they are a medley of patterns and colors.

After being circumcised, the young men "float" in society for up to two years, traveling in loose groups and living in temporary shelters called *inkangitie*. After that time they can build a manyatta. Before fully becoming a moran, however, they must enter a "holy house" at a special ceremony. Only a young man who has not slept with a circumcised woman can enter the holy house. The fear of violating this taboo is very strong, and young men who do not enter the house are beaten by their parents and carry the disrespect of the tribe all their lives.

The dancing of the morani celebrates everything that they consider beautiful and strong: morani dance competitively by jumping straight into the air, knees straight, over and over again, each leap trying to go higher than the last, as they sing and chant and encourage each

Masai ceremony of the Alamal Lenkapaata which is part of the Morani (warrior) coming of age for young Masai men.

Young Masai Morani (warriors) dancing traditionally with their hair caked with red ochre mud and their legs in an abstract pattern in a traditional Masai Manyatta with long mud huts in the Rift Valley, Kenya.

other. The morani also dance with their young girlfriends. Each couple performs sinuous motions repeatedly, then breaks off and another couple takes their place. A hypnotic rhythm develops as they follow the chanting and hand clapping of their mates.

Although they are now forbidden by the governments of Kenya and Tanzania to kill a lion—a traditional test of manhood—or to go cattle raiding, they retain all the trappings of a warrior, without the possibility of practicing their skill. They occasionally manage a cattle raid, but even without it, they still live with pride and dignity. Masai remain morani for about fifteen years, building up unusually strong relationships among their age-mates with whom they live during that time. Hundreds of boys may become morani at one time.

Traditionally, every fifteen years saw the advent of a new generation of warriors. Now, both colonial governments and independent black-ruled governments have tampered with this social process, and have been successful in reducing the time men spend as warriors. By forcing this change, the governments hope to mold the Masai male into a more tractable citizen, especially by forbidding such disruptive activities as lion killing and cattle raiding. But tinkering with the Masai system can have unforeseen and undesirable consequences. It takes a certain number of years before a moran is ready to take on the duties of that age-group. They need time to build up herds of cattle to be used for bride-price and to learn to perform the decision-making tasks expected. This change also leaves the younger boys without warriors to keep them in check, and to guide them through the years leading up to the circumcision ceremony.

More significantly, since 1978 it has been illegal to build a manyatta, and warriors from that time have been left with no place to live. Their mothers cannot live with them, they cannot tend their cattle or increase their herds, they have no wives or jobs. Since, once they become warriors, they are not allowed to enter another person's house to eat, they are forced to steal other peoples' cattle and live off the land.

Circumcision exists for women as well as for men. From the age of nine until puberty, young girls live with the morani as sexual partners; it is an accepted part of Masai life that girls do not reach puberty as virgins. It is because of this practice that syphilis causes the most serious problems for the Masai. The girls, unfamiliar with their bodies, contract the disease and leave it untreated until sterility results. This sexual activity changes dramatically when a girl reaches puberty. At that time, she is circumcised and forbidden to stay with the warriors. This is to prevent her from becoming pregnant before she is married. As soon as she recovers from the circumcision, or clitoridectomy, an operation that destroys her ability to experience orgasm, she is considered ready for marriage. Circumcision is seen as a means of equalizing men and women. By removing any vestige of the appearance of the organs of the opposite sex, it purifies the gender. Although female circumcision has long been banned by the Kenyan government, few girls manage to escape the operation.

While the entire tribe devotes itself to the rituals that perpetuate the male age-set system, girls travel individually through life in their roles as lovers, wives, and child bearers, in all instances subservient to the boys and men. They have no comparable age-set system and hence do not develop the intensely felt friendships of the men who move through life together in groups, and who, during the period of senior warriorhood live together, away from their families.

It is during this period that the mothers move away from their homes. They build manyattas in which they live with their sons who have achieved the status of senior morani, along with their sons' girlfriends, and away from their own small children. The husbands, other wives, and the other women of the tribe, take care of these children.

The male-female relationship is dictated according to the male age-sets. When a newly circumcised girl marries, she joins the household of her husband's family, and likely will be one among several of his wives. Her role is to milk the cows, to build the house, and to bear children, especially male children. Only through childbirth can she achieve high status; all men, on the other hand, achieve status simply by graduating from one age-set to the next.

A childless Masai woman is virtually without a role in her society. One of the rarest ceremonies among the Masai is a blessing for women who have not given birth and for women who want more children. While the women play a peripheral role in the men's ceremonies, the men are vital to the women's, for it is a man who blesses the women. To prepare for the ritual, the women brew great quantities of beer and offer beer and lambs to the men who are to bless them.

In their preparation for this ceremony, and in conducting matters that pertain to their lives, the women talk things out democratically, as do the men. They gather in the fields and each woman presents her views. Not until all who want to speak have done so does the group move toward a consensus. As with the men, a good speaker is highly valued and her views are listened to attentively. But these sessions are restricted to women's issues; the men have the final say over all matters relating to the tribe. Boys may gather in councils as soon as they have completed the Alamal Lenkapaata; girls don't have similar opportunities. They follow their lovers, the morani, devotedly, yet as soon as they reach the age when they can marry, they are wrenched out of this love relationship and given in marriage to much older men, men who have cattle for bride-price.

Because morani do not marry until they are elevated to elderhood, girls must accept husbands who are easily twice their age. But just as the husband has more than one wife, she will have lovers, who are permitted as long as they are members of her husband's circumcision group, not the age group for whom she was a girlfriend. This is often the cause of tension among the Masai. All the children she bears are considered to be her husband's even though they may not be his biologically. While incest taboos are clearly observed and various other taboos also pertain, multiple partners are expected. Polygamy in Masailand (and anywhere it prevails) dictates that some men will not marry at all. These men are likely to be those without cattle, men who cannot bring bride-price. For the less traditional, the payment of bride-price is sometimes made in cash, rather than in cattle, and to earn money, men go to the cities to seek work. Masai tend to find jobs that permit them to be outside and free; for this reason, many of the night watchmen in the capital city of Nairobi are Masai. They sit around fires at night, chatting, in an urban version of their life in the countryside. . . .

RAIDING, THEFT, AND THE LAW

Though now subject to national laws, the Masai do not turn to official bodies or courts for redress. They settle their own disputes democratically, each man giving his opinion until the matter at hand is settled. Men decide all matters for the tribe (women do not take part in these discussions), and they operate virtually without chiefs. The overriding concern is to be fair in the resolution of problems because kinship ties the Masai together in every aspect of their lives. Once a decision is made, punishment is always levied in the form of a fine. The Masai have no jails, nor do they inflict physical punishment. For a people who value cattle as much as they do, there is no greater sacrifice than to give up some of their animals.

The introduction of schools is another encroachment upon traditional life which was opposed by the Masai. While most African societies resisted sending their children to school, the Masai reacted with particular intensity. They compared school to death or enslavement; if children did go to school, they would be lost to the Masai community. They would forget how to survive on the land, how to identify animals by their tracks, and how to protect the cattle. All of these things are learned by example and by experience.

David Read is a white Kenyan, fluent in Masai who said that, as a boy: "I may not have been able to read or write, but I knew how to live in the bush. I could hunt my dinner if I had to."

The first school in their territory was opened in 1919 at Narok but few children attended. The Masai scorned the other tribes, such as the Kikuyu, who later embraced Western culture and

soon filled the offices of the government's bureaucracies. The distance between the Masai and the other tribes became even greater. The Masai were seen as a painful reminder of the primitivism that Europeans as well as Africans had worked so hard to erase. Today, however, many Masai families will keep one son at home to maintain traditional life, and send another one to school. In this way, they experience the benefits of literacy, opportunities for employment, money, connections to the government, and new knowledge, especially veterinary practices, while keeping their traditions intact. Masai who go to school tend to succeed, many of them graduating from college with science degrees. Some take up the study of animal diseases, and bring this knowledge back to help their communities improve the health of their cattle. The entire Masai herd was once nearly wiped out during the rinderpest epidemic in the late nineteenth century. Today, the cattle are threatened by tsetse flies. But where the Masai were able to rebuild their herds in the past, today, they would face tremendous pressure to give up cattle raising entirely.

LIVING CONDITIONS

While the Masai are admired for their great beauty, their living conditions are breeding grounds for disease. Since they keep their small livestock (sheep and goats) in the huts where they live, they are continually exposed to the animals' excrement. The cattle are just outside, in an open enclosure, and their excrement is added to the mix. Flies abound wherever cattle are kept, but with the animals living right next to the huts, they are ever-present. Like many tribal groups living in relative isolation, the Masai are highly vulnerable to diseases brought in by others. In the 1890s, when the rinderpest hit their cattle, the Masai were attacked by smallpox which, coupled with drought, reduced their numbers almost to the vanishing point.

For the most part, the Masai rely on the remedies of their traditional medicine and are renowned for their extensive knowledge and use of natural plants to treat illnesses and diseases of both people and cattle. Since they live in an

area that had hardly any permanent sources of water, the Masai have learned to live without washing. They are said to have one bath at birth, another at marriage. Flies are pervasive; there is scarcely a picture of a Masai taken in their home environment that does not show flies alit on them.

Their rounded huts, looking like mushrooms growing from the ground, are built by the women. On a frame of wooden twigs, they begin to plaster mud and cow dung. Layers and layers of this are added until the roof reaches the desired thickness. Each day, cracks and holes are repaired, especially after the rains, using the readily available dung. Within the homes, they use animal hides. Everything they need can be made from the materials at hand. There are a few items such as sugar, tea, and cloth that they buy from the *dukas,* or Indian shops, in Narok, Kajiado, and other nearby towns, but money is readily obtained by selling beaded jewelry, or simply one's own image. Long ago, the Masai discovered their photogenic qualities. If they cannot survive as warriors by raiding, they will survive as icons of warriors, permitting tourists to take their pictures for a fee, and that fee is determined by hard bargaining. One does not simply take a picture of a Masai without payment; that is theft.

Their nomadic patterns have been greatly reduced; now they move only the cattle as the seasons change. During the dry season, the Masai stay on the higher parts of the escarpment and use the pastures there which they call *osukupo.* This offers a richer savannah with more trees. When the rains come, they move down to the pastures of the Rift Valley to the plains called *okpurkel.*

Their kraals are built a few miles from the water supply. The cattle drink on one day only, then are grazed the next, so they can conserve the grazing by using a larger area than they would be able to if they watered the cattle every day. But their great love of cattle has inevitably brought them to the point of overstocking. As the cattle trample their way to and from the waterhole, they destroy all vegetation near it, and the soil washes away. Scientists studying Masai land use have concluded that with the change from a totally nomadic way of life, the natural environmental resistance of this system was destroyed; there is no self-regulating mechanism left. Some Masai have permitted wheat farming on their land for the exploding Kenyan population, taking away the marginal lands that traditionally provided further grazing for their cattle.

PRESSURE TO CHANGE

In June 1901, Sir Charles Eliot, colonial governor of Kenya, said, "I regard the Masai as the most important and dangerous of the tribes with whom we have to deal in East Africa and I think it will be long necessary to maintain an adequate military force in the districts which they inhabit."

The traditional Masai way of life has been under attack ever since. The colonial British governments of Kenya and Tanzania (then Tanganyika) outlawed Masai cattle raiding and tried to stifle the initiation ceremony; the black governments that took over upon independence in the 1960s continued the process. The Masai resisted these edicts, ignored them, and did their best to circumvent them throughout the century. In some areas, they gave in entirely—cattle raiding, the principal activity of the morani—rarely occurs, but their ceremonies, the vital processes by which a boy becomes a moran and a moran becomes an elder, remain intact, although they have been banned over and over again. Stopping these ceremonies is more difficult than just proclaiming them to be over, as the Kenyan government did in 1985.

Some laws restrict the very essence of a Masai's readiness to assume the position of moran. Hunting was banned entirely in Kenya and nearly so in Tanzania (except for expensive permits issued to tourists, and restricted to designated hunting blocks), making it illegal for a moran to kill a lion to demonstrate his bravery and hunting skills. Although the Masai ignore the government whenever possible, at times such as this, conflict is unavoidable. Lions are killed occasionally, but stealthily; some modern Masai boys say, "Who needs to kill a lion? It doesn't prove anything."

The Kenyan governments requirement that Masai children go to school has also affected the traditional roles of girls and women, who traditionally married at age twelve or thirteen and left school. Now the government will send fathers and husbands to jail for taking these girls out of school. There was a case in Kenya in 1986 of a girl who wrote to the government protesting the fact that her father had removed her from school to prepare her for marriage. Her mother carries the letter to the appropriate government officials, the father was tried, and the girl was allowed to return to school.

Sometimes there is cooperation between governmental policy and traditional life-style. Ceremonies are scheduled to take place in school holidays, and while government policies continue to erode traditional customs, the educated and traditional groups within the Masai community try to support each other.

TRADITION IN THE FACE OF CHANGE

Although the Masai in both countries are descended from the same people, national policies have pushed the Kenyan Masai further away from their traditions. The Tanzanian Masai, for example, still dress occasionally in animal skins, decorated with beading. The Kenyan Masai dress almost entirely in cloth, reserving skins for ceremonial occasions.

In 1977, Kenya and Tanzania closed their common border, greatly isolating the Tanzanian Masai from Western contact. Though the border has been reopened, the impact on the Masai is clear. The Kenyan Masai became one of the sights of the tourist route while the Tanzanian Masai were kept from such interaction. This has further accelerated change among the Kenyan Masai. Tepilit Ole Saitoti sees a real difference in character between the Masai of Kenya and Tanzania. "Temperamentally," he says, "the Tanzanian Masai tend to be calmer and slower than those in Kenya."

Tribal people throughout Africa are in a constant state of change, some totally urbanized, their traditions nearly forgotten; others are caught in the middle, part of the tribe living traditionally, some moving to the city and adopting Western ways. The Masai have retained their culture, their unique and distinctive way of life, longer than virtually all the other tribes of East Africa, and they have done so while living in the very middle of the tourist traffic. Rather than disappear into the bush, the Masai use their attractiveness and mystique to their own benefit. Masai Mara and Amboseli, two reserves set aside for them, are run by them for their own profit.

Few tribes in Africa still put such a clear cultural stamp on an area; few have so successfully resisted enormous efforts to change them, to modernize and "civilize" them, to make them fit into the larger society. We leave it to Tepilit Ole Saitoti to predict the future of his own people: "Through their long and difficult history, the Masai have fought to maintain their traditional way of life. Today, however, they can no longer resist the pressures of the modern world. The survival of Masai culture has ceased to be a question; in truth, it is rapidly disappearing."

BIBLIOGRAPHY

Bleeker, Sonia, *The Masai, Herders of East Africa*, 1963.
Fedders, Andrew, *Peoples and Cultures of Kenya*, TransAfrica Books, Nairobi, 1979.
Fisher, Angela, *Africa Adorned*, Harry N. Abrams Inc., New York, 1984.
Kinde, S.H., *Last of the Masai*, London, 1901.
Kipkorir, B., *Kenya's People, People of the Rift Valley*, Evans Bros. Ltd., London, 1978.
Lamb, David, *The Africans*, Vintage Books, New York, 1984.
Moravia, Alberto, *Which Tribe Do You Belong To?*, Farrar, Straus & Firous, New York, 1974.
Read, David, *Barefoot Over the Serengeti*, Read, Nairobi, 1979.
Ole Saitoti, Tepilit, *Masai*, Barry N. Abrams, Inc., New York 1980.
—,*The Worlds of a Masai Warrior*, Random House, New York, 1986.
Ricciardi, Mirella, *Vanishing Africa*, Holt, Rinehard Winston, 1971.
Sankan, S.S., *The Masai*, Kenya Literature Bureau, Nairobi, 1971.
Thomson, Joseph, *Through Masai Land*, Sampson Low, Marston & Co., London 1885.
Tignor, Robert, *The Colonial Transformation of Kenya, The Kamba, Kikuyu and Masai from 1900 to 1939*, Princeton, NJ 1976.

Life Without Chiefs

Are we forever condemned to a world of haves and have-nots, rulers and ruled?
Maybe not, argues a noted anthropologist—if we can relearn some ancient lessons.

Marvin Harris

Marvin Harris is a graduate research professor of anthropology at the University of Florida and chair of the general anthropology division of the American Anthropological Association. His seventeen books include Cows, Pigs, Wars and Witches *and* Cannibals and Kings.

Can humans exist without some people ruling and others being ruled? To look at the modern world, you wouldn't think so. Democratic states may have done away with emperors and kings, but they have hardly dispensed with gross inequalities in wealth, rank, and power.

However, humanity hasn't always lived this way. For about 98 percent of our existence as a species (and for four million years before then), our ancestors lived in small, largely nomadic hunting-and-gathering bands containing about 30 to 50 people apiece. It was in this social context that human nature evolved. It has been only about ten thousand years since people began to settle down into villages, some of which eventually grew into cities. And it has been only in the last two thousand years that the majority of people in the world have not lived in hunting-and-gathering societies. This brief period of time is not nearly sufficient for noticeable evolution to have taken place. Thus, the few remaining foraging societies are the closest analogues

we have to the "natural" state of humanity.

To judge from surviving examples of hunting-and-gathering bands and villages, our kind got along quite well for the greater part of prehistory without so much as a paramount chief. In fact, for tens of thousands of years, life went on without kings, queens, prime ministers, presidents, parliaments, congresses, cabinets, governors, and mayors—not to mention the police officers, sheriffs, marshals, generals, lawyers, bailiffs, judges, district attorneys, court clerks, patrol cars, paddy wagons, jails, and penitentiaries that help keep them in power. How in the world did our ancestors ever manage to leave home without them?

Small populations provide part of the answer. With 50 people per band or 150 per village, everybody knew everybody else intimately. People gave with the expectation of taking and took with the expectation of giving. Because chance played a great role in the capture of animals, collection of wild foodstuffs, and success of rudimentary forms of agriculture, the individuals who had the luck of the catch on one day needed a handout on the next. So the best way for them to provide for their inevitable rainy day was to be generous. As expressed by anthropologist Richard Gould, "The greater the amount of risk, the greater the extent of sharing." Reciprocity is a small society's bank.

In reciprocal exchange, people do not specify how much or exactly what they expect to get back or when they expect to get it. That would besmirch the quality of that transaction and make it similar to mere barter or to buying and selling. The distinction lingers on in societies dominated by other forms of exchange, even capitalist ones. For we do carry out a give-and-take among close kin and friends that is informal, uncalculating, and imbued with a spirit of generosity. Teen-agers do not pay cash for their meals at home or for the use of the family car, wives do not bill their husbands for cooking a meal, and friends give each other birthday gifts and Christmas presents. But much of this is marred by the expectation that our generosity will be acknowledged with expression of thanks.

Where reciprocity really prevails in daily life, etiquette requires that generosity be taken for granted. As Robert Dentan discovered during his fieldwork among the Semai of Central Malaysia, no one ever says "thank you" for the meat received from another hunter. Having struggled all day to lug the carcass of a pig home through the jungle heat, the hunter allows his prize to be cut up into exactly equal portions, which he then gives away to the entire group. Dentan explains that to express gratitude for the portion received indicates that you are the kind of ungenerous person who calculates how much you give and take: "In this con-

From *New Age Journal*, November/December 1989, pp. 42-45, 105-109. Excerpts from *Our Kind* by Marvin Harris. Copyright © 1990 by Marvin Harris. Reprinted by permission of HarperCollins Publishers.

text, saying 'thank you' is very rude, for it suggests, first, that one has calculated the amount of a gift and, second, that one did not expect the donor to be so generous." To call attention to one's generosity is to indicate that others are in debt to you and that you expect them to repay you. It is repugnant to egalitarian peoples even to suggest that they have been treated generously.

Canadian anthropologist Richard Lee tells how, through a revealing incident, he learned about this aspect of reciprocity. To please the !Kung, the "bushmen" of the Kalahari desert, he decided to buy a large ox and have it slaughtered as a present. After days of searching Bantu agricultural villages for the largest and fattest ox in the region, he acquired what appeared to be a perfect specimen. But his friends took him aside and assured him that he had been duped into buying an absolutely worthless animal. "Of course, we will eat it," they said, "but it won't fill us up—we will eat and go home to bed with stomachs rumbling." Yet, when Lee's ox was slaughtered, it turned out to be covered with a thick layer of fat. Later, his friends explained why they had said his gift was valueless, even though they knew better than he what lay under the animal's skin:

"Yes, when a young man kills much meat he comes to think of himself as a chief or a big man, and he thinks of the rest of us as his servants or inferiors. We can't accept this, we refuse one who boasts, for someday his pride will make him kill somebody. So we always speak of his meat as worthless. This way we cool his heart and make him gentle."

Lee watched small groups of men and women returning home every evening with the animals and wild fruits and plants that they had killed or collected. They shared everything equally, even with campmates who had stayed behind and spent the day sleeping or taking care of their tools and weapons.

"Not only do families pool that day's production, but the entire camp—residents and visitors alike—shares equally in the total quantity of food available," Lee observed. "The evening meal of any one family is made up of portions of food from each of the other families resident. There is a constant flow of nuts, berries, roots, and melons from one family fireplace to another, until each person has received an equitable portion. The following morning a different combination of foragers moves out of camp, and when they return late in the day, the distribution of foodstuffs is repeated."

In small, prestate societies, it was in everybody's best interest to maintain each other's freedom of access to the natural habitat. Suppose a !Kung with a lust for power were to get up and tell his campmates, "From now on, all this land and everything on it belongs to me. I'll let you use it but only with my permission and on the condition that I get first choice of anything you capture, collect, or grow." His campmates, thinking that he had certainly gone crazy, would pack up their few belongings, take a long walk, make a new camp, and resume their usual life of egalitarian reciprocity. The man who would be king would be left by himself to exercise a useless sovereignty.

THE HEADMAN: LEADERSHIP, NOT POWER

To the extent that political leadership exists at all among band-and-village societies, it is exercised by individuals called headmen. These headmen, however, lack the power to compel others to obey their orders. How can a leader be powerful and still lead?

The political power of genuine rulers depends on their ability to expel or exterminate disobedient individuals and groups. When a headman gives a command, however, he has no certain physical means of punishing those who disobey. So, if he wants to stay in "office," he gives few commands. Among the Eskimo, for instance, a group will follow an outstanding hunter and defer to his opinion with respect to choice of hunting spots. But in all other matters, the leader's opinion carries no more weight than any other man's. Similarly, among the !Kung, each band has its recognized leaders, most of whom are males. These men speak out more than others and are listened to with a bit more deference. But they have no formal authority and can only persuade, never command. When Lee asked the !Kung whether they had headmen—meaning powerful chiefs— they told him, "Of course we have headmen! In fact, we are all headmen. Each one of us is headman over himself."

Headmanship can be a frustrating and irksome job. Among Indian groups such as the Mehinacu of Brazil's Zingu National Park, headmen behave something like zealous scoutmasters on overnight cookouts. The first one up in the morning, the headman tries to rouse his companions by standing in the middle of the village plaza and shouting to them. If something needs to be done, it is the headman who starts doing it, and it is the headman who works harder than anyone else. He sets an example not only for hard work but also for generosity: After a fishing or hunting expedition, he gives away more of his catch than anyone else does. In trading with other groups, he must be careful not to keep the best items for himself.

In the evening, the headman stands in the center of the plaza and exhorts his people to be good. He calls upon them to control their sexual appetites, work hard in their gardens, and take frequent baths in the river. He tells them not to sleep during the day or bear grudges against each other.

COPING WITH FREELOADERS

During the reign of reciprocal exchange and egalitarian headmen, no individual, family, or group smaller than the band or village itself could control access to natural resources. Rivers, lakes, beaches, oceans, plants and animals, the soil and subsoil were all communal property.

Among the !Kung, a core of people born in a particular territory say that they "own" the water holes and hunting rights, but this has no effect on the people who happen to be visiting and living with them at any given time. Since !Kung from neighboring bands are related through marriage, they often visit each other for months at a time and have free use of whatever resources they need without having to ask permission. Though people from distant bands must make a request to use another band's territory, the "owners" seldom refuse them.

The absence of private possession in land and other vital resources means that a form of communism probably existed among prehistoric hunting and collecting bands and small villages. Perhaps I should emphasize that this did not rule out the existence of private property. People in simple band-and-village societies own personal effects such as weapons, clothing, containers, ornaments, and tools. But why should anyone want to steal such objects? People who have a bush camp and move about a lot have no use for extra possessions. And since the group is small enough that everybody knows everybody else, stolen items cannot be used anonymously. If you want something, better to ask for it openly, since by the rules of reciprocity such requests cannot be denied.

I don't want to create the impression that life within egalitarian band-and-village societies unfolded entirely without disputes over possessions. As in every social group, nonconformists and malcontents tried to use the system for their own advantage. Inevitably there were freeloaders, individuals who consistently took more than they gave and lay back in their hammocks while others did the work. Despite the absence of a criminal justice system, such behavior eventually was punished. A widespread belief among band-and-village peoples attributes death and misfortune to the malevolent conspiracy of sorcerers. The task of identifying these evildoers falls to a group's shamans, who remain responsive to public opinion during their divinatory trances. Well-liked individuals who enjoy strong support from their families need not fear the shaman. But quarrelsome, stingy people who do not give as well as take had better watch out.

FROM HEADMAN TO BIG MAN

Reciprocity was not the only form of exchange practiced by egalitarian band-and-village peoples. Our kind long ago found other ways to give and take. Among them the form of exchange known as redistribution played a crucial role in creating distinctions of rank during the evolution of chiefdoms and states.

Redistribution occurs when people turn over food and other valuables to a prestigious figure such as a headman, to be pooled, divided into separate portions, and given out again. The primordial form of redistribution was probably keyed to seasonal hunts and harvests, when more food than usual became available.

True to their calling, headmen-redistributors not only work harder than their followers but also give more generously and reserve smaller and less desirable portions for themselves than for anyone else. Initially, therefore, redistribution strictly reinforced the political and economic equality associated with reciprocal exchange. The redistributors were compensated purely with admiration and in proportion to their success in giving bigger feasts, in personally contributing more than anybody else, and in asking little or nothing for their effort, all of which initially seemed an innocent extension of the basic principle of reciprocity.

But how little our ancestors understood what they were getting themselves into! For if it is a good thing to have a headman give feasts, why not have several headmen give feasts? Or, better yet, why not let success in organizing and giving feasts be the measure of one's legitimacy as a headman? Soon, where conditions permit, there are several would-be headmen vying with each other to hold the most lavish feasts and redistribute the most food and other valuables. In this fashion there evolved the nemesis that Richard Lee's !Kung informants had warned about: the youth who wants to be a "big man."

A classic anthropological study of big men was carried out by Douglas Oliver among the Siuai, a village people who live on the South Pacific island of Bougainville, in the Solomon Islands. In the Siuai language, big men were known as *mumis*. Every Siuai boy's highest ambition was to become a mumi. He began by getting married, working hard, and restricting his own consumption of meats and coconuts. His wife and parents, impressed with the seriousness of his intentions, vowed to help him prepare for his first feast. Soon his circle of supporters widened and he began to construct a clubhouse in which his male followers could lounge about and guests could be entertained and fed. He gave a feast at the consecration of the clubhouse; if this was a success, the circle of people willing to work for him grew larger still, and he began to hear himself spoken of as a mumi. Larger and larger feasts meant that the mumi's demands on his supporters became more irksome. Although they grumbled about how hard they had to work, they remained loyal as long as their mumi continued to maintain and increase his renown as a "great provider."

Finally the time came for the new mumi to challenge the older ones. He did this at a *muminai* feast, where both sides kept a tally of all the pigs, coconut pies, and sago-almond puddings given away by the host mumi and his followers to the guest mumi and his followers. If the guests could not reciprocate with a feast as lavish as that of the challengers, their mumi suffered a great social humiliation, and his fall from mumihood was immediate.

At the end of a successful feast, the greatest of mumis still faced a lifetime of personal toil and dependence on the moods and inclinations of his followers. Mumihood did not confer the power to coerce others into doing one's bidding, nor did it elevate one's standard of living above anyone else's. In fact, because giving things away was the essence of mumihood, great mumis consumed less meat and other delicacies than ordinary men. Among the Kaoka, another Solomon Islands group, there is the saying, "The giver of the feast takes the bones and the stale cakes; the meat and the fat go to the others." At one great feast attended by 1,100 people, the host mumi, whose name was Soni, gave away thirty-two pigs and a large quantity of sago-almond puddings. Soni himself and some of his closest followers went hungry. "We shall eat Soni's renown," they said.

FROM BIG MAN TO CHIEF

The slide (or ascent?) toward social stratification gained momentum wherever extra food produced by the inspired diligence of redistributors could be stored while awaiting muminai feasts, potlatches, and other occasions of redistribution. The more concentrated and abundant the harvest and the less perishable the crop, the greater its potential for endowing the big man with power. Though others would possess some stored-up foods of their own, the redistributor's stores would be the largest. In times of scarcity, people would come to him, expecting to be fed; in return, he could call upon those who had special skills to make cloth, pots, canoes, or a fine house for his own use. Eventually, the redistributor no longer needed to work in the fields to gain and surpass big-man status. Management of the harvest surpluses, a portion of which continued to be given to him for use in communal feasts and other communal projects (such as trading expeditions and warfare), was sufficient to validate his status. And, increasingly, people viewed this status as an office, a sacred trust, passed on from one generation to the next according to the rules of hereditary succession. His dominion was no longer a small, autonomous village but a large political community. The big man had become a chief.

Returning to the South Pacific and the Trobriand Islands, one can catch a glimpse of how these pieces of encroaching stratification fell into place. The Trobrianders had hereditary chiefs who held sway over more than a dozen villages containing several thousand people. Only chiefs could wear certain shell ornaments as the insignia of high rank, and it was forbidden for commoners to stand or sit in a position that put a chief's head at a lower elevation. British anthropologist Bronislaw Malinowski tells of seeing all the people present in the village of Bwoytalu drop from their verandas "as if blown down by a hurricane" at the sound of a drawn-out cry warning that an important chief was approaching.

Yams were the Trobrianders' staff of life; the chiefs validated their status by storing and redistributing copious quantities of them acquired through donations from their brothers-in-law at harvest time. Similar "gifts" were received by husbands who were commoners, but chiefs were polygymous and, having as many as a dozen wives, received many more yams than anyone else. Chiefs placed their yam supply on display racks specifically built for this purpose next to their houses. Commoners did the same, but a chief's yam racks towered over all the others.

This same pattern recurs, with minor variations, on several continents. Striking parallels were seen, for example, twelve thousand miles away from the Trobrianders, among chiefdoms that flourished throughout the southeastern region of the United States—specifically among the Cherokee, former inhabitants of Tennessee, as described by the eighteenth-century naturalist William Bartram.

At the center of the principal Cherokee settlements stood a large circular house where a council of chiefs discussed issues involving their villages and where redistributive feasts were held. The council of chiefs had a paramount who was the principal figure in the Cherokee redistributive network. At the harvest time a large crib, identified as the "chief's granary," was erected in each field. "To this," explained Bartram, "each family carries and deposits a certain quantity according to his ability or inclination, or none at all if he so chooses." The chief's granaries functioned as a public treasury in case of crop failure, a source of food for strangers or travelers, and as military store. Although every citizen enjoyed free access to the store, commoners had to acknowledge that it really belonged to the supreme chief, who had "an exclusive right and ability . . . to distribute comfort and blessings to the necessitous."

Supported by voluntary donations, chiefs could now enjoy lifestyles that set them increasingly apart from their followers. They could build bigger and finer houses for themselves, eat and dress more sumptuously, and enjoy the sexual favors and personal services of several wives. Despite these harbingers, people in chiefdoms voluntarily invested unprecedented amounts of labor on behalf of communal projects. They dug moats, threw up defensive earthen embankments, and erected great log palisades around their villages. They heaped up small mountains of rubble and soil to form platforms and mounds on top of which they built temples and big houses for their chief. Working in teams and using nothing but levers and rollers, they moved rocks weighing fifty tons or more and set them in precise lines and perfect circles, forming sacred precincts for communal rituals marking the change of seasons.

If this seems remarkable, remember that donated labor created the megalithic alignments of Stonehenge and Carnac, put up the great statues on Easter Island, shaped the huge stone heads of the Olmec in Vera Cruz, dotted Polynesia with ritual precincts set on great stone platforms, and filled the Ohio, Tennessee, and Mississippi valleys with hundreds of large mounds. Not until it was too late did people realize that their beautiful chiefs were about to keep the meat and fat for themselves while giving nothing but bones and stale cakes to their followers.

IN THE END

As we know, chiefdoms would eventually evolve into states, states into empires. From peaceful origins, humans created and mounted a wild beast that ate continents. Now that beast has taken us to the brink of global annihilation.

Will nature's experiment with mind and culture end in nuclear war? No one knows the answer. But I believe it is essential that we understand our past before we can create the best possible future. Once we are clear about the roots of human nature, for example, we can refute, once and for all, the notion that it is a biological imperative for our kind to form hierarchical groups. An observer viewing human life shortly after cultural takeoff would easily have concluded that our species was destined to be irredeemably egalitarian except for distinctions of sex and age. That someday the world would be divided into aristocrats and commoners, masters and slaves, billionaires and homeless beggars would have seemed wholly contrary to human nature as evidenced in the affairs of every human society then on Earth.

Of course, we can no more reverse the course of thousands of years of cultural evolution than our egalitarian ancestors could have designed and built the space shuttle. Yet, in striving for the preservation of mind and culture on Earth, it is vital that we recognize the significance of cultural takeoff and the great difference between biological and cultural evolution. We must rid ourselves of the notion that we are an innately aggressive species for whom war is inevitable. We must reject as unscientific claims that there are superior and inferior races and that the hierarchical divisions within and between societies are the consequences of natural selection rather than of a long process of cultural evolution. We must struggle to gain control over cultural selection through objective studies of the human condition and the recurrent process of history. Not only a more just society, but our very survival as a species may depend on it.

From peaceful origins, humans created and mounted a wild beast that ate continents. Now that beast has taken us to the brink of global annihilation.

Symbolism of the Turban

Cultural Change in Rajasthan

Christi Ann Merrill

Christi Ann Merrill studied Indian history and culture at the University of Rajasthan.

This story is the final installment of a three-part series on cultural change in Rajasthan. Part one, "Puppetry in Jaipur," appeared in *World & I,* December 1990, and part two, "Revival in Hand-Block Printing," appeared in January 1991.

Pumpa Khan is a Rajasthani folk musician who has traveled all over the world. He recalls the beautiful streets of Paris and the friendly manner of people in Washington, D.C. Wherever he goes, be it Moscow, London, or Tokyo, he always wears his turban. "I started wearing one when I was ten or twelve, and I wear it everywhere," he says. Then a mischievous smile flickers beneath his bushy mustache as he adds, "Even in the airplane."

In the harsh desert region where Pumpa Khan grew up, wearing a turban is mandatory. The mass of twisted cotton serves as needed insulation from the glaring sun; the ends of the sheer fabric can be used to cover the face when dust storms tear across the dunes; and, during emergencies, the turban can be unwound and tied to a bucket to draw water from a well. A turban is, after all, simply ten meters of cloth wound round one's head. A man can use his turban as a pillow when he sleeps on the cool desert floor at night or to lash bundles onto his camel cart. Yet the turban is also a lingering symbol of the lore of spilled blood, a reminder of the bone-breaking, word-slashing culture that was old Rajasthan.

A SYMBOL OF STRENGTH

Historically, turbans were used to conceal knives and cushion blows, to stanch the blood of open wounds, and to bind opponents after a brawl. As long ago as 3,000 B.C., notes Ruth Edwards Kilgour in *A Pageant of Hats, Ancient and Modern,* "The warriors of India wore a tall, conical, black head-dress made by wrapping cloth around the head. . . . The holder not only for knives but for the dreaded *chakra,*" a metal disk sharpened 360 degrees to a deadly razor's edge.

"When danger threatened," Kilgour observes, "the wearer lifted the chakra from his turban, spun it on his forefinger, and hurled it at his enemy," severing a nose, splitting open a lip, or lopping off an ear. Thus, a man with a bare head was unprotected, vulnerable, and impotent.

Throughout the ages, a warrior's appearance did as much to enhance his reputation as did his prowess in battle. Whether it was the amount of gold a king wore around his neck or the color and shape of a foot soldier's turban, a man's attire proclaimed the breadth of his powers. A great deal of attention was bestowed on appearance, as is evident in the following description of a chieftain's army on its way to battle, written during the Grupta period (A.D. 320–470) and cited in Chandra:

Their shanks were covered with delicately tinted cloth. Their copper-coloured legs were chequered with mud-stained wraps and a heightened white was produced by trousers soft and dark as bees. They wore tunics of dark blue lapis-lazuli shade. Chinese cuirasses were thrown over them. They also wore coats and doublets and other bodices speckled with the mixture of various colours and shawls of the shade of a parrot's tail. They wore turbans to

which were stuck the stalks of ear-lotuses and their heads were often wrapped in shawls [of] soft saffron hue.

Legends of great warriors often mention such details of adornment and dress. A man's costume symbolized his standing in the social hierarchy; the turban, in particular, was a worthy stead for the warrior himself. It also became an integral part of ritual language.

Oaths were sworn on turbans and feuds were kindled or alliances struck, depending upon the way a man honored another's crown. In the days when women committed *sati* (self-immolation), stories were told of wives going to their doom with their dead husbands' turbans still intact in their burning laps. Even today a man will indicate his submission to another by placing his turban at the other's feet.

With the arrival of the Mogul conquerors in the eleventh century, the battles intensified and the styles of dress and life became increasingly decadent. The Persian warriors came with their own traditions of turbans, as elegant and meaningful as the Indian custom. Sir Thomas Roe, an emissary of the British East India Company, seems awed by the countenance of the Mogul Emperor Jahangir (1605–1626), in the following account:

The King descended the stayres with such an acclamation of "health to the king" as would have out cryed cannons . . . his sword and buckler, sett all over with great diamonds and rubyes, the belts of gould suteable . . . On his head he wore a rich turbant with a plume of herne tops, not many but long; on one syde hung a ruby ensett, as bigg as a walnut; on the other syde a diamond as great; in the middle an emeralld like a hart, much bigger.

This article appeared in *The World & I,* February 1991, pp. 672-683 and is reprinted by permission. *The World & I,* a publication of The Washington Times Corporation. Copyright © 1991.

1.

2.

3.

TYING A TURBAN

Pumpa Khan is a performer, whether he is onstage in Paris playing the jew's harp, or joking with friends as they sit in the shade of a tree. "Time me," he challenges anyone who will pay attention and proceeds to uncoil his turban. With the eight meters of purple fabric lying on the ground, he shakes and twists the cloth; then come coils and turns, until thirty seconds later—magically it seems—a pert turban once more crowns his head. He twists the ends of his mustache between his thumb and forefinger as a flourish.

Most men cannot remember the first time they wore a turban—there is no special rite of passage as such—but talk of a brother or uncle giving them offhand suggestions as they struggled in front of a mirror to tie it as they had seen others do. Their efforts may appear self-conscious and affected at first, but soon they become as instinctive as washing one's hands or blowing out a candle.

"When you start tying turbans, they come out funny," recalls Multan Khan with an amused expression. "It takes time, but you can learn only by doing." It takes two minutes to learn the rudiments, and a lifetime, or at least a good part of one's childhood, to learn to tie a turban consistently.

Although there are some individual differences in how a turban is tied, a man generally begins by shaking out the length of cloth to make it easier to manipulate. He then gathers up the edge of cloth that will be wound first, closest to his head. Next he starts to wind the cloth clockwise around his head, tucking the end under the first loop.

As he winds, he shakes and gathers the cloth, so that there will be no bulges or crinkles. It is important that he make the round tight enough that the cloth will hold but not so tight that it will constrict.

After the first few rounds come the twists and signatures that mark a man's background and individuality. Some men will tie the *gol* (round) style, common among peasants, which is achieved by winding the cloth from low to high, high to low around the circumference, making a neat round turban. Rajputs generally wear the *Jodhpuri safa*, which is tied by twisting the cloth at one's left ear to create a wavelike shape, leaving the end of the cloth to dangle down the back like a tail. Musicians from western Rajasthani villages usually wear a style that is characterized by a split down the crown, which is made by bringing the length of cloth alternately around the ear and then over the top. The *Rebari* turban is made by piling the coiled red fabric loosely on top in large, free rounds.

—C.A.M.

Steps in tying a turban: (1) The cloth, having been shaken, is gathered up by one end. (2) The end is tucked underneath as the fabric is wound clockwise around the head. (3) After several rounds, the end is pulled taut to make the turban tight below the ears. (4) The cloth is then wrapped around the head according to the style of the turban. (5) The other end of the cloth is tucked inside the top and the completed turban is adjusted for comfort and appearance.

4.

5.

Such pageantry stirred up trepidation in potential enemies, envy in lateral allies, and reverence in loyal subjects. For a ruler at any level, shameless opulence became a crucial tactical maneuver.

UNRAVELING THE TURBAN

These political strategies were made superfluous when Mogul strength waned and the East India Company assumed the stature of a colonial power. The displays of might and wealth that had been so impressive when the Muslims and Hindus were vying for dominance began to look exotic and even excessive in the more restrained courts of the British Raj. In his book on Indian royalty, *A Second Paradise: Indian Courtly Life 1590–1947,* Naveen Patnaik notes that the decadent dress of Indian rulers made them feel peripheral to the British: "Attending the viceregal durbars as virtual vassals, the Indian ruler, garbed in magnificent robes and jewels, circulated under huge chandeliers and oil paintings like brilliantly plumaged birds." With their symbols of power now regarded as decorative objects, the rulers found their weighty jeweled turbans increasingly top-heavy and awkward.

As Indian society approached the twentieth century, English notions of style became increasingly prevalent. "The wearing of turbans is somewhat declining," wrote A. Yusuf Ali in 1900, "with the advent of western tastes and fashions." Of course, the first to change were people of the higher castes, particularly Indians living in cities. In those days, when India was the crown jewel of the British Empire, the princes and kings of India enjoyed a privileged status in Europe. They flew to Cannes or the Alps and dashed from ball to party to coronation in the company of Europe's high society. They exuded an air of grace and mystery, especially when wearing their traditional—and very stately—attire. "When I was living in London, India was part of the Empire," remembers fashion force Diana Vreeland. "I used to pass Indians every night on the way to dinner. They looked so chic in their turbans and dinner jackets. And the

women were knockdown beautiful." Yet pictures of the time seem to indicate that Indians were more comfortable with European clothing in general and donned their traditional costumes only on certain occasions.

In the twentieth century, Indian culture seemed to assume a dual personality: one side was English, worldly, and modern, and the other was strictly Indian, traditional as could be. One personification of this dual nature was Jai Singh, world-famous polo player, socialite, and maharaja of Jaipur. His third wife, the equally well-known Gayatri Devi, wrote in her memoirs of the feverish excitement when the maharaja's "beautiful polo ponies [arrived] with their grooms wearing flamboyant Rajput turbans," while he, on the other hand, drove up in his green Rolls Royce, impeccably dressed in a "casual, informal style." His outfit was one any gentleman polo player in the world would have felt comfortable wearing. Yet when attending a marriage, funeral, or important religious ceremony, the maharaja would assume a guise very much in keeping with the rich heritage of his clan.

Although Rajput leaders certainly had more opportunity to be affected by foreign cultures, the changes were felt in all levels of urban society. By the 1960s, well after India had achieved independence, turbans were seen in the cities of Rajasthan only in very specific contexts. College campuses and office buildings maintained their aura of English culture and thus discouraged people from wearing traditional dress. Consequently, the stereotypical Rajasthani male—a strong man with dark eyes and a long, dark mustache, wearing crisp white clothes and a large bright turban—usually was seen only at train stations and tea stalls in the bazaar, places in the city where villagers went. City dwellers usually wore turbans only at religious ceremonies, formal events, and family affairs, occasions when it was important to reaffirm cultural identity.

IDIOM OF THE LAND

Ironically, it was the influx of tourists that helped rekindle the flame of tradi-

tion: hotel servants, folk musicians, and local craftsmen were asked to wear their turbans to satisfy tourists' expectations. Some had grown up in villages where turbans were part of daily life; others saw wearing them as something they had to do to keep their jobs.

Gazi Khan is a good example of a man who sees wearing a turban only as part of the show he puts on. A 22-year-old folk musician, born into a family of Muslim musicians from the Jaisalmer district deep in the desert, he explains: "I only wear a turban when I perform. People expect me to wear one, to look Rajasthani. But I do not usually wear one.

"When I went to Paris alone to perform," he continues, "my uncle had to tie a turban for me before I left, one I could carry with me to wear as needed. I guarded that turban with my life! If it had come unraveled, then what would I have done? I could not walk onstage without one! But I have never learned to tie a turban because I don't usually wear one. I went to school. I am educated." Like many men his age, he equates turbans with ignorance, unworldliness.

Even if it is the vogue to dispense with them, turbans continue to speak a very complex and current language even today. Turbans remain an essential part of ritual garb: They are still exchanged to formalize matters in an engagement ceremony, and mourners go to funerals wearing their white, khaki, or brown turbans to express condolence. In spite of its decline, the turban is a natural part of the idiom of this land, and without it a very strange silence would reign.

In Rajasthan, being "bareheaded" is synonymous with insolence, and a "brother with whom I exchanged turbans" has sworn eternal fidelity. If a man says that he "threw dirt on my turban," he is alluding to a subtle and yet penetrating insult, while another may cry out dramatically, "I lay my turban at your feet," when he has surrendered himself body and soul. Although these phrases often are used figuratively, the phrases are also taken quite literally.

Multan Khan, a nephew of Pumpa,

Above: *A driver maneuvers his camel cart through the streets of Jaipur. When needed, he will use his turban to lash bundles onto the cart.* Below: *Women hold up freshly dyed turban cloth to dry.*

that, he relented. He forgave me and came to the wedding."

Such ritualized expression does not easily translate into spoken words, and examples of such delicate encounters are many. Multan's brother, Niyaz Khan, says a turban can be used by a musician to indicate displeasure with his patron. "The turban I wear actually belongs to my patron," he explains. "Everything that I use is owned by him. He formally adopts us as his musicians by giving us turbans, and if we are upset with our treatment we can threaten to give them back. If we are enraged, we may even threaten to burn his turbans in front of him," Niyaz pauses and the other musicians seated beside him nod in agreement.

"Actually," he adds, "I have never heard of that happening. A few people have gone so far as to threaten, but no one has ever burned the turban. That is the gravest insult, and we all know that

tells this story: "My cousin and I were so angry with each other we were not even speaking. Our families lived side by side in the village and would not talk. But when it was time for my brother's marriage, I thought they would help with the arrangements, greeting guests. They were family, and usually forget their quarrels when an important occasion arrives. But still he refused to forget the matter, would not even talk to me. I went before him many times, begging and pleading. Then at last, I took off my turban and went to lay it at his feet. When he saw

for a musician to go to such lengths, the patron's clan must be a cursed one. No musician would ever set foot in that house again." Without a turban to burn, how would a musician be able to communicate his rage?

REKINDLING RESPECT

Like many Rajasthani villagers, the older members of this group of musicians have grown up in a context where turbans were a natural part of daily life. It is this easy familiarity that people like Gaj Singh, maharaja of the

former Jodhpur state (royal titles were officially revoked in 1971), hope to promote. He has been instrumental in establishing a collection of turbans at the Mehrangarh Museum in the fort in Jodhpur (a collection that has toured the world) and has organized workshops and seminars on the art of turban tying. There are thousands of styles, many of which are becoming lost as new generations fail to learn to tie them properly. It is not uncommon, for example, for a bridegroom to go to a wedding without a turban because he does not know how to tie one. Twenty years ago, people say, that would have been unheard of.

Mahendar Singh of Nagar, the project manager of the Mehrangarh Museum Trust and an undisputed expert on turbans, told a colorful story about the maharaja of Jodhpur, which illustrates the inherently haphazard nature of cultural preservation. Among the museum's collection there is a cotton *khirkiya pag* (an elaborate style of turban worn by royalty), a brocade and pearl turban worn by Rajputs 250 years ago, and a bow-shaped *Mathuria Brahmin* turban, once worn by the priestly caste. There is also a less ornate but still flamboyant red turban that belonged to a *Rebari* (shepherd); Mahendar Singh explained that the red turban had been tied by a boy from a nearby village. The maharaja, having toured the museum and photographed the collection, was impressed by the boy's unique manner of tying his turban. He gave a photograph of the turban to Mahendar Singh and told him to find the boy so they could hire him to teach others to tie turbans. Mahendar Singh felt at a loss but was lucky enough to bump into the boy that night at the hospital; the young villager had gone to the city to visit an ailing aunt. Now the boy works regularly for the trust.

The maharaja himself first wore a turban when he was four years old. He sat on the ceremonial ground at the palace twelve days after his father's death so noblemen could tie the white turban that signified the transfer of the throne. Then he was sent off to be educated in England.

"When His Highness returned from England after college," Mahendar Singh recalls, "crowds were gathered at the station to see him come in. He stepped off the train wearing full Rajasthani dress, turban and all. Of course, no one expected it; he had lived in England for all those years. They thought he would wear a suit and cap. Seeing him dressed like that, in the clothes of our people, everyone was pleased and very proud." Even today, the maharaja insists on wearing a turban for his engagements in the villages.

Mahendar Singh explains: "We drive along until we are two or three kilometers outside of a village. Then we stop the car while His Highness puts on his turban."

"I keep it in my suitcase when I travel," says the maharaja. "The round turbans are perfect for that. They are better than a hat," he claims.

While the maharaja hopes that more and more young men will follow his example, perhaps it is Mahendar Singh who best represents the contradictions facing the new generation. "Six years ago the rajmata [queen mother] of Jodhpur came to the fort," begins Mahendar Singh, "and when I came to bow before her she asked me 'Where is your turban?' 'I don't have one,' I answered. 'And you knew I was coming?' she asked. I mumbled an affirmative and felt very embarrassed. 'See me at the palace tomorrow,' she ordered and went on her way."

Mahendar Singh smiles as he remembers the event and continues with his story: "The next day, when I went to the palace, I was very nervous. I was trembling. 'Here,' she said, and presented me with a beautiful *mul-mul* (gauzy muslin) turban, a yellow tie-dyed pattern with red dots. 'You are the expert on turbans, and you do not even wear one yourself. Take this turban, learn how to tie it, and come back wearing it in three days.' The turban she gave me was so beautiful, I was obliged to learn to tie it myself. I went back to her a week later and said,

THE CASTE SYSTEM IN PRESENT-DAY RAJASTHAN

At tea stalls and bus stations in the city, villagers still wear the distinctive head gear that denotes particular regions or castes: *Rebari* (shepherds) with their vivid red, loosely tied *pagari; Bishnois* (a Hindu sect of pacifists, usually agriculturalists) turbaned only in white; *Gawariya* (nomadic tradesmen), who wind thirty feet of cotton in to a bulky *safa* into which they tuck the combs, mirrors, and novelty items they sell wherever they wander; and *Rajputs* (royalty), who wear the solid saffron or five-colored striped safa with the proud tail down the back.

Although the caste system no longer officially exists, individuals continue to classify themselves and others according to those age-old categories. When two strangers meet, they immediately survey each other for hints of caste: how the other person is dressed, how he talks, his general mien. Once they settle into a friendly banter one may ask the other his last name—the more subtle way to detect caste—or he may demand quite bluntly to which caste the man belongs. Seldom do people seem offended or even surprised by such questions.

The classifications of caste prescribe an individual's social niche: with whom he socializes, whom he marries, what he does for work, and where he lives. From birth to death, his life follows a well-traveled path, a prospect many find invitingly secure. Of course, such a system also fosters its own brand of nepotism. Mahatma Gandhi was among the more outspoken leaders critical of such institutional discrimination.

Ironically enough, the farmers and herdsmen and other groups who benefit little from a hierarchical structure are the ones who seem the most reluctant to change.

Perhaps the most arresting prospect is separating the turban from the caste system. Although he has been a great supporter of the headdress, Maharaja Gaj Singh of Jodhpur is uncomfortable with the turban as a cultural symbol because of its unpleasant associations with a very hierarchical, feudal society. To combat the association of turban with caste, he generally wears a round turban, whose lack of the significant tail denotes a lower status. Even so, because the traditions surrounding turban wear and the caste system are so deeply ingrained, it is very difficult to have one without the other.

—C.A.M.

'Look at this. I tied it myself.' And since that time I have worn a turban to every wedding, every function. Now my nephews and other young boys are coming to me to learn how it is done. I feel quite proud."

ADDITIONAL READING

A. Yusuf Ali, *A Monograph on Silk Fabrics*, Northwest Provinces and Oudh Government Press, Allahabad, 1900.

Meer Hassan Ali, *Observations on the Mussulmauns of India*, Oxford University Press, Oxford, 1917.

Moti Chandra, *Costumes, Textiles, Cosmetics and Coiffure in Ancient and Medieval India*, Oriental Publishers, Delhi, 1973.

Gayatri Devi, *A Princess Remembers*, J. B. Lippincott Co., Philadelphia and New York, 1976.

Ruth Edwards Kilgour, *A Pageant of Hats, Ancient and Modern*, Robert McBride Co., New York, 1958.

Naveen Patnaik, *A Second Paradise: Indian Courtly Life 1590–1947*, Doubleday, New York, 1985.

Diana Vreeland and Gael Love, "Naveen Patnaik," *Interview* magazine, January 1986, p. 90.

Gauging the Winds of War

Anthropologists seek the roots of human conflict

Bruce Bower

In a 1971 Motown hit single, Edwin Starr posed the musical question, "War—what is it good for?" His gruff response: "Absolutely nothin'."

Despite the grimly predictable tragedies of armed conflict, almost all ancient and modern societies studied by anthropologists have engaged in at least periodic bouts of warfare. The ubiquity of organized fighting between human groups—currently brought home by the war in the Middle East—has fired up the scientific study of warfare over the last 30 years and has sparked some bruising academic skirmishes.

A handful of warfare researchers described their findings and theories at last November's meeting of the American Anthropological Association in New Orleans. These investigators do not praise fighting, but they assume that anything so common in human experience serves some purpose. They search for the "absolutely somethin' " that lights the fuse of violence in bands of foragers, tribes of hunter-gatherers, rudimentary political states and modern nations alike.

In the 1960s, as U.S. involvement in Vietnam deepened, anthropological theories of war's causes and consequences flourished, numbering at least 16 by 1973, observes Keith F. Otterbein of the State University of New York at Buffalo. However, he says, only about half of those theories still receive strong scientific support, and no persuasive new theories have emerged.

Current notions about the roots of war stem mainly from studies of nonindustrial societies lacking centralized political power and extensive military organizations. In Otterbein's view, all of these theoretical approaches focus on three themes:

• "ultimate" causes of war that influence the goals people fight for, such as competition within a society for scarce resources or mates, and intense divisions between groups of related men.

• "proximate" causes of war, such as a society's military preparedness and the goals of its leaders, often centering on the desire for land, natural resources or control of trade routes.

• consequences of war that influence further conflict, including population decline, improved access to resources, and increased prestige and power accorded to victorious warriors.

Although some anthropologists and sociobiologists contend that a genetic tendency toward physical violence greases the human war machine, theories of innate aggression attract few advocates today, Otterbein maintains. Nevertheless, disputes over the alleged biological roots of combat continue to erupt, ignited in many cases by the work of Napoleon A. Chagnon of the University of California, Santa Barbara, whose studies of warfare have become the most widely publicized research in this field.

Since 1964, Chagnon has conducted fieldwork among the 15,000 Yanomamo Indians who inhabit some 200 villages in the Amazonian jungle of Brazil and Venezuela. He has long stressed the ferocity and frequency of combat between Yanomamo villages. Some other anthropologists who have studied the jungle tribe argue that Chagnon emphasizes a misleading slice of Yano-mamo life.

Chagnon's latest report, in the Feb. 26, 1988 SCIENCE, concludes that revenge fuels protracted, bloody battles between groups of men from different Yanomamo villages. Competition for food, water, territory or women creates the initial friction, he says. Minor bow-and-arrow confrontations ensue, escalating rapidly when a death results and the victim's male relatives exact revenge through raids on the offending village.

Blood vengeance apparently raises the social status and reproductive success of Yanomamo warriors, who represent nearly half of the men in the tribe, Chagnon maintains. On average, killers have more than twice as many wives and three times as many children as their peaceable counterparts.

Chagnon refrains from arguing that warfare generally proves biologically advantageous among the Yanomamo or in any other culture. He does contend, however, that reproductive success and fighting prowess probably go hand-in-hand in many human groups, and that this may help explain the great prestige attached to military conquest in both modern and ancient states.

Even if Chagnon's Yanomamo data hold up, responds anthropologist John H. Moore, successful warriors in similar tribal societies sometimes contribute few genes to subsequent generations. Moore, of the University of Oklahoma in Norman, cites the 19th-century Cheyenne Indians of the North American plains as a case in point. The Cheyenne, with a population of about 3,000 divided into bands of 150 to 400 individuals, engaged in fierce warfare with other Indian tribes as well as with U.S. military forces, achieving historical notoriety with their defeat of Custer at the battle of Little Big Horn. In addition to seven warrior bands led by numerous war chiefs, Cheyenne society included 44 peace chiefs, sometimes more than one to a band, who led polygynous extended families.

U.S. Census data collected in 1880 and 1892 reveal that men in the Cheyenne peace bands had a striking reproductive advantage over warriors, reports

Moore in the June 1990 CURRENT ANTHROPOLGY. The war chiefs stressed celibacy and ritual suicide, while the peace chiefs had numerous wives and children, he notes.

Moore asserts that many societies without centralized political systems, including the Cheyenne, undergo periodic cultural reorganizations, and he says researchers have no evidence suggesting that recent Yanomamo behavior reflects all or most of human prehistory, or even the Yanomamo of several generations ago.

Another critic of Chagnon's research, Marvin Harris of the University of Florida in Gainesville, theorizes that war occurs among hunter-gatherers and other "band-and-village" peoples when population growth creates increasingly intense competition for food, especially protein-rich game. He maintains that warfare, for all its brutality, effectively prunes these populations, preventing malnutrition and hunger among survivors—whether the combatants hail from Yanomamo villages or from horticultural groups in Papua New Guinea.

"Bank-and-village societies must pay a heavy price for keeping population and food supply in balance, and warfare is part of that price," Harris writes in *Our Kind* (1989, Harper & Row, New York). Conflicts sometimes veer out of control, wiping out more lives than malnutrition would have claimed, but "no system is fail-safe," he notes.

Harris' theory may help explain widespread fighting among North America's Anasazi Indians around 700 years ago, says Jonathan Haas of the Field Museum of Natural History in Chicago. Although Anasazi culture extended back at least to 500 A.D., Haas points out that burnt houses, decapitated skeletons and other archaeological evidence of warfare date only to the second half of the 13th century A.D. At that time, the ingredients for war coalesced, he says: A burgeoning population fostered the emergence of distinct cultural groups with an "us versus them" mentality, and periodic droughts reduced crop yields and drained food reserves.

When the Anasazi abandoned their population centers at the end of the 13th century and the droughts also eased, warfare again diminished, Haas observes.

"Tribal peoples cycle in and out of warfare because of environmental stress," he says. "Warfare has increased with the evolution of states because environmental stresses are more unrelenting now."

The nearly unrelenting warfare of most early states, which spread throughout the world from 3200 B.C. until around 1800 A.D., often reflects the "predatory accumulation" practiced by rulers sitting atop centralized political hierarchies, asserts Stephen P. Reyna of the University of New Hampshire in Durham. However, early or "archaic" states possessed nowhere near the political complexity or destructive means of modern "nation-states," he notes.

A violent conflict in the Chad Basin of north central Africa around 200 years ago illustrates the dynamics of warfare between archaic states, Reyna says. A leader of one state accused a neighboring leader of a crime against Islam—incest with his daughter—and the charge sparked a war. But the real problem stemmed from the rapid growth of both states due to a brutal type of arms race, Reyna holds. These leaders had engaged in constant warfare with weaker neighbors to accumulate wealth and larger armies. In a vicious cycle, each victory enabled them to accumulate even more means of destruction to wage more successful wars, he says. Eventually their "fields of empire" overlapped, and war between the two soon followed.

Reyna notes that the incest charge, though probably unfounded, served a strategic purpose: It led to the defection of several generals aligned with the accused ruler, undermining his army and helping to seal his eventual defeat.

Such hostilities grew out of a long history of warfare among human groups, says Robert L. Carneiro of the American Museum of Natural History in New York City. In his view, war played a critical role in the evolution of large political and social systems.

The origins of war probably stretch back through a couple of million years to Stone Age times, Carneiro contends. Stone Age battles—fought to avenge murders, wife-stealing or other trespasses often observed among modern hunter-gatherers—served to push small bands of humans apart and keep them separate.

But around 10,000 years ago, the nature of warfare changed, he maintains. The spread of agriculture increased permanent settlements and human populations. Adjacent villages then began to fight over access to farmland. Instead of pushing the communities apart in traditional Stone Age fashion, these wars forged the emergence of the chiefdom, a forced coalition of several formerly independent villages under the control of a paramount chief. With chiefdoms came district chiefs, village chiefs, advisers and other early representatives of social and political complexity.

Archaeological signs of war, such as the number of weapons found in graves and heavily fortified occupation sites, increase with the growth of the chiefdoms, Carneiro observes. The push from chiefdoms to even larger state-societies did not occur swiftly or irreversibly throughout the world, he says, but early hotbeds of state growth appeared where limited areas of prime farmland prevented vanquished villagers from fleeing to greener pastures. Prime examples include Mesopotamia, the Nile valley and the Peruvian coast.

"War was the one instrument capable of surmounting autonomous villages and deserves careful study as a cause of social evolution," Carneiro says.

Perhaps the most wide-ranging warfare study to date was conducted during the 1980s by Carol R. Ember and Melvin Ember of Human Relations Area Files, a privately funded research organization in New Haven, Conn. The team analyzed anthropological descriptions of 186 nonindustrial societies, virtually all of which operated on a much smaller scale than modern nation-states. Descriptions ranged from 18th-century writings on Native American tribes to recent accounts of African hunter-gatherers.

Two independent coders read the voluminous literature and rated the presence and frequency of warfare, aggressive acts, natural disasters and other social and psychological factors, focusing on a 25-year period in each society.

The Embers say their unpublished findings offer a tentative theory of war, at least among "simple" societies: The societies that engage in the most warfare express considerably more fear of food shortages caused by expected but unpredictable natural disasters, such as drought, flood or infestation. The fear of others—indicated by child-rearing practices stressing mistrust of neighbors—further fuels the tendency to fight, the researchers say.

Their data provide no backing for other explanations of warfare. For example, the Embers found that societies already experiencing chronic food and protein shortages did not engage in excessive fighting. The study also failed to support the idea that a shortage of women stimulates warfare and regulates population.

Some researchers have suggested a penchant for warfare among sexually restrictive societies and among societies with high levels of interpersonal aggression, as reflected in elevated rates of murder and theft. The Embers' study showed no such links.

Parents in warlike societies do tend to encourage toughness and aggression among boys, but warfare apparently *causes* this practice rather than vice versa, the Embers argue. When these societies lose wars and come under the control of outside forces, harsh child-rearing methods diminished sharply, they found.

Three-quarters of the sample's "simple" societies fought wars every two years, Carol Ember notes, although "this doesn't mean war is inevitable."

The Embers hope to expand their analyses to modern nation-states. In the meantime, they suspect that the link between the risk of war and the fear of unpredictable disasters extends to a wide variety of situations.

Several researchers say contact with Westerners has whipped up local conflicts in Africa and elsewhere since the early days of European colonialism.

More than a century ago, for example, Tuareg tribes of northern Africa limited their attacks to small-scale raids on caravans passing through their territory, say Candelario Saenz of the State University of New York at Purchase. The Tuareg extorted camels and other goods from the caravans to support their pastoral way of life, Saenz says. But when France took control of Algeria in the late 1800s, it imposed numerous restrictions on trade in the region. Tuareg groups soon entered into a period of nearly constant warfare among themselves as they competed for the rapidly decreasing supply of goods passing along traditional trade routes, Saenz says.

Another instance of Western contact helping to foment violence occurred more recently in the ethnically mixed African nation of Mauritania, say Michael M. Horowitz of the State University of New York at Binghamton, who has conducted fieldwork there for the past four years.

The completion of a large dam on the Senegal River several years ago expanded farmable floodplains and drew the promise of considerable outside investment by Western agricultural companies, Horowitz says. But the local population, long dependent on farming this fertile river valley, already occupied much of the area.

"The Mauritanian government is now killing and torturing these people to get the land," Horowitz says. "In the process, they've created 100,000 refugees and intensified violence between ethnic groups."

Whether stimulated by Western contact or not, most of the 120 wars documented since the end of World War II similarly pit large states against smaller nations or ethnic groups the states claim to represent, says Jason Clay of Cultural Survival, a public-interest organization in Cambridge, Mass.

In the aftermath of the international conflict sparked by the aggressions of the Axis powers, he notes, dictatorships and one-party states ironically solidified their power in many parts of the world, including Africa, the Soviet Union and Eastern Europe. Diverse nations and groups of people with separate languages and cultural histories were yoked to the goals of unresponsive, unelected leaders of both the political right and left, Clay says.

Moreover, those leaders socked away whatever taxes, internal resources, foreign aid and international loans they could extract for themselves, leaving the rest of the populace destitute, he maintains.

"The destruction of social and political life at the local level and the stripping away of resources by modern one-party states has led to longer, more widespread wars," Clay argues. "We'll have more violence at the regional level and the settling of old scores as states fall apart in the post–Cold War world."

Although Clay's dire prediction gathers support from the bloody Soviet crackdown on Lithuania's independence movement and the increasing tensions in other Soviet republics, anthropological research provides room for optimism, say R. Brian Ferguson of Rutgers University in Newark, N.J.

"War is not the natural human condition," Ferguson says. "Research shows that war varies over time due to factors such as trade, population growth and outside contacts."

Often, leaders must paint the enemy as inhuman in order to motivate people to kill, he says—and even then, many soldiers come out of combat with severe psychological aftereffects.

"We need to dispense with the idea that people love violence and are doomed to fight," Ferguson concludes.

Other Families, Other Ways

Since most people in small-scale societies of the past spent their whole lives within a local area, it is understandable that their primary interactions—economic, religious, and otherwise—were with their relatives. As shown in "Memories of a !Kung Girlhood," every age group, from children to the very old, played an active and indispensable role in the survival of the collective unit. It also makes sense that, through marriage customs, they strengthened those kinship relationships that clearly defined their mutual rights and obligations. Indeed, the resulting family structure may be surprisingly flexible and adaptive, as witnessed in "When Brothers Share a Wife," by Melvyn C. Goldstein. It is for these reasons that anthropologists have looked upon family and kinship as the key mechanisms through which culture is transmitted from one generation to the next. Since social changes would have been slow to take place throughout the world, and as social horizons have widened accordingly, family relationships and community alliances are increasingly based upon new sets of principles. There is no question that kinship networks have diminished in size and strength as we have increasingly become involved with others as co-workers in a market economy. Our associations depend more and more upon factors such as personal aptitudes, educational backgrounds, and job opportunities. Yet, the family is still there. It is smaller, but it still functions in its age-old nurturing and protective role. Beyond the immediate family, the situation is still in a state of flux. Certain ethnic groups, especially those living in poverty, still have a need for a broader network, and in some ways seem to be reformulating those ties.

Where the changes described in this section will lead us, and which ones will ultimately prevail, we do not know. One thing is certain: anthropologists will be there to document the trends, for the discipline of anthropology has had to change as well. One important feature of the essays in this section is that they are all representative of the growing interest of anthropologists in the study of complex societies—especially American society, where old theoretical perspectives are increasingly inadequate.

Current trends do not necessarily mean the eclipse of the kinship unit, however, as "Young Traders of Northern Nigeria" illustrates. The message is that the large family network is still the best guarantee of individual survival and well-being in an urban setting. According to the Bruce Dollar article, even in China, where a mere 45 years ago women's feet were bound, jobs for women and day care for children have made home life easier and have actually strengthened the family.

Looking Ahead: Challenge Questions

In what ways is the !Kung childhood similar to childhood in American culture?

What can contemporary hunter-collector societies tell us about the quality of life in the prehistoric past?

Why is "fraternal polyandry" socially acceptable in Tibet, but not in our society?

What are the implications of Western education for the ability of Hausa women to earn an income?

How are attitudes of cooperation, sharing, and altruism instilled in individuals in an industrial society?

How do differences in child care relate to economic circumstances?

Unit 4

Memories of a !Kung Girlhood

***A woman of the hunter-gatherers recalls her childhood;
the differences in her way of life
fade in the face of basic human similarities.***

Marjorie Shostak

Marjorie Shostak is a writer and photographer who first became interested in the !Kung while working with her husband, an anthropologist. For two years, from 1969 to 1971, she lived and worked among the !Kung San of Botswana as a research assistant to Irven DeVore, an anthropologist at Harvard University. After developing fluency in the !Kung language, Shostak began to tape interviews with !Kung women. In 1975 she returned to Botswana for six months to complete the life histories of several women and to correct ambiguous translations. At the same time she collaborated with four other researchers in a study of hormone level and mood fluctuations in relation to menstrual cycles.

I remember when my mother was pregnant with Kumsa. I was still small (about four years old) and I asked, "Mommy, that baby inside you . . . when that baby is born, will it come out from your bellybutton?" She said, "No, it won't come out from there. When you give birth, a baby comes from here." And she pointed to her genitals.

When she gave birth to Kumsa, I wanted the milk she had in her breasts, and when she nursed him, my eyes watched as the milk spilled out. I cried all night . . . cried and cried.

Once when my mother was with him and they were lying down asleep, I took him away from her and put him down on the other side of the hut. Then I lay down beside her. While she slept I squeezed some milk and started to nurse, and nursed and nursed and nursed. Maybe she thought it was him. When she woke and saw me she cried, "Where . . . tell me . . . what did you do with Kumsa? Where is he?"

I told her he was lying down inside the hut. She grabbed me and pushed me hard away from her. I lay there and cried. She took Kumsa, put him down beside her, and insulted me by cursing my genitals.

"Are you crazy? Nisa-Big Genitals, what's the matter with you? What craziness grabbed you that you took a baby, dropped him somewhere else, and then lay down beside me and nursed? I thought it was Kumsa."

When my father came home, she told him, "Do you see what kind of mind your daughter has? Hit her! She almost killed Kumsa. This little baby, this little thing here, she took from my side and dropped him somewhere else.

I was lying here holding him and fell asleep. She came and took him away, left him by himself, then lay down where he had been and nursed. Now, hit her!"

I said, "You're lying! Me . . . daddy, I didn't nurse. Really I didn't. I don't even want her milk anymore."

He said, "If I ever hear of this again, I'll hit you. Now, don't ever do that again!"

I said, "Yes, he's my little brother, isn't he? My little baby brother and I *love* him. I won't do that again. He can nurse all by himself. Daddy, even if you're not here, I won't try to steal Mommy's breasts. They belong to my brother."

We lived and lived, and as I kept growing, I started to carry Kumsa around on my shoulders. My heart was happy and I started to love him. I carried him everywhere. I would play with him for a while, and whenever he started to cry, I'd take him over to mother to nurse. Then I'd take him back with me and we'd play together again.

That was when Kumsa was still little. But once he was older and started to talk and then to run around, that's when we were mean to each other all the time. Sometimes we hit each other. Other times I grabbed him and bit him and said, "Ooooh . . . what is this thing that has such a horrible face and no brains and is so mean? Why is it so mean to me when I'm not doing anything to it?" Then he said, "I'm going to *hit* you!" And I said, "You're just a *baby!* I, *I* am the one who's going to hit *you.* Why are you so miserable to me?" I insulted him and he insulted me and then I insulted him back. We just stayed together and played like that.

Once, when our father came back carrying meat, we both called out, "Ho, ho, Daddy! Ho, ho, Daddy!" But when I heard him say, "Daddy, Daddy," I yelled, "Why are you greeting my father? He's *my* father, isn't he? You can only say, 'Oh, hello Father.'" But he called out, "Ho, ho . . . Daddy!" I said, "Be quiet! Only *I* will greet him. Is he your father? I'm going to hit you!"

We fought and argued until Mother finally stopped us. Then we just sat around while she cooked the meat.

This was also when I used to take food. It happened over all kinds of food—sweet *nin* berries or *klaru* bulbs . . . other times it was mongongo nuts. Sometimes before my mother left to go gathering, she'd leave food inside a leather pouch and hang it high on one of the branches inside the hut.

But as soon as she was gone, I'd take some of whatever food was left in the bag. If it was *klaru,* I'd find the biggest bulbs and take them. I'd hang the bag back on the branch and go sit somewhere to eat them.

One time I sat down in the shade of a tree while my parents gathered food nearby. As soon as they had moved away from me, I climbed the tree where they had left a pouch hanging, full of *klaru,* and took the bulbs.

I had my own little pouch, the one my father had made me, and I took the bulbs and put them in the pouch. Then I climbed down and sat waiting for my parents to return.

They came back. "Nisa, you ate the *klaru!*" What do you have to say for yourself?" I said, "Uhn uh, I didn't eat them."

I started to cry. Mother hit me and yelled, "Don't take things. You can't seem to understand! I tell you but you

don't listen. Don't your ears hear when I talk to you?"

I said, "Uhn uh. Mommy's been making me feel bad for too long now. She keeps saying I steal things and hits me so that my skin hurts. I'm going to stay with Grandma!"

But when I went to my grandmother, she said, "No, I can't take care of you now. If I try you will be hungry. I am old and just go gathering one day at a time. In the morning I just rest. We

would sit together and hunger would kill you. Now go back and sit beside your mother and father."

I said, "No, Daddy will hit me. Mommy will hit me. I want to stay with you."

So I stayed with her. Then one day she said, "I'm going to bring you back to your mother and father." She took me to them, saying, "Today I'm giving Nisa back to you. But isn't there someone here who will take good care of

---

About the !Kung

Nisa is a 50-year-old !Kung woman, one of an estimated 13,000 !Kung San living on the northern fringe of the Kalahari Desert in southern Africa. Much of her life—as daughter, sister, wife, mother, and lover—has been spent in the semi-nomadic pursuit of food and water in the arid savanna.

Like many !Kung, Nisa is a practiced storyteller. The !Kung have no written language with which to record their experiences, and people sit around their fires for hours recounting recent events and those long past. Voices rise and fall, hands move in dramatic gestures, and bird and animal sounds are imitated as stories are told and retold, usually with much exaggeration.

I collected stories of Nisa's life as part of my anthropological effort to record the lives of !Kung women in their own words. Nisa enjoyed working with the machine that "grabs your voice" and the interviews with her produced 25 hours of tape and 425 pages of transcription. The excerpts included here are faithful to her narrative except where awkward or discontinuous passages have been modified or deleted, and where long passages have been shortened.

Although most of Nisa's memories are typical of !Kung life, her early memories, like those of most people, are probably idiosyncratic mixtures of fact and fantasy. Her memories of being hit for taking food are probably not accurate. The !Kung tend to be lenient and indulgent with their children, and researchers have rarely observed any physical punishment or the withholding of food.

Strong feelings of sibling rivalry, like those that Nisa describes, are common. !Kung women wean their children as soon as they find they are pregnant again because they believe the milk belongs to the fetus. Children are not usually weaned until they are three or four years old, which tends to make them resent their younger siblings. Nisa's complaints about being given too little food probably stem from her jealousy of her little brother.

Despite the lack of privacy, !Kung parents are generally discreet in their sexual activity. As children become aware of it, they engage each other in sexual play. Parents say they do not approve of this play but do little to stop it.

Many !Kung girls first marry in their early teens, but these relationships are not consummated until the girls begin menstruating around the age of 16. Early marriages are relatively unstable. Nisa was betrothed twice before marrying Tashay.

The exclamation point at the beginning of !Kung represents one of the many click sounds in the !Kung language. Clicks are made by the tongue breaking air pockets in different parts of the mouth; but the notation for clicks has been eliminated from the translation in all cases except for the name of the !Kung people. Nisa, for instance, should be written as N≠isa.

Marjorie Shostak

her? You don't just hit a child like this one. She likes food and likes to eat. All of you are lazy and you've just left her so she hasn't grown well. You've killed this child with hunger. Look at her now, how small she still is."

Oh, but my heart was happy! Grandmother was scolding Mother! I had so much happiness in my heart that I laughed and laughed. But then, when Grandmother went home and left me there, I cried and cried.

My father started to yell at me. He didn't hit me. His anger usually came out only from his mouth. "You're so senseless! Don't you realize that after you left, everything felt less important? We wanted you to be with us. Yes, even your mother wanted you and missed you. Today, everything will be all right when you stay with us. Your mother will take you where she goes; the two of you will do things together and go gathering together."

Then when my father dug *klaru* bulbs, I ate them, and when he dug *chon* bulbs, I ate them. I ate everything they gave me, and I wasn't yelled at any more.

Mother and I often went to the bush together. The two of us would walk until we arrived at a place where she collected food. She'd set me down in the shade of a tree and dig roots or gather nuts nearby.

Once I left the tree and went to play in the shade of another tree. I saw a tiny steenbok, one that had just been born, hidden in the grass and among the leaves. It was lying there, its little eye just looking out at me.

I thought, "What should I do?" I shouted, *"Mommy!"* I just stood there and it just lay there looking at me.

Suddenly I knew what to do—I ran at it, trying to grab it. But it jumped up and ran away and I started to chase it. It was running and I was running and it was crying as it ran. Finally, I got very close and put my foot in its way, and it fell down. I grabbed its legs and started to carry it back. It was crying, "Ehn . . . ehn . . . ehn. . . ."

Its mother had been close by and when she heard it call, she came running. As soon as I saw her, I started to run again. I wouldn't give it back to its mother!

I called out, "Mommy! Come! Help me with this steenbok! Mommy! The steenbok's mother is coming for me! Run! Come! Take this steenbok from me."

But soon the mother steenbok was no longer following, so I took the baby, held its feet together, and banged it hard against the sand until I killed it. It was no longer crying; it was dead. I felt wonderfully happy. My mother came running and I gave it to her to carry.

The two of us spent the rest of the day walking in the bush. While my mother was gathering, I sat in the shade of a tree, waiting and playing with the dead steenbok. I picked it up. I tried to make it sit up, to open its eyes. I looked at them. After mother had dug enough *sha* roots, we left and returned home.

My father had been out hunting that day and had shot a large steenbok with his arrows. He had skinned it and brought it back hanging on a branch.

"Ho, ho. Daddy killed a steenbok!" I said. "Mommy! Daddy! I'm not going to let anyone have any of *my* steenbok. Now *don't* give it to anyone else. After you cook it, just my little brother and I will eat it, just the two of us."

I remember another time when we were traveling from one place to another and the sun was burning. It was the hot, dry season and there was no water anywhere. The sun was burning! Kumsa had already been born and I was still small.

After we had been walking a long time, my older brother Dau spotted a beehive. We stopped while he and my father chopped open the tree. All of us helped take out the honey. I filled my own little container until it was completely full.

We stayed there, eating the honey, and I found myself getting very thirsty. Then we left and continued to walk, I carrying my honey and my digging stick. Soon the heat began killing us and we were all dying of thirst. I started to cry because I wanted water so badly.

After a while, we stopped and sat down in the shade of a baobab tree. There was still no water anywhere. We just sat in the shade like that.

Finally my father said, "Dau, the rest of the family will stay here under this baobab. But you, take the water

containers and get us some water. There's a well not too far away."

Dau collected the empty ostrich egg-shell containers and the large clay pot and left. I lay there, already dead from thirst and thought, "If I stay with Mommy and Daddy, I'll surely die of thirst. Why don't I follow my big brother and go drink water with him?"

With that I jumped up and ran after him, crying out, calling to him, following his tracks. But he didn't hear me. I kept running . . . crying and calling out.

Finally, he heard something and turned to see. There I was. "Oh, no!" he said. "Nisa's followed me. What can I do with her now that she's here?" He just stood there and waited for me to catch up. He picked me up and carried me high up on his shoulder, and along we went. He really liked me!

The two of us went on together. We walked and walked and walked and walked. Finally, we reached the well. I ran to the water and drank, and soon my heart was happy again. We filled the water containers, put them in a twine mesh sack, and my brother carried it on his back. Then he took me and put me on his shoulder again.

We walked the long way back until we arrived at the baobab where our parents were sitting. They drank the water. Then they said, "How well our children have done, bringing us this water!" We are alive once again!"

We just stayed in the shade of the baobab. Later we left and traveled to another water hole where we settled for a while. My heart was happy . . . eating honey and just living.

We lived there, and after some time passed, we saw the first rain clouds. One came near but just hung in the sky. More rain clouds came over and they too just stood there. Then the rain started to spill itself and it came pouring down.

The rainy season had finally come. The sun rose and set, and the rain spilled itself and fell and kept falling. It fell without ceasing. Soon the water pans were full. And my heart! My heart within me was happy and we lived and ate meat and mongongo nuts. There was more meat and it was all delicious.

And there were caterpillars to eat, those little things that crawl along going "mmm . . . mmmmm . . . mmmmm. . . ." People dug roots and collected nuts and berries and brought home more and more food. There was plenty to eat, and people kept bringing meat back on sticks and hanging it in the trees.

My heart was bursting. I ate lots of food and my tail was wagging, always wagging about like a little dog. I'd laugh with my little tail, laugh with a little donkey's laugh, a tiny thing that is. I'd throw my tail one way and the other, shouting, "Today I'm going to eat caterpillars . . . *cat-er-pillars!*" Some people gave me meat broth to drink, and others prepared the skins of caterpillars and roasted them for me to eat, and I ate and ate and ate. Then I went to sleep.

But that night, after everyone was dead asleep, I peed right in my sleeping place. In the morning, when everyone got up, I just lay there. The sun rose and had set itself high in the sky, and I was still lying there. I was afraid of people shaming me. Mother said, "Why is Nisa acting like this and refusing to leave her blankets when the sun is sitting up in the sky? Oh . . . she has probably wet herself!"

When I did get up, my heart felt miserable. I thought, "I've peed on myself and now everyone's going to laugh at me." I asked one of my friends, "How come, after I ate all those caterpillars, when I went to sleep I peed in my bed?" Then I thought, "Tonight, when this day is over, I'm going to lie down separate from the others. If I pee in my bed again, won't mother and father hit me?"

When a child sleeps beside her mother, in front, and her father sleeps behind and makes love to her mother, the child watches. Her parents don't fear her, a small child, because even if the child sees, even if she hears, she is unaware of what it is her parents are doing. She is still young and without sense. Perhaps this is the way the child learns. The child is still senseless, without intelligence, and just watches.

If the child is a little boy, when he plays with other children, he plays sex with them and teaches it to himself, just like a baby rooster teaches itself. The little girls also learn it by themselves.

Little boys are the first ones to know its sweetness. Yes, a young girl, while she is still a child, her thoughts don't know it. A boy has a penis, and maybe, while he is still inside his mother's belly, he already knows about sex.

When you are a child you play at nothing things. You build little huts and play. Then you come back to the village and continue to play. If people bother you, you get up and play somewhere else.

Once we left a pool of rain water where we had been playing and went to the little huts we had made. We stayed there and played at being hunters. We went out tracking animals, and when we saw one, we struck it with our make-believe arrows. We took some leaves and hung them over a stick and pretended it was meat. Then we carried it back to our village. When we got back, we stayed there and ate the meat and then the meat was gone. We went out again, found another animal, and killed it.

Sometimes the boys asked if we wanted to play a game with our genitals and the girls said no. We said we didn't want to play that game, but would like to play other games. The boys told us that playing sex was what playing was all about. That's the way we grew up.

When adults talked to me I listened. Once they told me that when a young woman grows up, she takes a husband. When they first talked to me about it, I said: "What? What kind of thing am I that I should take a husband? Me, when I grow up, I won't marry. I'll just lie by myself. If I married a man, what would I think I would be doing it for?"

My father said: "Nisa, I am old. I am your father and I am old; your mother's old, too. When you get married, you will gather food and give it to your husband to eat. ~~He also will do things for you and give you things you can wear. But if you refuse to take a husband, who will give you food to eat? Who will give you things to have? Who will give you things to wear?"

Social Roles

I said to my father and mother, "No. There's no question in my mind—I refuse a husband. I won't take one. Why should I? As I am now, I am still a child and won't marry."

Then I said to Mother, "Why don't you marry the man you want for me and sit him down beside Father? Then you'll have two husbands."

Mother said: "Stop talking nonsense. I'm not going to marry him; you'll marry him. A husband is what I want to give you. Yet you say I should marry him. Why are playing with me with this talk?"

We just continued to live after that, kept on living and more time passed. One time we went to the village where Old Kantla and his son Tashay were living. My friend Nhuka and I had gone to the water well to get water, and Tashay and his family were there, having just come back from the bush. When Tashay saw me, he decided he wanted to marry me. He called Nhuka over and said, "Nhuka, that young woman, that beautiful young woman . . . what is her name?"

Nhuka told him my name was Nisa, and he said, "That young woman . . . I'm going to tell Mother and Father about her. I'm going to ask them if I can marry her."

The next evening there was a dance at our village, and Tashay and his parents came. We sang and danced into the night. Later his father said, "We have come here, and now that the dancing is finished, I want to speak to you. Give me your child, the child you gave birth to. Give her to me, and I will give her to my son. Yesterday, while we were at the well, he saw your child. When he returned he told me in the name of what he felt that I should come and ask for her today so I could give her to him."

My mother said, "Yes . . . but I didn't give birth to a woman, I bore a child. She doesn't think about marriage, she just doesn't think about the inside of her marriage hut."

Then my father said, "Yes, I also conceived that child, and it is true: She just doesn't think about marriage. When she marries a man, she leaves him and marries another man and leaves him and gets up and marries another man and leaves him. She refuses men completely. There are two men whom she has already refused. So when I look at Nisa today, I say she is not a woman."

Then Tashay's father said, "Yes, I have listened to what you have said.

That, of course, is the way of a child; it is a child's custom to do that. She gets married many times until one day she likes one man. Then they stay together. That is a child's way."

They talked about the marriage and agreed to it. In the morning Tashay's parents went back to their camp, and we went to sleep. When the morning was late in the sky, his relatives came back. They stayed around and his parents told my aunt and my mother that they should all start building the marriage hut. They began building it together, and everyone was talking and talking. There were a lot of people there. Then all the young men went and brought Tashay to the hut. They stayed around together near the fire. I was at Mother's hut. They told two of my friends to get me. But I said to myself, "Ooooh . . . I'll just run away."

When they came, they couldn't find me. I was already out in the bush, and I just sat there by the base of a tree. Soon I heard Nhuka call out, "Nisa . . . Nisa . . . my friend . . . there are things there that will bite and kill you. Now leave there and come back here."

They came and brought me back. Then they laid me down inside the hut. I cried and cried, and people told me: "A man is not something that kills you; he is someone who marries you, and becomes like your father or your older brother. He kills animals and gives you things to eat. Even tomorrow he would do that. But because you are crying, when he kills an animal, he will eat it himself and won't give you any. Beads, too. He will get some beads, but he won't give them to you. Why are you afraid of your husband and why are you crying?"

Social Roles

I listened and was quiet. Later Tashay lay down by the mouth of the hut, near the fire, and I was inside. He came in only after he thought I was asleep. Then he lay down and slept. I woke while it was still dark and thought,

"How am I going to jump over him? How can I get out and go to Mother's hut?" Then I thought, "This person has married me . . . yes." And, I just lay there. Soon the rain came and beat down and it fell until dawn broke.

In the morning, he got up first and sat by the fire. I was frightened. I was so afraid of him, I just lay there and waited for him to go away before I got up.

We lived together a long time and began to learn to like one another before he slept with me. The first time I didn't refuse. I agreed just a little and he lay with me. But the next morning my insides hurt. I took some leaves and wound them around my waist, but it continued to hurt. Later that day I went with the women to gather mongongo nuts. The whole time I thought "Ooooh . . . what has he done to my insides that they feel this way."

That evening we lay down again. But this time I took a leather strap, held my skin apron tightly against me, tied up my genitals with it, and then tied the strap to the hut's frame. I didn't want him to take me again. The two of us lay there and after a while he started to touch me. When he reached my stomach, he felt the leather strap. He felt around to see what it was. He said, "What is this woman doing? Yesterday she lay with me so nicely when I came to her. Why has she tied up her genitals this way?"

He sat me up and said, "Nisa . . . Nisa . . . what happened? Why are you doing this?" I didn't answer him.

"What are you so afraid of that you tied your genitals?"

I said, "I'm not afraid of anything."

He said, "No, now tell me what you are afraid of. In the name of what you did, I am asking you."

I said, "I refuse because yesterday when you touched me my insides hurt."

He said, "Do you see me as someone who kills people? Am I going to eat you? I am not going to kill you. I have

married you and I want to make love to you. Have you seen any man who has married a woman and who just lives with her and doesn't have sex with her?"

I said, "No, I still refuse it! I refuse sex. Yesterday my insides hurt, that's why."

He said, "Mmm. Today you will lie there by yourself. But tomorrow I will take you."

The next day I said to him, "Today I'm going to lie here, and if you take me by force, you will have me. You will have me because today I'm just going to lie here. You are obviously looking for some 'food,' but I don't know if the food I have is food at all, because even if you have some, you won't be full."

I just lay there and he did his work.

We lived and lived, and soon I started to like him. After that I was a grown person and said to myself, "Yes, without doubt, a man sleeps with you. I thought maybe he didn't."

We lived on, and then I loved him and he loved me, and I kept on loving him. When he wanted me I didn't refuse and he just slept with me. I thought, "Why have I been so concerned about my genitals? They are, after all, not so important. So why was I refusing them?"

I thought that and gave myself to him and gave and gave. We lay with one another, and my breasts had grown very large. I had become a woman.

FOR FURTHER INFORMATION:

Lee, Richard, B., and Irven DeVore, eds. *Kalahari Hunter-Gatherers: Studies of the !Kung San and Their Neighbors.* Harvard University Press, 1976.

Lee, Richard B., and Irven DeVore, eds. *Man the Hunter.* Aldine, 1968.

Marshall, Lorna. *The !Kung of Nyae Nyae.* Harvard University Press, 1976.

Shostak, Marjorie. "Life before Horticulture: An African Gathering and Hunting Society." *Horticulture,* Vol. 55, No. 2, 1977.

When Brothers Share a Wife

Among Tibetans, the good life relegates many women to spinsterhood

Melvyn C. Goldstein

Melvyn C. Goldstein, now a professor of anthropology at Case Western Reserve University in Cleveland, has been interested in the Tibetan practice of fraternal polyandry (several brothers marrying one wife) since he was a graduate student in the 1960s.

Eager to reach home, Dorje drives his yaks hard over the 17,000-foot mountain pass, stopping only once to rest. He and his two older brothers, Pema and Sonam, are jointly marrying a woman from the next village in a few weeks, and he has to help with the preparations.

Dorje, Pema, and Sonam are Tibetans living in Limi, a 200-square-mile area in the northwest corner of Nepal, across the border from Tibet. The form of marriage they are about to enter—fraternal polyandry in anthropological parlance—is one of the world's rarest forms of marriage but is not uncommon in Tibetan society, where it has been practiced from time immemorial. For many Tibetan social strata, it traditionally represented the ideal form of marriage and family.

The mechanics of fraternal polyandry are simple. Two, three, four, or more brothers jointly take a wife, who leaves her home to come and live with them. Traditionally, marriage was arranged by parents, with children, particularly females, having little or no say. This is changing somewhat nowadays, but it is still unusual for children to marry without their parents' consent. Marriage ceremonies vary by income and region and range from all the brothers sitting together as grooms to only the eldest one formally doing so. The age of the brothers plays an important role in determining this: very young brothers almost never participate in actual marriage ceremonies, although they typically join the marriage when they reach their midteens.

The eldest brother is normally dominant in terms of authority, that is, in managing the household, but all the brothers share the work and participate as sexual partners. Tibetan males and females do not find the sexual aspect of sharing a spouse the least bit unusual, repulsive, or scandalous, and the norm is for the wife to treat all the brothers the same.

Offspring are treated similarly. There is no attempt to link children biologically to particular brothers, and a brother shows no favoritism toward his child even if he knows he is the real father because, for example, his other brothers were away at the time the wife became pregnant. The children, in turn, consider all of the brothers as their fathers and treat them equally, even if they also know who is their real father. In some regions children use the term "father" for the eldest brother and "father's brother" for the others, while in other areas they call all the brothers by one term, modifying this by the use of "elder" and "younger."

Unlike our own society, where monogamy is the only form of marriage permitted, Tibetan society allows a variety of marriage types, including monogamy, fraternal polyandry, and polygyny. Fraternal polyandry and monogamy are the most common forms of marriage, while polygyny typically occurs in cases where the first wife is barren. The widespread practice of fraternal polyandry, therefore, is not the outcome of a law requiring brothers to marry jointly. There is choice, and in fact, divorce traditionally was relatively simple in Tibetan society. If a brother in a polyandrous marriage became dissatisfied and wanted to separate, he simply left the main house and set up his own household. In such cases, all the children stayed in the main household with the remaining brother(s), even if the departing brother was known to be the real father of one or more of the children.

The Tibetans' own explanation for choosing fraternal polyandry is materialistic. For example, when I asked Dorje why he decided to marry with his two brothers rather than take his own wife, he thought for a moment, then said it prevented the division of his family's farm (and animals) and thus facilitated all of them achieving a higher standard of living. And when I later asked Dorje's bride whether it wasn't difficult for her to cope with three brothers as husbands, she laughed and echoed the rationale of avoiding fragmentation of the family and land, adding that she expected to be better off economically, since she would have three husbands working for her and her children.

Exotic as it may seem to Westerners, Tibetan fraternal polyandry is thus in many ways analogous to the way primogeniture functioned in nineteenth-century England. Primogeniture dictated that the eldest son inherited the family estate, while younger sons had to leave home and seek their own employment—for example, in the military or the clergy. Primogeniture maintained family estates intact over generations by permitting only one heir per generation. Fraternal polyandry also accomplishes this but does so by keeping all the brothers together with just one wife so that there is only one *set* of heirs per generation.

While Tibetans believe that in this way fraternal polyandry reduces the risk of family fission, monogamous marriages among brothers need not necessarily precipitate the division of the family estate: brothers could continue to live together, and the family land could continue to be worked jointly. When I asked Tibetans about this, however, they invariably responded that such joint families are unstable because each wife is primarily oriented to her own children and interested in their success and well-being over that of the children of the other wives. For example, if the youngest brother's wife had three sons while the eldest brother's wife had only one daughter, the wife of the youngest brother might begin to demand more resources for her children since, as males, they represent the future of the family. Thus, the children from different wives in the same generation are competing sets of heirs, and this makes such families inherently unstable. Tibetans perceive that conflict will spread from the wives to their husbands and consider this likely to cause family fission. Consequently, it is almost never done.

Although Tibetans see an economic advantage to fraternal polyandry, they do not value the sharing of a wife as an end in itself. On the contrary, they articulate a number of problems inherent in the practice. For example, because authority is customarily exercised by the eldest brother, his younger male siblings have

Family Planning in Tibet

An economic rationale for fraternal polyandry is outlined in the diagram below, which emphasizes only the male offspring in each generation. If every wife is assumed to bear three sons, a family splitting up into monogamous households would rapidly multiply and fragment the family land. In this case, a rule of inheritance, such as primogeniture, could retain the family land intact, but only at the cost of creating many landless male offspring. In contrast, the family practicing fraternal polyandry maintains a steady ratio of persons to land.
Joe LeMonnier

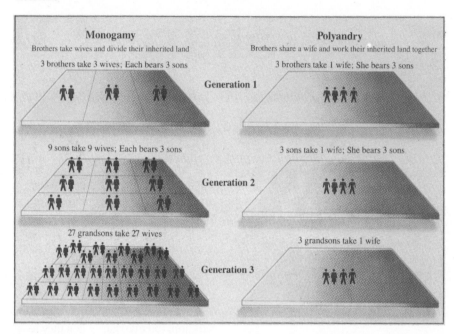

to subordinate themselves with little hope of changing their status within the family. When these younger brothers are aggressive and individualistic, tensions and difficulties often occur despite there being only one set of heirs.

In addition, tension and conflict may arise in polyandrous families because of sexual favoritism. The bride normally sleeps with the eldest brother, and the two have the responsibility to see to it that the other males have opportunities for sexual access. Since the Tibetan subsistence economy requires males to travel a lot, the temporary absence of one or more brothers facilitates this, but there are also other rotation practices. The cultural ideal unambiguously calls for the wife to show equal affection and sexuality to each of the brothers (and vice versa), but deviations from this ideal occur, especially when there is a sizable difference in age between the partners in the marriage.

Dorje's family represents just such a

potential situation. He is fifteen years old and his two older brothers are twenty-five and twenty-two years old. The new bride is twenty-three years old, eight years Dorje's senior. Sometimes such a bride finds the youngest husband immature and adolescent and does not treat him with equal affection; alternatively, she may find his youth attractive and lavish special attention on him. Apart from that consideration, when a younger male like Dorje grows up, he may consider his wife "ancient" and prefer the company of a woman his own age or younger. Consequently, although men and women do not find the idea of sharing a bride or a bridegroom repulsive, individual likes and dislikes can cause familial discord.

Two reasons have commonly been offered for the perpetuation of fraternal polyandry in Tibet: that Tibetans practice female infanticide and therefore have to marry polyandrously, owing to a shortage of females; and that Tibet, lying at extremely high altitudes, is so barren and bleak that Tibetans would starve without resort to this mechanism. A Jesuit who lived in Tibet during the eighteenth century articulated this second view: "One reason for this most odious custom is the sterility of the soil, and the small amount of land that can be cultivated owing to the lack of water. The crops may suffice if the brothers all live together, but if they form separate families they would be reduced to beggary."

Both explanations are wrong, however. Not only has there never been institutionalized female infanticide in Tibet, but Tibetan society gives females considerable rights, including inheriting the family estate in the absence of brothers. In such cases, the woman takes a bridegroom who comes to live in her family and adopts her family's name and identity. Moreover, there is no demographic evidence of a shortage of females. In Limi, for example, there were (in 1974) sixty females and fifty-three males in the fifteen- to thirty-five-year age category, and many adult females were unmarried.

The second reason is also incorrect. The climate in Tibet is extremely harsh, and ecological factors do play a major role perpetuating polyandry, but polyandry is not a means of preventing starvation. It is characteristic, not of the poorest segments of the society, but rather of the peasant landowning families.

In the old society, the landless poor could not realistically aspire to prosperity, but they did not fear starvation. There was a persistent labor shortage throughout Tibet, and very poor families with little or no land and few animals could subsist through agricultural labor, tenant farming, craft occupations such as carpentry, or by working as servants. Although the per person family income could increase somewhat if brothers married polyandrously and pooled their wages, in the absence of inheritable land, the advantage of fraternal polyandry was not generally sufficient to prevent them from setting up their own households. A more skilled or energetic younger brother could do as well or better alone, since he would completely control his income and would not have to share it with his siblings. Consequently, while there was and is some polyandry among the poor, it is much less frequent and more prone to result in divorce and family fission.

An alternative reason for the persistence of fraternal polyandry is that it reduces population growth (and thereby reduces the pressure on resources) by relegating some females to lifetime spinsterhood. Fraternal polyandrous marriages in Limi (in 1974) averaged 2.35 men per woman, and not surprisingly, 31 percent of the females of child-bearing age (twenty to forty-nine) were unmarried. These spinsters either continued to live at home, set up their own households, or worked as servants for other families. They could also become Buddhist nuns. Being unmarried is not synonymous with exclusion from the reproductive pool. Discreet extramarital relationships are tolerated, and actually half of the adult unmarried women in Limi had one or more children. They raised these children as single mothers, working for wages or weaving cloth and blankets for sale. As a group, however, the unmarried woman had far fewer offspring than the married women, averaging only 0.7 children per woman, compared with 3.3 for married women, whether polyandrous, monogamous, or polygynous. While polyandry helps regulate population, this function of polyandry is not consciously perceived by Tibetans and is not the reason they consistently choose it.

If neither a shortage of females nor the fear of starvation perpetuates fraternal polyandry, what motivates brothers, particularly younger brothers, to opt for this system of marriage? From the perspective of the younger brother in a landholding family, the main incentive is the attainment or maintenance of the good life. With polyandry, he can expect a more secure and higher standard of living, with access not only to this family's land and animals but also to its inherited collection of clothes, jewelry, rugs, saddles, and horses. In addition, he will experience less work pressure and much greater security because all responsibility does not fall on one "father." For Tibetan brothers, the question is whether to trade off the greater personal freedom inherent in monogamy for the real or potential economic security, affluence, and social prestige associated with life in a larger, labor-rich polyandrous family.

A brother thinking of separating from his polyandrous marriage and taking his own wife would face various disadvantages. Although in the majority of Tibetan regions all brothers theoretically have rights to their family's estate, in reality Tibetans are reluctant to divide their land into small fragments. Generally, a younger brother who insists on leaving the family will receive only a small plot of land, if that. Because of its power and wealth, the rest of the family usually can block any attempt of the younger brother to increase his share of land through litigation. Moreover, a younger brother may not even get a house and cannot expect to receive much above the minimum in terms of movable possessions, such as furniture, pots, and pans. Thus, a brother contemplating going it on his own must plan on achieving economic security and the good life not through inheritance but through his own work.

The obvious solution for younger brothers—creating new fields from virgin land—is generally not a feasible option. Most Tibetan populations live at high altitudes (above 12,000 feet), where arable land is extremely scarce. For example, in Dorje's village, agriculture ranges only from about 12,900 feet, the lowest point in the area, to 13,300 feet. Above that altitude, early frost and snow destroy the staple barley crop. Furthermore, because of the low rainfall caused by the Himalayan rain shadow, many areas in Tibet and northern Nepal that are within the appropriate altitude range for agriculture have no reliable sources of irrigation. In the end, although there is plenty of unused land in such areas, most of it is either too high or too arid.

Even where unused land capable of being farmed exists, clearing the land and building the substantial terraces necessary for irrigation constitute a great undertaking. Each plot has to be completely dug out to a depth of two to two and half feet so that the large rocks and boulders can be removed. At best, a man might be able to bring a few new fields under cultivation in the first years after separating from his brothers, but he could not expect to acquire substantial amounts of arable land this way.

In addition, because of the limited farmland, the Tibetan subsistence economy characteristically includes a strong emphasis on animal husbandry. Tibetan farmers regularly maintain cattle, yaks, goats, and sheep, grazing them in the areas too high for agriculture. These herds produce wool, milk, cheese, butter, meat, and skins. To obtain these resources, however, shepherds must accompany the animals on a daily basis. When first setting up a monogamous household, a younger brother like Dorje would find it difficult to both farm and manage animals.

In traditional Tibetan society, there was an even more critical factor that operated to perpetuate fraternal polyandry—a form of hereditary servitude somewhat analogous to serfdom in Europe. Peasants were tied to large estates held by aristocrats, monasteries, and the Lhasa government. They were allowed the use of some farmland to produce their own subsistence but were required to provide taxes in kind and corvée (free labor) to their lords. The corvée was a substantial hardship, since a peasant household was in many cases required to furnish the lord with one laborer daily for most of the year and more on specific occasions such as the harvest. This enforced labor, along with the lack of new land and ecological pressure to pursue both agriculture and animal husbandry, made polyandrous families particularly beneficial. The polyandrous family allowed an internal division of adult labor, maximizing economic advantage. For example, while the wife worked the family fields, one brother could perform the lord's corvée, another could look after the animals, and a third could engage in trade.

Although social scientists often discount other people's explanations of why they do things, in the case of Tibetan fraternal polyandry, such explanations are very close to the truth. The custom, however, is very sensitive to changes in its political and economic milieu and, not surprisingly, is in decline in most Tibetan areas. Made less important by the elimination of the traditional serf-based economy, it is disparaged by the dominant non-Tibetan leaders of India, China, and Nepal. New opportunities for economic and social mobility in these countries, such as the tourist trade and government employment, are also eroding the rationale for polyandry, and so it may vanish within the next generation.

Young Traders of Northern Nigeria

Enid Schildkrout

Thirty years ago, Erik Erikson wrote that "the fashionable insistence on dramatizing the dependence of children on adults often blinds us to the dependence of the older generation on the younger one." As a psychoanalyst, Erikson was referring mainly to the emotional bonds between parents and children, but his observation is a reminder that in many parts of the world, adults depend on children in quite concrete ways. In northern Nigeria, children with trays balanced on their heads, carrying and selling a variety of goods for their mothers or themselves, are a common sight in villages and towns. Among the Muslim Hausa, aside from being a useful educational experience, this children's trade, as well as children's performance of household chores and errands, complements the activity of adults and is socially and emotionally significant.

Children's services are especially important to married Hausa women, who, in accordance with Islamic practices, live in purdah, or seclusion. In Nigeria, purdah is represented not so much by the wearing of the veil but by the mud-brick walls surrounding every house or compound and by the absence of women in the markets and the streets. Women could not carry out their domestic responsibilities, not to mention their many income-earning enterprises, without the help of children, who are free from the rigid sexual segregation that so restricts adults.

Except for elderly women, only children can move in and out of their own and other people's houses without violating the rules of purdah. Even children under three years of age are sent on short errands, for example, to buy things for their mothers.

Hausa-speaking people are found throughout West Africa and constitute the largest ethnic group in northern Nigeria, where they number over eighteen million. Their adherence to Islam is a legacy of the centuries during which Arabs came from the north to trade goods of North African and European manufacture. The majority of the Hausa are farmers, but markets and large commercial cities have existed in northern Nigeria since long before the period of British colonial rule. The city of Kano, for example, which was a major emporium for the trans-Saharan caravan trade, dates back to the eighth century. Today it has a population of about one million.

Binta is an eleven-year-old girl who lives in Kano, in a mud-brick house that has piped water, but no electricity. The household includes her father and mother, her three brothers, her father's second wife and her three children, and a foster child, who is the daughter of one of Binta's cousins. By Kano standards, it is a middle-income family. Binta's father sells shoes, and her mother cooks and sells bean cakes and *tuwo*, the stiff porridge made of guinea corn (*Shorghum vulgare*), which is the Hausa's staple. Binta described for me one day's round of activities, which began very early when she arose to start trading.

"After I woke up, I said my prayers and ate breakfast. Then I went outside the house to sell the bean cakes my mother makes every morning. Soon my mother called me in and asked me to take more bean cakes around town to sell; she spoke to me about making an effort to sell as much as I usually do. I sold forty-eight bean cakes at one kobo each [one kobo is worth one and a half cents]. After I returned home, some people came to buy more cakes from me. Then I went out for a second round of trading before setting out for Arabic school. I study the Koran there every morning from eight to nine.

"When school was over, I washed and prepared to sell *tuwo*. First my mother sent me to another neighborhood to gather the customers' empty bowls. I also collected the money from our regular customers. My mother put the *tuwo* in the bowls and told me the amount of money to collect for each. Then I delivered them to the customers.

"On my way home, a man in the street, whom I know, sent me on an errand to buy him fifteen kobo worth of food; he gave me a reward of one kobo. I then sold some more *tuwo* outside our house by standing there and shouting for customers. When the *tuwo* was finished, I was sent to another house to buy some guinea corn, and one of the women there asked me to bring her one of my mother's big pots. The pot was too heavy for me to carry, but finally one of my brothers helped me take it to her.

"When I returned, my mother was busy pounding some grain, and she sent me out to have some locust beans pounded. She then sent me to pick up three bowls of pounded guinea corn, and she gave me money to take to the woman who had pounded it. The woman told me to remind my mother that she still owed money from the day before.

"When I came home I was sent out to trade again, this time with salt, bouillon cubes, and laundry detergent in small packets. Afterward I prepared some pancakes using ingredients I bought myself—ten kobo worth of flour, one kobo worth of salt, five kobo worth of palm oil, and ten kobo worth of firewood. I took this food outside to sell it to children.

"My mother then gave me a calabash of guinea corn to take for grinding; my younger sister also gave me two calabashes of corn to take. The man who ran the grinding machine advised me that I should not carry so large a load, so I made two trips on the way back. He gave me and my younger brothers, who accompanied me, on kobo each.

"I was then told to take a bath, which I did. After that I was sent to visit a sick relative who was in the hospital. On the way I met a friend, and we took the bus together. I also bought some cheese at the market for five kobo. I met another friend on the way home, and she bought some fish near the market for ten kobo and gave me some. I played on the way to the hospital. When I got home, I found the women of the house preparing a meal. One of them was already eating, and I was invited to eat with her.

"After nightfall, I was sent to take some spices for pounding, and I wasted a lot of time there. The other children and I went to a place where some fruits and vegetables are sold along the street. We bought vegetables for soup for fifty kobo, as my mother had asked me to do. By the time I got home it was late, so I went to sleep."

Binta's many responsibilities are typical for a girl her age. Like many women, Binta's mother relies upon her children in carrying out an occupation

at home. Although purdah implies that a woman will be supported by her husband and need not work, most Hausa women do work, keeping their incomes distinct from the household budget. Women usually cook one main meal a day and purchase their other meals from other women. In this way they are able to use their time earning a living instead of performing only unpaid domestic labor.

Among the Hausa, men and women spend relatively little time together, eating separately and, except in certain ritual contexts, rarely doing the same things. Differences in gender are not as important among children, however. In fact, it is precisely because children's activities are not rigidly defined by sex that they are able to move between the world of women, centered in the inner courtyard of the house, and the world of men, whose activities take place mainly outside the home. Children of both sexes care for younger children, go to the market, and help their mothers cook.

Both boys and girls do trading, although it is more common for girls. From the age of about five until marriage, which is very often at about age twelve for girls, many children like Binta spend part of every day selling such things as fruits, vegetables, and nuts; bouillon cubes, bread, and small packages of detergent, sugar, or salt; and bowls of steaming rice or *tuwo*. If a woman embroiders, children buy the thread and later take the finished product to the client or to an agent who sells it.

Women in purdah frequently change their occupations depending on the availability of child helpers. In Kano, women often trade in small commodities that can be sold in small quantities, such as various kinds of cooked food. Sewing, embroidery, mat weaving, and other craft activities (including, until recently, spinning) are less remunerative occupations, and women pursue them when they have fewer children around to help. Unlike the situation common in the United States, where children tend to hamper a woman's ability to earn money, the Hausa woman finds it difficult to earn income without children's help. Often, if a

woman has no children of her own, a relative's child will come to live with her.

Child care is another service children perform that benefits women. It enables mothers to devote themselves to their young infants, whom they carry on their backs until the age of weaning, between one and two. Even though women are always at home, they specifically delegate the care of young children to older ones. The toddler moves from the mother's back into a group of older children, who take the responsibility very seriously. Until they are old enough, children do not pick up infants or very young children, but by the age of nine, both boys and girls bathe young children, play with them, and take them on errands. The older children do a great deal of direct and indirect teaching of younger ones. As soon as they can walk, younger children accompany their older siblings to Arabic school. There the children sit with their age-mates, and the teacher gives them lessons according to their ability.

Much of a child's activity is directed toward helping his or her parents, but other relatives—grandparents, aunts, uncles, and stepmothers—and adults living in the same house as servants or tenants may call on a child for limited tasks without asking permission of the parents. Like other Muslims, Hausa men may have up to four wives, and these women freely call on each other's children to perform household chores. Even strangers in the street sometimes ask a child to do an errand, such as delivering a message, particularly if the chore requires entering a house to which the adult does not have access. The child will be rewarded with a small amount of money or food.

Adults other than parents also reprimand children, who are taught very early to obey the orders of grownups. Without ever directly refusing to obey a command, however, children do devise numerous strategies of non-compliance, such as claiming that another adult has already co-opted their time or simply leaving the scene and ignoring the command. Given children's greater mobility, there is little an adult can do to enforce compliance.

Besides working on behalf of adults, children also participate in a "children's economy." Children have their own money—from school allowances given to them daily for the purchase of snacks, from gifts, from work they may have done, and even from their own investments. For example, boys make toys for sale, and they rent out valued property, such as slide viewers or bicycles. Just as women distinguish their own enterprises from the labor they do as wives, children regard the work they do for themselves differently from the work they do on behalf of their mothers. When Binta cooks food for sale, using materials she has purchased with her own money, the profits are entirely her own, although she may hand the money over to her mother for safekeeping.

Many girls begin to practice cooking by the age of ten. They do not actually prepare the family meals, for this heavy and tedious work is primarily the wives' responsibility. But they do carry out related chores, such as taking vegetables out for grinding, sifting flour, and washing bowls. Many also cook food for sale on their own. With initial help from their mothers or other adult female relatives, who may given them a cooking pot, charcoal, or a small stove, children purchase small amounts of ingredients and prepare various snacks. Since they sell their products for less than the adult women do, and since the quantities are very small, their customers are mainly children. Child entrepreneurs even extend credit to other children.

Aisha is a ten-year-old girl who was notoriously unsuccessful as a trader. She disliked trading and regularly lost her mother's investment. Disgusted, her mother finally gave her a bit of charcoal, some flour and oil, and a small pot. Aisha set up a little stove outside her house and began making small pancakes, which she sold to very young children. In three months she managed to make enough to buy a new dress, and in a year she bought a pair of shoes. She had clearly chosen her occupation after some unhappy trials at street trading.

Hausa women usually engage in some form of enterprise; most of their profits are invested in their children's marriage expenses. Working at home, a woman weaves a mat for sale.

In the poorest families, as in Aisha's, the profit from children's work goes toward living expenses. This may occur in households that are headed by divorced or widowed women. It is also true for the *almajirai*, or Arabic students, who often live with their teachers. The proceeds of most children's economic activity, however, go to the expenses of marriage. The income contributes to a girl's dowry and to a boy's bridewealth, both of which are considerable investments.

The girl's dowry includes many brightly painted enamel, brass, and glass bowls, collected years before marriage. These utensils are known as *kayan daki*, or "things of the room." After the wedding they are stacked in a large cupboard beside the girl's bed. Very few of them are used, but they are always proudly displayed, except during the mourning period if the husband dies. *Kayan daki* are not simply for conspicuous display, however. They remain the property of the woman unless she sells them or gives them away. In the case of divorce or financial need, they can provide her most important and immediate source of economic security.

Kayan daki traditionally consisted of brass bowls and beautifully carved calabashes. Today the most common form is painted enamel bowls manufactured in Nigeria or abroad. The styles and designs change frequently, and the cost is continually rising.

Among the wealthier urban women and the Western-educated women, other forms of modern household equipment, including electric appliances and china tea sets, are becoming part of the dowry.

The money a young girl earns on her own, as well as the profits she brings home through her trading, are invested by her mother or guardian in *kayan daki* in anticipation of her marriage. Most women put the major part of their income into their daughters' *kayan daki* as well as helping their sons with marriage expenses. When a woman has many children, the burden can be considerable.

For girls, marriage, which ideally coincides with puberty, marks the transition to adult status. If a girl marries as early as age ten, she does not cook for her husband or have sexual relations with him for some time, but she enters purdah and loses the freedom of childhood. Most girls are married by age fifteen, and for many the transition is a difficult one.

Boys usually do not marry until they are over twenty and are able to support a family. They also need to have raised most of the money to cover the cost of getting married. Between the ages of eight and ten, however, they gradually begin to move away from the confines of the house and to regard it as a female domain. They begin taking their food outside and eating it with friends, and they roam much farther than girls in their play activities. By the onset of puberty, boys have begun to observe the rules of purdah by refraining from entering the houses of all but their closest relatives. In general, especially if they have sisters, older boys spend less time than girls doing chores and errands and more time playing and, in recent years, going to school. Traditionally, many boys left home to live and study with an Arabic teacher. Today many also pursue Western education, sometimes in boarding school. Although the transition to adulthood is less abrupt for boys, childhood for both sexes ends by age twelve to fourteen.

As each generation assumes the responsibilities of adulthood and the restrictions of sexual separation, it must rely on the younger members of society who can work around the purdah system. Recently, however, the introduction of Western education has begun to threaten this traditional arrangement, in part just by altering the pattern of children's lives.

The Nigerian government is now engaged in a massive program to provide Western education to all school-age children. This program has been undertaken for sound economic and political reasons. During the colonial period, which ended in the early 1960s, the British had a "hands-off"

policy regarding education in northern Nigeria. They ruled through the Islamic political and judicial hierarchy and supported the many Arabic schools, where the Koran and Islamic law, history, and religion were taught. The British discouraged the introduction of Christian mission schools in the north and spent little on government schools.

The pattern in the rest of Nigeria was very different. In the non-Muslim areas of the country, mission and government schools grew rapidly during the colonial period. The result of this differential policy was the development of vast regional imbalances in the extent and level of Western education in the country. This affected the types of occupational choices open to Nigerians from different regions. Despite a longer tradition of literacy in Arabic in the north, few northerners were eligible for those civil service jobs that required literacy in English, the language of government business. This was one of the many issues in the tragic civil war that tore Nigeria apart in the 1960s. The current goal of enrolling all northern children in public schools, which offer training in English and secular subjects, has, therefore, a strong and valid political rationale.

Western education has met a mixed reception in northern Nigeria. While

it has been increasingly accepted for boys—as an addition to, not a substitute for, Islamic education—many parents are reluctant to enroll their daughters in primary school. Nevertheless, there are already more children waiting to get into school than there are classrooms and teachers to accommodate them. If the trend continues, it will almost certainly have important, if unintended, consequences for purdah and the system of child enterprise that supports it.

Children who attend Western school continue to attend Arabic school, and thus are removed from the household for much of the day. For many women this causes considerable difficulty in doing daily housework. It means increased isolation and a curtailment of income-producing activity. It creates a new concern about where to obtain the income for children's marriages. As a result of these practical pressures, the institution of purdah will inevitably be challenged. Also, the schoolgirl of today may develop new skills and new expectations of her role as a woman that conflict with the traditional ways. As Western education takes hold, today's young traders may witness a dramatic change in Hausa family life—for themselves as adults and for their children.

Child Care in China

Bruce Dollar

Societies differ as to how they characteristically raise (socialize) their children. The following selection describes some of the cultural values, beliefs, and institutions of modern China that directly affect the development of its children and the roles of other family members. The institutionalized child care programs in China will be of particular interest to those concerned with the growing use of day care centers in the United States.

The old art of China watching is giving way to China witnessing, and one quality of the new China seems inevitably to impress all recent visitors is the extraordinary vibrancy of Chinese children, from the very youngest to the adolescents, who already tower so noticeably over their grandparents. During my own recent trip within China, my companions and I saw for ourselves the exuberant self-confidence that seems to infuse all Chinese kids, whether they are performing for strangers, participating in a classroom exercise, or playing by themselves.

"Ours is a socialist society; everything is done according to plan." This pronouncement, with which our various Chinese hosts so frequently prefaced their answers to our questions, provides a starting point for understanding how this spirit of exuberance has been achieved. Although Chinese society is largely decentralized to encourage local self-sufficiency and diversification, the whole is knit together by an administrative structure that is more or less uniform from city to city and, somewhat less, from commune (or network of villages) to commune. It is a framework that provides an efficient system of communication and has helped produce a remarkable social cohesion based on commonly held goals and values—which themselves are informed by the teachings of Mao Tse-tung.

The consensus is particularly apparent with respect to the care and training of the young. This is hardly surprising when one considers the enormous stock the Chinese place in producing what they call "revolutionary successors," an apt phrase in a country where revolutionary consciousness has been maintained largely through vivid comparisons with the "bitter past," and where the problem of continuing the revolution into succeeding generations is paramount.

Thus, throughout our visit we constantly encountered—with amazing consistency at various points along a 2,500-mile itinerary—several major ideas about child rearing in the numerous conversations we had with people in child-related institutions: families, nurseries, kindergartens, and schools. These themes—especially the subordination of personal to social needs, respect for productive labor, altruism, cooperation, and the integration of physical with intellectual labor—together describe the kind of citizen China hopes to produce. The techniques employed to achieve these values are in practice virtually from infancy.

During the years before primary schools, which begins at the age of seven, a series of public child care facilities is available to parents who wish to use them. In the cities, where patterns are more uniform, a mother's maternity leave (paid) usually terminates 56 days after birth. Since breast-feeding is the rule in China, the mother may then place her child in the nursing room at her place of work. Most work institutions—factories, hospitals, and government offices, for example—provide this facility for their employees. In a typical arrangement the mother has two half hour breaks, plus lunch, to visit and nurse her baby during the work day. After work the baby returns home with the mother.

Nursing rooms provide care for infants up to one and a half years old; then they may be sent to one of the various kinds of nurseries. Some of these are attached to the work place or located in the home neighborhood; they may be open only during the work day, or they may be "live-in" nurseries, where children stay overnight and go home on weekends. Kindergartens, usually located in the residential areas, generally care for children from three and a half to seven years old and may also be either part-time or full-time.

In a country in which over 90 per cent of all women of working age do work, it might be expected that a similar percentage of children would therefore receive some kind of institutional care. But there are options. The most common is to leave the child in the care of grandparents, who frequently live with the family. Another alternative is to make arrangements with a friend or neighbor. Estimates vary from place to place, but in most cities no more than half the children of nursery school age are in attendance. For kindergarten the figures are higher, especially in the cities, where attendance is over 80 per cent.

Since child care is decentralized, different localities often make their own arrangements, which may not conform to the usual patterns. This is particularly true of rural areas, where a lack of resources and the persistence of custom probably account for a lower incidence of public child care facilities. One small village we visited, the Sha Shih Yu Brigade in northeast China, had no permanent facility; only during harvest time, when all hands were needed in the fields, was there organized care for small children. A child care center located in a coalmining area near Tangshan, on the other hand, served 314 children divided into at least five separate age groups, from 56 days to six years old.

How do these institutions work to socialize the children under their care? And what are they like for the kids? In spite of the diversity in organizational structure, the remarkable similarity from place to place, both in the values espoused and the methods used to inculcate them, seems to support a number of generalizations.

One quality that is sure to strike an American observer is the preponderance and the style of group activities. A common example is the "cultural performance," usually presented for visitors. Whether they are songs from a revolutionary opera, dances to celebrate a harvest, or a program of folk melodies played on traditional Chinese instruments, these performances are always presented by groups, and it is impossible to pick out a "star."

Although there were exceptions, many early child care facilities we visited seemed rather poorly supplied with the variety of toys and materials that the conventional wisdom in the United States says should be on hand to enrich and enliven a child's environment. Although this may have been due to a simple inability to pay for more equipment, the teachers we spoke to did not seem to consider it a shortcoming. Perhaps this is because Chinese children are generally expected to rely on each other for stimulation—at any rate, this seems to be the effect. The situation provides an interesting contrast to that in the United States, where

the highly desired "rich environment" often means that kids interact with inanimate materials more than they do with other people.

The small children we saw were not without playthings, however. There was always at least one toy for each child—typically a rubber or plastic doll of a worker, a peasant, or a soldier. Rocking horses were also common, as were military toys and playground equipment that could accommodate many children. But in general the emphasis was on group play. One recent American visitor to a Chinese nursery school reports noticing that the blocks seemed awfully heavy for the small children. "Exactly!" beamed the teachers. "That fosters mutual help."

Chinese teachers actively encourage such group behavior as cooperation, sharing, and altruism. "We praise a child when he shows concern for others' interests," said one kindergarten teacher. "For example, at meal time teachers give out bowls and chop sticks. If a youngster gets a nicer bowl and gives it to someone else, we praise him for it. Or when the children are asked to select a toy and a child gives the best one to a classmate, we praise that, too."

Even in a competitive situation, this teacher said, helping another is more important than winning. "When the children run in a relay race, sometimes one will fall down, especially if he's small. If another child stops to help him get up or to see if he's all right, even though his own team might fall behind, we encourage this." The approach contrasts markedly with methods used in the Soviet Union, another country that stresses the collective in its child-rearing practices. There, competition is discouraged between individuals but promoted between groups. Each child is made aware of his importance within his group—say, a row in his classroom—and then competes fiercely for the rewards of a group victory. The Chinese seem genuinely to eschew even this form of competition in favor of straightforward mutual help and cooperation.

But how do teachers deal with improper behavior and matters of discipline? Here is how the question was answered in a conversation with three staff members of a full-time kindergarten in Peking:

Q: What kinds of behavior do you discourage in the children?
A: We criticize those who take toys or other things from others. Or if children beat each other—we criticize that.
Q: Exactly how do you handle such a situation—say, two kids fighting?
A: First, the teacher must understand the reason for the fight. For instance, one might have taken a toy from the other, and the second child hit him. In that case, the teacher will criticize both. This criticism is carried out alone, unless it took place in the class; in that case it will be done in front of the class so that all the children will understand what was wrong. Criticism is to make children understand what was wrong and why.
Q: What kind of punishment do you use?
A: There is no punishment.
Q: Well, what if a child were really intractable? Would you use some mild sanction, such as depriving him of some free play time on the playground?
A: (At this point all three women broke into smiles at our incredulity. Waving their hands back and forth to underscore their words, they said): No, no, nothing like that. We believe in persuasion.
Q: Do other children ever participate in criticism?
A: Generally, no. Unless a third child saw what happened—then he'll be asked to tell.
Q: Let's say the incident was unobserved by any third party and the two kids involved give conflicting versions of what happened. Then how does the teacher act?
A: If the teacher finds a contradiction when both tell what happened, she will try to educate the children. She will note that everyone can make a mistake, including teachers. The mistake that led to the fight is not important, she will say, but telling the truth is very important. At this point the children will probably tell the truth.

This sounded like fine theory, but it provoked some skepticism among those of us who had been teachers. What about teachers who do not have the patience to use such positive techniques? we asked. How do you deal with teachers who don't observe

For a child in China today, the experience of "multiple mothering" is very likely. If the mother elects not to leave her child in a nursing room where she works, chances are the child will be in the care of its grandmother or a neighbor.

the school's policy? The reply: "We all—teachers and leadership—have the same goal: to cultivate revolutionary successors. So we all work together and help each other. We study our profession together. We have regular criticism and self-criticism sessions, and sometimes we help each other on specific problems."

If we had not already seen many teachers in action here and elsewhere on our trip, we might have been dissatisfied with this answer. But we were constantly struck by the teachers' apparent love for their work in all the early child care institutions we

visited. These women, we learned (there were no men), were chosen for their jobs after having shown a particular interest in children, and "sensitivity and love for children" were the criteria most often cited for their recruitment. Credentials were secondary. Since the Cultural Revolution, the amount of training teachers receive has ranged all the way from university graduation to short-term training classes and "learning through practice."

Three of us in the group who were especially interested in child rearing and education often asked to see child care centers and schools under

normal operating conditions. Our guides accommodated these requests by arranging for us to stay behind after the formal tour or make a low-key visit to a kindergarten, say, without the rest of the group. Some of our most revealing insights occurred during our observation of everyday free playground activities.

One afternoon, for example, at the child care center serving workers of the Fan Ga Chong coal mine area near Tangshan, I spent nearly an hour outside among the four-and-a-half-to-six-year-olds and their teachers, or "nurses." Here was the one place where I saw what might be called a disruptive child—a little boy who, in the United States, would probably have been labeled hyperkinetic and put on Ritalin. While the other 50 or so children busied themselves with various games—rope jumping, drop the handkerchief, tricycle riding, playing with toys and each other— this boy ran constantly from place to place, trying to be in on everything at once and occasionally interfering with someone else's fun. The nurses, who themselves were taking part in the games, were obviously aware of the boy's actions, but they made no fuss over him. Instead, each time he ran by a nurse, she would reach out, place her hand on the back of his head, and gently guide him away from trouble or toward an activity he might like—usually with a few soothing words. Soon he was off again, and once or twice it was necessary to intervene when he began picking on another child. But always the adults acted cheerfully and patiently, and the boy never became a center of attention. His actions were the closest thing to aggressive or disruptive behavior among children that I saw on the entire trip.

After visiting several classrooms at the Pei Hai Kindergarten, a full-time kindergarten located in a park in Peking, I spent an even longer time on the playground watching free play. Once again I was struck by the way teachers enthusiastically joined in. The children, well over a hundred of them, had formed into a variety of play groups. Some played on slides, a merry-go-round, monkey bars, and swings. Some were organized into class-sized groups for games. Others were in smaller groups, jumping rope or kicking a ball around. There were kids in pairs and kids alone. One gleeful little boy, holding aloft a leafy twig, ran, danced, and twirled with it till he fell down from dizziness. And ranging over the whole playground, sweeping past and through everyone else's games, was a whooping pack of boys chasing a soccer ball, a laughing teacher in the lead.

In one group that especially caught my eye, seven or eight girls were jumping rope, taking turns at the ends of a pink plastic rope and lining up to jump one by one. No teacher was with them. They were very absorbed and used chants and songs to accompany each jumper. Several times while I watched, a minor controversy of some kind would erupt and everything would come to a halt. Maybe it concerned whose turn was next on the rope or how many times one had jumped before missing. Whatever it was, the whole group would come together and heatedly debate their points. With no single girl taking charge, they would quickly work out a settlement that seemed to satisfy everyone and then resume their jumping with all the gusto of before. These little girls were good jumpers, incidentally. So good that after a while they attracted an audience: six little boys found chairs, lined them up to form a small gallery, and proceeded to join in the jumping chants, applauding for each jumper. Great fun for all, highly organized, and by all indications spontaneous and undirected by adults.

In the United States the growing demand for facilities for the care of infants and preschool children has provoked a chorus of urgent questions: Doesn't a baby need a single individual to relate to and identify with as mother? How can a mother be sure that those to whom she entrusts her child will teach the same values she holds? Isn't it the mother's natural role to care for her own children? What is the effect of insitutionalized child care on the family?

Obviously, the answers the Chinese have found to these questions are not directly applicable to this country. Yet the insights they provide can be instructive as we seek our own solutions.

There is a strong likelihood that the average child in China will undergo "multiple mothering" of some kind. Even if the mother does not choose to leave her infant in the nursing room where she works, chances are the child will wind up in the care of a neighbor or the grandmother. Offsetting this diversity of "mothers," however, is the near-uniform consensus of values and methods of child rearing I have described. This consistency seems to go a long way toward providing young children with the kind of security we in the United States might normally associate only with single mothering.

Another aspect of multiple or "shared" mothering, as Ruth Sidel, author of the excellent recent book *Women & Child Care in China*, points out, "is that infants can thrive physically and emotionally if the mother-surrogates are constant, warm, and giving. Babies in China are not subjected to serial mothering; we were repeatedly told that aunties (i.e., nurses) and teachers rarely leave their jobs. And they are warm and loving with the children. The children show none of the lethargy or other intellectual, emotional, or physical problems of institutionalized children. Quite the opposite!"

"Everything is planned," and the position of mothers in China is the consequence of a society-wide effort to provide for the economic liberation of women. In keeping with Mao Tse-tung's edict calling for "genuine equality between the sexes," a broad series of programs, including birth control information and prenatal care with maternity leave, in addition to the system of child care facilities, is underway to assume the full participation of women in "building socialism." The objects of unspeakable oppression in prerevolutionary society, Chinese women today have been thoroughly integrated into the labor force, both in factory and commune. And a growing number of them are entering professions—for example, 50 per cent of the medical students are now women.

Despite the enormous progress, even the Chinese will concede that full parity with men is not yet a reality. Top governmental, military, and management posts continue to be mostly male preserves. However, women do wield considerable political and administrative power at the local level, where they often run the smallest governmental units, the neighborhood revolutionary committees.

But the key to liberation is still

economic independence, which depends on the availability of work. Since 1971 a new source of work for women has appeared: the so-called housewives' factories. These have been organized locally by women who live in housing areas like the Kung Kiang Workers' Residential Area in Shanghai, and whose husbands work in the various nearby factories. As they described it to us, the housewives were looking for ways in which they could contribute productively to the revolution without having to leave the residential area. So they set up their own light industries in workshops near their homes, and by working full- or part-time were able to produce needed commodities, such as flashlight bulbs or men's trousers, while earning extra money for themselves. The entire operation in each case was staffed and run by women.

Since nearly all working-age women in China today work and are no longer economically dependent on their husbands or families, one might well wonder about the effects of these conditions on the family.

By all available evidence the family is thriving in China, and the individual household continues to be the basic social unit. A featured item in every home we visited, as ubiquitous as a portrait of Chairman Mao, was a display of a great many photographs of family members, usually pressed under a piece of glass on top of a bureau or framed on the wall. Our host or hostess would invariably point this out with pride. Signs of active and full participation in family life were everywhere, and all generations were included. A man out with his children is a common sight, as is a child with a grandmother or grandfather.

Parents are obviously revered by children, and so are grandparents. In fact, the complete absence of a "generation gap" is a striking phenomenon to an American. Not only are grandparents well integrated into family life, but old people who have no family or who are disabled live in well-tended "respect for aged" homes and are given important functions that serve the neighborhood.

Far from undermining the family structure, we were repeatedly told, jobs for women and day care for children have made home life easier, having eliminated many former sources of friction and frustration. A major factor here is undoubtedly the mass commitment to working for the betterment of China. Personal gratification seems to derive from each individual's knowledge that he or she makes an important contribution, no matter how small, to the national effort and that the benefits of this contribution, and others like it, will be distributed to all.

Sex Roles and Statuses

The feminist movement in the United States has had a significant impact on the development of anthropology. Feminists have rightly charged that anthropologists have tended to gloss over the lives of women in studies of society and culture. In part, this is because, up until recent times, most anthropologists have been men. The result has been an undue emphasis upon male activities as well as male perspectives in descriptions of particular societies.

These charges, however, have proven to be a firm corrective. In the last few years women and, more particularly, the sexual division of labor and its relation to social and political status have begun to be studied by anthropologists. In addition, these changes in emphasis have been accompanied by an increase in the number of women in the field.

Feminist anthropologists have begun to critically attack many established anthropological truths. They have shown, for example, that field studies of nonhuman primates, which were often used to demonstrate the evolutionary basis of male dominance, distorted the actual evolutionary record by focusing primarily on baboons. (Male baboons are especially dominant and aggressive.) Other, less-quoted primate studies show how dominance and aggression are highly situational phenomena, sensitive to ecological variation. Feminist anthropologists have also shown that the subsistence contribution of women has likewise been ignored by anthropologists. A classic case is that of the !Kung, a hunting and gathering people in Southern Africa, whose women provide the bulk of the foodstuffs, including most of the available protein, and who, coincidentally, enjoy a more egalitarian relationship with the men.

Recent studies have concerned themselves with determining how and why the relationships between the sexes have changed over time and what have been the consequences of women's generally subordinate status. Although the subordination of women can be extreme (see "A Matter of Honor" by Longina Jukubowska), Ernestine Friedl, in "Society and Sex Roles," explains that the sex that controls the valued goods of exchange in a society is the dominant gender and, since this is a matter of cultural variation, male authority cannot be biologically predetermined. While Lori Heise ("The Global War Against Women") and Maxine Margolis ("Blaming the Victim") show that sexual equality is still far from being a reality in many parts of the world, Helen Fisher ("A Primitive Prescription for Equality") sees a reemergence of the economically autonomous woman in modern industrial society, and with it the sexual equality of our paleolithic past.

Looking Ahead: Challenge Questions

What is it about foraging societies that encourages an egalitarian relationship between the sexes?

What kinds of shifts in the social relations of production are necessary for women to achieve equality with men?

Under what circumstances does divorce become common?

Why is elopement a breach of the "code of honor" among Bedouins?

What kinds of personal dilemmas do women face in a changing society?

What kinds of historical, religious, and legal legacies have contributed to violence against women around the world?

How does the "blaming the victim" rationale help to keep women subordinate?

In what ways is the rise of the economically autonomous woman bringing about the revival of ancient hunter-gatherer traditions?

Society and Sex Roles

Ernestine Friedl

Ernestine Friedl is a professor of anthropology at Duke University; a former president of the American Anthropological Association, a fellow of the American Academy of Arts and Sciences, and an advisory editor to Human Nature. *She received her Ph.D. from Columbia University in 1950. Until recently, Friedl was a firm believer in the relative equality of women in the field of anthropology and had little interest in the anthropological study of women. None of her field work among the Pomo and Chippewa Indians of North America, or in rural and urban Greece was concerned with women's issues.*

In the early 1970s, while serving on the American Anthropological Association Committee on the Status of Women, Friedl became convinced that women were discriminated against as much in anthropology as in the other academic disciplines. Since that time, she has devoted her efforts to the cross-cultural study of sex roles and has written one book on the topic, Women and Men: An Anthropologist's View. *Friedl now accounts for her own success in part by the fact that she attended an all-women's college and taught for many years at the City University of New York, a university system that included a women's college.*

"Women must respond quickly to the demands of their husbands," says anthropologist Napoleon Chagnon describing the horticultural Yanomamo Indians of Venezuela. When a man returns from a hunting trip, "the woman, no matter what she is doing, hurries home and quietly but rapidly prepares a meal for her husband. Should the wife be slow in doing this, the husband is within his rights to beat her. Most reprimands...take the form of blows with the hand or with a piece of firewood. . . .Some of them chop their wives with the sharp edge of a machete or axe, or shoot them with a barbed arrow in some nonvital area, such as the buttocks or leg."

Among the Semai agriculturalists of central Malaya, when one person refuses the request of another, the offended party suffers *punan,* a mixture of emotional pain and frustration. "Enduring *punan* is commonest when a girl has refused the victim her sexual favors," reports Robert Dentan. "The jilted man's 'heart becomes sad.' He loses his energy and his appetite. Much of the time he sleeps, dreaming of his lost love. In this state, he is in fact very likely to injure himself 'accidentally.' " The Semai are afraid of violence; a man would never strike a woman.

The social relationship between men and women has emerged as one of the principal disputes occupying the attention of scholars and the public in recent years. Athough the dis-cord is sharpest in the United States, the controversy has spread throughout the world. Numerous national and international conferences, including one in Mexico sponsored by the United Nations, have drawn together delegates from all walks of life to discuss such questions as the social and political rights of each sex, and even the basic nature of males and females.

Whatever their position, partisans often invoke examples from other cultures to support their ideas about the proper role of each sex. Because women are clearly subservient to men in many societies, like the Yanomamo, some experts conclude that the natural pattern is for men to dominate. But among the Semai no one has the right to command others, and in West Africa women are often chiefs. The place of women in these societies supports the argument of those who believe that sex roles are not fixed, that if there is a natural order, it allows for many different arrangements.

The argument will never be settled as long as the opposing sides toss examples from the world's cultures at each other like intellectual stones. But the effect of biological differences on male and female behavior can be clarified by looking at known examples of the earliest forms of human society and examining the relationship between technology, social organization, environment, and sex roles. The problem is to determine the conditions in which different degrees of male dominance are found, to try to discover the social and cultural arrangements that give rise to equality or inequality between the sexes, and to attempt to apply this knowledge to our understanding of the changes taking place in modern industrial society.

As Western history and the anthropological record have told us, equality between the sexes is rare; in most known societies females are subordinate. Male dominance is so widespread that it is virtually a human universal; societies in which women are consistently dominant do not exist and have never existed.

Evidence of a society in which women control all strategic resources like food and water, and in which women's activities are the most prestigious has never been found. The Iroquois of North America and the Lovedu of Africa came closest. Among the Iroquois, women raised food, controlled its distribution, and helped to choose male political leaders. Lovedu women ruled as queens, exchanged valuable cattle, led ceremonies, and controlled their own sex lives. But among both the Iroquois and the Lovedu, men owned the land and held other positions of power and prestige. Women were equal to men; they did not have ultimate authority over them. Neither culture was a true matriarchy.

Patriarchies are prevalent, and they appear to be strongest in societies in which men control significant goods that are exchanged with people outside the family. Regardless of who produces food, the person who gives it to others creates the obligations and alliances that are at the center of all political relations. The greater the male monopoly on the distribution of scarce items, the stronger their control of women seems to be. This is most obvious in relatively simple hunter-gatherer societies.

Hunter-gatherers, or foragers, subsist on wild plants, small land animals, and small river or sea creatures gathered by hand; large land animals and sea mammals hunted

with spears, bows and arrows, and blow guns; and fish caught with hooks and nets. The 300,000 hunter-gatherers alive in the world today include the Eskimos, the Australian aborigines, and the Pygmies of Central Africa.

Foraging has endured for two million years and was replaced by farming and animal husbandry only 10,000 years ago; it covers more than 99 percent of human history. Our foraging ancestry is not far behind us and provides a clue to our understanding of the human condition.

Hunter-gatherers are people whose ways of life are technologically simple and socially and politically egalitarian. They live in small groups of 50 to 200 and have neither kings, nor priests, nor social classes. These conditions permit anthropologists to observe the essential bases for inequalities between the sexes without the distortions induced by the complexities of contemporary industrial society.

The source of male power among hunter-gatherers lies in their control of a scarce, hard to acquire, but necessary nutrient—animal protein. When men in a hunter-gatherer society return to camp with game, they divide the meat in some customary way. Among the !Kung San of Africa, certain parts of the animal are given to the owner of the arrow that killed the beast, to the first hunter to sight the game, to the one who threw the first spear and to all men in the hunting party. After the meat has been divided, each hunter distributes his share to his blood relatives and his in-laws, who in turn share it with others. If an animal is large enough, every member of the band will receive some meat.

Vegetable foods, in contrast, are not distributed beyond the immediate household. Women give food to their children, to their husbands, to other members of the household, and rarely, to the occasional visitor. No one outside the family regularly eats any of the wild fruits and vegetables that are gathered by the women.

The meat distributed by the men is a public gift. Its source is widely

known, and the do ciprocal gift when from a successful honor as a supplie and simultaneousl to him.

These obligations constitute a form of power or control over others, both men and women. The opinions of hunters play an important part in decisions to move the village; good hunters attract the most desirable women; people in other groups join camps with good hunters; and hunters, because they already participate in an internal system of exchange, control exchange with other groups for flint, salt, and steel axes. The male monopoly on hunting unites men in a system of exchange and gives them power; gathering vegetable food does not give women equal power even among foragers who live in the tropics, where the food collected by women provides more than half the hunter-gatherer diet.

If dominance arises from a monopoly on big-game hunting, why has the male monopoly remained unchallenged? Some women are strong enough to participate in the hunt and their endurance is certainly equal to that of men. Dobe San women of the Kalahari Desert in Africa walk an average of 10 miles a day carrying from 15 to 33 pounds of food plus a baby.

Women do not hunt, I believe, because of four interrelated factors: variability in the supply of game; the different skills required for hunting and gathering; the incompatibility between carrying burdens and hunting; and the small size of semi-nomadic foraging populations.

Because the meat supply is unstable, foragers must make frequent expeditions to provide the band with gathered food. Environmental factors such as seasonal and annual variation in rainful often affect the size of the wildlife population. Hunters cannot always find game, and when they do encounter animals, they are not always successful in killing their prey. In northern latitudes, where meat is the primary food, periods of starvation are known in every

...eration. The irregularity of the game supply leads hunter-gatherers in areas where plant foods are available to depend on these predictable foods a good part of the time. Someone must gather the fruits, nuts, and roots and carry them back to camp to feed unsuccessful hunters, children, the elderly, and anyone who might not have gone foraging that day.

Foraging falls to the women because hunting and gathering cannot be combined on the same expedition. Although gatherers sometimes notice signs of game as they work, the skills required to track game are not the same as those required to find edible roots or plants. Hunters scan the horizon and the land for traces of large game; gatherers keep their eyes to the ground, studying the distribution of plants and the texture of the soil for hidden roots and animal holes. Even if a woman who was collecting plants came across the track of an antelope, she could not follow it; it is impossible to carry a load and hunt at the same time. Running with a heavy load is difficult, and should the animal be sighted, the hunter would be off balance and could neither shoot an arrow nor throw a spear accurately.

Pregnancy and child care would also present difficulties for a hunter. An unborn child affects a woman's body balance, as does a child in her arms, on her back, or slung at her side. Until they are two years old, many hunter-gatherer children are carried at all times, and until they are four, they are carried some of the time.

An observer might wonder why young women do not hunt until they become pregnant, or why mature women and men do not hunt and gather on alternate days, with some women staying in camp to act as wet nurses for the young. Apart from the effects hunting might have on a mother's milk production, there are two reasons. First, young girls begin to bear children as soon as they are physically mature and strong enough to hunt, and second, hunter-gatherer bands are so small that there are unlikely to be enough lactating women to serve as wet nurses. No hunter-gatherer group could afford to maintain a specialized female hunting force.

Because game is not always available, because hunting and gathering are specialized skills, because women carrying heavy loads cannot hunt, and because women in hunter-gatherer societies are usually either pregnant or caring for young children, for most of the last two million years of human history men have hunted and women have gathered.

If male dominance depends on controlling the supply of meat, then the degree of male dominance in a society should vary with the amount of meat available and the amount supplied by the men. Some regions, like the East African grasslands and the North American woodlands, abounded with species of large mammals; other zones, like tropical forests and semi-deserts, are thinly populated with prey. Many elements affect the supply of game, but theoretically, the less meat provided exclusively by the men, the more egalitarian the society.

All known hunter-gatherer societies fit into four basic types; those in which men and women work together in communal hunts and as teams gathering edible plants, as did the Washo Indians of North America; those in which men and women each collect their own plant foods although the men supply some meat to the group, as do the Hadza of Tanzania; those in which male hunters and female gatherers work apart but return to camp each evening to share their acquisitions, as do the Tiwi of North Australia; and those in which the men provide all the food by hunting large game, as do the Eskimo. In each case the extent of male dominance increases directly with the proportion of meat supplied by individual men and small hunting parties.

Among the most egalitarian of hunter-gatherer societies are the Washo Indians, who inhabited the valleys of the Sierra Nevada in what is now southern California and Nevada. In the spring they moved north to Lake Tahoe for the large fish runs of sucker and native trout. Everyone—men, women, and children—participated in the fishing. Women spent the summer gathering edible berries and seeds while the men continued to fish. In the fall some men hunted deer but the most important source of animal protein was the jack rabbit, which was captured in communal hunts. Men and women together drove the rabbits into nets tied end to end. To provide food for the winter, husbands and wives worked as teams in the late fall to collect pine nuts.

Since everyone participated in most food-gathering activities, there were no individual distributors of food and relatively little difference in male and female rights. Men and women were not segregated from each other in daily activities; both were free to take lovers after marriage; both had the right to separate whenever they chose; menstruating women were not isolated from the rest of the group; and one of the two major Washo rituals celebrated hunting while the other celebrated gathering. Men were accorded more prestige if they had killed a deer, and men directed decisions about the seasonal movement of the group. But if no male leader stepped forward, women were permitted to lead. The distinctive feature of groups such as the Washo is the relative equality of the sexes.

The sexes are also relatively equal among the Hadza of Tanzania but this near-equality arises because men and women tend to work alone to feed themselves. They exchange little food. The Hadza lead a leisurely life in the seemingly barren environment of the East African Rift Gorge that is, in fact, rich in edible berries, roots, and small game. As a result of this abundance, from the time they are 10 years old, Hadza men and women gather much of their own food. Women take their young children with them into the bush, eating as they forage, and collect only enough food for a light family meal in the evening. The men eat berries and roots as they hunt for small game, and should they bring down a rabbit or a hyrax, they eat the meat on the spot. Meat is

In the maritime Inuit (Eskimo) societies, inequality between the sexes is matched by the ability to supply food for the group. The men hunt for meat and control the economy. Women perform all the other duties that support life in the community, and are virtually treated as objects. (Photo credit: American Museum of Natural History—Dr. F. Rainey)

carried back to the camp and shared with the rest of the group only on those rare occasions when a poisoned arrow brings down a large animal—an impala, a zebra, an eland, or a giraffe.

Because Hadza men distribute little meat, their status is only slightly higher than that of the women. People flock to the camp of a good hunter and the camp might take on his name because of his popularity, but he is in no sense a leader of the group. A Hadza man and a woman have an equal right to divorce and each can repudiate a marriage simply by living apart for a few weeks. Couples tend to live in the same camp as the wife's mother but they sometimes make long visits to the camp of the husband's mother. Although a man may take more than one wife, most Hadza males cannot afford to

indulge in this luxury. In order to maintain a marriage, a man must supply both his wife and his mother-in-law with some meat and trade goods, such as beads and cloth, and the Hadza economy gives few men the wealth to provide for more than one wife and mother-in-law. Washo equality is based on cooperation; Hadza equality is based on independence.

In contrast to both these groups, among the Tiwi of Melville and Bathurst Islands off the northern coast of Australia, male hunters dominate female gatherers. The Tiwi are representative of the most common form of foraging society, in which the men supply large quantities of meat, although less than half the food consumed by the group. Each morning Tiwi women, most with babies on

their backs, scatter in different directions in search of vegetables, grubs, worms, and small game such as bandicoots, lizards, and opossums. To track the game, they use hunting dogs. On most days women return to camp with some meat and with baskets full of *korka*, the nut of a native palm, which is soaked and mashed to make a porridge-like dish. The Tiwi men do not hunt small game and do not hunt every day, but when they do they often return with kangaroo, large lizards, fish, and game birds.

The porridge is cooked separately by each household and rarely shared outside the family, but the meat is prepared by a volunteer cook, who can be male or female. After the cook takes one of the parts of the animal traditionally reserved for him or her, the animal's "boss," the one who caught it, distributes the rest to all near kin and then to all others residing with the band. Although the small game supplied by the women is distributed in the same way as the big game supplied by the men, Tiwi men are dominant because the game they kill provides most of the meat.

The power of the Tiwi men is clearest in their betrothal practices. Among the Tiwi, a woman must always be married. To ensure this, female infants are betrothed at birth and widows are remarried at the gravesides of their late husbands. Men form alliances by exchanging daughters, sisters, and mothers in marriage and some collect as many as 25 wives. Tiwi men value the quantity and quality of the food many wives can collect and the many children they can produce.

The dominance of the men is offset somewhat by the influence of adult women in selecting their next husbands. Many women are active strategists in the political careers of their male relatives, but to the exasperation of some sons attempting to promote their own futures, widowed mothers sometimes insist on selecting their own partners. Women also influence the marriages of their daughters and granddaughters, especially when the selected husband dies before the bestowed child moves to his camp.

Among the Eskimo, representative of the rarest type of forager society, inequality between the sexes is matched by inequality in supplying the group with food. Inland Eskimo men hunt caribou throughout the year to provision the entire society, and maritime Eskimo men depend on whaling, fishing, and some hunting to feed their extended families. The women process the carcasses, cut and sew skins to make clothing, cook, and care for the young; but they collect no food of their own and depend on the men to supply all the raw materials for their work. Since men provide all the meat, they also control the trade in hides, whale oil, seal oil, and other items that move between the maritime and inland Eskimos.

Eskimo women are treated almost exclusively as objects to be used, abused, and traded by men. After puberty all Eskimo girls are fair game for any interested male. A man shows his intentions by grabbing the belt of a woman and if she protests, he cuts off her trousers and forces himself upon her. These encounters are considered unimportant by the rest of the group. Men offer their wives' sexual services to establish alliances with trading partners and members of hunting and whaling parties.

Despite the consistent pattern of some degree of male dominance among foragers, most of these societies are egalitarian compared with agricultural and industrial societies. No forager has any significant opportunity for political leadership. Foragers, as a rule, do not like to give or take orders, and assume leadership only with reluctance. Shamans (those who are thought to be possessed by spirits) may be either male or female. Public rituals conducted by women in order to celebrate the first menstruation of girls are common, and the symbolism in these rituals is similar to that in the ceremonies that follow a boy's first kill.

In any society, status goes to those who control the distribution of valued goods and services outside the family. Equality arises when both sexes work side by side in food production, as do the Washo, and the products are simply distributed among the workers. In such circumstances, no person or sex has greater access to valued items than do others. But when women make no contribution to the food supply, as in the case of the Eskimo, they are completely subordinate.

When we attempt to apply these generalizations to contemporary industrial society, we can predict that as long as women spend their discretionary income from jobs on domestic needs, they will gain little social recognition and power. To be an effective source of power, money must be exchanged in ways that require returns and create obligations. In other words, it must be invested.

Jobs that do not give women control over valued resources will do little to advance their general status. Only as managers, executives, and professionals are women in a position to trade goods and services, to do others favors, and therefore to obligate others to them. Only as controllers of valued resources can women achieve prestige, power, and equality.

Within the household, women who bring in income from jobs are able to function on a more nearly equal basis with their husbands. Women who contribute services to their husbands and children without pay, as do some middle-class Western housewives, are especially vulnerable to dominance. Like Eskimo women, as long as their services are limited to domestic distribution they have little power relative to their husbands and none with respect to the outside world.

As for the limits imposed on women by their procreative functions in hunter-gatherer societies, childbearing and child care are organized around work as much as work is organized around reproduction. Some foraging groups space their children three to four years apart and have an average of only four to six children, far fewer than many women in other cultures. Hunter-gatherers nurse their infants for extended periods, sometimes for as long as four years. This custom suppresses ovulation and limits the size of their families. Sometimes, although rarely, they practice infanticide. By limiting reproduction, a woman who is gathering food has only one child to carry.

Different societies can and do adjust the frequency of birth and the care of children to accommodate whatever productive activities women customarily engage in. In horticultural societies, where women work long hours in gardens that may be far from home, infants get food to supplement their mothers' milk, older children take care of younger children, and pregnancies are widely spaced. Throughout the world, if a society requires a woman's labor, it finds ways to care for her children.

In the United States, as in some other industrial societies, the accelerated entry of women with preschool children into the labor force has resulted in the development of a variety of child-care arrangements. Individual women have called on friends, relatives, and neighbors. Public and private child-care centers are growing. We should realize that the declining birth rate, the increasing acceptance of childless or single-child families, and a de-emphasis on motherhood are adaptations to a sexual division of labor reminiscent of the system of production found in hunter-gatherer societies.

In many countries where women no longer devote most of their productive years to childbearing, they are beginning to demand a change in the social relationship of the sexes. As women gain access to positions that control the exchange of resources, male dominance may become archaic, and industrial societies may one day become as egalitarian as the Washo.

REFERENCES

Friedl, Ernestine, *Women and Men: An Anthropologist's View,* Holt, Rinehart and Winston, 1975.

Martin, M. Kay, and Barbara Voorhies, eds., *Female of the Species,* Columbia University Press, 1977.

Murphy, Yolanda, and Robert Murphy, *Women of the Forest,* Columbia University Press, 1974.

Reiter, Rayna, ed., *Toward an Anthropology of Women,* Monthly Review Press, 1975.

Rosaldo, M.Z., and Louise Lamphere, eds., *Women, Culture, and Society,* Stanford University Press, 1974.

Schlegel, Alice, ed., *Sexual Stratification; A Cross-Cultural View,* Columbia University Press, 1977.

Strathern, Marilyn, *Women in Between: Female Roles in a Male World,* Academic Press, 1972.

A Matter of Honor

Bedouin cultural codes and sense of honor persist despite the passing of the people's nomadic life-style

Longina Jakubowska

Longina Jakubowska teaches anthropology at the University of the Pacific in Stockton, California.

The world modernizes: Technology and consumerism spreads: a nomad hauls his herd in a truck; television antennas stick through tent roofs; a Walkman covers the ears of a shepherd. And today, no one is surprised. The Bedouin—pastoral Arab nomads who have roamed the deserts for centuries—hardly exist as such anymore. Most live in cities today.

The word *Bedouin* is derived from the Arabic *bada'* (desert). The Bedouin derived their livelihood from herding animals—camels, goats, sheep. Their life-style was a direct adaptation to the desert ecology; their movements and activities determined by the needs of their animals. Scarce reserves of underground water and sparse, unpredictable rainfall obliged movement over a large territory to ensure that herds had enough pasture and consequently people enough food. Nomads rarely consumed meat, considered a luxury, since doing so would deplete their capital. They mostly lived off animal byproducts (predominantly, processed milk), as well as dried fruits, dates, and some grains. There was a time when most of their needs were fulfilled by animal products— tents were woven from camel and goat wool, and gear was made from leather.

Given the limited resources of the desert, the nomads faced the constant challenge of maintaining a precarious balance between water supplies, pasture, and animal populations. Depletion of either meant demise. The land was sparsely populated and the lonely black tents of small Bedouin groups dotted the desert. Space and freedom of movement were essential to the nomadic existence, but the Bedouin nomads did not wander aimlessly; their movements were calculated, conducted seasonally, and limited to a territory they claimed as their ancestral tribal land. Territorial rights were closely guarded; infringements could, and frequently did, result in extended disputes or even an occasional war.

Fiercely independent, the Bedouin avoided involvement in the wars of others, even those conflicts that affected their own region. They remained disinterested in the politics of the entities surrounding them, until the middle of this century when the Bedouin became absorbed or encapsulated by the state structures. The process of settling the nomads in more permanent locations was strongly encouraged by all state governments in the Middle East and is now well under way. Nomadism is perceived as incompatible with modernity, and the nomads are also considered difficult to control. Yet the traditional Bedouin life-style still lingers in some areas, usually those which the state considers marginal.

"Settling-down" involves more than simply moving into houses. It necessitates a total restructuring of the society to be settled and a redefining of the sense of identity—which for the Bedouin is closely linked with the notion of honor.

The contrast between the Bedouin past and the present is striking. The change occurred rapidly, in less than one generation. Encased in the trappings of modernity, technological gadgets, and Western clothing, the Bedouin present a very different image today from that of the past. Most have moved to towns and adjusted to the market economy. They hold salaried jobs, work in construction, operate agricultural machines, and drive trucks. There is, however, continuity in their attitude toward employment. They prefer independence, the ability to set their own time schedule, and they frequently operate family businesses. Occasionally, forgetting the hardships of nomadic life, they reminisce nostalgically about when the Bedouin worried only about the rainfall and pasture, and tell stories to their children about the challenge and glory of *hel* (camel racing).

Contrary to expectations, settling-down has not greatly improved the quality of life for either Bedouin men or women. If anything, their behavior has become even more circumspect, and female honor is guarded even

The honor and authority of the father is central to Bedouin family and society.

also feared for their unequivocal honor code which does not allow for mistakes.

THE CONSEQUENCE OF AN ELOPEMENT

Changes in material culture and in the externals of life-style can be misleading: The beliefs and value systems taught to the generation of Bedouin born and brought up in the sedentary modern environment remain those of the nomadic tradition. The trial described below occurred a few years ago in southern Israel, but it could have happened in any other country in the Middle East, for the issues involved are of vital importance to the Bedouin cultural ethos. Despite the numerous changes that many of these societies experienced, the notion of honor has been altered little.

The trial took place early on a spring morning. The rains had stopped and the arid hills were, at least temporarily, green again. The busy morning activities in the small encampment of Sheikh Abu Rashid had subsided. Everything indicated that something unusual was about to happen. A long black tent, many times the size of the domestic tents that some of the Bedouin present remembered living in, had been erected. Firewood had been gathered in piles, animals stood nearby—unknowingly waiting to be slaughtered, and the rhythmic sounds of coffee mills could be heard. Everyone present awaited the arrival of the guests. The preparations that were under way in the camp (which consisted of tin shacks and wooden plank huts) were similar to those for a wedding, yet the joy of wedding preparations, usually marked by the shrilled ululations of women rejoicing because their sons were soon to become men, was missing.

There was another significant difference. Although Sheikh Abu Rashid was giving the last directions to his male and female kinfolk about the placement of the mattresses and pillows in the grand tent for the visitors to recline on, none of the implements—the tent, the firewood, the animals, nor the numerous other supplies including

closer. Compared with the sparsely populated desert, Bedouin towns are crowded, which greatly increases social interaction and potential sources of conflict. To maintain the code of modesty, women are forced to remain either inside their houses or to veil heavily, in a manner similar to peasant women. Since men are absent from the village most of the day, and since the behavior of women forms an intricate part of the honor code, there is even greater social control imposed on women. Furthermore, due to present patterns of employment, women are now completely excluded from involvement in the process of production, which diminishes their participation in decision-making and consequently harms their position in society.

So far the Bedouin exhibit considerable resiliency and cultural continuity. They remain the unquestionable ideal of the Arab ethos—honorable, pure, brave, independent, hospitable, and honest. It is widely believed that the Bedouin dialect is the untainted version of Arabic, the language in which the Prophet Muhammad spoke. Although highly praised, the Bedouin are tea and coffee and even the mattresses, belonged to him. All were brought by the men who were to be tried, the family of Ataywah. A Bedouin court, or *manshed*, was about to be convened.

In a distant hut, surrounded by the sheikh's female relatives, a young girl called Azizah was anxiously awaiting the events of the day. Some weeks ago she and her boyfriend had run away to the Negev desert hoping their families would agree to their marriage. It occasionally would happen; elopements were rare but legitimate means of eliciting consent to marriage. According to tradition, marriage unions were arranged by the respective families of groom and bride, as marriage is not a matter for the individual but the family to decide. There were concerns about access to wells and pastures, previous marriage arrangements to finalize, and weakened ties that needed strengthening; in short, alliances to be made. In the absence of other forms of social integration, kinship and marriage serve as the primary means of political and social action. Women link families together. This link, however, is highly vulnerable, and women are placed under a constant cloud of suspicion regarding their loyalty (or suspected disloyalty) to either their paternal or husband's families.

Azizah did not rebel against the norms underpinning the Bedouin institutions, but rather against a particular choice of husband her father had made on her behalf. She miscalculated, however, the degree of his involvement in the marriage negotiations and the extent of his commitment. Once the agreement was made it became a matter of honor to keep it.

Whatever credits or discredits a woman earns reflect back on her paternal family. An unruly daughter can damage family reputation. Public disclosure of the inability to exert control over one's women is disgraceful. Fathers are aware of the inherent power in command of women and frequently mediate between daughters' preferences and their own goals. In this case, however, marriage to a man chosen by the daughter, a man from the Ataywah, was incongruent with the father's family politics. Public opinion is a double-edged sword. Mustering public sympathy could have turned events to Azizah's advantage, but it would also have exposed her father's honor. The only means of saving his and the family's face was to bring a legal case against the family of the offender, the young man she eloped with.

THE IMPORTANCE OF THE CODES OF HONOR

In the Bedouin social framework, an individual's actions reflect on his paternal kin. Family, which includes generations and can reach hundreds of members, is the strongest unit of identification. The farther the distance between kin, the "weaker the blood" between them, the lesser are the responsibilities toward one another and the accountability for each other's behavior. This system of organization, called the segmentary lineage system in anthropological literature, is best illustrated by the Bedouin proverb:

Me against my brother
My brother and I against my cousin,
My cousin and I against a stranger.

Family lineage, called *hamula*, places a person in the social structure, gives identity, and offers protection and security. It circumscribes, however, freedom of individual action and imposes obligations and strict rules of behavior. The price of misconduct on the part of an individual is paid by the group.

The behavior of the young man was irresponsible and implicated his hamula. The verdict of guilt was already pronounced and the result of the trial known beforehand. His family had few excuses to make on his behalf and had to carry the burden of the trial—including its costs—and reparations to the girl's family. The financial as well as social losses were considerable and would take years to repay. There were no possibilities of appeal—to maintain their respectability the family had to act in a socially prescribed responsible fashion. Serious transgressions of norms and recidivist behavior, which threaten the economic well-being and the social standing of the family, could result in the offender's expulsion from the larger group. This grave consequence served as the final safeguard for the family. It had happened only a few times in the living memory of the Bedouin present. Such an outcast, expelled from under the protective umbrella of the hamula, becomes a person without roots or identity; without kin, he loses his social existence. The Bedouin apply a very revealing term to such a person, *enshamma*, meaning literally and metaphorically "the one under the sun."

One may wonder why, knowing the serious potential repercussions, the young man risked public condemnation. The possibility of public exposure and confrontation at the beginning of the affair was rather small, and he had made every effort to avoid it. However, the girl's father was so unrelenting that the couple had sought refuge with the well-respected Sheikh Abu Rashid, leader of a powerful tribe, relying on his reputation in the Negev to mediate a noncontroversial settlement in the dispute.

On the surface, the issue concerned arranging a marriage. Using an important personality as a broker was common in such negotiations. However, this was no longer only a question of marriage; the problem now addressed a principle of honor. The girl's father had refused to grant his permission to the marriage both before and after the elopement and demanded restitution of his honor, insulted by an unlawful act of taking his daughter against his wishes. Since the offensive act, the elopement, was a public statement, so had to be the admission of guilt. The guilty party had to show humility and restore the honor of the offended.

Honor is the basis of the moral code of an individual in Bedouin society. It is inherently personal, but as the individual constitutes an integral part of the kinship group, his honor extends to the kin. Honor is obtained not by performing unusual acts but by the ability to live according to the ideal. Honor is maintained through a series of challenges and ripostes; success garnishes respect; failure to react entails disgrace. Even blood can be spilled in

Women's roles are closely defined, and their behavior, which can bestow honor or dishonor upon one's family, is under constant scrutiny.

defense of honor. "Blood can be washed only by blood," the Bedouin say. A wounding or killing is a stain on the family honor; restitution can be accomplished only through a similar retaliatory act.

Blood feuds are spectacular examples of the honor code binding Bedouin kin groups. Although they occur rarely in the extreme, they command attention, appeal to the imagination, and linger in Bedouin memories. Events that occurred in a distant past are handed down to each generation. The Bedouin culture always emphasized the oral tradition; skillful storytellers once held great respect. Historical time was changed; events of hundreds of years ago appeared as yesterday's happenings. Stories of blood feuds, of warriors fighting inadvertent circumstances told at the evening fires become relevant to the present. They form the integral part of the Bedouin ethos, the code of honor.

Sheikh Abu Rashid had little choice

when the eloping couple approached him. He was expected to offer hospitality, protection, and to mediate in the dispute. Refusal would endanger his reputation. Heredity does not guarantee leadership among the Bedouin. So although Sheikh Abu Rashid came from a long line of tribal chiefs, he had to earn his title—by demonstrating charisma, powers of persuasion, and by gaining fame for his wisdom.

Hospitality among the Bedouin is proverbial. It also is the rule of the desert. Bound by ecological constraints and the frequent shortage of resources, the nomads customarily extend help to those in need. Visitors are fed, given shelter, and even clothing if necessary. Bedouin glorify hospitality. One is obliged by it even at the risk of starvation. Every Bedouin child can recall a tale that recounts the suffering of an impoverished nomad who, although his very life depended on it, slaughtered the last camel to feed the unsuspecting but

hungry guest. For his sacrifice he was held in the highest esteem. Furthermore, guests receive immunity and protection from their hosts. Hospitality is a sacred duty. Even one's enemies are granted this privilege and are entitled to safety of passage. Any attack on the guest would be perceived as an affront to the host.

It was common for eloped couples to seek refuge from their families at the powerful Bedouin houses. When Azizah and her young man arrived in the encampment of Sheikh Abu Rashid they were promptly separated from each other and housed in different places. Sheikh Abu Rashid could not afford, for his own sake, the reputation of his kin, and the proceedings of the case, to be placed under the slightest suspicion of fostering improper sexual behavior. He breathed easier upon learning that the girl's virginity was intact. Had the couple been involved

The "advantages" of modern life are affecting the core values of Bedouin society and could introduce an unprecedented separation between the generations.

sexually, the matter would have been even more grave.

The honor of Bedouin men is dependent upon the sexual conduct of women in their family. Male kin are required to protect female virtue. While male honor is flexible—depending on the man's behavior, it can be acquired, diminished, lost, or regained—female honor is rigid. A sexual offense on the part of a woman causes her honor to be lost, and it cannot be restored. Thus the core of male honor is the protection of one's female relatives' honor. According to the Bedouin ethical code, a transgression of sexual norms is a crime that may result in capital punishment.

Azizah's father pressed for court proceedings. *Manshed,* the highest Bedouin court, is convened extremely rarely, once in a few years or even a decade. Usually every effort is made not to escalate the conflict so that it can be resolved on a much smaller scale at lower levels of Bedouin social structure. Manshed deals with the most serious matters and achieves the greatest exposure, which was why the girl's father insisted on its taking place. As

one Bedouin said when addressing the sources of conflict in Bedouin society, Bedouin fight either over land or over women, and both concern honor.

THE TRIAL

Attendance at the manshed was enormous—over a hundred people arrived. As each visitor entered the tent, ceremonial greetings were exchanged and tea served. There were no women in sight, and adolescent boys quietly and busily attended to all the guests. The court was open to all men. Only the assailants' party, the family of Ataywah, was conspicuously missing. It was represented by Sheikh Abu Rashid. There was no set hour for the beginning of the proceedings, which began when all the important participants were present, notably the famous sheikhs of the area and authorities on Bedouin law. There was no set procedure either. All could voice their opinions. Knowledge and oratory skills prevailed in reaching the decision, which took until the late afternoon. The discussion of the case was inter-

twined with chatting about recent political events, questions about each other's families. It was interrupted by people taking leave for noon prayers and greeting those who were still arriving.

When a sense of consensus was reached, a tentative verdict was announced, the hearing of which could make an inexperienced observer shudder. The man's tongue was to be cut, for he talked to the girl; his hands were to be cut, for he touched her; his legs were to be cut, for he walked with her. Then a prolonged and heated bargaining started. It soon became clear that nobody had any intention of mutilating the culprit's body; the verdict was an expression of the severe nature of the crime committed. Instead the punishment was translated into monetary measures. The bargaining had all the makings of a ritual. There was more to follow. For every mile the man traveled with the girl, he was also to pay. All came to an enormous sum of 100 million lira, approximately $500,000. It was lowered considerably during further bargaining: in honor of the prophet Muhammad, on behalf of the people present and the costs of tea and coffee consumed by them, which they would have refused to drink otherwise.

A stream of new guests arrived in the afternoon. They came late intentionally, announced their names aloud, and refused to drink the customary cup of tea unless an additional sum of money was forgone. Only one representative of a hamula was allowed to make an appeal. The amount withdrawn from the one penalty depended on the respect commanded by his family. The family of the offender, although not present at the proceedings, kept a close watch over its developments. Through sending messengers and calling upon their allies, people were lobbied to make a plea on behalf of the Ataywah.

By the evening the sum was lowered to $100,000, but the bargaining did not cease yet. Dinner followed and this called for further negotiations. Meanwhile an elaborate meal was served,

for which fifteen sheep were slaughtered, but the guests refused to eat until the punishment was revised again.

It was late at night when the sheikhs pronounced their final verdict. Azizah was to come back to her family. The young man was found guilty of kidnapping, for such was the preferred interpretation of the affair, and had to pay 15 million lira ($75,000) to the girl's family. Also the family's car in which they eloped had to be returned to them. Sheikh Abu Rashid and two other prominent figures agreed to oversee the fulfillment of the sentence.

The punishment was severe. The young man, employed as a construction worker at the time, did not have the means to pay the penalty himself. The elopement proved to be a costly affair. The cost of materials and food supplied for the trial, together with the monetary amount of compensation, exceeded his probable lifetime earnings. These expenses were divided equally among his hamula, the members of

which from now on were obliged to commit their meager resources to paying the family debt, the debt of honor. The social costs were even greater. His family had to call upon old alliances and political favors, reserved for a time of crisis.

The girl returned to her father's household. Her future looked bleak. After causing so much discord, it was unlikely that she would still be welcomed as a match for the marriage her father arranged for her. Most probably Azizah would be married as a second wife, or else wedded to an elderly widower (which is certainly not regarded as the best option).

ADDITIONAL READING

Lila Abu-Lughod, *Veiled Sentiments: Honor & Poetry in a Bedouin Society*, University of California Press, 1986.

P. C. Dodd, "Family Honor & the Forces of Change in Arab Society," *International Journal of Middle East Studies*, 4 (1973): 40–54.

Emanuel Marx and Avshalom Shmueli, eds., *The Changing Bedouin*, Transaction Books, 1986.

The Global War Against Women

Lori Heise

Lori Heise is a senior researcher at the Worldwatch Institute. She prepared a recent report on this subject for World Watch *magazine.*

Violence against women—including assault, mutilation, murder, infanticide, rape and cruel neglect—is perhaps the most pervasive yet least recognized human-rights issue in the world. It is also a profound health problem sapping women's physical and emotional vitality and undermining their confidence—both vital to achieving widely held goals for human progress, especially in the Third World.

Despite its invisibility, the dimensions of the problem are vast. In Bangkok, Thailand, a reported 50 percent of married women are beaten regularly by their husbands. In the barrios of Quito, Ecuador, 80 percent of women are said to have been physically abused. And in Nicaragua, 44 percent of men admit to beating their wives or girlfriends. Equally shocking statistics can be found in the industrial world.

Then there are the less recognized forms of violence. In Nepal, female babies die from neglect because parents value sons over daughters; in Sudan, girls' genitals are mutilated to ensure virginity until marriage; and in India, young brides are murdered by their husbands when parents fail to provide enough dowry.

In all these instances, women are targets of violence because of their sex. This is not random violence. The risk factor is being female.

Most of these abuses have been reported in one or another country, at one or another time. But is only when you begin to amass statistics and reports from international organizations and countries around the world that the horrifying dimensions of this global war on women come into focus. For me the revelation came only recently after talking with scores of village women throughout the world.

I never intended to investigate violence; I was researching maternal and child health issues overseas. But I would commonly begin my interviews with a simple question: What is your biggest problem? With unnerving frequency, the answer came back: "My husband beats me."

These are women who daily have to walk four hours to gather enough wood for the evening meal, whose children commonly die of treatable illnesses, whose security can be wiped out with one failed rain. Yet when defining their own concerns, they see violence as their greatest dilemma. Those dedicated to helping Third World women would do well to listen.

More than simply a "women's issue," violence could thwart other widely held goals for human progress in the Third World. Study after study has shown that maternal education is the single most effective way to reduce child mortality—not because it imparts new knowledge or skills related to health, but because it erodes fatalism, improves self-confidence and changes the power balance within the family.

In effect, these studies say that women's sense of self is critical to reducing infant mortality. Yet acts of violence and society's tacit acceptance of them stand as constant reminders to women of their low worth. Where women's status is critical to achieving a development goal—such as controlling fertility and improving child survival—violence will remain a powerful obstacle to progress.

Measured by its human costs alone, female-focused violence is worthy of international attention and action. But it has seldom been raised at that level, much less addressed. Millions of dollars are spent each year to protect the human rights of fetuses. It is time to stand up for the human rights of women.

The Indian subcontinent is home to one of the most pernicious forms of wife abuse, known locally as "bride-burning" or "dowry deaths." Decades ago dowry referred to the gifts that a woman received from her parents upon marriage. Now dowry has become an important part of premarital negotiations and refers to the wealth that the bride's parents must pay the groom as part of the marriage settlement.

Once a gesture of love, ever-escalating dowry now represents a real financial burden to the parents of unwed daughters. Increasingly, dowry is being seen as a "get rich quick" scheme by prospective husbands, with young brides suffering severe abuse if promised money or goods do not materialize. In its most severe form, dowry harassment ends in suicide or murder, freeing the husband to pursue a more lucrative arrangement.

Dowry deaths are notoriously undercounted, largely because the husband and his relatives frequently try to disguise the murder as a suicide or an accident and the police are loathe to get involved. A frequent scam is to set the women alight with kerosene, and then claim she died in a kitchen accident—hence the term "bride-burning." In 1987 the police official recorded 1,786 dowry deaths in all of India, but the Ahmedabad Women's Action Group estimates that 1,000 women may have been burned alive that year in Gujurat State alone.

A quick look at mortality data from India reveals the reasonableness of this claim. In both urban Maharashtra and greater Bombay, 19 percent of all deaths among women 15 to 44 years old are due to "accidental burns." In other Third World countries, such as Guatemala, Ecuador and Chile, the same statistic is less [than] 1 percent.

Elsewhere in the world, the marriage transaction is reversed, with prospective husbands paying "bridewealth" to secure a woman's hand in marriage. In many cultures—especially in Africa—the exchange has become so commercialized that inflated bridewealth leaves the man with the distinct impression that he has "purchased" his wife.

The notion that bridewealth confers ownership was clearly depicted during recent parliamentary debates in Papua New Guinea over whether wife-beating should be made illegal. Transcripts show that most ministers were violently against the idea of parliament interfering in "traditional family life." Minister William Wi of North Waghi argued that wife-beating "is an accepted custom and we are wasting our time debating the issue." Another parliamentarian added: "I paid for my wife, so she should not overrule my decisions, because I am the head of the family."

It is this unequal power balance—institutionalized in the structure of the patriarchal family—that is at the root of wife-beating. As Cheryl Bernard, director of Austria's Ludwig Boltzmann Institute of Politics, notes: "Violence against women in the family takes place because the perpetrators feel, and their environment encourages them to feel, that this is an acceptable exercise of male prerogative, a legitimate and appropriate way to relieve their own tension in conditions of stress, to sanction female behavior . . . or just to enjoy a feeling of supremacy."

While stress and alcohol may increase the likelihood of violence, they do not "cause" it. Rather, it is the belief that violence is an acceptable way to resolve conflict, and that women are "appropriate" and "safe" targets for abuse, that leads to battering.

Today's cultures have strong historical, religious and legal legacies that reinforce the legitimacy of wife-beating. Under English common law, for example, a husband had the legal right to discipline his wife—subject to a "rule of thumb" that barred him from using a stick broader than his thumb. Judicial decisions in England and the United States upheld this right until well into the 19th century. Only last week, a New York judge let off with only five years' probation a Chinese immigrant who admitted bludgeoning his wife to death. The judge justified the light sentence partly by reference to traditional Chinese attitudes toward female adultery.

While less overt, the preference for male offspring in many cultures can be as damaging and I paid forpotentially fatal to females as rape or assault. The same sentiment that once motivated infanticide is now expressed in the systematic neglect of daughters—a neglect so severe in some countries that girls aged 2 to 4 die at nearly twice the rate of boys.

"Let it be late, but let it be a son," goes a saying in Nepal, a country that shares its strong preference for male children with the rest of the Indian subcontinent, as well as China, South Korea and Taiwan. In these cultures and others, sons are highly valued because only they can perpetuate the family line and perform certain religious rituals. Even more important, sons represent an economic asset to the family and a source of security for parents in their old age.

Studies confirm that where the preference for sons is strong, girls receive inferior medical care and education, and less food. In Punjab, India, for example, parents spend more than twice as much on medical care for boy infants as for girls.

In fact, the pressure to bear sons is so great in India and China that women have begun using amniocentesis as a sex identification test to selectively abort female fetuses. Until protests forced them to stop, Indian sex detection clinics boldly advertised it was better to spend $38 now on terminating a girl than $3,800 later on her dowry. Of 8,000 fetuses examined at six abortion clinics in Bombay, 7,999 were found to be female.

In parts of Africa and the Middle East, young girls suffer another form of violence, euphemistically known as female circumcision. More accurately, this operation—which removes all or part of the external female genitalia, including the clitoris—is a life-threatening form of mutilation. According to the World Health Organization, more than 80 million women have undergone sexual surgery in Africa alone.

While female circumcision has its origin in the male desire to control female sexuality, today a host of other superstitions and beliefs sustains the practice. Some Moslem groups mistakenly believe that it is demanded by the Islamic faith, although it has no basis in the Koran. Others believe the operation will increase fertility, affirm femininity or prevent still births. Yet ultimately what drives the tradition is that men will not marry uncircumcised women, believing them to be promiscuous, unclean and sexually untrustworthy.

The medical complications of circumcision are severe. Immediate risks include hemorrhage, tetanus and blood poisoning from unsterile and often primitive cutting implements (knife, razor blade or broken glass), and shock from the pain of the operation, which is carried out without anesthesia. Not uncommonly, these complications result in death.

The long-term effects, in addition to loss of all sexual feeling, include chronic urinary tract infections, pelvic infections that can lead to infertility, painful intercourse and severe scarring that can cause tearing of tissue and hemorrhage during childbirth. In fact, women who are infibulated—the most severe form of circumcision—must be cut open on their wedding night to make intercourse possible, and more cuts are necessary for delivery of a child.

Despite these horrific death effects, many still oppose the eradication of this practice. As late as June 1988, Muslim religious scholars in Somalia argued that milder forms of circumcision should be maintained to temper female sexuality. Others defend circumcision as an "important African tradition." But as the Kenyan women's magazine *Via* observes: "There is nothing 'African' about injustice or violence, whether it takes the form of mistreated wives and mothers, or slums or circumcision. Often the very men who . . . excuse injustice to women

with the phrase 'it is African' are wearing three-piece pin-striped suits and shiny shoes."

Fortunately, women have not sat idle in the face of such abuse. Around the world they are organizing shelters, lobbying for legal reform and fighting the sexism that underlies violence.

Most industrial countries and at least a dozen developing nations now have shelter movements to provide refuge for abused women and their children. Brazil has established almost 30 all-female police stations for victims of rape, battering and incest. And in Africa, women are organizing education campaigns to combat sexual surgery.

Elsewhere women have organized in their own defense. In San Juan de Miraflores, a shantytown of Lima, Peru, women carry whistles that they use to summon other women in case of attack.

Yet it will take more than the dedicated action of a few women to end crimes of gender. Most important is for women worldwide to recognize their common oppression. Violence against women cuts across all cultures and all socioeconomic groups. Indeed, we in America live in our own glass house: In the United States a woman is beaten every 15 seconds, and each day four women are killed by their batterers.

Such statistics are as important as they are shocking. Violence persists in part because it is hidden. If governments and women's groups can expose violence through surveys and better documentation, then ignorance will no longer be an excuse for inaction.

Also critical is challenging the legal framework that undergirds male violence, such as unequal inheritance, discriminatory family laws and a husband's right to chastise. Especially important are the social inequities and cultural beliefs that leave women economically dependent on men. As long as women must marry to survive, they will do whatever they must to secure a husband—including tolerating abuse and submitting themselves and their daughters to sexual surgery.

Action against violence, however, must proceed from the international community down as well as from the grass roots up. Where governments tacitly condone violence through their silence, or worse yet, legitimize it through discriminatory laws and customs, international pressure can be an important impetus for reform. Putting violence against women high on the world agenda is not appeasing a "special interest" group. It is restoring the birthright of half of humanity.

Blaming the Victim: Ideology and Sexual Discrimination in the Contemporary United States

Maxine Margolis

Women are a problem not only as individuals, but collectively as a separate group with special functions within the structure of society. As a group and generally, they are a problem to themselves, to their children and families, to each other, to society as a whole.

Lundberg and Farnham
1947, p. 1

Only an equal society can save the victim from being the victim.

Gloria Steinem
PBS Program on wife beating
May, 1977

It has long been a cardinal rule of anthropology that one of the main functions of a culture's social and economic structure is the creation of ideologies that perpetuate, or at least do not threaten, the status quo. The need for system-maintaining ideologies is particularly acute in stratified societies where the divisions between haves and have-nots always present potential challenges to the established order.

Blaming the Victim is one such system-maintaining ideology. It helps to preserve the status quo in the United States and other stratified societies by attributing myriad social ills—poverty, delinquency, illegitimacy, low educational attainment—to the norms and values of the victimized group, rather than to the external conditions of in-

equality and discrimination under which that group lives. According to William Ryan (1971:xii), who was the first to recognize and label this phenomenon, Blaming the Victim is "an ideology, a mythology" consisting of a "set of official certified non-facts and respected untruths."

The primary function of this ideology is to obscure the victimizing effects of social forces. Rather than analyzing the socially induced inequalities that need changing, it focuses instead on the group or individual that is being victimized. This results in distracting attention from the social injustice, thus allowing it to continue. To change things, according to the ideology, we must change the victims, rather than the circumstances under which they live.

In American society this ideology is most often applied to minority groups, particularly blacks. It is used to "explain" their low socioeconomic status, their "aberrant" family structure, and their general failure to reap the benefits of all—it is said—this society so freely offers. Then too, Blaming the Victim is a convenient tool used to account for the underdevelopment of the third world. According to the ideology, underdevelopment is due to some defect in the national character of the nations

affected, to their people's lack of achievement motivation or openness to innovation.

Here I will argue that in the contemporary United States Blaming the Victim is also used widely to rationalize the continued economic, political, and social inequality of women. The application of this ideology to women is somewhat problematic in that, unlike other minority groups, women, at least until recently, have not regarded themselves as the objects of collective victimization. Moreover, through the process of socialization, most women have internalized victim blaming—they blame themselves and other female victims for their economic, social, and political problems. Essentially they ask: "What am I doing to make people discriminate against me?"

In writing this paper, I soon realized that women are blamed for a host of society's ills which, strictly speaking, only indirectly victimize women. Rather, in such cases, the victims are their children, their husbands, and their close associates who, it is said, are damaged by female behavior. The best known example of this type of thinking is the claim that women who work neglect their children and, therefore, are entirely responsible for

From *Researching American Culture*, 1982, pp. 212-227, edited by Conrad P. Koltak. Copyright © 1982 by University of Michigan Press.

whatever emotional and behavioral problems arise in their offspring. But this is simply a new twist of the victim-blaming mentality since its function is the same: to obscure the current social order's role in creating all manner of social and psychological problems by placing the blame where it is often not warranted.

Then too, it is sometimes difficult to distinguish the tendency to blame the female victim from outright misogyny. Is, for example, Philip Wylie's (1955: chap. 11) charge that men and boys are infantilized by their archtypical "Moms"—whom he describes as women who are "twenty-five pounds overweight," who have "beady brains behind their beady eyes," and who spend their time playing bridge "with the stupid voracity of a hammerhead shark"—simple misogyny or does it have an element of the victim-blaming mentality in it? It is clear why the line between the two is often blurred: it is far easier to victimize a group whom you dislike. By defining women as inferior, less trustworthy, more emotional, and less motivated than men, mistreatment or, at least, unequal treatment is justified and the status quo is preserved.

It is not particularly important to a great many working women whether or not they earn as much as men, or have equal opportunities for training and promotion. [Smuts 1974:108]

Blaming the female victim finds its widest application in the world of work. Here it comes in a variety of guises and is used to "explain" why women are paid less than men and have fewer opportunities for occupational advancement. Women, it is said, work only for "pin money" since they have husbands to support them and, therefore, do not really "need" their jobs. Similarly, it is claimed that women have higher rates of absenteeism and job turnover than men do, along with less interest in moving up the career ladder. These purported characteristics of the female labor force are then used to rationalize the fact that women are overwhelmingly confined to low-paying, tedious, dead-end positions.

According to the "pin money" argu-ment, men must provide for their families, while women only work to supplement their husbands' income or for pocket money to buy "extras." Using this logic, employers rationalize paying women low wages on the grounds that they do not need their earnings to live on. And, lest it be thought that this justification for salary discrimination has succumbed to more enlightened thinking in this era of the Equal Pay Act and the feminist movement, the comments of a county commissioner in Utah should lay such hopes aside. When asked to explain why male employees had received a 22 percent wage increase and female employees a 5 percent increase, he replied: "We felt that with their husbands working, the ladies could stand the squeeze a little better" (quoted in *Ms. Magazine* 3 December, 1975).

This reasoning is specious since it misinterprets why women enter the labor force: the reasons are overwhelmingly economic. Of the nearly 38 million women employed in 1976, 84 percent were the sole support of themselves and their families, or were married to men whose 1975 incomes were under $15,000. Women's median contribution to family income was 40 percent, with 12 percent contributing one-half or more. Moreover, the only reason many families are able to maintain a middle-class standard of living is that they have two incomes. "Women flocking to work account for the vital margin between solvency and insolvency," says economic analyst Eliot Janeway (1977:66).

One of the most pernicious results of the pin money myth is the failure to take high levels of female unemployment seriously. The belief that women's jobless rates are less worrisome than those of "household heads" again belies the fact that most women work not for pocket money, but because they are the sole support of their families or because their earnings make up a substantial proportion of their household income. By ignoring these factors, a delegate to the 1976 Republican National Convention could pooh-pooh high unemployment rates.

The unemployment rate tells a dangerously false story for which women are particularly to blame. It's not an economic problem. It's a sociological problem. [Quoted in Porter 1976]

Another component of the Blaming the Victim mentality in the world of work is the purported tendency of women to have higher rates of absenteeism and job turnover than men. These supposed liabilities of employing female labor also have been used to justify lower wages for women as well as employers' reluctance to promote them to more responsible, better-paying positions. Here, it is argued that women are not attached to the labor force, that they just "up and quit their jobs" to get married, or, if already married, to have babies. Why then, it is asked, should employers invest in expensive job-training programs for women or allow them to take on positions of responsibility?

Once again, the facts are ignored by the victimizers. A Department of Labor study of job turnover over one year found that 10 percent of male workers and 7 percent of female workers had changed jobs during that period (U.S. Department of Labor 1975). The number of women who leave work when they marry or have children has declined in the last two decades, and even with breaks in employment, the average woman now spends twenty-five years in the labor force.

It is also claimed that women miss work more than men do since they are subject to "female problems" and are more likely to stay home under the pretext of one minor ailment or another. Here too, the facts speak to the contrary. A recent survey by the Public Health Service found little difference in absentee rates due to illness or injury; women averaged 5.6 days annually and men averaged 5.2 days annually (U.S. Department of Labor 1975). Moreover, women over forty-five had a lower absentee rate than did men in the same age bracket.

Although ideas have changed since the early years of this century, when menstruation, pregnancy, and menopause were viewed as serious illnesses that disabled women and made them ill-suited for paid employment, many hiring and promotion policies still view women as baby makers who, if they are not pregnant, will soon become so. This assumption then becomes the employer's rationale for passing over women for promotion. Nor does the situation improve for older women since the belief that menopausal women suffer emotional disturbances is often used to justify denying them good jobs.

In a similar vein, Dr. Edgar Berman, a member of the Democratic party's Committee on National Priorities, received widespread publicity in 1970 when he questioned women's ability to hold certain responsible positions due to their "raging hormonal influences." "Take a woman surgeon," said the illustrious doctor, "if she had premenstrual tension . . . I wouldn't want her operating on me." Of course, Dr. Berman ignores the research which suggests that men have four- to six-week cycles that vary predictably and also seem to be caused by changing hormonal levels (quoted in Corea 1977:98–99).

Victim blamers also assert that women don't get ahead in their jobs because they lack the ambition to do so. They claim that women don't want promotions, job training, or job changes that add to their work load: "What they seek first in work," says sociologist Robert W. Smuts (1974:108), "is an agreeable job that makes limited demands. . . . Since they have little desire for a successful career," Smuts continues, "they are likely to drift into traditional women's occupations." George Meany offered a similar rationale in commenting on the lack of women on the thirty-three-member executive council of the AFL-CIO: "We have some very capable women in our unions, but they only go up to a certain level. . . . They don't seem to have any desire to go further" (quoted in *Ms. Magazine,* July, 1977).

Data regarding women's purported lack of ambition are difficult to come by, given that relatively few women have been offered positions of responsibility in the business world. Nevertheless, there is no evidence that the

5.1 million women who held professional and technical jobs and the 1.6 million who worked as managers and administrators in 1974 performed any less ably than men in comparable positions.

Yet another assertion made by Blaming the Victim ideologues is that women are "naturally" good at tedious, repetitive jobs; that they have an aptitude, if not an affinity, for typing, filing, assembling small items, packaging, labeling, and so forth. This view is clearly spelled out in a pamphlet entitled *The Feminine Touch* issued by Employer's Insurance of Wausau.

The female sex tends to be better suited for the unvarying routine that many . . . jobs require. Women are not bored by repetitive tasks as easily as men.

It was also echoed by the chief detective in the notorious "Son of Sam" case who, in a *New York* article, was quoted as saying that he sent two female detectives to the hack bureau to go through tens of thousands of licenses because they were "judged better able to withstand such drudgery than men" (quoted in Daley 1977).

These stereotypes lack any data to back them up and are simply rationalizations that allow men to assign women to such tasks without guilt. They also help justify the continued ghettoization of women workers in certain "appropriate" female occupations where their purported aptitude for tedium can be put to good use.

Many women . . . exaggerate the severity of their complaints to gratify neurotic desires. The woman who is at odds with her biological self develops psychosomatic and gynecologic problems. [Greenhill 1965:154, 158]

Psychiatry and gynecology have provided lucrative settings for victim-blaming ideologues. Blaming the female victim is the unifying theme in the perception and treatment of such medically diverse spheres as depression, childbirth, contraception, abortion, menstruation, and menopause. The common thread in all is that women's psychological and medical complaints are suspect, that they exaggerate their ills to get attention, and

that most female ailments are of a psychogenic rather than a biogenic origin.

Most psychotherapists, wittingly or unwittingly, ignore the objective conditions under which female neurosis and depression arise, and help maintain the sexual status quo by suggesting individual rather than collective solutions to female discontent. The patient is encouraged to think that her depression, her neurosis, is unique, that they are conditions of her own making.

Nowhere is the Blaming the Victim syndrome more evident in the profession than in the diagnosis and treatment of female sexual problems. Lundberg and Farnham, in their misogynist tome *Modern Woman: The Lost Sex,* claimed that the failure of women to achieve sexual satisfaction is a neurosis that stems from a negative view of childbearing and from attempts to "emulate the male in seeking a sense of personal value by objective exploit" (1947:265). Similarly, Freudian psychoanalyst Helene Deutsch (1944) believed that frigidity in women resulted from nonconformity to the feminine role.

Blaming the individual woman for emotional problems that in many cases are related to her fulfillment of traditional, socially accepted female roles obscures the dilemmas inherent in these roles and relieves society of responsibility for her unhappiness. The psychiatrist Robert Seidenberg suggests that the housewife-mother role often gives rise to emotional problems in women who adhere to it. He found that the "trauma of eventlessness"— that is, the absence of stimuli, challenges, choices, and decision making, which characterizes many women's lives—can threaten their mental well-being as much as physical danger (quoted in Sklar 1976).

When women are used as guinea pigs—as in the case of the birth control pill and other contraceptive devices— their complaints of side effects are often dismissed as the reaction of neurotic females. For example, depression, a fairly common side effect of the pill, is discussed in a medical text in these terms:

Recent evidence suggests that a significant number of these depressive reactions are due to an unrecognized and deeply rooted wish for another child. [Ciriacy and Hughes 1973:300]

The fact that the development of birth control pills and other contraceptive methods has been largely aimed at women is the result of a number of assumptions made by the largely male research establishment. Not only do they believe that conception control is the responsibility of women, they fear the untoward effects of interfering with the male sex drive. Having a healthy supply of sperm is more important to men than ovulation is to women, claim these authorities.

Although the medical profession encourages women to employ problematic contraceptive techniques, it is far more reticent about permitting them to undergo early, medically safe abortions. The reasons are often of the victim-blaming ilk. A staff physician at a county hospital in Milwaukee compared abortions to such cosmetic procedures as face lifts and breast enlargements. "Women know what makes them pregnant and they should have responsibility," he is quoted as saying (quoted in the *Milwaukee Sentinel,* July, 1976).

Even pregnancy and childbirth do not escape the net cast by the medical victim blamers. Morning sickness, for example, is described in one gynecological text as possibly indicating "resentment, ambivalence, and inadequacy in women ill-prepared for motherhood" (quoted in Corea 1977:77). Thus, a condition that is experienced by 75 to 80 percent of all pregnant women, and seems to be related to higher levels of estrogen during pregnancy, is dismissed as a psychosomatic aberration. Others have claimed that many women exaggerate the pain of childbirth: "Exaggeration of the rigors of the process is self-enhancing and . . . affords a new and powerful means of control over the male," say Lundberg and Farnham (1947:294).

Menstrual cramps also are suspect. One gynecologic text writer (Greenhill 1965:154) argues that they often "reflect the unhealthy attitude toward femininity that is so predominant in our society." Other medical texts adopt a similar view. One attributes menstrual pain to a "faulty outlook . . . leading to an exaggeration of minor discomfort," while another states "the pain is always secondary to an emotional problem" (quoted in Lenanne and Lenanne 1973:288).

Victim blaming by the medical establishment reached a crescendo during Senate subcommittee hearings looking into unnecessary surgical procedures. There, the highest ranking staff physician of the American Medical Association argued that hysterectomy is justified—though the uterus was healthy—in women who feared pregnancy or cancer. The chief of obstetrics and gynecology at a Rhode Island hospital agrees: "The uterus is just a muscle" and "It's a liability after children are born because it's a cancer site." The doctor added that his reasoning "ideally" applied to breasts as well, but "this would be a hard concept to sell in this society" (quoted in *Ms. Magazine,* November, 1977). One fact little noted in these discussion is that while it is true that hysterectomy eliminates the possibility of later uterine cancer, the death rate from uterine cancer is lower than the mortality rate from hysterectomies.

Menopause is another medical area in which victim-blaming health practitioners have had a field day. The common medical depiction of menopausal women as aged hags suffering from hot flashes and severe depression has been adopted by the public at large. A judge in Toronto, for example, dismissed the testimony of a forty-eight-year-old woman, stating: "There comes a certain age in a woman's life . . . when the evidence is not too reliable" (quoted in *Ms Magazine,* July, 1977). This stereotype overlooks the fact that only between 20 and 30 percent of the female population have such symptoms. Moreover, it is usually assumed that depression is caused by the loss of reproductive capacity, while little attention is paid to the objective life conditions of many middle-aged women—their "empty nests," their husbands' inattention, their lack of challenging employment opportunities, and society's glorification of female youth and beauty. Surely these conditions do much to account for depression in middle-aged women. But rather than question traditional sex roles, or the unequal distribution of power between men and women in our society, the medical establishment appeals to the "empty uterus" as the source of female discontent.

Whether they like it or not, a woman's a sex object, and they're the ones who turn the men on. [Judge Archie Simonson, Dane County, Wisconsin, 1977]

Nowhere is victim blaming more pernicious than when it is used to rationalize sexual and physical aggression against women. The courtroom statements of Judge Archie Simonson of Wisconsin show that Blaming the Victim is still too often the norm in the perception of rape and the treatment of its victims. This is also true of wife beating. In fact, attitudes toward abused wives and rape victims are strikingly similar; just as the rape victim is supposed to be an irresistible temptress who deserves what she got, so, it is said, the abused wife provokes her husband into beating her. Then too, it is said that women secretly enjoy being beaten, just as they are supposed to be "turned on" by rape.

There are two components to victim blaming as a rationalization for rape. For one, it is assumed that all women covertly desire rape, and, for another, that no woman can be raped against her will, so that forcible rape doesn't really exist. In combination, these assumptions lead to the conclusion that if a woman is raped, she is at fault, or, as Brownmiller (1976:374) says: "She was asking for it" is the classic rapist's remark as he "shifts the burden of blame from himself to his victim."

Victim precipitation, a concept in criminology often used in rape cases, tries to determine if the victim's behavior contributed in any way to the crime. While an unlawful act has occurred, goes the argument, if the victim had acted differently—had not walked alone at night or allowed a strange male to enter her house—the crime might not have taken place. This point is illustrated by a court case in California in which the judge overturned the conviction of a man who had picked up a female hitchhiker and raped her. The ruling read, in part:

The lone female hitchhiker . . . advises all who pass by that she is willing to enter the vehicle of anyone who stops, and . . . so advertises that she has less concern for the consequences than the average female. Under such circumstances, it would not be unreasonable for a man in the position of the defendant . . . to believe that the female would consent to sexual relations. [*New York Times,* July 10, 1977]

Another example of this mentality is the minister who wrote in a letter to "Dear Abby" that a young girl whose father had sexually abused her had "tempted" him by "wearing tight fitting, revealing clothes." In light of these opinions, which reflect the deeply ingrained notion that women provoke rape by their behavior and dress, it is little wonder that rape victims often agonize over what they did to cause themselves to be raped.

These attitudes are also evident in the way rape victims are handled by the courts and the police: the victim is more often treated like the criminal than is the rapist. Some states still permit testimony about the victim's prior sexual experience and general moral demeanor, and Brownmiller (1976:419) cites a study of the jury system which reported that in cases of rape "the jury closely scrutinizes the female complainant" and "weighs the conduct of the victims in judging the guilt of the defendant."

Similar attitudes are reflected in a California police manual which states that "forcible rape is the most falsely reported crime," and Brownmiller (1976:408) notes that many police assume that rape complaints are made by "prostitutes who didn't get paid." If a woman is raped by a stranger, the charge usually is taken more seriously than if she is raped by a man she knows. The latter, the police claim, is a "woman who changed her mind."

No matter how women behave in rape cases they are still held responsible for the outcome. While popular opinions denies the possibility of forcible rape, a judge in England recently

suggested that a woman who was seriously injured fighting off a rapist had only herself to blame for being hurt. She should have given in to the rapist, said the judge. The *London Times* editorialized, "This almost suggests that refusing to be raped is a kind of contributory negligence" (quoted in *Ms. Magazine,* November, 1977). The accused rapist, a soldier in the Coldstream Guards, was freed pending appeal on the grounds that he has a "promising career"!

In dealing with sexual violence the victim blamers once again ignore the facts. As a whole, according to the National Commission of the Causes and Prevention of Violence, rape victims are responsible for less precipitant behavior than victims of other kinds of crimes (Brownmiller 1976:396). Nor are the vast majority of rape charges brought by "women who changed their mind"; a study showed that only 2 percent of rape complaints proved to be false, which is about the same rate as for other felonies (Brownmiller 1976:410). Finally, the idea that women secretly "enjoy" rape is too preposterous to take seriously. I heartily concur with Herschberger's (1970:24) remark that

the notion that a victim of sexual aggression is forced into an experience of sensory delight should be relegated to the land where candy grows on trees.

Since the evidence negates the widespread belief that rape victims are "responsible" for what happens to them, it is senseless to argue that if women took special precautions in their dress and behavior the problem would disappear. As Brownmiller (1976:449) convincingly argues: "there can be no private solutions to the problems of rape." Yet these attitudes persist since, by viewing rape as a "woman's problem" brought on by the victims themselves, both men and society are relieved of guilt.

As I suggested earlier, the explanation for and treatment of wife abuse are remarkably similar to that of rape, and the victim blaming is just as loud and clear. Police, who are notoriously loath to intervene in domestic disputes, too often take the attitude "well, if her

husband beat her, she probably deserved it." They often assume that women who accuse their husbands of beating them are vindictive, and will only prosecute if they are convinced that the wife is a "worthy victim." And in courtroom after courtroom, it is the battered woman's responsibility to persuade the judge that she is really a victim—a judge who may ask her what she did to provoke her husband's attack.

These attitudes are sometimes shared by members of the abused woman's family as well as society at large. In a newspaper article on wife abuse, a woman whose husband beat her while she was pregnant told of getting no support from her family or her doctor.

My mother said I must be doing things to make him mad, and my sister said it was all right for a man to beat his wife. I told my gynecologist that my husband was extremely violent and I was mortally afraid of him. Guess what he said? I should relax more. He prescribed tranquilizers. [*Gainesville Sun,* September 5, 1977]

Victim blamers have had a field day in looking for culprits in wife-abuse cases. A member of the New Hampshire Commission on the Status of Women, for example, suggested that the women's liberation movement was responsible for the increased incidence of wife beating and rape (reported on the "Today Show," September 16, 1977).

In fact that a mere two percent of battering husbands are ever prosecuted is clearly related to these attitudes. While assault and battery are quickly punished when they occur between strangers, punitive action is rare within a marital relationship. The extreme to which this can go is evidenced in a recent court decision in England. A man who killed his wife and pleaded guilty to "manslaughter" was sentenced to only three years probation on the grounds that his wife had "nagged him constantly for seventeen years." "I don't think I have ever come across a case where provocation has gone on for so long," said the judge (reported in the *Independent Florida Alligator,* October 20, 1977).

Many who are otherwise sympathetic to the battered wife are perplexed as to why she takes the abuse. But the reasons are not too difficult to discern. Not only are many women economically dependent on their husbands, but they also have been socialized to be victims. As Marjory Fields, a lawyer involved in wife abuse cases, has noted, "they not only take the beatings, they tend to feel responsible for them" (quoted in Gingold 1976:52).

Should something go wrong, as in the production of a Hitler, a woman is said to be at the root of the trouble—in this case Hitler's mother. [Herschberger 1970:16]

Victims blamers have devoted a good deal of their time and rhetoric to what can be termed "mother blame." In this category of victim blaming, it is not women themselves who are said to be adversely affected by their behavior, but rather their children and, ultimately, society at large. The psychiatric profession, in particular, has been responsible for popularizing the view that, in Chesler's (1972:378) words, "the lack of or superabundance of mother love causes neurotic, criminal . . . and psychopathic children." The absent or uncaring father and other forms of deprivation rarely are blamed for problem children and problem adults.

Mother blame is a natural outgrowth of the traditional, socially approved sexual division of labor that sees child rearing as exclusively "woman's work"; if something goes wrong, it must be mother who is to blame. Moreover, women are held responsible for their children's problems no matter what they do. If they work, they are accused of child neglect, while if they stay home and devote their time to child care, they are berated for smothering their offspring.

The theory that attributes juvenile delinquency and other behavior problems to maternal employment has been around for quite some time. During World War II, working mothers were widely criticized for rearing "latchkey children" who got into trouble for lack of supervision. Mother blame reached a peak shortly after the war with the publication of *Modern Woman: The Lost Sex.* In it, Lundberg and Farnham (1947:304–305) estimate that between 40 and 50 percent of all mothers are "rejecting, over-solicitous, or dominating," and that they produce "the delinquents, the behavior problem children, and some substantial proportion of criminals."

Some years later psychiatrist Abram Kardiner (1954:224) agreed with these sentiments when he wrote that "children reared on a part-time basis will show the effects of such care in the distortions of personality that inevitably result." After all, "motherhood is a full-time job."

Lest it be thought that mother blame is merely an artifact of the days of the feminine mystique, a recent newspaper editorial espoused it when attempting to explain the high crime rate.

Let's speculate that the workaday grind makes Mom more inaccessible, irritable . . . and spiteful, thereby rendering family life less pleasant . . . than the good old days when she stayed in the kitchen and baked apple pies. What could that be doing to the rising crime rate? Say fellows, could it be Mom's fault? [Editorial, *Gainesville Sun*, March 25, 1977]

These views, of course, ignore the studies that indicate that absent and low profile fathers are more responsible for delinquency in their children than are working mothers. Moreover, the most comprehensive study of maternal employment, *The Employed Mother in America* (Nye and Hoffman 1963), effectively rebuts the myths concerning the supposed ill effects of working mothers on their offspring, and concludes that "maternal employment . . . is not the overwhelming influential factor in children's lives that some have thought it to be" (Burchinal 1963:118; Siegal et al. 1963:80). But, as we have seen, victim blamers have little use for facts that contradict their strongly held beliefs.

What of the woman who stays home and devotes full time to child raising? She too is the target of the mother blamers who hold her accountable for an incredible variety of social problems. In his book *Generation of Vipers*, Phillip Wylie (1955) characterized such women as "Moms" who led empty lives and preyed upon their offspring, keeping them tied to their proverbial apron strings. This theme was also sounded by Edward Strecker (1946), a psychiatric consultant to the Army and Navy Surgeons General during World War II. In trying to account for the emotional disorders of 600,000 men unable to continue in military service, Strecker wrote, "in the vast majority of case histories, a Mom is at fault." But what causes "Moms" to be the way they are in the first place? In most cases, a Mom is a Mom because she is the immature result of a Mom, says Strecker (1946:23, 70).

If it weren't for Martha, there'd have been no Watergate. [Richard Nixon on David Frost interview, September, 1977]

Richard Nixon's statement holding Martha Mitchell responsible for Watergate is a timely reminder of the length to which victim blamers sometimes go. According to Nixon, Watergate occurred because "John Mitchell wasn't minding the store," but was preoccupied with his wife's emotional problems. This claim is particularly malicious given the often-noted fact that the large Watergate case was *all* male. A similarly absurd remark was made during the "Son of Sam" episode, when it was automatically assumed that a woman was at the root of "Sam's" problem. The killer "must have been terribly provoked by a woman," New York psychiatrist Hyman Spotnitz was quoted as saying in *Time* (July 11, 1977).

While Nixon's assertion was widely seen as self-serving, the opinions of psychiatrists and other authoritative victim blamers are taken quite seriously by the general public, including women. Women not only participate in this ideology, they often internalize it, blaming themselves and other women for a host of problems. This shows the effectiveness of the ideology in rationalizing subordination to the victims themselves. The very persistence of victim blaming, in fact, is partly due to the implicit participation of its targets. And men, of course, perpetuate the ideology since it is clearly in their own self-interest to do so. It helps maintain the status quo from which they benefit.

In recent years the ability of victim blaming to deflect attention from social institutions and obscure societal processes has been particularly valuable in "explaining" women's failure to make significant advances in employment and other realms. Despite the existence of the feminist movement and a plethora of equal opportunity laws, women still overwhelmingly remain in low-paid, low-prestige, female job ghettos. But, say the victim blamers, that is because they have no interest in getting ahead, they fear success, and don't want the added responsibility that comes with promotions. The goal of the victim blamers is clear: these purported qualities of the victimized group conveniently mask the fact of continued widespread sexual discrimination. But it must be emphasized that although the Blaming the Victim ideology does distort reality by covering up the inequalities in contemporary American life, it is not the *cause* of these deeply rooted social and economic inequalities: it is a rationalization for them.

A Primitive Prescription for Equality

Helen Fisher, an anthropologist at the American Museum of Natural History, argues that the "traditional" role of women is a recent invention—and that human society is now rediscovering its ancient roots

Conversation with Kathleen McAuliffe

Men and women are moving toward the kind of roles they had on the grasslands of Africa millions of years ago. But this "backward" trend is a step forward, toward equality between the sexes.

The rise of economically autonomous women is a new phenomenon that is in reality very old. For more than 99 percent of human evolution, we existed as hunters and gatherers, and women in those cultures enjoyed enormous clout because they probably brought back 60 to 80 percent of the food. At least that's the case in most contemporary hunting-gathering communities, such as the Kung bushmen of Africa, whose lifestyle is thought to mirror that of earliest Homo sapiens.

The recent trend toward divorce and remarriage is another example of a throwback to earlier times. The constant making and breaking of marital ties is a hallmark of hunting-gathering societies. The trend only seems novel to us because we are just now emerging from an agricultural tradition—a male-dominated culture that, while recent, lasted for a flash in the night on the time scale of human evolution. A peculiarity of the farming lifestyle is that men and women functioned as an isolated, economically dependent unit. Marriage was "till death do us part" for the simple reason that neither part-

ner could pick up half the property and march off to town.

But when men and women left farms for jobs and came back with money—movable, divisible property—we slipped right back into deeply ingrained behavior patterns that evolved long ago. Money makes it easy to walk out on a bad relationship. A man is going to think a lot harder about leaving a woman who picks his vegetables than leaving a woman who is the vice president of Citibank, because she can fend for herself and vice versa. Indeed, around the globe, wherever women are economically powerful, divorce rates are high. You see it in the Kung, and you see it in the United States: Between 1960 and 1980, when the number of women in the work force doubled, the divorce rate doubled, too.

THE "NEW" EXTENDED FAMILY

That figure seems bleak until we recall that the vast majority of couples who split up remarry—and that's as true in hunting-gathering communities as in postindustrial America. This suggests that the so-called new extended family may actually have evolved millennia ago. If so, perhaps our tendency to equate divorce with failure has made us blind to the advantages of the extended family: Children grow up with more adult role models and a larger network of relatives, increasing their

range of power and influence within society.

The trend toward smaller families may not be as modern as we think, either. Although women gatherers had four or five children, only two typically survived childhood—the number found in the average American family today. Even our style of rearing children is starting to parallel hunting-gathering communities, in which girls and boys are permitted to play together from a young age, and consequently experiment at sex earlier and engage in trial marriages. Clearly we've moved away from the agricultural custom of arranged marriages and cloistering girls to preserve their virginity.

Moreover, the home is no longer the "place of production," as it was in farm days. We don't make our soap, grow our vegetables and slaughter our chicken for the dinner table. Instead, we hunt and gather in the grocery store and return to our "home base" to consume the food we have collected. No wonder we are so in love with fast foods. It probably harks back to an eating strategy our primate relatives adopted over 50 million years ago.

PUTTING OUR HEADS TOGETHER

There's no mistaking the trend: Humans are once again on the move. Husband and wife are no longer bound to a single plot of land for their livelihood. Women are back in production as well as reproduction. As we head back to the future, there's every reason to believe the sexes will enjoy the kind of equality that is a function of our birthright. By equality, I mean a more equitable division of power—not that our roles will converge. Alike men and women have never been and never will be. Very simply, we *think* differently, which is again tied to our long hunting-gathering heritage.

For 2 million years, women carried around children and have been the nurturers. That's probably why tests show they are both more verbal and more attuned to nonverbal cues. Men, on the other hand, tend to have superior mathematical and visual-spatial skills because they roamed long distances from the campsite, had to scheme ways to trap prey and then had to find their way back.

The specialization is reflected in genuine gender differences in the brain today. Nature not only intended men and women to put their bodies together; we're meant to put our heads together as well.

That's what is so thrilling about what's happening now. All those male and female skills are beginning to work together again. At long last, society is moving in a direction that should be highly compatible with our ancient human spirit.

Religion, Belief, and Ritual

The anthropological concern for religion, belief, and ritual does not have to do with the scientific validity of such phenomena, but rather the way in which people relate various concepts of the "supernatural" to their everyday lives. With this more practical perspective, some anthropologists have found that traditional spiritual healing is just as applicable in the treatment of illness as modern medicine, that voodoo is a form of social control, and that the ritual and spiritual preparation for playing the game of baseball can be just as important as spring training.

Every society is composed of feeling, thinking, and acting human beings who at one time or another are either conforming to or altering the social order into which they were born. Religion is an ideological framework that gives special legitimacy and validity to human experience within any given sociocultural system. In this way, monogamy as a marriage form or monarchy as a political form ceases to be simply one of many alternative ways in which a society can be organized, but becomes, for the believer, the only legitimate way. Religion renders certain human values and activities sacred and inviolable, and it is this "mythic" function that helps to explain the strong ideological attachments that some people have regardless of the scientific merits of their points of view.

While, under some conditions, religion may in fact be "the opiate of the masses," under other conditions it may be a rallying point for social and economic protest. A contemporary example of the former might be the "Moonies" (members of the Unification Church), while a good example of the latter is the role of the black church in the American civil rights movement, along with the prominence of such religious figures as Martin Luther King, Jr., and Jesse Jackson.

Finally, a word of caution must be set forth concerning attempts to understand the belief systems of other cultures. At times the prevailing attitude seems to be that "what I believe in is religion and what you believe in is superstition." While anthropologists generally do not subscribe to this view, there is a tendency within the field to explain that which seems, on the surface, to be incomprehensible, impractical behavior as some form of "religious ritual." The following articles should serve as a strong warning concerning the pitfalls of that approach.

"The Mbuti Pygmies: Change and Adaptation" involves ritual that is subtle, informal, and yet absolutely necessary for social harmony and stability. In contrast, in "The Initiation of a Maasai Warrior," what seems to be a highly formal circumcision ceremony is ultimately revealed to be a deeply personal experience. The emphasis in "The Secrets of Haiti's Living Dead," "Dark Side of the Shaman," and "The Real Vampire" is upon both individual conformity and community solidarity.

Mystical beliefs and ritual are not absent from modern society. "Rituals of Death" draws striking parallels between capital punishment in the United States and human sacrifice among the Aztecs, and, in a lighter vein, "Body Ritual Among the Nacirema" reveals that even our daily routines have mystic overtones.

In summary, the articles in this section will show religion, belief, and ritual in relationship to practical human affairs.

Looking Ahead: Challenge Questions

How does ritual contribute to a sense of personal security, individual responsibility, and social equality?

How has voodoo become such an important form of social control in rural Haiti?

In what ways is the spirit world of a rural African village similar in function to a fiction writer's imagination?

How and why did the folklore of the vampire develop out of the peasant culture of Eastern Europe?

In what ways can capital punishment be seen as a ritual with social functions?

How important are ritual and taboo in our modern industrial society?

Psychotherapy in Africa

Thomas Adeoye Lambo

Thomas Adeoye Lambo is deputy director-general of the World Health Organization in Geneva and an advisory editor of Human Nature. *He was born in Abeokuta, Nigeria, in 1923 and lived there until he finished secondary school. He studied medicine at the University of Birmingham in England, later specializing in psychiatry. Lambo first received international acclaim in 1954 when he published reports on the neuropsychiatric problems of Nigeria's Yoruba tribe and on the establishment of the Aro village hospital. Lambo served as medical director of Aro until 1962, when he was appointed to the first Chair of Psychiatry at Nigeria's Ibadan University; in 1968 he became vice-chancellor of the University. Lambo's psychiatric research and approach to therapy have consistently blended biology, culture, and social psychology.*

Some years ago, a Nigerian patient came to see me in a state of extreme anxiety. He had been educated at Cambridge University and was, to all intents and purposes, thoroughly "Westernized." He had recently been promoted to a top-level position in the administrative service, bypassing many of his able peers. A few weeks after his promotion, however, he had had an unusual accident from which he barely escaped with his life. He suddenly became terrified that his colleagues had formed a conspiracy and were trying to kill him.

His paranoia resisted the usual methods of Western psychiatry, and he had to be sedated to relieve his anxiety. But one day he came to see me, obviously feeling much better. A few nights before, he said, his grandfather had appeared to him in a dream and had assured him of a long and healthy life. He had been promised relief from fear and anxiety if he would sacrifice a goat. My patient bought a goat the following day, car-

ried out all of the detailed instructions of his grandfather, and quickly recovered. The young man does not like to discuss this experience because he feels it conflicts with his educational background, but occasionally, in confidence, he says: "There is something in these native things, you know."

To the Western eye, such lingering beliefs in ritual and magic seem antiquated and possibly harmful—obstacles in the path of modern medicine. But the fact is that African cultures have developed indigenous forms of psychotherapy that are highly effective because they are woven into the social fabric. Although Western therapeutic methods are being adopted by many African therapists, few Africans are simply substituting new methods for traditional modes of treatment. Instead, they have attempted to combine the two for maximum effectiveness.

The character and effectiveness of medicine for the mind and the body always and everywhere depend on the culture in which the medicine is practiced. In the West, healing is often considered to be a private matter between patient and therapist. In Africa, healing is an integral part of society and religion, a matter in which the whole community is involved. To understand African psychotherapy one must understand African thought and its social roots.

It seems impossible to speak of a single African viewpoint because the continent contains a broad range of cultures. The Ga, the Masai, and the Kikuyu, for example, are as different in their specific ceremonies and customs as are the Bantus and the Belgians. Yet in sub-Saharan black Africa the different cultures do share a consciousness of the world. They have in common a characteristic per-

ception of life and death that makes it possible to describe their overriding philosophy. (In the United States, Southern Baptists and Episcopalians are far apart in many of their rituals and beliefs, yet one could legitimately say that both share a Christian concept of life.)

The basis of most African value systems is the concept of the unity of life and time. Phenomena that are regarded as opposites in the West exist on a single continuum in Africa. African thought draws no sharp distinction between animate and inanimate, natural and supernatural, material and mental, conscious and unconscious. All things exist in dynamic correspondence, whether they are visible or not. Past, present, and future blend in harmony; the world does not change between one's dreams and the daylight.

Essential to this view of the world is the belief that there is continuous communion between the dead and the living. Most African cultures share the idea that the strength and influence of every clan is anchored by the spirits of its deceased heroes. These heroes are omnipotent and indestructible, and their importance is comparable to that of the Catholic saints. But to Africans, spirits and deities are ever present in human affairs; they are the guardians of the established social order.

The common element in rituals throughout the continent—ancestor cults, deity cults, funeral rites, agricultural rites—is the unity of the people with the world of spirits, the mystical and emotional bond between the natural and supernatural worlds.

Because of the African belief in deities and ancestral spirits, many Westerners think that African thought is more concerned with the supernatural causes of events than with their natural causes. On one level this is true. Africans attribute nearly all forms of illness and disease, as well as personal and communal catastrophes, accidents, and deaths to the magical machinations of their enemies and to the intervention of gods and ghosts. As a result there is a deep faith in the power of symbols to produce the effects that are desired. If a man finds a hair, or a piece of material, or a bit of a fingernail belonging to his enemy, he believes he has only to use the object ritualistically in order to bring about the enemy's injury or death.

As my educated Nigerian patient revealed by sacrificing a goat, the belief in the power of the supernatural is not confined to uneducated Africans. In a survey of African students in British universities conducted some years ago, I found that the majority of them firmly believed that their emotional problems had their origin in, or could at least be influenced by, charms and diabolical activities of other African students or of people who were still in Africa. I recently interviewed the student officers at the Nigeria House in London and found no change in attitude.

The belief in the power of symbols and magic is inculcated at an early age. I surveyed 1,300 elementary-school children over a four-year period and found that 85 percent used native medicine of some sort— incantations, charms, magic—to help them pass exams, to be liked by teachers, or to ward off the evil effects of other student "medicines." More than half of these children came from Westernized homes, yet they held firmly to the power of magic ritual.

Although most Africans believe in supernatural forces and seem to deny natural causality, their belief system is internally consistent. In the Western world, reality rests on the human ability to master things, to conquer objects, to subordinate the outer world to human will. In the African world, reality is found in the soul, in a religious acquiescence to life, not in its mastery. Reality rests on the rela-

tions between one human being and another, and between all people and spirits.

The practice of medicine in Africa is consistent with African philosophy. Across the African continent, sick people go to acknowledged diviners and healers—they are often called witch doctors in the West—in order to discover the nature of their illness. In almost every instance, the explanation involves a deity or an ancestral spirit. But this is only one aspect of the diagnosis, because the explanation given by the diviner is also grounded in natural phenomena. As anthropologist Robin Horton observes: "The diviner who diagnoses the intervention of a spiritual agency is also expected to give some acceptable account of what moved the agency in question to intervene. And this account very commonly involves reference to some event in the world of visible, tangible happenings. Thus if a diviner diagnoses the action of witchcraft influence or lethal medicine spirits, it is usual for him to add something about the human hatreds, jealousies, and misdeeds that have brought such agencies into play. Or, if he diagnoses the wrath of an ancestor, it is usual for him to point to the human breach of kinship morality which has called down this wrath."

The causes of illness are not simply attributed to the unknown or dropped into the laps of the gods. Causes are always linked to the patient's immediate world of social events. As Victor Turner's study of the Ndembu people of central Africa revealed, diviners believe a patient "will not get better until all the tensions and aggressions in the group's interrelations have been brought to light and exposed to ritual treatment." In my work with the Yoruba culture, I too found that supernatural forces are regarded as the agents and consequences of human will. Sickness is the natural effect of some social mistake—breaching a taboo or breaking a kinship rule.

African concepts of health and illness, like those of life and death, are intertwined. Health is not regarded as

an isolated phenomenon but reflects the integration of the community. It is not the mere absence of disease but a sign that a person is living in peace and harmony with his neighbors, that he is keeping the laws of the gods and the tribe. The practice of medicine is more than the administration of drugs and potions. It encompasses all activities—personal and communal —that are directed toward the promotion of human well-being. As S.R. Burstein wrote, to be healthy requires "averting the wrath of gods or spirits, making rain, purifying streams or habitations, improving sex potency or fecundity or the fertility of fields and crops—in short, it is bound up with the whole interpretation of life."

Native healers are called upon to treat a wide range of psychiatric disorders, from schizophrenia to neurotic syndromes. Their labels may not be the same, but they recognize the difference between an incapacitating psychosis and a temporary neurosis, and between a problem that can be cured (anxiety) and one that cannot (congenital retardation or idiocy). In many tribes a person is defined as mad when he talks nonsense, acts foolishly and irresponsibly, and is unable to look after himself.

It is often assumed that tribal societies are a psychological paradise and that mental illness is the offspring of modern civilization and its myriad stresses. The African scenes in Alex Haley's *Roots* tend to portray a Garden of Eden, full of healthy tribesmen. But all gardens have snakes. Small societies have their own peculiar and powerful sources of mental stress. Robin Horton notes that tribal societies have a limited number of roles to be filled, and that there are limited choices for individuals. As a result each tribe usually has a substantial number of social misfits. Traditional communities also have a built-in set of conflicting values: aggressive ambition versus a reluctance to rise above one's neighbor; ruthless individualism versus acceptance of one's place in the lineage system. Inconsistencies such as these, Horton believes, "are often as sharp as those so well known in modern industrial societies. . . .One may even suspect that some of the young Africans currently rushing from the country to the towns are in fact escaping from a more oppressive to a less oppressive psychological environment."

Under typical tribal conditions, traditional methods are perfectly effective in the diagnosis and treatment of mental illness. The patient goes to the tribal diviner, who follows a complex procedure. First the diviner (who may be a man or a woman) determines the "immediate" cause of the illness—that is, whether it comes from physical devitalization or from spiritual possession. Next he or she diagnoses the "remote" cause of the ailment: Had the patient offended one of his ancestor spirits or gods? Had a taboo been violated? Was some human agent in the village using magic or invoking the help of evil spirits to take revenge for an offense?

The African diviner makes a diagnosis much as a Western psychoanalyst does: through the analysis of dreams, projective techniques, trances and hypnotic states (undergone by patient and healer alike), and the potent power of words. With these methods, the diviner defines the psychodynamics of the patient and gains insight into the complete life situation of the sick person.

One projective technique of diagnosis—which has much in common with the Rorschach test—occurs in *Ifa* divination, a procedure used by Yoruba healers. There are 256 *Odus* (incantations) that are poetically structured; each is a dramatic series of words that evoke the patient's emotions. Sometimes the power of the *Odus* lies in the way the words are used, the order in which they are arranged, or the starkness with which they express a deep feeling. The incantations are used to gain insight into the patient's problem. Their main therapeutic value, as in the case with the Rorschach ink blots, is to interpret omens, bring up unconscious motives, and make unknown desires and fears explicit.

Once the immediate and remote causes are established, the diagnosis is complete and the healer decides on the course of therapy. Usually this involves an expiatory sacrifice meant to restore the unity between man and deity. Everyone takes part in the treatment; the ritual involves the healer, the patient, his family, and the community at large. The group rituals —singing and dancing, confessions, trances, storytelling, and the like— that follow are powerful therapeutic measures for the patient. They release tensions and pressures and promote positive mental health by tying all individuals to the larger group. Group rituals are effective because they are the basis of African social life, an essential part of the lives of "healthy" Africans.

Some cultures, such as the N'jayei society of the Mende in Sierra Leone and the Yassi society of the Sherbro, have always had formal group therapy for their mentally ill. When one person falls ill, the whole tribe attends to his physical and spiritual needs.

Presiding over all forms of treatment is the healer, or *nganga.* My colleagues and I have studied and worked with these men and women for many years, and we are consistently impressed by their abilities. Many of those we observed are extraordinary individuals of great common sense, eloquence, boldness, and charisma. They are highly respected within their communities as people who through self-denial, dedication, and prolonged meditation and training have discovered the secrets of the healing art and its magic (a description of Western healers as well, one might say).

The traditional *nganga* has supreme self-confidence, which he or she transmits to the patient. By professing an ability to commune with supernatural beings—and therefore to control or influence them—the healer holds boundless power over members of the tribe. Africans regard the *nganga*'s mystical qualities and eccentricities fondly, and with awe. So strongly do people believe in the *nganga*'s ability to find out which ancestral spirit is responsible for the psychological distress of the patient, that pure suggestion alone can be very effective.

For centuries the tribal practice of communal psychotherapy served African society well. Little social stigma was attached to mental illness; even chronic psychotics were tolerated in their communities and were able to function at a minimal level. (Such tolerance is true of many rural cultures.) But as the British, Germans, French, Belgians, and Portuguese colonized many African countries, they brought a European concept of mental illness along with their religious, economic, and educational systems.

They built prisons with special sections set aside for "lunatics"— usually vagrant psychotics and criminals with demonstrable mental disorders—who were restricted with handcuffs and ankle shackles. The African healers had always drawn a distinction between mental illness and criminality, but the European colonizers did not.

In many African cultures today, the traditional beliefs in magic and religion are dying. Their remaining influence serves only to create anxiety and ambivalence among Africans who are living through a period of rapid social and economic change. With the disruption and disorganization of family units, we have begun to see clinical problems that once were rare: severe depression, obsessional neurosis, and emotional incapacity. Western medicine has come a long way from the shackle solution, but it is not the best kind of therapy for people under such stress. In spite of its high technological and material advancement, modern science does not satisfy the basic metaphysical and social needs of many people, no matter how sophisticated they are.

In 1954 my colleagues and I established a therapeutic program designed to wed the best practices of traditional and contemporary psychology. Our guiding premise was to make use of the therapeutic practices that already existed in the indigenous culture, and to recognize the power of the group in healing.

We began our experiment at Aro, a rural suburb of the ancient town of Abeokuta, in western Nigeria. Aro consists of four villages that lie in close proximity in the beautiful rolling countryside. The villages are home Yoruba tribesmen and their relatives, most of whom are peasant farmers, fishermen, and craftsmen.

Near these four villages we built a day hospital that could accommodate up to 300 patients, and then we set up a village care system for their treatment. Our plan was to preserve the fundamental structure of African culture: closely knit groups, well-defined kin networks, an interlocking system of mutual obligations and traditional roles.

Patients came to the hospital every morning for treatment and spent their afternoons in occupational therapy, but they were not confined to the hospital. Patients lived in homes in the four villages or, if necessary, with hospital staff members who lived on hospital grounds—ambulance drivers, clerks, dispensary attendants, and gardeners. (This boarding-out procedure resembles a system that has been practiced for several hundred years in Gheel, a town in Belgium, where the mentally ill live in local households surrounding a central institution.)

We required the patients, who came from all over Nigeria, to arrive at the village hospital with at least one relative—a mother, sister, brother, or aunt—who would be able to cook for them, wash their clothes, take them to the hospital in the morning, and pick them up in the afternoon.

These relatives, along with the patients, took part in all the social activities of the villages: parties, plays, dances, storytelling. Family participation was successful from the beginning. We were able to learn about the family influences and stresses on the patient, and the family

members learned how to adjust to the sick relative and deal with his or her emotional needs.

The hospital staff was drawn from the four villages, which meant that the hospital employees were the "landlords" of most of the patients, in constant contact with them at home and at work. After a while, the distinction between the two therapeutic arenas blurred and the villages became extensions of the hospital wards.

Doctors, nurses, and superintendents visited the villages every day and set up "therapy" groups—often for dancing, storytelling, and other rituals—as well as occupational programs that taught patients traditional African crafts.

It is not enough to treat patients on a boarding-out or outpatient basis. If services are not offered to them outside of the hospital, an undue burden is placed on their families and neighbors. This increases the tension to which patients are exposed. An essential feature of our plan was to regard the villages as an extension of the hospital, subject to equally close supervision and control.

But we neither imposed the system on the local people nor asked them to give their time and involvement without giving them something in return. We were determined to inflict no hardships. The hosptial staff took full responsibility for the administration of the villages and for the health of the local people. They held regular monthly meetings with the village elders and their councils to give the villagers a say in the system. The hospital also arranged loans to the villagers to expand, repair, or build new houses to take care of the patients; it paid for the installation of water pipes and latrines; it paid for a mosquito eradication squad; it offered jobs to many local people and paid the "landlords" a small stipend.

Although these economic benefits aided the community, no attempt was ever made to structure the villages in any way, or to tell the villagers what to do with the patients or how to treat them. As a result of economic bene-

fits, hospital guidance, and a voice in their own management, village members supported the experiment.

In a study made after the program began, we learned that patients who were boarded out under this system adapted more quickly and responded more readily to treatment than patients who lived in the hospital. Although the facilities available in the hospital were extensive—drug medication, group therapy sessions, modified insulin therapy, electroconvulsive shock treatments—we found that the most important therapeutic factor was the patient's social contacts, especially with people who were healthier than the patient. The village groups, unlike the hospital group, were unrehearsed, unexpected, and voluntary. Patients could choose their friends and activities; they were not thrown together arbitrarily and asked to "work things out." We believe that the boarded-out patients improved so quickly because of their daily contact with settled, tolerant, healthy people. They learned to function in society again without overwhelming anxiety.

One of the more effective and controversial methods we used was to colaborate with native healers. Just as New Yorkers have faith in their psychoanalysts, and pilgrims have faith in their priests, the Yoruba have faith in the *nganga;* and faith, as we are learning, is half the battle toward cure.

Our unorthodox alliance proved to be highly successful. The local diviners and religious leaders helped many of the patients recover, sometimes through a simple ceremony at a village shrine, sometimes in elaborate forms of ritual sacrifice, sometimes by interpreting the spiritual or magical causes of their dreams and illnesses.

At the beginning of the program patients were carefully selected for admission, but now patients of every sort are accepted: violent persons, catatonics, schizophrenics, and others whose symptoms make them socially unacceptable or emotionally withdrawn. The system is particularly effective with emotionally disturbed and psychotic children, who always come to the hospital with a great number of concerned relatives. Children who have minor neurotic disorders are kept out of the hospital entirely and treated exclusively and successfully in village homes.

The village care system was designed primarily for the acutely ill and for those whose illness was manageable, and the average stay for patients at Aro was, and is, about six months. But patients who were chronically ill and could not recover in a relatively short time posed a problem. For one thing, their relatives could not stay with them in the villages because of family and financial obligations in their home communities. We are working out solutions for such people on a trial-and-error basis. Some of the incapacitated psychotic patients now live on special farms; others live in Aro villages near the hospital and earn their keep while receiving regular supervision. The traditional healers keep watch over these individuals and maintain follow-up treatment.

We have found many economic, medical, and social advantages to our program. The cost has been low because we have concentrated on using human resources in the most effective and strategic manner. Medically and therapeutically, the program provides a positive environment for the treatment of character disorders, sociopathy, alcoholism, neuroses, and anxiety. Follow-up studies show that the program fosters a relatively quick recovery for these problems and that the recidivism rate and the need for aftercare are significantly reduced. The length of stay at Aro, and speed of recovery,

is roughly one third of the average stay in other hospitals, especially for all forms of schizophrenia. Patients with neurotic disorders respond most rapidly. Because of its effectiveness, the Aro system has been extended to four states in Nigeria and to five countries in Africa, including Kenya, Ghana, and Zambia. At each new hospital the program is modified to fit local conditions.

Some observers of the Aro system argue that it can operate only in nonindustrial agrarian communities, like those in Africa and Asia, where families and villages are tightly knit. They say that countries marked by high alienation and individualism could not import such a program. Part of this argument is correct. The Aro approach to mental health rests on particularly African traditions, such as the *nganga,* and on the belief in the continuum of life and death, sickness and health, the natural and the supernatural.

But some lessons of the Aro plan have already found their way into Western psychotherapy. Many therapists recognize the need to place the sick person in a social context; a therapist cannot heal the patient without attending to his beliefs, family, work, and environment. Various forms of group therapy are being developed in an attempt to counteract the Western emphasis on curing the individual in isolation. Lately, family therapy has been expanded into a new procedure called network therapy in which the patient's entire network of relatives, coworkers, and friends become involved in the treatment.

Another lesson of Aro is less obvious than the benefits of group support. It is the understanding that

treatment begins with a people's indigenous beliefs and their world view, which underlie psychological functioning and provide the basis for healing. Religious values that give meaning and coherence to life can be the healthiest route for many people. As Jung observed years ago, religious factors are inherent in the path toward healing, and the native therapies of Africa support his view.

A supernatural belief system, Western or Eastern, is not a sphere of arbitrary dreams but a sphere of laws that dictate the rules of kinship, the order of the universe, the route of happiness. The Westerner sees only part of the African belief system, such as the witch doctor, and wonders how wild fictions can take root in a reasonable mind. (His own fictions seem perfectly reasonable, of course.) But to the African, the religious-magical system is a great poem, allegorical of human experience, wise in its portrayal of the world and its creatures. There is more method, more reason, in such madness than in the sanity of most people today.

REFERENCES

Burstein, S.R. "Public Health and Prevention of Disease in Primitive Communities." *The Advancement of Science,* Vol. 9, 1952, pp. 75- 81.

Horton, Robin. "African Traditional Thought and Western Science." *Africa,* Vol. 37, 1967, pp. 50-71.

Horton, Robin. *The Traditional Background of Medical Practice in Nigeria.* Institute of Africa Studies, 1966.

Lambo, T.A. "A World View of Mental Health: Recent Developments and Future Trends." *American Journal of Orthopsychiatry,* Vol. 43, 1973, pp. 706-716.

Lambo, T.A. "Psychotherapy in Africa." *Psychotherapy and Psychosomatics,* Vol. 24, 1974, pp. 311-326.

The Mbuti Pygmies: Change and Adaptation

Colin M. Turnbull

THE EDUCATIONAL PROCESS

. . . In the first three years of life every Mbuti alive experiences almost total security. The infant is breast-fed for those three years, and is allowed almost every freedom. Regardless of gender, the infant learns to have absolute trust in both male and female parent. If anything, the father is just another kind of mother, for in the second year the father formally introduces the child to its first solid food. There used to be a beautiful ritual in which the mother presented the child to the father in the middle of the camp, where all important statements are made (anyone speaking from the middle of the camp must be listened to). The father took the child and held it to his breast, and the child would try to suckle, crying "*ema, ema,*" or "mother." The father would shake his head, and say "no, father . . . *eba,*" but like a mother (the Mbuti said), then give the child its first solid food.

At three the child ventures out into the world on its own and enters the *bopi*, what we might call a playground, a tiny camp perhaps a hundred yards from the main camp, often on the edge of a stream. The *bopi* were indeed playgrounds, and often very noisy ones, full of fun and high spirits. But they were also rigorous training grounds for eventual economic responsibility. On entry to the *bopi*, for one thing, the child discovers the importance of age as a structural principle, and the relative unimportance of gender and biological kinship. The *bopi* is the private world of the children. Younger youths may occasionally venture in, but if adults or elders try, as they sometimes do when angry at having their afternoon snooze interrupted, they invariably get driven out, taunted, and ridiculed. Children, among the Mbuti, have rights, but they also learn that they have responsibilities. Before the hunt sets out each day it is the children, sometimes the younger youths, who light the hunting fire.

Ritual among the Mbuti is often so informal and apparently casual that it may pass unnoticed at first. Yet insofar as ritual involves symbolic acts that represent unspoken, perhaps even unthought, concepts or ideals, or invoke other states of being, alternative frames of mind and reference, then Mbuti life is full of ritual. The hunting fire is one of the more obvious of such rituals. Early in the morning children would take firebrands from the *bopi*, where they always lit their own fire with embers from their family hearths, and set off on the trail by which the hunt was to leave that day (the direction of each day's hunt was always settled by discussion the night before). Just a short distance from the camp they lit a fire at the base of a large tree, and covered it with special leaves that made it give off a column of dense smoke. Hunters leaving the camp, both men and women, and such youths and children as were going with them, had to pass by this fire. Some did so casually, without stopping or looking, but passing through the smoke. Others reached into the smoke with their hands as they passed, rubbing the smoke into their bodies. A few always stopped, for a moment, and let the smoke envelop them, only then almost dreamily moving off.

And indeed is *was* a form of intoxication, for the smoke invoked the spirit of the forest, and by passing through it the hunters sought to fill themselves with that spirit, not so much to make the hunt successful as to minimize the

---

sacrilege of killing. Yet they, the hunters, could not light the fire themselves. After all, they were already contaminated by death. Even youths, who daily joined the hunt at the edges, catching any game that escaped the nets, by hand, if they could, were not pure enough to invoke the spirits of forestness. But young children were uncontaminated, as yet untainted by contact with the original sin of the Mbuti. It was their responsibility to light the fire, and if it was not lit then the hunt would not take place, or as the Mbuti put it, the hunt *could* not take place.

In this way even the children in Mbuti society, at the first of the four age levels that dominate Mbuti social structure, are given very real social responsibility and see themselves as a part of that structure, by virtue of their purity. After all, they have just been born from the source of all purity, the forest itself. By the same reasoning, the elders, who are about to return to that ultimate source of all being, through death, are at least closer to purity than the adults, who are daily contaminated by killing. Elders no longer go on the hunt. So, like the children, the elders have important sacred ritual responsibilities in the Mbuti division of labor by age.

In the *bopi* the children play, but they have no "games" in the strict sense of the word. Levi-Strauss has perceptively compared games with rituals, suggesting that whereas in a game the players start theoretically equal but end up unequal, in a ritual just the reverse takes place. All are equalized. Mbuti children could be seen every day playing in the *bopi*, but not once did I see a game, not one activity that smacked of any kind of competition, except perhaps that competition that it is necessary for us all to feel from time to time, competition with our own private and personal inadequacies. One such pastime (rather than game) was tree climbing. A dozen or so children would climb up a young sapling. Reaching the top, their weight brought the sapling bending down until it almost touched the ground. Then all the children leapt off together, shrieking as the young tree sprang upright again with a rush. Sometimes one child, male or female, might stay on a

little too long, either out of fear, or out of bravado, or from sheer carelessness or bad timing. Whatever the reason, it was a lesson most children only needed to be taught once, for the result was that you got flung upward with the tree, and were lucky to escape with no more than a few bruises and a very bad fright.

Other pastimes taught the children the rules of hunting and gathering. Frequently elders, who stayed in camp when the hunt went off, called the children into the main camp and enacted a mock hunt with them there. Stretching a discarded piece of net across the camp, they pretended to be animals, showing the children how to drive them into the nets. And, of course, the children played house, learning the patterns of cooperation that would be necessary for them later in life. They also learned the prime lesson of egality, other than for purposes of division of labor making no distinction between male and female, this nuclear family or that. All in the *bopi* were *apua'i* to each other, and so they would remain throughout their lives. At every age level—childhood, youth, adulthood, or old age—everyone of that level is *apua'i* to all the others. Only adults sometimes (but so rarely that I think it was only done as a kind of joke, or possibly insult) made the distinction that the Bira do, using *apua'i* for male and *amua'i* for female. Male or female, for the Mbuti, if you are the same age you are *apua'i*, and that means that you share everything equally, regardless of kinship or gender.

YOUTH AND POLITICS

Sometime before the age of puberty boys or girls, whenever they feel ready, move back into the main camp from the *bopi* and join the youths. This is when they must assume new responsibilities, which for the youths are primarily political. Already, in the *bopi*, the children become involved in disputes, and are sometimes instrumental in settling them by ridicule, for nothing hurts an adult more than being ridiculed by children. The art of reason, however, is something they learn from the youths,

and it is the youths who apply the art of reason to the settlement of disputes.

When puberty comes it separates them, for the first time in their experience, from each other as *apua'i*. Very plainly girls are different from boys. When a girl has her first menstrual period the whole camp celebrates with the wild *elima* festival, in which the girl, and some of her chosen girl friends, are the center of all attention, living together in a special *elima* house. Male youths sit outside the *elima* house and wait for the girls to come out, usually in the afternoon, for the *elima* singing. They sing in antiphony, the girls leading, the boys responding. Boys come from neighboring territories all around, for this is a time of courtship. But there are always eligible youths within the camp as well, and the *elima* girl may well choose girls from other territories to come and join her, so there is more than enough excuse for every youth to carry on several flirtations, legitimate or illegitimate. I have known even first cousins to flirt with each other, but learned to be prudent enough not to pull out my kinship charts and point this out—well, not in public anyway.

The *elima* is more than a premarital festival, more than a joint initiation of youth into adulthood, and more than a rite of passage through puberty, though it is all those things. It is a public recognition of the opposition of male and female, and every *elima* is used to highlight the *potential* for conflict that lies in that opposition. As at other times of crisis, at puberty, a time of change and uncertainty, the Mbuti bring all the major forms of conflict out into the open. And the one that evidently most concerns them is the male/female opposition.

The adults begin to play a special form of "tug of war" that is clearly a ritual rather than a game. All the men are on one side, the women on the other. At first it looks like a game, but quickly it becomes clear that the objective is for *neither* side to win. As soon as the women begin to win, one of them will leave the end of the line and run around to join the men, assuming a deep male voice and in other ways ridicul-

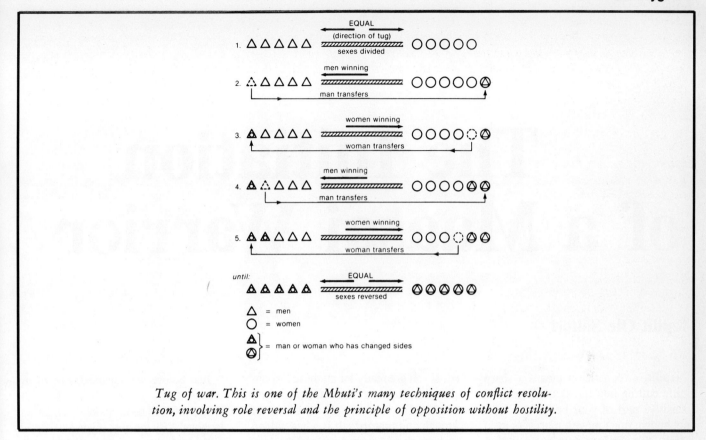

Tug of war. This is one of the Mbuti's many techniques of conflict resolution, involving role reversal and the principle of opposition without hostility.

ing manhood. Then, as the men begin to win, a male will similarly join the women, making fun of womanhood as he does so. Each adult on changing sides attempts to outdo all the others in ridiculing the opposite sex. Finally, when nearly all have switched sides, and sexes, the ritual battle between the genders simply collapses into hysterical laughter, the contestants letting go of the rope, falling onto the ground, and rolling over with mirth. Neither side wins, both are equalized very nicely, and each learns the essential lesson, that there should be *no* contest. . . .

The Initiation of a Maasai Warrior

Tepilit Ole Saitoti

"Tepilit, circumcision means a sharp knife cutting into the skin of the most sensitive part of your body. You must not budge; don't move a muscle or even blink. You can face only one direction until the operation is completed. The slightest movement on your part will mean you are a coward, incompetent and unworthy to be a Maasai man. Ours has always been a proud family, and we would like to keep it that way. We will not tolerate unnecessary embarrassment, so you had better be ready. If you are not, tell us now so that we will not proceed. Imagine yourself alone remaining uncircumcised like the water youth [white people]. I hear they are not circumcised. Such a thing is not known in Maasailand; therefore, circumcision will have to take place even if it means holding you down until it is completed."

My father continued to speak and every one of us kept quiet. "The pain you will feel is symbolic. There is a deeper meaning in all this. Circumcision means a break between childhood and adulthood. For the first time in your life, you are regarded as a grownup, a complete man or woman. You will be expected to give and not just to receive. To protect the family always, not just to be protected yourself. And your wise judgment will for the first time be taken into consideration. No family affairs will be discussed without your being consult-

ed. If you are ready for all these responsibilities, tell us now. Coming into manhood is not simply a matter of growth and maturity. It is a heavy load on your shoulders and especially a burden on the mind. Too much of this—I am done. I have said all I wanted to say. Fellows, if you have anything to add, go ahead and tell your brother, because I am through. I have spoken."

After a prolonged silence, one of my half-brothers said awkwardly, "Face it, man . . . it's painful. I won't lie about it, but it is not the end. We all went through it, after all. Only blood will flow, not milk." There was laughter and my father left.

My brother Lellia said, "Men, there are many things we must acquire and preparations we must make before the ceremony, and we will need the cooperation and help of all of you. Ostrich feathers for the crown and wax for the arrows must be collected."

"Are you *orkirekenyi?*" one of my brothers asked. I quickly replied no, and there was laughter. *Orkirekenyi* is a person who has transgressed sexually. For you must not have sexual intercourse with any circumcised woman before you yourself are circumcised. You must wait until you are circumcised. If you have not waited, you will be fined. Your father, mother, and the circumciser will take a cow from you as punishment.

Just before we departed, one of my closest friends said, "If you kick the knife, you will be in trouble." There was laughter. "By the way, if you have decided to kick the circumciser, do it well. Silence him once and for all." "Do it the way you kick a football in school." "That will fix him," another added, and we all laughed our heads off again as we departed.

The following month was a month of preparation. I and others collected wax, ostrich feathers, honey to be made into honey beer for the elders to drink on the day of circumcision, and all the other required articles.

Three days before the ceremony my head was shaved and I discarded all my belongings, such as my necklaces, garments, spear, and sword. I even had to shave my pubic hair. Circumcision in many ways is similar to Christian baptism. You must put all the sins you have committed during childhood behind and embark as a new person with a different outlook on a new life.

The circumciser came the following day and handed the ritual knives to me. He left drinking a calabash of beer. I stared at the knives uneasily. It was hard to accept that he was going to use them on my organ. I was to sharpen them and protect them from people of ill will who might try to blunt them, thus rendering them inefficient during the ritual and thereby bringing shame on our family. The knives threw a chill down my spine; I was not sure I was sharpening them properly, so I took them to my closest brother for him to check out, and he assured me that the knives were all right. I hid them well and waited.

Tension started building between me and my relatives, most of whom worried that I wouldn't make it through the ceremony valiantly. Some even snarled at me, which was their way of encouraging me. Others threw insults and abusive words my way. My sister Loiyan in particular was more troubled by the whole affair than anyone in the whole family. She had to assume my mother's role during the circumcision. Were I to fail my initiation, she would have to face the consequences. She would be spat upon and even beaten for representing the mother of an unworthy son. The same fate would befall my father, but he seemed unconcerned. He had this weird belief that because I was not particularly handsome, I must be brave. He kept saying, "God is not so bad as to have made him ugly and a coward at the same time."

Failure to be brave during circumcision would have other unfortunate consequences: the herd of cattle belonging to the family still in the compound would be beaten until they stampeded; the slaughtered oxen and honey beer prepared during the month before the ritual would go to waste; the initiate's food would be spat upon and he would have to eat it or else get a severe beating. Everyone would call him Olkasiodoi, the knife kicker.

Kicking the knife of the circumciser would not help you anyway. If you struggle and try to get away during the ritual, you will be held down until the operation is completed. Such failure of nerve would haunt you in the future. For example, no one will choose a person who kicked the knife for a position of leadership. However, there have been instances in which a person who failed to go through circumcision successfully became very brave afterwards because he was filled with anger over the incident; no one dares to scold him or remind him of it. His agemates, particularly the warriors, will act as if nothing had happened.

During the circumcision of a woman, on the other hand, she is allowed to cry as long as she does not hinder the operation. It is common to see a woman crying and kicking during circumcision. Warriors are usually summoned to help hold her down.

For woman, circumcision means an end to the company of Maasai warriors. After they recuperate, they soon get married, and often to men twice their age.

The closer it came to the hour of truth, the more I was hated, particularly by those closest to me. I was deeply troubled by the withdrawal of all the support I needed. My annoyance turned into anger and resolve. I decided not to budge or blink, even if I were to see my intestines flowing before me. My resolve was hardened when newly circumcised warriors came to sing for me. Their songs were utterly insulting, intended to annoy me further. They tucked their wax arrows under my crotch and rubbed them on my nose. They repeatedly called me names.

By the end of the singing, I was fuming. Crying would have meant I was a coward. After midnight they left me alone and I went into the house and tried to sleep but could not. I was exhausted and numb but remained awake all night.

At dawn I was summoned once again by the newly circumcised warriors. They piled more and more insults on me. They sang their weird songs with even more vigor and excitement than before. The songs praised warriorhood and encouraged one to achieve it at all costs. The songs continued until the sun shone on the cattle horns clearly. I was summoned to the main cattle gate, in my hand a ritual cowhide from a cow that had been properly slaughtered during my naming ceremony. I went past Loiyan, who was milking a cow, and she muttered something. She was shaking all over. There was so much tension that people could hardly breathe.

I laid the hide down and a boy was ordered to pour ice-cold water, known as *engare entolu* (ax water), over my head. It dripped all over my naked body and I shook furiously. In a matter of seconds I was summoned to sit down. A large crowd of boys and men formed a semicircle in front of me; women are not allowed to watch male circumcision and vice-versa. That was the last thing I saw clearly. As soon as I sat down, the circumciser appeared, his knives at the ready. He spread my legs and said, "One cut," a pronouncement necessary to prevent an initiate from claiming that he had been taken by surprise. He splashed a white liquid, a ceremonial paint called *enturoto*, across my face. Almost immediately I felt a spark of pain under my belly as the knife cut through my penis' foreskin. I happened to choose to look in the direction of the operation. I continued to observe the circumciser's fingers working mechanically. The pain became numbness and my lower body felt heavy, as if I were weighed down by a heavy burden. After fifteen minutes or so, a man who had been supporting from behind pointed at something, as if to assist the circumciser. I came to learn later that the circumciser's eyesight had been failing him and that my brothers had been mad at him because the operation had taken longer than was usually necessary. All the same, I remained pinned down until the operation was over. I heard a call for milk to wash the knives, which signaled the end, and soon the ceremony was over.

With words of praise, I was told to wake up, but I remained seated. I waited for the customary presents in appreciation of my bravery. My father gave me a cow and so did my brother Lillia. The man who had supported my back and my brother-in-law gave me a heifer. In all I had eight animals given to me. I was carried inside the house to my own bed to recuperate as activities intensified to celebrate my bravery.

I laid on my own bed and bled profusely. The blood must be retained within the bed, for according to Maasai tradition, it must not spill to the ground. I was drenched in my own blood. I stopped bleeding after about half an hour but soon was in intolerable pain. I was supposed to squeeze my organ and force blood to flow out of the wound, but no one had told me, so the blood coagulated and caused unbearable pain. The circumciser was brought to my aid and showed me what to do, and soon the pain subsided.

The following morning, I was escorted by a small boy to a nearby valley to walk and relax, allowing my wound to drain. This was common for everyone who had been circumcised, as well as for women who had just given birth. Having lost a lot of blood, I was extremely weak. I walked very slowly, but in spite of my caution I fainted. I tried to hang on to bushes and shrubs, but I fell, irritating my wound. I came out of unconsciousness quickly, and the boy who was escorting me never realized what had happened. I was so scared that I told him to lead me back home. I could have died without there being anyone around who could have helped me. From that day on, I was selective of my company while I was feeble.

In two weeks I was able to walk and was taken to join other newly circumcised boys far away from our settlement. By tradition Maasai initiates are required to decorate their headdresses with all kinds of colorful birds they have killed. On our way to the settlement, we hunted birds and teased girls by shooting them with our wax blunt arrows. We danced and ate and were well treated wherever we went. We were protected from the cold and rain during the healing period. We were not allowed to touch food, as we were regarded as unclean, so whenever we ate we had to use specially prepared sticks instead. We remained in this pampered state until our wounds healed and our headdresses were removed. Our heads were shaved, we discarded our black cloaks and bird headdresses and embarked as newly shaven warriors, Irkeleani.

As long as I live I will never forget the day my head was shaved and I emerged a man, a Maasai warrior. I felt a sense of control over my destiny so great that no words can accurately describe it. I now stood with confidence, pride, and happiness of being, for all around me I was desired and loved by beautiful, sensuous Maasai maidens. I could now interact with women and even have sex with them, which I not been allowed before. I was now regarded as a responsible person.

In the old days, warriors were like gods, and women and men wanted only to be the parent of a warrior. Everything else would be taken care of as a result. When a poor family had a warrior, they

ceased to be poor. The warrior would go on raids and bring cattle back. The warrior would defend the family against all odds. When a society respects the individual and displays confidence in him the way the Maasai do their warriors, the individual can grow to his fullest potential. Whenever there was a task requiring physical strength or bravery, the Maasai would call upon their warriors. They hardly ever fall short of what is demanded of them and so are characterized by pride, confidence, and an extreme sense of freedom. But there is an old saying in Maasai: "You are never a free man until your father dies." In other words, your father is paramount while he is alive and you are obligated to respect him. My father took advantage of this principle and held a tight grip on all his warriors, including myself. He always wanted to know where we all were at any given time. We fought against his restrictions, but without success. I, being the youngest of my father's five warriors, tried even harder to get loose repeatedly, but each time I was punished severely.

Roaming the plains with other warriors in pursuit of girls and adventure was a warrior's pastime. We would wander from one settlement to another, singing, wrestling, hunting, and just playing. Often I was ready to risk my father's punishment for this wonderful freedom.

One clear day my father sent me to take sick children and one of his wives to the dispensary in the Korongoro Highlands. We rode in the L.S.B. Leakey lorry. We ascended the highlands and were soon attended to in the local hospital. Near the conservation offices I met several acquaintances, and one of them told me of an unusual circumcision that was about to take place in a day or two. All the local warriors and girls were preparing to attend it.

The highlands were a lush green from the seasonal rains and the sky was a purple-blue with no clouds in sight. The land was overflowing with milk, and the warriors felt and looked their best, as they always did when there was plenty to eat and drink. Everyone was at ease. The demands the community usually made on warriors during the dry sea-

son when water was scarce and wells had to be dug were now not necessary. Herds and flocks were entrusted to youths to look after. The warriors had all the time for themselves. But my father was so strict that even at times like these he still insisted on overworking us in one way or another. He believed that by keeping us busy, he would keep us out of trouble.

When I heard about the impending ceremony, I decided to remain behind in the Korongoro Highlands and attend it now that the children had been treated. I knew very well that I would have to make up a story for my father upon my return, but I would worry about that later. I had left my spear at home when I boarded the bus, thinking that I would be coming back that very day. I felt lighter but now regretted having left it behind; I was so used to carrying it wherever I went. In gales of laughter resulting from our continuous teasing of each other, we made our way toward a distant kraal. We walked at a leisurely pace and reveled in the breeze. As usual we talked about the women we desired, among other things.

The following day we were joined by a long line of colorfully dressed girls and warriors from the kraal and the neighborhood where we had spent the night, and we left the highland and headed to Ingorienito to the rolling hills on the lower slopes to attend the circumcision ceremony. From there one could see Oldopai Gorge, where my parents lived, and the Inaapi hills in the middle of the Serengeti Plain.

Three girls and a boy were to be initiated on the same day, an unusual occasion. Four oxen were to be slaughtered, and many people would therefore attend. As we descended, we saw the kraal where the ceremony would take place. All those people dressed in red seemed from a distance like flamingos standing in a lake. We could see lines of other guests heading to the settlements. Warriors made gallant cries of happiness known as *enkiseer*. Our line of warriors and girls responded to their cries even more gallantly.

In serpentine fashion, we entered the gates of the settlement. Holding spears in our left hands, we warriors walked proudly, taking small steps, swaying like palm trees, impressing our girls, who walked parallel to us in another line, and of course the spectators, who gazed at us approvingly.

We stopped in the center of the kraal and waited to be greeted. Women and children welcomed us. We put our hands on the children's heads, which is how children are commonly saluted. After the greetings were completed, we started dancing.

Our singing echoed off the kraal fence and nearby trees. Another line of warriors came up the hill and entered the compound, also singing and moving slowly toward us. Our singing grew in intensity. Both lines of warriors moved parallel to each other, and our feet pounded the ground with style. We stamped vigorously, as if to tell the next line and the spectators that we were the best.

The singing continued until the hot sun was overhead. We recessed and ate food already prepared for us by other warriors. Roasted meat was for those who were to eat meat, and milk for the others. By our tradition, meat and milk must not be consumed at the same time, for this would be a betrayal of the animal. It was regarded as cruel to consume a product of the animal that could be obtained while it was alive, such as milk, and meat, which was only available after the animal had been killed.

After eating we resumed singing, and I spotted a tall, beautiful *esiankiki* (young maiden) of Masiaya whose family was one of the largest and richest in our area. She stood very erect and seemed taller than the rest.

One of her breasts could be seen just above her dress, which was knotted at the shoulder. While I was supposed to dance generally to please all the spectators, I took it upon myself to please her especially. I stared at and flirted with her, and she and I danced in unison at times. We complemented each other very well.

During a break, I introduced myself to the *esiankiki* and told her I would like to see her after the dance. "Won't you need a warrior to escort you home later when the evening threatens?" I said. She replied, "Perhaps, but the evening is still far away."

I waited patiently. When the dance ended, I saw her departing with a group of other women her age. She gave me a sidelong glance, and I took that to mean come later and not now. With so many others around, I would not have been able to confer with her as I would have liked anyway.

With another warrior, I wandered around the kraal killing time until the herds returned from pasture. Before the sun dropped out of sight, we departed. As the kraal of the *esiankiki* was in the lowlands, a place called Enkoloa, we descended leisurely, our spears resting on our shoulders.

We arrived at the woman's kraal and found that cows were now being milked. One could hear the women trying to appease the cows by singing to them. Singing calms cows down, making it easier to milk them. There were no warriors in the whole kraal except for the two of us. Girls went around into warriors' houses as usual and collected milk for us. I was so eager to go and meet my *esiankiki* that I could hardly wait for nightfall. The warriors' girls were trying hard to be sociable, but my mind was not with them. I found them to be childish, loud, bothersome, and boring.

As the only warriors present, we had to keep them company and sing for them, at least for a while, as required by custom. I told the other warrior to sing while I tried to figure out how to approach my *esiankiki*. Still a novice warrior, I was not experienced with women and was in fact still afraid of them. I could flirt from a distance, of course. But sitting down with a woman and trying to seduce her was another matter. I had already tried twice to approach women soon after my circumcision and had failed. I got as far as the door of one woman's house and felt my heart beating like a Congolese drum; breathing became difficult and I had to turn back. Another time I managed to get in the house and suceeded in sitting on the bed, but then I started trembling until the whole bed was shaking, and conversation became difficult. I left the house and the woman, amazed and speechless, and never went back to her again.

Tonight I promised myself I would be brave and would not make any silly, ridiculous moves. "I must be mature and not afraid," I kept reminding myself, as I remembered an incident involving one of my relatives when he was still very young and, like me, afraid of women. He went to a woman's house and sat on a stool for a whole hour; he was afraid to awaken her, as his heart was pounding and he was having difficulty breathing.

When he finally calmed down, he woke her up, and their conversation went something like this:

"Woman, wake up."

"Why should I?"

"To light the fire."

"For what?"

"So you can see me."

"I already know who you are. Why don't *you* light the fire, as you're nearer to it than me?"

"It's your house and it's only proper that you light it yourself."

"I don't feel like it."

"At least wake up so we can talk, as I have something to tell you."

"Say it."

"I need you."

"I do not need one-eyed types like yourself."

"One-eyed people are people too."

"That might be so, but they are not to my taste."

They continued talking for quite some time, and the more they spoke, the braver he became. He did not sleep with her that night, but later on he persisted until he won her over. I doubted whether I was as strong-willed as he, but the fact that he had met with success encouraged me. I told my warrior friend where to find me should he need me, and then I departed.

When I entered the house of my *esiankiki,* I called for the woman of the house, and as luck would have it, my lady responded. She was waiting for me. I felt better, and I proceeded to talk to her like a professional. After much talking back and forth, I joined her in bed.

The night was calm, tender, and loving, like most nights after initiation ceremonies as big as this one. There must have been a lot of courting and lovemaking.

Maasai women can be very hard to deal with sometimes. They can simply reject a man outright and refuse to change their minds. Some play hard to get, but in reality are testing the man to see whether he is worth their while. Once a friend of mine while still young was powerfully attracted to a woman nearly his mother's age. He put a bold move on her. At first the woman could not believe his intention, or rather was amazed by his courage. The name of the warrior was Ngengeiya, or Drizzle.

"Drizzle, what do you want?"

The warrior stared her right in the eye and said, "You."

"For what?"

"To make love to you."

"I am your mother's age."

"The choice was either her or you."

This remark took the woman by surprise. She had underestimated the saying "There is no such thing as a young warrior." When you are a warrior, you are expected to perform bravely in any situation. Your age and size are immaterial.

"You mean you could really love me like a grown-up man?"

"Try me, woman."

He moved in on her. Soon the woman started moaning with excitement, calling out his name. "Honey Drizzle, Honey Drizzle, you *are* a man." In a breathy, stammering voice, she said, "A real man."

Her attractiveness made Honey Drizzle ignore her relative old age. The Maasai believe that if an older and a younger person have intercourse, it is the older person who stands to gain. For instance, it is believed that an older woman having an affair with a young man starts to appear younger and healthier, while the young man grows older and unhealthy.

The following day when the initiation rites had ended, I decided to return home. I had offended my father by staying away from home without his consent, so I prepared myself for whatever punishment he might inflict on me. I walked home alone.

The Secrets of Haiti's Living Dead

A Harvard botanist investigates mystic potions, voodoo rites, and the making of zombies.

Gino Del Guercio

Gino Del Guercio is a national science writer for United Press International, currently on leave studying television production as a Macy fellow at Boston's WGBH.

Five years ago, a man walked into l'Estère, a village in central Haiti, approached a peasant woman named Angelina Narcisse, and identified himself as her brother Clairvius. If he had not introduced himself using a boyhood nickname and mentioned facts only intimate family members knew, she would not have believed him. Because, eighteen years earlier, Angelina had stood in a small cemetery north of her village and watched as her brother Clairvius was buried.

The man told Angelina he remembered that night well. He knew when he was lowered into his grave, because he was fully conscious, although he could not speak or move. As the earth was thrown over his coffin, he felt as if he were floating over the grave. The scar on his right cheek, he said, was caused by a nail driven through his casket.

The night he was buried, he told Angelina, a voodoo priest raised him from the grave. He was beaten with a sisal whip and carried off to a sugar plantation in northern Haiti where, with other zombies, he was forced to work as a slave. Only with the death of the zombie master were they able to escape, and Narcisse eventually returned home.

Legend has it that zombies are the living dead, raised from their graves and animated by malevolent voodoo sorcerers, usually for some evil purpose. Most Haitians believe in zombies, and Narcisse's claim is not unique. At about the time he reappeared, in 1980, two women turned up in other villages saying they were zombies. In the same year, in northern Haiti, the local peasants claimed to have found a group of zombies wandering aimlessly in the fields.

But Narcisse's case was different in one crucial respect; it was documented. His death had been recorded by doctors at the American-directed Schweitzer Hospital in Deschapelles. On April 30, 1962, hospital records show, Narcisse walked into the hospital's emergency room spitting up blood. He was feverish and full of aches. His doctors could not diagnose his illness, and his symptoms grew steadily worse. Three days after he entered the hospital, according to the records, he died. The attending physicians, an American among them, signed his death certificate. His body was placed in cold storage for twenty hours, and then he was buried. He said he remembered hearing his doctors pronounce him dead while his sister wept at his bedside.

At the Centre de Psychiatrie et Neurologie in Port-au-Prince, Dr. Lamarque Douyon, a Haitian-born, Canadian-trained psychiatrist, has been systematically investigating all reports of zombies since 1961. Though convinced zombies were real, he had been unable to find a scientific explanation for the phenomenon. He did not believe zombies were people raised from the dead, but that did not make them any less interesting. He speculated that victims were only made to *look* dead, probably by means of a drug that dramatically slowed metabolism. The victim was buried, dug up within a few hours, and somehow reawakened.

The Narcisse case provided Douyon with evidence strong enough to warrant a request for assistance from colleagues in New York. Douyon wanted to find an ethnobotanist, a traditional-medicines expert, who could track down the zombie potion he was sure existed. Aware of the medical potential of a drug that could dramatically lower metabolism, a group organized by the late Dr. Nathan Kline—a New York psychiatrist and pioneer in the field of psychopharmacology—raised the funds necessary to send someone to investigate.

The search for that someone led to the Harvard Botanical Museum, one of the world's foremost institutes of ethnobiology. Its director, Richard Evans Schultes, Jeffrey professor of biology, had spent thirteen years in the tropics studying native medicines. Some of his best-known work is the investigation of curare, the substance used by the nomadic people of the Amazon to poison their darts. Refined into a powerful muscle relaxant called D-tubocurarine, it is now an essential component of the anesthesia used during almost all surgery.

Schultes would have been a natural for the Haitian investigation, but he was too busy. He recommended another Harvard ethnobotanist for the assignment, Wade Davis, a 28-year-old Canadian pursuing a doctorate in biology.

Davis grew up in the tall pine forests of British Columbia and entered Harvard in 1971, influenced by a Life magazine story on the student strike of 1969. Before Harvard, the only Americans he had known were draft dodgers, who seemed very exotic. "I used to fight forest fires with them," Davis says. "Like everybody else, I thought America was where it was at. And I wanted to go to Harvard because of that Life article. When I got there, I realized it wasn't quite what I had in mind."

Davis took a course from Schultes, and when he decided to go to South America to study plants, he approached his professor for guidance. "He was an extraordinary figure," Davis remembers. "He was a man who had done it all. He had lived alone for years in the Amazon." Schultes sent Davis to the rain forest with two letters of introduction and two pieces of advice: wear a pith helmet and try ayahuasca, a powerful hallucinogenic vine. During that expedition and others, Davis proved himself an "outstanding field man," says his mentor. Now, in early 1982, Schultes called him into his office and asked if he had plans for spring break.

"I always took to Schultes's assignments like a plant takes to water," says Davis, tall and blond, with inquisitive blue eyes. "Whatever Shultes told me to do, I did. His letters of introduction opened up a whole world." This time the world was Haiti.

Davis knew nothing about the Caribbean island—and nothing about African traditions, which serve as Haiti's cultural basis. He certainly did not believe in zombies. "I thought it was a lark," he says now.

Davis landed in Haiti a week after his conversation with Schultes, armed with a hypothesis about how the zombie drug—if it existed—might be made. Setting out to explore, he discovered a country materially impoverished, but rich in culture and mystery. He was impressed by the cohesion of Haitian society; he found none of the crime,

social disorder, and rampant drug and alcohol abuse so common in many of the other Caribbean islands. The cultural wealth and cohesion, he believes, spring from the country's turbulent history.

During the French occupation of the late eighteenth century, 370,000 African-born slaves were imported to Haiti between 1780 and 1790. In 1791, the black population launched one of the few successful slave revolts in history, forming secret societies and overcoming first the French plantation owners and then a detachment of troops from Napoleon's army, sent to quell the revolt. For the next hundred years Haiti was the only independent black republic in the Caribbean, populated by people who did not forget their African heritage. "You can almost argue that Haiti is more African than Africa," Davis says. "When the west coast of Africa was being disrupted by colonialism and the slave trade, Haiti was essentially left alone. The amalgam of beliefs in Haiti is unique, but it's very, very African."

Davis discovered that the vast majority of Haitian peasants practice voodoo, a sophisticated religion with African roots. Says Davis, "It was immediately obvious that the stereotypes of voodoo weren't true. Going around the countryside, I found clues to a whole complex social world." Vodounists believe they communicate directly with, indeed are often possessed by, the many spirits who populate the everyday world. Vodoun society is a system of education, law, and medicine; it embodies a code of ethics that regulates social behavior. In rural areas, secret vodoun societies, much like those found on the west coast of Africa, are as much or more in control of everyday life as the Haitian government.

Although most outsiders dismissed the zombie phenomenon as folklore, some early investigators, convinced of its reality, tried to find a scientific explanation. The few who sought a zombie drug failed. Nathan Kline, who helped finance Davis's expedition, had searched unsuccessfully, as had Lamarque Douyon, the Haitian psychiatrist. Zora Neale Hurston, an American black woman, may have come closest. An anthropological pioneer, she went to Haiti in the Thirties, studied vodoun

society, and wrote a book on the subject, *Tell My Horse,* first published in 1938. She knew about the secret societies and was convinced zombies were real, but if a powder existed, she too failed to obtain it.

Davis obtained a sample in a few weeks.

He arrived in Haiti with the names of several contacts. A BBC reporter familiar with the Narcisse case had suggested he talk with Marcel Pierre. Pierre owned the Eagle Bar, a bordello in the city of Saint Marc. He was also a voodoo sorcerer and had supplied the BBC with a physiologically active powder of unknown ingredients. Davis found him willing to negotiate. He told Pierre he was a representative of "powerful but anonymous interests in New York," willing to pay generously for the priest's services, provided no questions were asked. Pierre agreed to be helpful for what Davis will only say was a "sizable sum." Davis spent a day watching Pierre gather the ingredients—including human bones—and grind them together with mortar and pestle. However, from his knowledge of poison, Davis knew immediately that nothing in the formula could produce the powerful effects of zombification.

Three weeks later, Davis went back to the Eagle Bar, where he found Pierre sitting with three associates. Davis challenged him. He called him a charlatan. Enraged, the priest gave him a second vial, claiming that this was the real poison. Davis pretended to pour the powder into his palm and rub it into his skin. "You're a dead man," Pierre told him, and he might have been, because this powder proved to be genuine. But, as the substance had not actually touched him, Davis was able to maintain his bravado, and Pierre was impressed. He agreed to make the poison and show Davis how it was done.

The powder, which Davis keeps in a small vial, looks like dry black dirt. It contains parts of toads, sea worms, lizards, tarantulas, and human bones. (To obtain the last ingredient, he and Pierre unearthed a child's grave on a nocturnal trip to the cemetery.) The poison is rubbed into the victim's skin. Within hours he begins to feel nauseated and has difficulty breathing. A pins-

and-needles sensation afflicts his arms and legs, then progresses to the whole body. The subject becomes paralyzed; his lips turn blue for lack of oxygen. Quickly—sometimes within six hours—his metabolism is lowered to a level almost indistinguishable from death.

As Davis discovered, making the poison is an inexact science. Ingredients varied in the five samples he eventually acquired, although the active agents were always the same. And the poison came with no guarantee. Davis speculates that sometimes instead of merely paralyzing the victim, the compound kills him. Sometimes the victim suffocates in the coffin before he can be resurrected. But clearly the potion works well enough often enough to make zombies more than a figment of Haitian imagination.

Analysis of the powder produced another surprise. "When I went down to Haiti originally," says Davis, "my hypothesis was that the formula would

contain *concombre zombi,* the 'zombie's cucumber,' which is a *Datura* plant. I thought somehow *Datura* was used in putting people down." *Datura* is a powerful psychoactive plant, found in West Africa as well as other tropical areas and used there in ritual as well as criminal activities. Davis had found *Datura* growing in Haiti. Its popular name suggested the plant was used in creating zombies.

But, says Davis, "there were a lot of problems with the *Datura* hypothesis. Partly it was a question of how the drug was administered. *Datura* would create a stupor in huge doses, but it just wouldn't produce the kind of immobility that was key. These people had to appear dead, and there aren't many drugs that will do that."

One of the ingredients Pierre included in the second formula was a dried fish, a species of puffer or blowfish, common to most parts of the world. It gets its name from its ability to fill itself with

water and swell to several times its normal size when threatened by predators. Many of these fish contain a powerful poison known as tetrodotoxin. One of the most powerful nonprotein poisons known to man, tetrodotoxin turned up in every sample of zombie powder that Davis acquired.

Numerous well-documented accounts of puffer fish poisoning exist, but the most famous accounts come from the Orient, where *fugu* fish, a species of puffer, is considered a delicacy. In Japan, special chefs are licensed to prepare *fugu*. The chef removes enough poison to make the fish nonlethal, yet enough remains to create exhilarating physiological effects—tingles up and down the spine, mild prickling of the tongue and lips, euphoria. Several dozen Japanese die each year, having bitten off more than they should have.

"When I got hold of the formula and saw it was the *fugu* fish, that suddenly

Richard Schultes

His students continue his tradition of pursuing botanical research in the likeliest of unlikely places.

Richard Evans Schultes, Jeffrey professor of biology emeritus, has two homes, and they could not be more different. The first is Cambridge, where he served as director of the Harvard Botanical Museum from 1970 until last year, when he became director emeritus. During his tenure he interested generations of students in the exotic botany of the Amazon rain forest. His impact on the field through his own research is worldwide. The scholarly ethnobotanist with steel-rimmed glasses, bald head, and white lab coat is as much a part of the Botanical Museum as the thousands of plant specimens and botanical texts on the museum shelves.

In his austere office is a picture of a crew-cut, younger man stripped to the waist, his arms decorated with

tribal paint. This is Schultes's other persona. Starting in 1941, he spent thirteen years in the rain forests of South America, living with the Indians and studying the plants they use for medicinal and spiritual purposes.

Schultes is concerned that many of the people he has studied are giving up traditional ways. "The people of so-called primitive societies are becoming civilized and losing all their forefathers' knowledge of plant lore," he says. "We'll be losing the tremendous amounts of knowledge they've gained over thousands of years. We're interested in the practical aspects with the hope that new medicines and other things can be developed for our own civilization."

Schultes's exploits are legendary in the biology department. Once, while gathering South American plant specimens hundreds of miles from civilization, he contracted beriberi. For forty days he fought creeping paralysis and overwhelming fatigue as he paddled back to a doctor. "It was an extraordinary feat of endurance," says disciple Wade

Davis. "He is really one of the last nineteenth-century naturalists."

Hallucinogenic plants are one of Schultes's primary interests. As a Harvard undergraduate in the Thirties, he lived with Oklahoma's Kiowa Indians to observe their use of plants. He participated in their peyote ceremonies and wrote his thesis on the hallucinogenic cactus. He has also studied other hallucinogens, such as morning glory seeds, sacred mushrooms, and ayahuasca, a South American vision vine. Schultes's work has led to the development of anesthetics made from curare and alternative sources of natural rubber.

Schultes's main concern these days is the scientific potential of plants in the rapidly disappearing Amazon jungle. "If chemists are going to get material on 80,000 species and then analyze them, they'll never finish the job before the jungle is gone," he says. "The short cut is to find out what the [native] people have learned about the plant properties during many years of living in the very rich flora."

—G.D.G.

threw open the whole Japanese literature," says Davis. Case histories of *fugu* poisoning read like accounts of zombification. Victims remain conscious but unable to speak or move. A man who had "died" after eating *fugu* recovered seven days later in the morgue. Several summers ago, another Japanese poisoned by *fugu* revived after he was nailed into his coffin. "Almost all of Narcisse's symptoms correlated. Even strange things such as the fact that he said he was conscious and could hear himself pronounced dead. Stuff that I thought had to be magic, that seemed crazy. But, in fact, that is what people who get *fugu*-fish poisoning experience."

Davis was certain he had solved the mystery. But far from being the end of his investigation, identifying the poison was, in fact, its starting point. "The drug alone didn't make zombies," he explains. "Japanese victims of puffer-fish poisoning don't become zombies, they become poison victims. All the drug could do was set someone up for a whole series of psychological pressures that would be rooted in the culture. I wanted to know why zombification was going on," he says.

He sought a cultural answer, an explanation rooted in the structure and beliefs of Haitian society. Was zombification simply a random criminal activity? He thought not. He had discovered that Clairvius Narcisse and "Ti Femme," a second victim he interviewed, were village pariahs. Ti Femme was regarded as a thief. Narcisse had abandoned his children and deprived his brother of land that was rightfully his. Equally suggestive, Narcisse claimed that his aggrieved brother had sold him to a *bokor,* a voodoo priest who dealt in black magic; he made cryptic reference to having been tried and found guilty by the "masters of the land."

Gathering poisons from various parts of the country, Davis had come into direct contact with the vodoun secret societies. Returning to the anthropological literature on Haiti and pursuing his contacts with informants, Davis came to understand the social matrix within which zombies were created.

Davis's investigations uncovered the importance of the secret societies. These groups trace their origins to the bands of escaped slaves that organized the revolt against the French in the late eighteenth century. Open to both men and women, the societies control specific territories of the country. Their meetings take place at night, and in many rural parts of Haiti the drums and wild celebrations that characterize the gatherings can be heard for miles.

Davis believes the secret societies are responsible for policing their communities, and the threat of zombification is one way they maintain order. Says Davis, "Zombification has a material basis, but it also has a societal logic." To the uninitiated, the practice may appear a random criminal activity, but in rural vodoun society, it is exactly the opposite—a sanction imposed by recognized authorities, a form of capital punishment. For rural Haitians, zombification is an even more severe punishment than death, because it deprives the subject of his most valued possessions: his free will and independence.

The vodounists believe that when a person dies, his spirit splits into several different parts. If a priest is powerful enough, the spiritual aspect that controls a person's character and individuality, known as *ti bon ange,* the "good little angel," can be captured and the corporeal aspect, deprived of its will, held as a slave.

From studying the medical literature on tetrodotoxin poisoning, Davis discovered that if a victim survives the first few hours of the poisoning, he is likely to recover fully from the ordeal. The subject simply revives spontaneously. But zombies remain without will, in a trance-like state, a condition vodounists attribute to the power of the priest. Davis thinks it possible that the psychological trauma of zombification may be augmented by *Datura* or some other drug; he thinks zombies may be fed a *Datura* paste that accentuates their disorientation. Still, he puts the material basis of zombification in perspective: "Tetrodotoxin and *Datura* are only templates on which cultural forces and beliefs may be amplified a thousand times."

Davis has not been able to discover how prevalent zombification is in Haiti.

"How many zombies there are is not the question," he says. He compares it to capital punishment in the United States: "It doesn't really matter how many people are electrocuted, as long as it's a possibility." As a sanction in Haiti, the fear is not of zombies, it's of becoming one.

Davis attributes his success in solving the zombie mystery to his approach. He went to Haiti with an open mind and immersed himself in the culture. "My intuition unhindered by biases served me well," he says. "I didn't make any judgments." He combined this attitude with what he had learned earlier from his experiences in the Amazon. "Schultes's lesson is to go and live with the Indians as an Indian." Davis was able to participate in the vodoun society to a surprising degree, eventually even penetrating one of the Bizango societies and dancing in their nocturnal rituals. His appreciation of Haitian culture is apparent. "Everybody asks me how did a white person get this information? To ask the question means you don't understand Haitians— they don't judge you by the color of your skin."

As a result of the exotic nature of his discoveries, Davis has gained a certain notoriety. He plans to complete his dissertation soon, but he has already finished writing a popular account of his adventures. To be published in January by Simon and Schuster, it is called *The Serpent and the Rainbow,* after the serpent that vodounists believe created the earth and the rainbow spirit it married. Film rights have already been optioned; in October Davis went back to Haiti with a screenwriter. But Davis takes the notoriety in stride. "All this attention is funny," he says. "For years, not just me, but all Schultes's students have had extraordinary adventures in the line of work. The adventure is not the end point, it's just along the way of getting the data. At the Botanical Museum, Schultes created a world unto itself. We didn't think we were doing anything above the ordinary. I still don't think we do. And you know," he adds, "the Haiti episode does not begin to compare to what others have accomplished—particularly Schultes himself."

Dark Side of the Shaman

The traditional healer's art has its perils

Michael Fobes Brown

Michael Fobes Brown, an associate professor in the Department of Anthropology and Sociology at Williams College, Williamstown, Massachusetts, has spent the past year as a resident scholar at the School of American Research in Santa Fe. His most recent book is War of Shadows: The Struggle for Utopia in the Peruvian Amazon *(Berkeley and Los Angeles, University of California Press, 1991), coauthored with Eduardo Fernández.*

Sante Fe, New Mexico, is a stronghold of that eclectic mix of mysticism and folk medicine called "New Age" thought. The community bulletin board of the public library, just around the corner from the plaza and the venerable Palace of the Governors, serves as a central bazaar for spiritual guides advertising instruction in alternative healing methods. Many of these workshops—for example, classes in holistic massage and rebirthing—have their philosophical roots in the experiments of the 1960s. Others resist easy classification: What, I've wondered, is Etheric Body Healing and Light Body Work, designed to "resonate the light forces within our being"? For thirty-five dollars an hour, another expert offers consultations in "defense and removal psychic attack." Most of the classes, however, teach the healing arts of non-Western or tribal peoples. Of particular interest to the New Agers of Santa Fe is the tradition known as shamanism.

Shamans, who are found in societies all over the world, are believed to communicate directly with spirits to heal people struck down by illness. Anthropologists are fond of reminding their students that shamanism, not prostitution, is the world's oldest profession. When, in my role as curious ethnographer, I've asked Santa Feans about their interest in this exotic form of healing, they have expressed their admiration for the beauty of the shamanistic tradition, the ability of shamans to "get in touch with their inner healing powers," and the superiority of spiritual treatments over the impersonal medical practice of our own society. Fifteen years ago, I would have sympathized with these romantic ideas. Two years of fieldwork in an Amazonian society, however, taught me that there is peril in the shaman's craft.

A man I shall call Yankush is a prominent shaman among the Aguaruna, a native people who make their home in the tropical forest of northeastern Peru. Once feared headhunters, the Aguaruna now direct their considerable energies to cultivating cash crops and protecting their lands from encroachment by settlers fleeing the poverty of Peru's highland and coastal regions.

Yankush is a vigorous, middle-aged man known for his nimble wit and ready laugh. Like every other able-bodied man in his village, Yankush works hard to feed his family by hunting, fishing, and helping his wife cultivate their fields. But when his kinfolk or friends fall ill, he takes on the role of *iwishín*—shaman—diagnosing the cause of the affliction and then, if possible, removing the source of the ailment from the patient's body.

In common with most peoples who preserve a lively shamanistic heritage, the Aguaruna believe that life-threatening illness is caused by sorcerers. Sorcerers are ordinary people who, driven by spite or envy, secretly introduce spirit darts into the bodies of their victims. If the dart isn't soon removed by a shaman, the victim dies. Often the shaman describes the dart as a piece of bone, a tiny thorn, a spider, or a blade of grass.

The Aguaruna do not regard sorcery as a quaint and colorful bit of traditional lore. It is attempted homicide, plain and simple. That the evidence of sorcery can only be seen by a shaman does not diminish the ordinary person's belief in the reality of the sorcerer's work, any more than our inability to see viruses with the naked eye leads us to question their existence. The Aguaruna insist that sorcerers, when discovered, must be executed for the good of society.

Shaman and sorcerer might seem locked in a simple struggle of good against evil, order against chaos, but things are not so straightforward. Shamans and sorcerers gain their power from the same source, both receiving spirit darts from a trusted instructor. Because the darts attempt to return to their original owner, apprentice shamans and sorcerers must induce them to remain in their bodies by purifying themselves. They spend months in jungle isolation, fasting and practicing sexual abstinence. By wrestling with the terrifying apparitions that come to plague their dreams, they steel themselves for a life of spiritual struggle.

There the paths of sorcerer and shaman divide. The sorcerer works in secret, using spirit darts to inflict suffering on his enemies. The shaman operates in the public eye and uses his own spirit darts to thwart the sorcerer's schemes of pain and untimely death. (I say "he," because to my knowledge all Aguaruna shamans are men. Occasionally, however, a woman is accused of sorcery.) Yet because shamans possess spirit darts, and with them the power to kill, the boundary between sorcerer and shaman is sometimes indistinct.

The ambiguities of the shaman's role were brought home to me during a healing session I attended in Yankush's house. The patients were two women: Yamanuanch, who complained of pains in her stomach and throat, and Chapaik, who suffered discomfort in her back and lower abdomen. Their illnesses did not seem life threatening, but they were persistent enough to raise fears that sorcery was at the root of the women's misery.

As darkness fell upon us, the patients and their kin waited for Yankush to enter into a trance induced by a bitter, hallucinogenic concoction he had taken just before sunset (it is made from a vine known as *ayahuasca*). While the visitors exchanged gossip and small talk, Yankush sat facing the wall of his house, whistling healing songs and waving a bundle of leaves that served as a fan and soft rattle. Abruptly, he told the two women to lie on banana leaves that had been spread on the floor, so that he could use his visionary powers to search their bodies for tiny points of light, the telltale signature of the sorcerer's darts. As Yankush's intoxication increased, his meditative singing gave way to violent retching. Gaining control of himself, he sucked noisily on the patients' bodies in an effort to remove the darts.

Family members of the patients shouted words of concern and support. "Others know you are curing. They can hurt you, be careful!" one of the spectators warned, referring to the sorcerers whose work the shaman hoped to undo. Torn by anxiety, Chapaik's husband addressed those present: "Who has done this bewitching? If my wife dies, I could kill any man out of anger!" In their cries of encouragement to Yankush, the participants expressed their high regard for the difficult work of the shaman, who at this point in the proceedings was frequently doubled over with nausea caused by the drug he had taken.

Suddenly there was a marked change of atmosphere. A woman named Chimi called out excitedly, "If there are any darts there when she gets back home, they may say that Yankush put them there. So take them all out!" Chimi's statement was an unusually blunt rendering of an ambivalence implicit in all relations between Aguaruna shamans and their clients. Because shamans control spirit darts, people fear that a shaman may be tempted to use the cover of healing as an opportunity to bewitch his own clients for personal reasons. The clients therefore remind the shaman that they expect results—and if such results are not forthcoming, the shaman himself may be suspected of, and punished for, sorcery.

Yankush is such a skilled healer that this threat scarcely caused him to miss a step. He sucked noisily on Yamanuanch's neck to cure her sore throat and, after singing about the sorcery darts lodged in her body, announced she would recover. For good measure, he recommended injections of a commercial antibiotic. Yankush also took pains to emphasize the intensity of his intoxication. Willingness to endure the rigors of a large dose of *ayahuasca* is a sign of his good faith as a healer. "Don't say I wasn't intoxicated enough," he reminded the participants.

As Yankush intensified his singing and rhythmic fanning of the leaf-bundle, he began to have visions of events taking place in distant villages. Suddenly he cried out, "In Achu they killed a person. A sorcerer was killed." "Who could it be?" the other partici-

pants asked one another, but before they could reflect on this too long, Yankush had moved on to other matters. "I'm concentrating to throw out sickness, like a tireless jaguar," he sang, referring to Chapaik, who complained of abdominal pains. "With my help she will become like the tapir, which doesn't know how to refuse any kind of food."

After two hours of arduous work, Yankush steered the healing session to its conclusion by reassuring the patients that they were well on their way to recovery. "In her body the sickness will end," he sang. "It's all right. She won't die. It's nothing," he added, returning to a normal speaking voice. Before departing, the patients and their kin discussed the particulars of Yankush's dietary recommendations and made plans for a final healing session to take place at a later date. As the sleepy participants left Yankush's house for their beds in other parts of the village, they expressed their contentment with the results of his efforts.

During the year I lived near Yankush, he conducted healing sessions like this one about twice a month. Eventually, I realized that his active practice was only partly a matter of choice. To allay suspicions and demonstrate his good faith as a healer, he felt compelled to take some cases he might otherwise have declined. Even so, when I traveled to other villages, people sometimes asked me how I could live in a community where a "sorcerer" practiced on a regular basis.

When a respected elder died suddenly of unknown causes in 1976, Yankush came under extraordinary pressure to identify the sorcerer responsible. From the images of his *ayahuasca* vision he drew the name of a young man from a distant region who happened to be visiting a nearby village. The man was put to death in a matter of days. Because Yankush was widely known to have fingered the sorcerer, he became the likely victim of a reprisal raid by members of the murdered man's family. Yankush's willingness to accept this risk in order to protect his community from future acts of sorcery was a source of his social prestige, but it was also a burden. I rarely saw him leave his house without a loaded shotgun.

In calling attention to the violent undercurrents of shamanism, my intention is not to disparage the healing traditions of the Aguaruna or of any other tribal people. I have no doubt that the cathartic drama I witnessed in Yankush's house made the two patients feel better. Medical anthropologists agree that rituals calling forth expressions of community support and concern for sick people often lead to a marked improvement in their sense of well-being. Shamans also serve their communities by administering herbal medications and other remedies and even, as in Yankush's case, helping to integrate traditional healing arts with the use of modern pharmaceuticals. At the same time, however, they help sustain a belief in sorcery that exacts a high price in anxiety and, from time to time, in human life.

In their attempts to understand this negative current, anthropologists have studied how shamanism and accusations of sorcery define local patterns of power and control. Belief in sorcery, for example, may provide a system of rules and punishments in societies that lack a police force, written laws, and a formal judicial system. It helps people assign a cause to their misfortunes. And it sustains religions that link human beings with the spirit world and with the tropical forest itself.

What I find unsettling, rather, is that New Age America seeks to embrace shamanism without any appreciation of its context. For my Santa Fe acquaintances, tribal lore is a supermarket from which they choose some tidbits while spurning others. They program computers or pursue other careers by day so that by night they can wrestle with spirit-jaguars and search for their power spots. Yankush's lifetime of discipline is reduced to a set of techniques for personal development, stripped of links to a specific landscape and cultural tradition.

New Age enthusiasts are right to admire the shamanistic tradition, but while advancing it as an alternative to our own healing practices, they brush aside its stark truths. For throughout the world, shamans see themselves as warriors in a struggle against the shadows of the human heart. Shamanism affirms life but also spawns violence and death. The beauty of shamanism is matched by its power—and like all forms of power found in society, it inspires its share of discontent.

The Real Vampire

Forensic pathology and the lore of the undead

Paul Barber

I saw the Count lying within the box upon the earth, some of which the rude falling from the cart had scattered over him. He was deathly pale, just like a waxen image, and the red eyes glared with the horrible vindictive look which I knew too well . . .

The eyes saw the sinking sun, and the look of hate in them turned to triumph.

But, on the instant, came the sweep and flash of Jonathan's great knife. I shrieked as I saw it shear through the throat; whilst at the same moment Mr. Morris's bowie knife plunged into the heart.

It was like a miracle; but before our very eyes, and almost in the drawing of a breath, the whole body crumbled into dust and passed from our sight.

—Bram Stoker, *Dracula*

If a typical vampire of folklore were to come to your house this Halloween, you might open the door to encounter a plump Slavic fellow with long fingernails and a stubbly beard, his mouth and left eye open, his face ruddy and swollen. He would wear informal attire—a linen shroud—and he would look for all the world like a disheveled peasant.

If you did not recognize him, it would be because you expected to see—as would most people today—a tall, elegant gentleman in a black cloak. But that would be the vampire of fiction—the count, the villain of Bram Stoker's novel and countless modern movies, based more or less on Vlad Tepes, a figure in Romanian history who was a prince, not a count; ruled in Walachia, not Transylvania; and was never viewed by the local populace as a vampire. Nor would he be recognized as one, bearing so little resemblance to the original Slavic revenant (one who returns from the dead)—the one actually called *upir* or *vampir*. But

in folklore, the undead are seemingly everywhere in the world, in a variety of disparate cultures. They are people who, having died before their time, are believed to return to life to bring death to their friends and neighbors.

We know the European version of the vampire best and have a number of eyewitness accounts telling of the "killing" of bodies believed to be vampires. When we read these reports carefully and compare their findings with what is now known about forensic pathology, we can see why people believed that corpses came to life and returned to wreak havoc on the local population.

Europeans of the early 1700s showed a great deal of interest in the subject of the vampire. According to the *Oxford English Dictionary,* the word itself entered the English language in 1734, at a time when many books were being written on the subject, especially in Germany.

One reason for all the excitement was the Treaty of Passarowitz (1718), by which parts of Serbia and Walachia were turned over to Austria. The occupying forces, which remained there until 1739, began to notice, and file reports on, a peculiar local practice: exhuming bodies and "killing" them. Literate outsiders began to attend such exhumations. The vampire craze was an early "media event," in which educated Europeans became aware of practices that were by no means of recent origin.

In the early 1730s, a group of Austrian medical officers were sent to the Serbian village of Medvegia to investigate some very strange accounts. A number of people in the village had died recently, and the villagers blamed

the deaths on vampires. The first of these vampires, they said, had been a man named Arnold Paole, who had died some years before (by falling off a hay wagon) and had come back to haunt the living.

To the villagers, Paole's vampirism was clear: When they dug up his corpse, "they found that he was quite complete and undecayed, and that fresh blood had flowed from his eyes, nose, mouth, and ears; that the shirt, the covering, and the coffin were completely bloody; that the old nails on his hands and feet, along with the skin, had fallen off, and that new ones had grown; and since they saw from this that he was a true vampire, they drove a stake through his heart, according to their custom, whereby he gave an audible groan and bled copiously."

This new offensive by the vampires—the one that drew the medical officers to Medvegia—included an attack on a woman named Stanacka, who "lay down to sleep fifteen days ago, fresh and healthy, but at midnight she started up out of her sleep with a terrible cry, fearful and trembling, and complained that she had been throttled by the son of a Haiduk by the name of Milloe, who had died nine weeks earlier, whereupon she had experienced a great pain in the chest and became worse hour by hour, until finally she died on the third day."

In their report, *Visum et Repertum* (Seen and Discovered), the officers told not only what they had heard from the villagers but also, in admirable clinical detail, what they themselves had seen when they exhumed and dissected the bodies of the supposed victims of the vampire. Of one corpse, the authors observed, "After the opening of the body there was found in the *cavitate pectoris* a quantity of fresh extravascular blood. The *vasa* [vessels] of the *arteriae* and *venae,* like the *ventriculis cordis,* were not, as is usual, filled with coagulated blood, and the whole *viscera,* that is, the *pulmo* [lung], *hepar* [liver], *stomachus, lien* [spleen], *et intestina* were quite fresh as they would be in a healthy person." But while baffled by the events, the medical officers did not venture opinions as to their meaning.

Modern scholars generally disregard such accounts—and we have many of them—because they invariably contain "facts" that are not believable, such as the claim that the dead Arnold Paole, exhumed forty days after his burial, groaned when a stake was driven into him. If that is untrue—and it surely seems self-evident that it must be untrue—then the rest of the account seems suspect.

Yet these stories invariably contain details that could only be known by someone who had exhumed a decomposing body. The flaking away of the skin described in the account of Arnold Paole is a phenomenon that forensic pathologists refer to as "skin slippage." Also, pathologists say that it is no surprise that Paole's "nails had fallen away," for that too is a normal event. (The Egyptians knew this and dealt with it either by tying the nails onto the mummified corpse or by attaching them with little golden thimbles.) The reference to "new nails" is presumably the interpretation of the glossy nail bed underneath the old nails.

Such observations are inconvenient if the vampire lore is considered as something made up out of whole cloth. But since the exhumations actually took place, then the question must be, how did our sources come to the conclusions they came to? That issue is obscured by two centuries of fictional vampires, who are much better known than the folkloric variety. A few distinctions are in order.

The folklore of the vampire comes from peasant cultures across most of Europe. As it happens, the best evidence of actual exhumations is from Eastern Europe, where the Eastern Orthodox church showed a greater tolerance for pagan traditions than the Catholic church in Western Europe.

The fictional vampire, owing to the massive influence of Bram Stoker's *Dracula,* moved away from its humble origin. (Imagine Count Dracula—in formal evening wear—undergoing his first death by falling off a hay wagon.)

Most fiction shows only one means of achieving the state of vampirism: people become vampires by being bitten by one. Typically, the vampire looms over the victim dramatically, then bites into the neck to suck blood. When vampires and revenants in European folklore suck blood—and many do not—they bite their victims somewhere on the thorax. Among the Kashubes, a Slavic people of northern Europe, vampires chose the area of the left breast; among the Russians, they left a small wound in the area of the heart; and the Danzig (now Gdansk), they bit the victim's nipples.

People commonly believed that those who were different, unpopular, or great sinners returned from the dead. Accounts from Russia tell of people who were unearthed merely because while alive they were alcoholics. A more universal category is the suicide. Partly because of their potential for returning from the dead or for drawing their nearest and dearest into the grave after them, suicides were refused burial in churchyards.

One author lists the categories of revenants by disposition as "the godless [people of different faiths are included], evildoers, suicides, sorcerers, witches, and werewolves; among the Bulgarians the group is expanded by robbers, highwaymen, arsonists, prostitutes, deceitful and treacherous barmaids and other dishonorable people."

A very common belief, reported not only from Eastern Europe but also from China, holds that a person may become a revenant when an animal jumps over him. In Romania there is a belief that a bat can transform a corpse into a vampire by flying over it. This circumstance deserves remark if only because of its rarity, for as important as bats are in the fiction of vampires, they are generally unimportant in the folklore. Bats came into vampire fiction by a circuitous route: the vampire bat of Central and South America was named after the vampire of folklore, because it sucks (or rather laps up) blood after biting its victim. The bat was then assimilated into the fiction: the modern (fictional) vampire is apt to transform himself into a bat and fly off to seek his victims.

Potential revenants could often be identified at birth, usually by some defect, as when (among the Poles of Upper Silesia and the Kashubes) a child was born with teeth or a split lower lip or features viewed as somehow bestial—for example, hair or a taillike extension of the spine. A child born with a red caul, or amniotic membrane, covering its head was regarded as a potential vampire.

The color red is related to the undead. Decomposing corpses often acquire a ruddy color, and this was generally taken for evidence of vampirism. Thus, the folkloric vampire is never pale, as one would expect of a corpse; his face is commonly described as florid or of a healthy color or dark, and this may be attributed to his habit of drinking blood. (The Serbians, referring to a red-faced, hard-drinking man, assert that he is "blood red as a vampire.")

In various parts of Europe, vampires, or revenants, were held responsible for any number of untoward events. They tipped over Gypsy caravans in Serbia, made loud noises on the frozen sod roofs of houses in Iceland (supposedly by beating their heels against them), caused epidemics, cast spells on crops, brought on rain and hail, and made cows go dry. All these activities attributed to vampires do occur: storms and scourges come and go, crops don't always thrive, cows do go dry. Indeed, the vampire's crimes are persistently "real-life" events. The issue often is not whether an event occurred but why it was attributed to the machinations of the vampire, an often invisible villain.

Bodies continue to be active long after death, but we moderns distinguish between two types of activity: that which we bring about by our will (in life) and that which is caused by other entities, such as microorganisms (in death). Because we regard only the former as "our" activity, the body's posthumous movements, changes in dimension, or the like are not real for us, since we do not will them. For the most part, however, our ancestors made no such distinction. To them, if after death the body changed in color, moved, bled, and so on (as it does), then it continued to experience a kind of life. Our view of death has made it difficult for us to understand earlier views, which are often quite pragmatic.

Much of what a corpse "does" results from misunderstood processes of decomposition. Only in detective novels does this process proceed at a predictable rate. So when a body that had seemingly failed to decompose came to the attention of the populace, theories explaining the apparent anomaly were likely to spring into being. (Note that when a saint's body failed to decompose it was a miracle, but when the body of an unpopular person failed to decompose it was because he was a vampire.) But while those who exhumed the bodies of suspected vampires invariable noted what they believed was the lack of decomposition, they almost always presented evidence that the body really was decomposing. In the literature, I have so far found only two instances of exhumations that failed to yield a "vampire." (With so many options, the body almost certainly will do something unexpected, hence scary, such as showing blood at the lips.) Our natural bias, then as now, is for the dramatic and the exotic, so that an exhumation that did not yield a vampire could be expected to be an early dropout from the folklore and hence the literature.

But however mythical the vampire was, the corpses that were taken for vampires were very real. And many of the mysteries of vampire lore clear up when we examine the legal and medical evidence surrounding these exhumation. "Not without astonishment," says an observer at the exhumation of a Serbian vampire in 1725, "I saw some fresh blood in his mouth, which, according to the common observation, he had sucked from the people killed by him." Similarly, in *Visum et Repertum,* we are told that the people exhuming one body were surprised by a "plumpness" they asserted had come to the corpse in the grave. Our sources deduced a cause-and-effect relationship from these two observations. The vampire was larger than he was because he was full to bursting with the fresh blood of his victims.

The observations are clinically accurate: as a corpse decomposes, it normally bloats (from the gases given off by decomposition), while the pressure from the bloating causes blood from the lungs to emerge at the mouth. The blood is real, it just didn't come from "victims" of the deceased.

But how was it that Arnold Paole, exhumed forty days after his death, groaned when his exhumers drove a stake into him? The peasants of Medvegia assumed that if the corpse groaned, it must still be alive. But a corpse does emit sounds, even when it is only moved, let alone if a stake were driven into it. This is because the compression of the chest cavity forces air past the glottis, causing a sound similar in quality and origin to the groan or cry of a living person. Pathologists shown such accounts point out that a corpse that did not emit such sounds when a stake was driven into it would be unusual.

To vampire killers who are digging up a corpse, anything unexpected is taken for evidence of vampirism. Calmet, an eighteenth-century French ecclesiastic, described people digging up corpses "to see if they can find any of the usual marks which leads them to conjecture that they are the parties who molest the living, as the mobility and suppleness of the limbs, the fluidity of the blood, and the flesh remaining uncorrupted." A vampire, in other words, is a corpse that lacks rigor mortis, has fluid blood, and has not decomposed. As it happens, these distinctions do not narrow the field very much: Rigor mortis is a temporary condition, liquid blood is not at all unusual in a corpse (hence the "copious bleeding" mentioned in the account of Arnold Paole), and burial slows down decomposition drastically (by a factor of eight, according to a standard textbook on fo-

rensic pathology). This being the case, exhumations often yielded a corpse that nicely fit the local model of what a vampire was.

None of this explains yet another phenomenon of the vampire lore—the attack itself. To get to his victim, the vampire is often said to emerge at night from a tiny hole in the grave, in a form that is invisible to most people (sorcerers have made a good living tracking down and killing such vampires). The modern reader may reject out of hand the hypothesis that a dead man, visible or not, crawled out of his grave and attacked the young woman Stanacka as related in *Visum et Repertum.* Yet in other respects, these accounts have been quite accurate.

Note the sequence of events: Stanacka is asleep, the attack takes place, and she wakes up. Since Stanacka was asleep during the attack, we can only conclude that we are looking at a culturally conditioned interpretation of a nightmare—a real event with a fanciful interpretation.

The vampire does have two forms: one of them the body in the grave; the other—and this is the mobile one—the image, or "double," which here appears as a dream. While we interpret this as an event that takes place within the mind of the dreamer, in nonliterate cultures the dream is more commonly viewed as either an invasion by the spirits of whatever is dreamed about (and these can include the dead) or evidence that the dreamer's soul is taking a nocturnal journey.

In many cultures, the soul is only rather casually attached to its body, as is demonstrated by its habit of leaving the body entirely during sleep or unconsciousness or death. The changes that occur during such conditions—the lack of responsiveness, the cessation or slowing of breathing and pulse—are attributed to the soul's departure. When the soul is identified with the image of the body, it may make periodic forays into the minds of others when they dream. The image is the essence of the person, and its presence in the mind of another is evidence that body and soul are separated. Thus, one reason that the dead are believed to live on is that their image can appear in people's dreams and memories even after death. For this reason some cultures consider it unwise to awaken someone suddenly: he may be dreaming, and his soul may not have a chance to return before he awakens, in which case he will die. In European folklore, the dream was viewed as a visit from the person dreamed about. (The vampire is not the only personification of the dream: the Slavic *mora* is a living being whose soul goes out of the body at night, leaving it as if dead. The *mora* first puts men to sleep, and then frightens them with dreams, chokes them, and sucks their blood. Etymologically, *mora* is cognate with the *mare* or nightmare, with German *Mahr,* and with the second syllable of the French *cauchemar.*

When Stanacka claimed she was attacked by Milloe, she was neither lying nor even making an especially startling accusation. Her subsequent death (probably from some form of epidemic disease; others in the village were dying too) was sufficient proof to her friends and relatives that she had in fact been attacked by a dead man, just as she had said.

This is why our sources tell us seemingly contradictory facts about the vampire. His body does not have to leave the grave to attack the living, yet the evidence of the attack—the blood he has sucked from his victims—is to be seen on the body. At one and the same time he can be both in the grave in his physical form and out of it in his spirit form. Like the fictional vampire, the vampire of folklore must remain in his grave part of the time—during the day—but with few exceptions, folkloric

vampires do not travel far from their home towns.

And while the fictional vampire disintegrates once staked, the folkloric vampire can prove much more troublesome. One account tells that "in order to free themselves from this plague, the people dug the body up, drove a consecrated nail into its head and a stake through its heart. Nonetheless, that did not help: the murdered man came back each night." In many of these cases, vampires were cremated as well as staked.

In Eastern Europe the fear of being killed by a vampire was quite real, and the people devised ways to protect themselves from attacks. One of the sources of protection was the blood of the supposed vampire, which was baked in bread, painted on the potential victim, or even mixed with brandy and drunk. (According to *Visum et Repertum,* Arnold Paole had once smeared himself with the blood of a vampire—that is, a corpse—for protection.) The rationale behind this is a common one in folklore, expressed in the saying "similia similiis curantur" (similar things are cured by similar things). Even so, it is a bit of a shock to find that our best evidence suggests that it was the human beings who drank the blood of the "vampires," and not the other way around.

Perhaps foremost among the reasons for urgency with which vampires were sought—and found—was sheer terror. To understand its intensity we need only recall the realities that faced our informants. Around them people were dying in clusters, by agencies that they did not understand. As they were well

aware, death could be extremely contagious: if a neighbor died, they might be next. They were afraid of nothing less than death itself. For among many cultures it was death that was thought to be passed around, not viruses and bacteria. Contagion was meaningful and deliberate, and its patterns were based on values and vendettas, not on genetic predisposition or the domestic accommodations of the plague-spreading rat fleas. Death came from the dead who, through jealousy, anger, or longing, sought to bring the living into their realm. And to prevent this, the living attempted to neutralize or propitiate the dead until the dead became powerless—not only when they stopped entering dreams but also when their bodies stopped changing and were reduced to inert bones. This whole phenomenon is hard for us to understand because although death is as inescapable today as it was then, we no longer personify its causes.

In recent history, the closest parallel to this situation may be seen in the AIDS epidemic, which has caused a great deal of fear, even panic, among people who, for the time being at least, know little about the nature of the disease. In California, for instance, there was an attempt to pass a law requiring the quarantine of AIDS victims. Doubtless the fear will die down if we gain control over the disease— but what would it be like to live in a civilization in which all diseases were just as mysterious? Presumably one would learn—as was done in Europe in past centuries—to shun the dead as potential bearers of death.

Rituals of Death

Capital Punishment and Human Sacrifice

Elizabeth D. Purdum and J. Anthony Paredes

We were perplexed by the resurgence of enthusiasm for the death penalty in the United States. According to a 1986 *Gallup Report,* support for the death penalty in America has reached a near-record high in 50 years of polling, with 70 percent of Americans favoring execution of convicted murderers (Gallup, 1986). In a 1983 poll conducted in Florida, 72 percent of respondents were found to support the death penalty, compared with 45 percent in 1964 (Cambridge Survey Research, 1985). Still more perplexing is the finding that nearly half of those supporting the death penalty agree that "only the poor and unfortunate are likely to be executed" (Ellsworth and Ross, 1983:153). Equally startling is the revelation that although deterrence is often given as a primary justification for the death penalty, most people would continue to support it even if convinced that it had no greater deterrent effect than that of a life sentence (P. Harris, 1986). In addition, there is little if any evidence that capital punishment reduces the crime rate; there seems, rather, to be some historical evidence for a reverse correlation. Pickpocketing, a crime then punishable by hanging, was rampant among spectators at executions in England circa 1700 (Lofland, 1977). Bowers and Pierce (1980) argue, on the basis of increased murder rates in New York State in the month following executions, that capital punishment has a "brutalizing" effect and leads to more, not less, violence. Why, then, does capital punishment receive such widespread support in modern America?

Capital Punishment—Another "Riddle of Culture"

In theory, capital punishment should be no more a puzzle than any other seemingly bizarre, nonrational custom. Either human cultures are amenable to scientific explanation or they are not. And we anthropologists have not been timid about tackling everything from Arunta penile subincision to Hindu cow love as problems for scientific explication. As a first step in this task, we will compare capital punishment in Florida, the leader in the United States in death sentencing since Florida's 1972 capital punishment statute was affirmed by the U.S. Supreme Court in 1976, with certain forms of human sacrifice as practiced by the Aztecs of Mexico in the sixteenth century. This is not a capricious comparison. John Cooper (1976) pointedly seeks the "socio-religious origins of capital punishment" in ancient rites of, to use his term, "propitiatory death." But his study is narrowly constrained by canons of Western philosophy and history. By making a more exotic comparison, we hope to point the way to more nomothetic principles for understanding state-sanctioned homicide in complex societies. Albert Camus (1959) also perceived elements of religious ritual in French capital punishment, but argued that the practice continued only because hidden from the view of the general public. Anticipating our comparisons here, anthropologist Colin Turnbull concludes in his article "Death by Decree" that the key to understanding capital punishment is to be found in its ritual element (1978). John Lofland (1977) has compared the dramaturgy of state executions circa 1700 in England with those of contemporary America, concluding that modern executions in their impersonal, unemotional, and private aspects appear humane, yet deny the reality of death and strip the condemned of any opportunity to die with dignity or courage.

It was the public media spectacle surrounding recent executions in Florida that triggered the thoughts leading to this paper. Detailed, minute-by-minute accounts of Florida's first post–1976 execution, widely reported press conferences with death row inmates, television images of the ambulance bearing the body of an executed criminal, news photos of mourners and revelers outside the prison on the night before an execution—all these served to transform a closely guarded, hidden expression of the ultimate power of the state into a very public ceremonial event. We were reminded of the pomp and circumstance for the masses accompanying the weird rites of Tenochtitlan that greeted sixteenth-century Spaniards. In such similarities, we thought, might lie the key to a dispassionate, anthropological understanding of capital punishment in modern America.

Before proceeding we must note that the Aztec state itself imposed capital punishment for a variety of crimes, ranging from murder to fornication to violations of the dress code for commoners. The available sources indicate, however, that among the Aztecs capital punishment was swift, rather unceremonious, and even brutish. It is the high drama of Aztec rituals of human sacrifice that shows the closest parallels with the bureaucratically regulated procedures for electrocution of the condemned at Starke, Florida, in the 1980s.

The Victims of Execution and Sacrifice

The death penalty is imposed on only a small percentage of Americans convicted of homicide—5 percent, according to a 1980 Georgia study (Baldus et al., 1983). Today there are 2,182 people on death row in the United States; 296 of these are in Florida (NAACP Legal Defense and Educational Fund, 1988). Since 1976, 18 persons have been executed in Florida. Prior to 1972, when the Supreme Court voided state death penalty statutes, it was clear that the death penalty was disproportionately applied to black men. Fifty-four percent of the 3,859 people executed in the United States between 1930 and 1967 were nonwhite. Among those executed for rape during the same period, 405 of 455 were black (U.S. Department of Justice, 1986). Nakell and Hardy's study of homicide cases in North Carolina from 1977 and 1978 revealed the effects of race of victim and race of defendant throughout the criminal justice process (1987). The relationship between race and execution consistently holds even when one controls for such factors as differential conviction rates and the relationship between the defendant and the victim (Radelet, 1981).

Recent studies (for example, Baldus et al., 1983a; Bowers and Pierce, 1980b; Gross and Mauro, 1984; Pasternoster, 1983; and Radelet, 1981) suggest that the defendant's race, since the reinstatement of the death penalty in 1976, is less important than it once was

in predicting death sentences. These studies conclude that a more significant factor is the race of the victim: that is, people who kill whites are more likely to receive the death penalty than people who kill blacks.

Statistics aside, people familiar with death row inmates readily acknowledge that they are marginal members of society—economically, socially, and, even, in the case of Florida, geographically. Many come from backgrounds of extreme poverty and abuse. Michael Radelet and his colleagues (1983) report one common denominator among families who have members in prison: low socioeconomic status. Poverty makes it hard, if not impossible, for families to maintain ties with prisoners. Many inmates on death row have few family or social ties. Only about 15 of the 208 men on death row in Florida in 1983 had visitors each week; 60 others had visitors about once a month; and fewer than half received a visitor in any given year (Radelet et al., 1983). Many of Florida's inmates are from out of state. More than a few of Florida's death row inmates are also crazy, retarded, or both. For instance, Arthur Goode, who was convicted of murdering a nine-year-old boy, ate a half-gallon of butter pecan ice cream, his requested "last meal," then gave as his final statement his desire to marry a young boy. In the three weeks before his execution, Goode wrote letters to the governor and other prominent officials complaining of the lack of toilet paper to blow his nose (Radelet and Barnard, 1986). There is an inmate who believes that one of the people helping him with his court appeals is alternately a dead disc jockey or one of his own seven wives. Or, there is James Douglas Hill, a 26-year-old with an IQ of 66 and a serious speech impediment, who, having learned to read and write while in prison, sent to his mother this message:

Hi mom me hour are you doing to day fine i hope i am doing ok for now But i miss you so varry varry much that i can cry But i am to Big to cry. . . . i miss you i miss you love James all way. By now. (Sherrill, 1984:555)

In 1987 James Douglas Hill was released on bail when substantial doubt about his guilt surfaced.

Detailed statistics on *whom* the Aztecs put to death in their rites of human sacrifice are not available, nor is the exact number of sacrificial victims. Nonetheless, the Aztecs of Central Mexico sacrificed humans on a scale unprecedented in any other society. Putting aside the question of whether the Aztecs were nutritionally motivated toward this human slaughter (Harner, 1977), annual estimates for central Mexico in the first decades of the sixteenth century vary from 20,000 (Cortes, as quoted by Fagan, 1984:230) to 250,000 sacrificed victims (Woodrow Borah, as quoted by Harner, 1977:119).

Most of the sacrificial victims were able-bodied male war captives from neighboring kingdoms, but the Aztecs reportedly also sacrificed large numbers of children—sold to the priests by the poor. The children's tears were believed to be particularly appealing to Tlaloc, the rain god. Women were also sometimes sacrificed, some of them presented as impersonations of certain female deities. Similarly, one of the most frequently recounted, and often highly romanticized, forms of Aztec human sacrifice was that in which a flawless young war captive was pampered and indulged for a year as the embodiment of a god, then killed with great ritual and sadness while the victim dutifully played his role in the deicidal drama. Most Aztec war captives enjoyed no such protracted special treatment. How god-impersonators were selected we do not know. Neither do we know how many war captives' lives were spared, if any, nor how many were doomed to a life of slavery.

Paralleling the numerous means of execution employed in the United States—electrocution, hanging, firing squad, deadly gas, lethal injection—the Aztecs sacrificed their victims with a variety of techniques. These included beheading, burning, and flights of arrows, but the most common method was to spread the victim on a large, elaborately carved stone, cut open his chest with an obsidian knife, then tear out his heart. We present here a brief, composite account of "ordinary" war captive sacrifice using the method of coronary excision.

Announcement of Death

According to Fray Diego Duran's account of the aftermath of a battle between the Aztecs and the Tepeacas, the Tepeacan captives were taken back to the Aztec capital, Tenochtitlan, with collars around their necks and their hands bound behind them. The captives "went along singing sadly, weeping and lamenting their fate," knowing they were to be sacrificed. Once they were in the capital, priests threw incense on them, offered them maize bread, and said:

We welcome you
To this city of Mexico Tenochtitlan
. . . .
Do you think that you have come to live;
You have come to die.
. . . .
We salute you and comfort you with these words:
You have not come because of weakness,
But because of your manliness.
You will die here but your fame will live forever.
    (Duran, 1964:101)

The announcement of a Florida death row inmate's impending death comes with the signing of a death warrant by the state governor, once all routine appeals and bids for clemency have failed. The criteria by which the decision is made to sign a warrant against a particular person at a particular time are not publicly known.

A death warrant is a single-page document in legal language, bordered in black. Each one bears the state seal and is officially witnessed by the secretary of state—not by some seemingly more likely authority such as the attorney general. Each death warrant is publicized by a news release issued shortly after the governor signs. Between 1972 and the end of 1988, Florida's three governors signed over two hundred death warrants. Once the warrant is signed in Tallahassee, the superintendent of Florida State Prison at Starke, 150 miles away, is immediately notified. Prison guards are sent to get

the person named in the warrant from his or her cell. They bring the prisoner, who may have no forewarning of what is about to happen, to the assistant superintendent's office. There the superintendent or his designee reads the warrant aloud to the condemned. Following a string of "whereas's" tracing the history of the case, the warrant concludes:

Now, therefore, I, [names governor], as Governor of the State of Florida and pursuant to the authority and responsibility vested by the Constitution and the laws of Florida do hereby issue this warrant directing the Superintendent of the Florida State Prison to cause the sentence of death to be executed upon [names person] on some day of the week beginning [for instance] Noon, Tuesday, the 29th day of October, 1989, and ending Noon, Tuesday, the 5th day of November, 1989, in accord with the provisions of the laws of the State of Florida.

The warrant is usually dated four weeks before the last day the warrant is in effect. Reportedly, warrants are never issued for executions to take place during the time the state supreme court is not in session or during the Christmas season. After the warrant is read, the prisoner is permitted to telephone a lawyer and a family member, if he or she has any.

Treatment After Announcement of Death

Aztec war captives were served "Divine Wine" (probably pulque) and paraded past images of the Aztec gods and past the emperor, Montezuma. They were given cloaks, loincloths, and sandals—sandals being a mark of nobility. Next, the prisoners were taken to the central marketplace, where they were given flowers and "shields of splendid featherwork" and forced to dance upon a platform. The condemned were also given tobacco to smoke, which, according to Duran, "comforted them greatly" (Duran, 1964:102).

The war captives were dispersed among the several wards of the city, and men were assigned to guard and maintain them with the charge:

Take care that they do not escape
Take care that they do not die!
Behold, they are children of the Sun!
Feed them well; let them be fat and desirable for the sacrifice
    . . . (Duran, 1964:108)

Duran (1964) reports that captives were treated well and honored as if they were gods.

Many days passed during which craftsmen were instructed to carve a stone for the sacrificial altar. A few days later the altar was ready, and temple youths were given instructions about how the sacrifice was to be conducted. Guests were invited from neighboring states, and booths were decorated for spectators.

In Florida, the reading of the death warrant initiates a period officially designated as "death watch," marked by moving the person to a cell in "Q Wing," where he or she will be closer to the electric chair and isolated from other death row inmates. Most of the person's possessions are taken away, including photographs and tennis shoes, the only personally owned item of apparel that inmates are ordinarily allowed; the condemned is allowed to retain only those items listed in the "Execution Guidelines," a 39-page single-spaced document (Florida State Prison, 1983). The only books on the list are "religious tracts as distributed by Institution Chaplain, maximum possession ten (10)." Magazine and newspaper subscriptions may continue, but no new periodicals may be ordered. In a curious specific parallel with Aztec practice, there are no special restrictions on tobacco for prisoners on Q Wing. Three meals a day are fed to all "condemned inmates," and dietary restrictions for "medical reasons" continue to be observed. Indeed, meticulous, detailed instructions are given to prison personnel to ensure that the condemned person is kept in good health and not provided with any item that might be used to harm himself or attempt suicide. Moreover, under current procedures if a prisoner is determined to have become insane on death row, he or she is spared execution until restored to mental health (Radelet and Barnard, 1986).

Once death watch begins, social visits are "noncontact" and held in the "maximum security visiting park" any two days, Monday through Friday, 9 A.M. to 3 P.M. Other death row inmates are permitted "contact" social visits for six hours on Saturdays or Sundays. Legal visits for the condemned may continue to be the "contact" type during the death warrant, but only until one week before execution, when these visits, too, become noncontact. Media visits are scheduled through prison officials on Tuesday, Wednesday, and Thursday until Phase II of death watch begins, five days before the execution is scheduled to occur.

With Phase II of death watch, more property is taken from the prisoner. The condemned is allowed only a few so-called comfort items: "one TV located outside cell, 1 radio, 1 deck of cards, 1 Bible, 1 book, periodical, magazine or newspaper." Very specific day-by-day regulations and procedures now go into effect, beginning with "Execution Day–Minus Five (5)," when the "execution squad" is identified. Likewise, on Execution Day–Minus Four (4), testing of the electrical equipment to be used for execution begins. During Phase II the inmate is subjected to further limitations on visits, but during the 48 hours before the scheduled execution, the condemned may have an interview with a media representative of his or her choice. Execution Day–Minus Four (4) is a particularly busy day: the condemned reinventories his or her property and specifies in writing its disposition; specifies in writing his or her funeral arrangements; and is measured for a suit of clothing—the suit will be cheap—in which the condemned will, if he or she wants, be buried. On Day–Minus Three (3) there are "no activities," and Day–Minus Two (2) is devoted primarily to testing the equipment and "execution squad drill." On Execution Day–Minus One (1) the pace quickens, and it is on this day that the chef takes the person's order for the last meal.

Each time the prisoner is moved during Phase II of death watch, the entire prison is locked down and the condemned undergoes a complete body search upon being returned to his or her cell. A guard sits outside the condemned inmate's cell, as one always does during an active death warrant, but now the guard records every 15 minutes what the prisoner is doing.

Final Preparations for Death

On the day of an Aztec sacrifice, the visiting nobles were seated in their decorated booths and the prisoners were placed in a line before them and made to dance. The victims were smeared with plaster; white feathers were tied to their hair; their eyelids were blackened and their lips painted red. Priests who would perform the actual sacrifice stood in a long row according to their rank. Each priest was disguised as a god and carried a richly decorated sword and shield. The priests sat under a beautifully adorned arbor erected at the summit of a large, truncated pyramid. Chanters came forth and began to dance and sing.

In Florida, sometime around midnight on the night before an execution, the condemned is usually allowed a last one-hour contact visit. The person is permitted to see his own clergyman if he has one, but only the prison chaplain will be permitted to accompany the inmate to the place of execution. At 4:30 A.M. the prisoner is served his or her last meal, to be eaten on a paper plate with a spoon; if the prisoner has requested a steak, the chef has cut the meat into bite-sized pieces beforehand and arranged them to appear to be an intact steak. No later than 5:30 A.M., the official witnesses to the execution, 12 in number (one of whom may be designated by the condemned), must assemble at the main prison gate. At 5:50 A.M. the media witnesses, also 12 in number, are picked up at the "media onlooker area." Both types of witnesses will later be "escorted to the witness room of the execution chamber." At 6:00 A.M. an administrative assistant, three designated electricians, a physician, and a physician's assistant are assembled in the death chamber. The administrative assistant establishes telephone contact with the state governor's office. Meanwhile, the condemned inmate has his or her head and right calf shaved (to better conduct electricity), takes a shower under the supervision of a high-ranking prison official, and is dressed in his or her new burial clothes, omitting the suit jacket and shoes. Until recently, by informal custom the prison superintendent would then have a drink of whiskey with the condemned in his cell, but public outcry was so great that the practice was discontinued. At 6:50 "conducting gel" is applied to the person's head and leg. The superintendent reads the death warrant to the condemned a final time.

The Moment of Death

Each Aztec victim was taken singly to the sacrificial stone and tethered to it by a rope. In one form of sacrifice, in a mockery of self-defense, the victim was then given a sword edged with feathers rather than obsidian. The high priest rose and descended to the stone, walked around it twice and returned to his seat. Next, an old man disguised as an ocelot gave the captive four wooden balls and a drink of "Divine Wine" and instructed him to defend himself. Many victims tried to defend themselves against a series of ceremonially garbed priest-warriors, but others "unwilling to undergo such ceremony cast themselves upon the stone seeking a quick death" (Duran, 1964:112). Death was inevitable: as soon as the captive was wounded, four priests painted black, with long braided hair and garments resembling chasubles, spread-eagled the victim on the stone, each priest holding a limb. The high priest cut open the victim's chest with an obsidian knife, pulled out the victim's heart and offered the organ to the sun. The heart was deposited in a jar or placed on a brazier, and the next victim was brought forward.

The superintendent of Florida State Prison at Starke and two other prison officials escort the condemned inmate to the death chamber at 6:56 A.M. The person is strapped into the electric chair. At 7:00 A.M. the condemned is permitted to make a last statement. The governor directs the superintendent to proceed with the execution, traditionally concluding with the words "God save us all." The witnesses have been seated in their peculiarly carved, white high-backed chairs. The electrician places the sponge and cap on the inmate's head. The assistant superintendent engages the circuit breaker. The electrician activates the panel, the superintendent signals the executioner to throw the switch, and the "automatic cycle will begin." The actual executioner is an anonymous private citizen dressed in a black hood and robe who will be paid $150 for his services. Once the automatic cycle has run its course, the superintendent invites the doctor to conduct the examination. If all has gone well, the condemned is pronounced dead and the time recorded. A designated prison official proclaims, "The sentence of _____ has been carried out. Please exit to the rear at this time." By custom, someone in attendance waves a white cloth just outside the prison to signal the crowd assembled in a field across from it—reporters, death penalty opponents and proponents, and any others—that the deed is done. Official guidelines for the execution of more than one inmate on a single day exist, but we will dispense with those here.

After Death

Fray Bernardino de Sahagun (1951:24) reports that after each Aztec captive had been slain, the body was taken gently away and rolled down the stairs of the sacrificial pyramid. At the bottom, the victim's head was cut off for display on a rack and the remainder of the corpse was taken to one of the special houses, *calpulli,* where "they divided [the bodies] up in order to eat them." Meanwhile, those who had taken part in the sacrifice entered a temple, removed their ritual garb, and were rewarded with fine clothes and a feast. The lords from the provinces who had been brought to observe were

"shocked and bewildered."

As soon as a Florida inmate is pronounced dead in the electric chair, ambulance attendants are called into the chamber; they remove the inmate from the chair and take the body to a waiting ambulance, which transports the corpse to the medical examiner's office. There an autopsy is performed. Until recently, portions of the brain were removed for secret study by a University of Florida researcher investigating the relationship between "head trauma and violent behavior." This procedure was followed for 11 of the 13 men executed between 1979 and 1985, but was stopped in response to negative publicity. Once the autopsy is completed, the corpse is released to the funeral home for cremation or burial. If the deceased has made no arrangements for a private funeral, his or her body is interred on the prison grounds. The executioner, meanwhile, is returned to his secret pick-up point and compensated. There is a "debriefing" at the prison of all the other participants in the execution save one.

The Native Explanations

What explanations are given by Aztecs and modern Americans for these decidedly gruesome acts? While we will probably never know what the Aztec man in the street thought of the sacrificial murders committed by his priests and nobles, official theology, if we may trust the sources, held that the gods had to be fed and placated to keep the crops growing, the sun high, and the universe in healthy order. Unfortunately for war captives, one of the gods' favorite foods was human hearts.

The explanations given by Americans for capital punishment generally are clothed in more pragmatic, secular terms. Most commonly, supporters of capital punishment invoke stimulus-response psychology and declare that such punishment will prevent others from committing heinous crimes. For instance, following the execution of an admitted child-murderer, Florida's governor declared that "he hoped the execution would be a warning to others

who harbored the desire to mistreat children" (Sherrill, 1984:553). Other explanations emphasize the lower cost of execution as compared with long-term imprisonment, the need to provide families of murder victims with a sense of justice and mental repose, and what might be called the "social hygiene" approach: "[S]ome people just ought to be eliminated—we kill rattlesnakes, we don't keep them as pets," declared one Florida Supreme Court justice (*Tallahassee Democrat,* 15 Sept. 1985).

Despite the rationalistic cast of the most common public explanations for capital punishment, at least some of the explanations, or justifications, that surface into public view are unabashedly religious. The author of a letter to the *Tallahassee Democrat* (6 Feb. 1985) cited scripture to argue that earthly governments have the God-given right and authority "to make and enforce laws, including the right to take human life." He urged his readers to submit " 'to every ordinance of man for the Lord's sake,' " for in so doing evildoers will be punished, those who do well will be praised, and " 'ye will put to silence the ignorance of foolish men' (I Peter 2:13–15)." We suspect that beneath more sophisticated explanations for capital punishment there is, if not an outright appeal to supernatural authority, the same deep-seated set of nameless fears and anxieties that motivate humans everywhere to commit ceremonial acts that reassure and give substance to the Durkheimian view that "religion is society collectively worshipping itself."

Conclusion

The perceptive reader will have recognized the sometimes startling points of similarity between the conduct of some forms of Aztec human sacrifice and capital punishment in Florida. There are, of course, some profoundly important points of difference as well. We will not belabor the obvious here, but given the many commonalities in the organization, procedures, and even physical appurtenances between Aztec human sacrifice and Florida capital punishment, it is reasonable to propose that whatever psychosocial functions human sacrifice might have served in the Aztec empire, they are matched by similar functions for capital punishment in the United States. Just as Aztec ripping out of human hearts was couched in mystical terms of maintaining universal order and well-being of the state (putting aside the question of the utility of such practices as terror tactics with which to intimidate neighboring societies), we propose that capital punishment in the United States serves to assure many that society is not out of control after all, that the majesty of the Law reigns, and that God is indeed in his heaven. Precise, emic ("native") corroboration of our interpretation of capital punishment as the ultimate validator of law is provided by an automobile bumper sticker first seen in Tallahassee in 1987, shortly after the Florida legislature passed a controversial statute requiring automobile passengers to wear safety belts:

I'LL BUCKLE UP—
WHEN BUNDY DOES
IT'S THE LAW

"Bundy" is Theodore Bundy, Florida's most famous prisoner sentenced to be "buckled up" in the electric chair.

Sources as diverse as the populist *National Enquirer* (Mitteager, 1985) and the eminent legal scholar Lawrence Friedman (1973) instruct their readers that the crime rate is actually far lower today than 100 years ago. But through the mass media, the average American is subjected to a daily diet of fanatical terrorists, crazed rapists, revolting child molesters, and ghoulish murderers, to say nothing of dishonest politicians, unruly protestors, welfare and tax cheats, greedy gurus and philandering preachers, marauding street gangs, sexual perverts, and drug fiends, while all the time having to deal with the everyday personal irritations of a society in which, as Marvin Harris (1981) tells us, nothing works, mothers leave home, and gays come out of the closet. In an ironic twist on the anthropological debate (e.g., Isaac, 1983; Ortiz de Montellano, 1982; Price, 1978) over Harner's proposed materialist ex-

planation of Aztec human sacrifice, we hypothesize that the current groundswell of support for capital punishment in the United States springs from the universal, ancient human impulse to do something in times of stress, even if it is only ritual. Bronislaw Malinowski observed that "there are no peoples however primitive without religion and magic" (1954:17); neither are there peoples so civilized that they are devoid of magic. All peoples turn to magic when knowledge, technology, and experience fail (Malinowski, 1954). In the face of all the evidence that capital punishment does no more to deter crime than the bloody rituals of Tenochtitlan did to keep the sun in the sky, we must seek some broader, noninstrumental function that the death penalty serves. We propose, in short, that modern capital punishment is an institutionalized *magical* response to perceived disorder in American life and in the world at large, an attempted magical solution that has an especial appeal to the beleaguered, white, God-fearing men and women of the working class. And in certain aspiring politicians they find their sacrificial priests.

References

Baldus, David C.; Charles A. Pulaski, Jr.; and George Woodworth. 1983. "Comparative Review of Death Sentences: An Empirical Study of the Georgia Experience." *Journal of Criminal Law and Criminology* 74:661–753.

Bowers, William, J., and Glenn L. Pierce. 1980. "Deterrence or Brutalization: What Is the Effect of Executions?" *Crime and Delinquency* 26:453–84.

—————. 1980. "Arbitrariness and Discrimination Under Post-*Furman* Capital Statutes." *Crime and Delinquency* 26:563–635.

Cambridge Survey Research. 1985. "An Analysis of Attitudes Toward Capital Punishment in Florida." Prepared for Amnesty International.

Camus, Albert. 1959. *Reflections on the Guillotine.* Michigan City, Ind.: Fridtjof-Karla.

Cooper, John W. 1976. "Propitiation as Social Maintenance: A Study of Capital Punishment Through the Sociology of Religion." M.A. thesis, Florida State University.

Duran, Fray Diego. 1964. *The Aztecs.* New

York: Orion Press.

Ellsworth, Phoebe C., and Lee Ross. 1983. "Public Opinion and Capital Punishment: A Close Examination of the Views of Abolitionists and Retentionists." *Crime and Delinquency* 29:116–69.

Fagan, Brian M. 1984. *The Aztecs.* New York: W. H. Freeman.

Florida State Prison. 1983. "Execution Guidelines During Active Death Warrant." Starke: Florida State Prison. Reprinted in part at pp. 235–40 of Amnesty International, *United States of America: The Death Penalty.* London: Amnesty International, 1987.

Friedman, Lawrence M. 1973. *A History of American Law.* New York: Simon and Schuster.

Gallup, George. 1986. "The Death Penalty." *Gallup Report* 244–45 (Jan.–Feb.) 10–16.

Gross, Samuel R., and Robert Mauro. 1984. "Patterns of Death: An Analysis of Racial Disparities in Capital Sentencing and Homicide Victimization." *Stanford Law Review* 37:27–153.

Harner, Michael. 1977. "The Ecological Basis for Aztec Sacrifice." *American Ethnologist* 4:117–35.

Harris, Marvin. 1981. *America Now: The Anthropology of a Changing Culture.* New York: Simon and Schuster.

Harris, Philip W. 1986. "Over-Simplification and Error in Public Opinion Surveys on Capital Punishment." *Justice Quarterly* 3:429–55.

Isaac, Barry L. 1983. "The Aztec 'Flowery War': A Geopolitical Explanation." *Journal of Anthropological Research* 39:415–32.

Lofland, John. 1977. "The Dramaturgy of State Executions." Pp. 275–325 in *State Executions Viewed Historically and Sociologically,* by Horace Bleackley. Montclair, N.J.: Patterson Smith.

Malinowski, Bronislaw. 1954. *Magic, Science and Religion and Other Essays.* Garden City, N.Y.: Doubleday.

Mitteager, James. 1985. "Think Crime Is Bad Now? It Was Much Worse 100 Years Ago." *National Enquirer,* 25 Nov., p. 25.

NAACP Legal Defense and Educational Fund. 1988. "Death Row, U.S.A." Unpublished compilation, available from 99 Hudson St., New York, N.Y. 10013.

Nakell, Barry, and Kenneth A. Hardy. 1987. *The Arbitrariness of the Death Penalty.* Philadelphia: Temple University Press.

Ortiz de Montellano, Bernard R. 1982. "The Body Dangerous: Physiology and Social Stratification." *Reviews in Anthropology* 9:97–107.

Paternoster, Raymond. 1983. "Race of Victim and Location of Crime: The Decision to Seek the Death Penalty in South Carolina." *Journal of Criminal Law and Criminology* 74:754–85.

Price, Barbara J. 1978. "Demystification, Enriddlement and Aztec Cannibalism: A

Materialist Rejoinder to Harner." *American Ethnologist* 5:98–115.

Radelet, Michael L. 1981. "Racial Characteristics and the Imposition of the Death Penalty." *American Sociological Review* 46:918–27.

Radelet, Michael L., and George W. Barnard. 1986. "Ethics and the Psychiatric Determination of Competency to Be Executed." *Bulletin of the American Acad-* emy of Psychiatry and the Law 14:37–53.

Radelet, Michael L.; Margaret Vandiver; and Felix M. Berardo. 1983. "Families, Prisons, and Men with Death Sentences: The Human Impact of Structured Uncertainty." *Journal of Family Issues* 4:593–612.

Sahagun, Fray Bernardino de. 1951. *General History of the Things of New Spain,* Santa Fe, N.M.: School of American Research and the University of Utah.

Sherrill, Robert. 1984. "In Florida, Insanity Is No Defense." *The Nation* 239:539, 552–56.

Turnbull, Colin. 1978. "Death by Decree." *Natural History* 87 (May):51–66.

U.S. Department of Justice. 1986. *Capital Punishment, 1984.* Washington, D.C.: U.S. Government Printing Office.

Body Ritual Among the Nacirema

Horace Miner
University of Michigan

The anthropologist has become so familiar with the diversity of ways in which different peoples behave in similar situations that he is not apt to be surprised by even the most exotic customs. In fact, if all of the logically possible combinations of behavior have not been found somewhere in the world, he is apt to suspect that they must be present in some yet undescribed tribe. This point has, in fact, been expressed with respect to clan organization by Murdock (1949:71). In this light, the magical beliefs and practices of the Nacirema present such unusual aspects that it seems desirable to describe them as an example of the extremes to which human behavior can go.

Professor Linton first brought the ritual of the Nacirema to the attention of anthropologists twenty years ago (1936:326), but the culture of this people is still very poorly understood. They are a North American group living in the territory between the Canadian Cree, the Yaqui and Tarahumare of Mexico, and the Carib and Arawak of the Antilles. Little is known of their origin, though tradition states that they came from the east. According to Nacirema mythology, their nation was originated by a culture hero, Notgnishaw, who is otherwise known for two great feats of strength—the throwing of a piece of wampum across the river Pa-To-Mac and the chopping down of a cherry tree in which the Spirit of Truth resided.

Nacirema culture is characterized by a highly developed market economy which has evolved in a rich natural habitat. While much of the people's time is devoted to economic pursuits, a large part of the fruits of these labors and a considerable portion of the day are spent in ritual activity. The focus of this activity is the human body, the appearance and health of which loom as a dominant concern in the ethos of the people. While such a concern is certainly not unusual, its ceremonial aspects and associated philosophy are unique.

The fundamental belief underlying the whole system appears to be that the human body is ugly and that its natural tendency is to debility and disease. Incarcerated in such a body, man's only hope is to avert these characteristics through the use of the powerful influences of ritual and ceremony. Every household has one or more shrines devoted to this purpose. The more powerful individuals in the society have several shrines in their houses and, in fact, the opulence of a house is often referred to in terms of the number of such ritual centers it possesses. Most houses are of wattle and daub construction, but the shrine rooms of the more wealthy are walled with stone. Poorer families imitate the rich by applying pottery plaques to their shrine walls.

While each family has at least one such shrine, the rituals associated with it are not family ceremonies but are private and secret. The rites are normally only discussed with children, and then only during the period when they are being initiated into these mysteries. I was able, however, to establish sufficient rapport with the natives to examine these shrines and to have the rituals described to me.

The focal point of the shrine is a box or chest which is built into the wall. In this chest are kept the many charms and magical potions without which no native believes he could live. These preparations are secured from a variety of specialized practitioners. The most powerful of these are the medicine men, whose assistance must be rewarded with substantial gifts. However, the medicine men do not provide the curative potions for their clients, but decide what the ingredients should be and then write them down in an ancient and secret language. This writing is understood only by the medicine men and by the herbalists who, for another gift, provide the required charm.

The charm is not disposed of after it has served its purpose, but is placed in the charm-box of the household shrine. As these magical materials are specific for certain ills, and the real or imagined maladies of the people are many, the charm-box is usually full to overflowing. The magical packets are so numerous that people forget what their purposes were and fear to use them again. While the natives are very vague on this point, we can only assume that the idea in retaining all the old magical materials is that their presence in the charm-box, before which the body rituals are conducted, will in some way protect the worshipper.

Beneath the charm-box is a small font. Each day every member of the family, in succession, enters the shrine room, bows his head before the charm-box, mingles different sorts of holy water in the font, and proceeds with a brief rite of ablution. The holy waters are secured from the Water Temple of the community, where the priests conduct elaborate ceremonies to make the liquid ritually pure.

In the hierarchy of magical practitioners, and below the medicine men in prestige, are specialists whose designation is best translated "holy-mouth-men." The Nacirema have an almost pathological horror and fascination with the mouth, the condition of which is believed to have a supernatural influence on all social relationships. Were it not for the rituals of the mouth, they believe that their teeth would fall out, their gums bleed, their jaws shrink, their friends desert them, and their lovers reject them. (They also belive that a strong relationship exists between oral and moral characteristics. For example, there is a ritual ablution of the mouth for children which is supposed to improve their moral fiber.)

The daily body ritual performed by everyone includes a mouth-rite. Despite the fact that these people are so punctilious about care of the mouth, this rite involves a practice which strikes the uninitiated stranger as revolting. It was reported to me that the ritual consists of inserting a small bundle of hog hairs into the mouth, along with certain magical powders, and then moving the bundle in a highly formalized series of gestures.

In addition to the private mouth-rite, the people seek out a holy-mouth-man once or twice a year. These practitioners have an impressive set of paraphernalia, consisting of a variety of augers, awls, probes, and prods. The use of these objects in the exorcism of the evils of the mouth involves almost unbelievable ritual torture of the client. The holy-mouth-man opens the client's mouth and, using the above mentioned tools, en-

larges any holes which decay may have created in the teeth. Magical materials are put into these holes. If there are no naturally occurring holes in the teeth, large sections of one or more teeth are gouged out so that the supernatural substance can be applied. In the client's view, the purpose of these ministrations is to arrest decay and to draw friends. The extremely sacred and traditional character of the rite is evident in the fact that the natives return to the holy-mouth-men year after year, despite the fact that their teeth continue to decay.

It is to be hoped that, when a thorough study of the Nacirema is made, there will be a careful inquiry into the personality structure of these people. One has but to watch the gleam in the eye of a holy-mouth-man, as he jabs an awl into an exposed nerve, to suspect that a certain amount of sadism is involved. If this can be established, a very interesting pattern emerges, for most of the population shows definite masochistic tendencies. It was to these that Professor Linton referred in discussing a distinctive part of the daily body ritual which is performed only by men. This part of the rite involves scraping and lacerating the surface of the face with a sharp instrument. Special women's rites are performed only four times during each lunar month, but what they lack in frequency is made up in barbarity. As part of this ceremony, women bake their heads in small ovens for about an hour. The theoretically interesting point is that what seems to be a preponderantly masochistic people have developed sadistic specialists.

The medicine men have an imposing temple, or *latipso*, in every community of any size. The more elaborate ceremonies required to treat very sick patients can only be performed at this temple. These ceremonies involve not only the thaumaturge but a permanent group of vestal maidens who move sedately about the temple chambers in distinctive costume and headdress.

The *latipso* ceremonies are so harsh that it is phenomenal that a fair

proportion of the really sick natives who enter the temple ever recover. Small children whose indoctrination is still incomplete have been known to resist attempts to take them to the temple because "that is where you go to die." Despite this fact, sick adults are not only willing but eager to undergo the protracted ritual purification, if they can afford to do so. No matter how ill the supplicant or how grave the emergency, the guardians of many temples will not admit a client if he cannot give a rich gift to the custodian. Even after one has gained admission and survived the ceremonies, the guardians will not permit the neophyte to leave until he makes still another gift.

The supplicant entering the temple is first stripped of all his or her clothes. In every-day life the Nacirema avoids exposure of his body and its natural functions. Bathing and excretory acts are performed only in the secrecy of the household shrine, where they are ritualized as part of the body-rites. Psychological shock results from the fact that body secrecy is suddenly lost upon entry into the *latipso*. A man, whose own wife has never seen him in an excretory act, suddenly finds himself naked and assisted by a vestal maiden while he performs his natural functions into a sacred vessel. This sort of ceremonial treatment is necessitated by the fact that the excreta are used by a diviner to ascertain the course and nature of the client's sickness. Female clients, on the other hand, find their naked bodies are subjected to the scrutiny, manipulation and prodding of the medicine men.

Few supplicants in the temple are well enough to do anything but lie on their hard beds. The daily ceremonies, like the rites of the holy-mouth-men, involve discomfort and torture. With ritual precision, the vestals awaken their miserable charges each dawn and roll them about on their beds of pain while performing ablutions, in the formal movements of which the maidens are highly trained. At other times they insert magic wands in the supplicant's mouth or force him to eat substances which are supposed to be healing. From time to time the medicine men come to their clients and jab magically treated needles into their flesh. The fact that these temple ceremonies may not cure, and may even kill the neophyte, in no way decreases the people's faith in the medicine men.

There remains one other kind of practioner, known as a "listener." This witch-doctor has the power to exorcise the devils that lodge in the heads of people who have been bewitched. The Nacirema believe that parents bewitch their own children. Mothers are particularly suspected of putting a curse on children while teaching them the secret body rituals. The counter-magic of the witch-doctor is unusual in its lack of ritual. The patient simply tells the "listener" all his troubles and fears, beginning with the earliest difficulties he can remember. The memory displayed by the Nacirema in these exorcism sessions is truly remarkable. It is not uncommon for the patient to bemoan the rejection he felt upon being weaned as a babe, and a few individuals even see their troubles going back to the traumatic effects of their own birth.

In conclusion, mention must be made of certain practices which have their base in native esthetics but which depend upon the pervasive aversion to the natural body and its functions. There are ritual fasts to make fat people thin and ceremonial feasts to make thin people fat. Still other rites are used to make women's breasts large if they are small, and smaller if they are large. General dissatisfaction with breast shape is symbolized in the fact that the ideal form is virtually outside the range of human variation. A few women afflicted with almost inhuman hypermammary development are so idolized that they make a handsome living by simply going from village to village and permitting the natives to stare at them for a fee.

Reference has already been made to the fact that excretory functions are ritualized, routinized, and relegated to secrecy. Natural reproductive functions are similarly distorted. Intercourse is taboo as a topic and scheduled as an act. Efforts are made to avoid pregnancy by the use of magical materials or by limiting intercourse to certain phases of the moon. Conception is actually very infre-

quent. When pregnant, women dress so as to hide their condition. Parturition takes place in secret, without friends or relatives to assist, and the majority of women do not nurse their infants.

Our review of the ritual life of the Nacirema has certainly shown them to be a magic-ridden people. It is hard to understand how they have managed to exist so long under the burdens which they have imposed upon themselves. But even such exotic customs as these take on real meaning when they are viewed with the insight provided by Malinowski when he wrote (1948:70):

Looking from far and above, from our high places of safety in the developed civilization, it is easy to see all the crudity and irrelevance of magic. But without its power and guidance early man could not have mastered his practical difficulties as he has done, nor could man have advanced to the higher stages of civilization.

REFERENCES

Linton, Ralph. 1936. *The Study of Man*. New York, D. Appleton-Century Co.
Malinowski, Bronislaw. 1948. *Magic, Science, and Religion*. Glencoe, The Free Press.
Murdock, George P. 1949. *Social Structure*. New York, The Macmillan Co.

Sociocultural Change:
The Impact of the West

The origins of academic anthropology lie in the colonial and imperial ventures of the nineteenth and twentieth centuries. During these periods, many people of the world were brought into a relationship with Europe and the United States that was usually exploitative and often socially and culturally disruptive. For almost a century, anthropologists have witnessed this process and the transformations that have taken place in those social and cultural systems brought under the umbrella of a world economic order. Early anthropological studies—even those widely regarded as pure research—directly or indirectly served colonial interests. Many anthropologists certainly believed that they were extending the benefits of Western technology and society while preserving the cultural rights of those people whom they studied. But other representatives of poor nations challenge this view, and are far less generous in describing the past role of the anthropologist. Most contemporary anthropologists, however, have a deep moral commitment to defending the legal, political, and economic rights of the people with whom they work.

When anthropologists discuss social change, they usually mean change brought about in preindustrial societies, through longstanding interaction with the nation states of the industrialized world. In early anthropology, contact between the West and the remainder of the world was characterized by the terms "acculturation" and "culture contact." These terms were used to describe the diffusion of cultural traits between the developed and less developed countries. Often this was analyzed as a one-way process in which cultures of the Third World were seen, for better or worse, as receptacles for Western cultural traits. Nowadays, many anthropologists believe that the diffusion of cultural traits across social, political, and economic boundaries was emphasized at the expense of the real issues of dominance, subordinance, and dependence that characterized the colonial experience. Just as importantly, many anthropologists recognize that the present-day forms of cultural, economic, and political interaction between the developed and the so-called underdeveloped world are best characterized as neocolonial.

Most of the articles in this section take the perspective that anthropology should be critical as well as descriptive. They raise questions about cultural contact, and about the political economies of underdeveloped countries, that are both interesting and troublesome.

In keeping with the notion that the negative impact of the West on traditional cultures began with colonial domination, this section opens with "Death and Taxes" and "Why Can't People Feed Themselves?" These articles show that the "progress" of the West has meant poverty and hunger for peasant societies.

Each succeeding article emphasizes a different aspect of culture affected by the impact of the West. "Growing Up as a Fore" points to the problems of maintaining individual identity in a changing society. "The Transformation of the Kalahari !Kung" details the change in values associated with food-getting. "Has Success Spoiled the Sherpas?" assesses the impact of Western education and tourism on a traditional economy. "Dark Dreams About the White Man" reveals that even the dreams of natives are invaded by the white man. "Trouble in Paradise," "Amazon Tragedy," "Bicultural Conflict," and "Inuit Youth in a Changing World" describe the personal devastation inflicted upon people who are caught between two worlds, the traditional and the modern.

"Back on the Land" helps us to understand that, even considering all that has happened to non-Western peoples, they have not been passive recipients of change. Rather, they have been actively adjusting and, to some degree directing, their responses to the new challenges facing them. With the advantages of new technology, some have even managed to salvage a part of their past.

Finally, "Easter Island: Scary Parable" delivers the sternest warning of all: If the downward spiral of human degradation is not broken soon, it will be too late.

Looking Ahead: Challenge Questions

What parallels can be drawn between the Spanish conquest in the Americas and the expansion of the Roman Empire? How did they differ?

What have been the effects of colonialism on formerly subsistence-oriented socioeconomic systems? What is a subsistence system?

Do cash crops inevitably lead to class distinctions and poverty?

What was it about the Fore culture that made it so

vulnerable to the harmful effects of the change from a subsistence economy to a cash-crop economy?

What impact has the tourist trade and the developing educational opportunities had upon the Sherpa life-style?

How has culture contact affected the dreams of the Mehinaku?

In what ways are traditional peoples struggling to maintain their cultures?

What ethical obligations do industrial societies have toward respecting the human rights and cultural diversity of traditional communities?

What happened to Easter Island civilization?

Death and Taxes

Every empire has its price

Samuel M. Wilson

Samuel M. Wilson is an assistant professor of anthropology at the University of Texas, Austin.

"Taxation is made more shameful and burdensome," wrote Salvian the Presbyter in the fifth century, "because all do not bear the burden of all. They extort tribute from the poor man for the taxes of the rich, and the weaker carry the load for the stronger" (*The Writings of Salvian the Presbyter,* Catholic University Press, 1947). Salvian was complaining of the tax burden imposed on conquered territory by the Roman Empire, but the same sentiments might have been expressed by New World peoples as they were incorporated into the expanding Spanish empire. In a large part of the New World, most notably in regions ruled by the Aztec and Inca empires, people probably grumbled about taxes long before the arrival of the Europeans. From the smallest agrarian chiefdom to empires spanning continents, governments throughout history have lived off the surplus produced by the populace, and they have engineered economies to insure that such a surplus was produced.

When they conquered the most complex societies of the New World, the Spaniards substituted their own systems of taxation for those already in place. How, we may wonder, did the conquistadors come to the conclusion that New World people owed them anything? Montezuma might have pondered this as he sat under house arrest in the Spaniards' quarters in Tenochtitlán. For most early Spanish conquerors, however, it was a given.

Columbus took it for granted and had a tribute system in place on Hispaniola by 1494:

All the natives between the ages of fourteen and seventy years bound themselves to pay him tribute in the products of the country at so much per head, promising to fulfill their engagement. Some of the conditions of this agreement were as follows: the mountaineers of Cibao were to bring to the town every three months a specified measure filled with gold. They reckon by the moon and call the months moons. The islanders who cultivated the lands which spontaneously produced spices and cotton, were pledged to pay a fixed sum per head [*De Orbe Novo,* by Peter Martyr D'Anghera. Burt Franklin, 1912].

Perhaps for sixteenth-century Europeans (as in twentieth-century conventional wisdom) taxes were one of the two inescapable things. Or perhaps Spain, in demanding tribute from conquered peoples, took Rome as its model. Gaul and Britain and Spain itself—or the peoples and lands that then constituted Spain—had paid tribute to Rome a thousand years before Columbus sailed.

Within the Roman system, as in almost all tax systems, the state's objective was to extract the greatest amount of money, goods, and services for the least cost. During the period of the Roman Republic, the imposition of tribute on conquered territories was an important motivation for the conquests in the first place. Nevertheless, to subjugate the provinces completely and hold them to the letter of tribute demands was probably impossible and certainly not expedient. Conquered territories attempted to minimize their tribute burden without attracting the attention of the imperial army. The Romans, too, were eager to preserve the peace.

For example, Julius Caesar's strategy for extracting tribute from the province of Gaul depended on convincing local leaders that producing tax revenues was in their interest. In Caesar's words (written in the third person):

During the winter which he spent in Belgic Gaul Caesar made it his single aim to keep the tribes loyal, and to see that none had any pretext for revolt or any hope of profiting by it. The last thing he wanted was to have to fight a campaign immediately before his departure; for it would mean leaving Gaul in a state of rebellion when the time came to withdraw his army, and all the tribes would be only too willing to take up arms when they could do so without immediate risk. So he made their condition of subjection more tolerable by addressing the tribal governments in complimentary terms, refraining from the imposition of any fresh [tax] burdens, and bestowing rich presents upon the principal citizens. By these means it was easy to induce a people exhausted by so many defeats to live at peace [*The Conquest of Gaul,* Penguin Books, Ltd., 1951].

Spanish tacticians also knew that much was to be gained by co-opting the local rulers. They coerced and courted them into becoming agents of the empire who would collect tribute and keep the peace. Spain's treatment of its New World territories was similar in other respects to Rome's relationship to its provinces. To generate income, Spain placed the greatest effort in areas of greatest return (like the gold- and silver-mining regions), just as Rome exploited Britain's mineral wealth. Spain pensioned off its soldiers with grants of New World lands and the labor of conquered people, just as Rome granted parcels of conquered land to retiring soldiers to repay them cheaply and to further subdue the provinces. And like Rome, Spain kept the cost of having an army within bounds by using the threat of force more often than force itself.

As did Rome and Spain, the Inca empire in the Andes undertook its conquests with the smallest standing army possible. But their might was still adequate to subjugate unwilling populations whose traditional leadership had nothing to gain and everything to lose by imperial conquest. And like the Romans, the Inca relied on the cooperation of local elites to fill the imperial coffers.

The Inca policy of gentle persuasion involved taking provincial hostages to the Inca capital, Cuzco, to live in great style. These guests were steeped in the city's language and culture. Undoubtedly, it would have been impressed on them that the treatment they received depended entirely upon their participation in extracting tribute from their homelands. Garcilaso de la Vega, whose mother was a member of the Inca elite and whose father was a Spanish nobleman, described the strategy of the Inca emperor:

They also carried off the leading chief and all his children to Cuzco, where they were treated with kindness and favor so that by frequenting the court they would learn not only its laws, customs, and correct speech, but also the rites, ceremonies, and superstitions of the Incas. This done, the [chief] was restored to his former dignity and authority, and the Inca, as king, ordered the vassals to serve and obey him as their natural lord.

The Inca bestowed . . . gifts on newly conquered Indians, so that however brutish and barbarous they had been they were subdued by affection and attached to his service by a bond so strong that no province ever dreamed of rebelling. And in order to remove all occasion for complaint and to prevent dissatisfaction from leading to rebellion, he confirmed and promulgated anew all the former laws, liberties, and statutes so that they might be more esteemed and respected, and he never changed a word of them unless they were contrary to the idolatry and laws of his empire [*Royal Commentaries of the Incas,* translated by Harold Livermore, University of Texas Press, 1966].

The Aztec empire, centered in the capital city Tenochtitlán, also resembled republican Rome in its treatment of peripheral territories. In his recent book *Trade, Tribute, and Transportation* (University of Oklahoma Press), historical anthropologist Ross Hassig emphasized three correspondences in his analysis of the Aztec empire before and during the Spanish conquest:

While the similarities between the Romans and the Aztecs can be overstated, they did share certain characteristics: (1) expansion of political dominance without direct territorial control, (2) a focus on the internal security of the empire by exercising influence on a limited range of activities within the client states, and (3) the achievement of such influence by generally retaining rather than replacing local officials.

When the Inca and Aztec empires fell to Spain, the conquerors seemed in a good position to replace the top strata of New World bureaucratic structures, leaving lower strata intact to funnel tribute upward. But substituting tribute to Spain for tribute to Cuzco or Tenochtitlán was a disaster for several reasons. Foremost, the conquest brought massive loss of life through the introduction of Old World diseases. The indigenous economies were completely disrupted by epidemics that in many areas killed 70 to 90 percent of the population in less than a century, providing a grimly literal example of a shrinking tax base. In the New World, death and taxes were more closely linked than in the proverbial sense.

Second, the expanding European empire did not merely replace the top tier of the indigenous tribute system; it short-circuited the entire structure. Under the Aztec system, for example, tribute flowed through a pyramidal series of institutions, from local governments to regional centers to provincial capitals to Tenochtitlán. With the imposition of Spanish control, these intermediate stops were bypassed; tribute went from local regions directly to Mexico City and from there to Spain. Regional centers and administrative systems withered and disappeared, undercutting the native political order.

Finally, European governments and entrepreneurs were interested in forms of wealth that were tangible and transportable. Taxes in the form of labor—such as the Inca *mita* system, which supplied a work force for state projects—were less appealing. Thus, local groups that had previously met their obligations by working for the state

Spaniards under Balboa (center) quarrel over the gold objects bestowed on them by Panciaco, the chief who showed them the way to the Pacific Ocean. In the background of this late sixteenth century illustration by Flemish engraver Theodore de Bry, the Europeans reward Panciaco with baptism.

From *Discovering the New World*, by Michael Alexander

from time to time were forced to pay tribute in goods.

As bad as this was, the situation was still worse for those New World people who were unaccustomed to life within the sphere of tribute-demanding empires. For them, being forced to pay taxes in the form of money or goods or labor was an impossible order: little or no surplus was generated by their subsistence economies, and no tribute-collecting mechanisms were in place. As a result, most of these peoples were pushed from their lands or trampled in the course of European expansion.

Today, of course, we enjoy the advantage of governing ourselves, instead of paying tribute to some foreign imperial power. And yet, as Thomas Paine observed in *Common Sense,*

Government even in the best state is but a necessary evil; in its worst state an intolerable one; for when we suffer, or are exposed to the same miseries *by a government,* which we might expect in a country *without government,* our calamity is heightened by reflecting that we furnish the means by which we suffer.

Why Can't People Feed Themselves?

Frances Moore Lappé and Joseph Collins

Frances Moore Lappé and Dr. Joseph Collins are founders and directors of the Institute for Food and Development Policy, located in San Francisco and New York.

Question: You have said that the hunger problem is not the result of overpopulation. But you have not yet answered the most basic and simple question of all: Why can't people feed themselves? As Senator Daniel P. Moynihan put it bluntly, when addressing himself to the Third World, "Food growing is the first thing you do when you come down out of the trees. The question is, how come the United States can grow food and you can't?"

Our Response: In the very first speech I, Frances, ever gave after writing *Diet for a Small Planet,* I tried to take my audience along the path that I had taken in attempting to understand why so many are hungry in this world. Here is the gist of that talk that was, in truth, a turning point in my life:

When I started I saw a world divided into two parts: a *minority* of nations that had "taken off" through their agricultural and industrial revolutions to reach a level of unparalleled material abundance and a *majority* that remained behind in a primitive, traditional, undeveloped state. This lagging behind of the majority of the world's peoples must be due, I thought, to some internal deficiency or even to several of them. It seemed obvious that the underdeveloped countries must be deficient in natural resources—particularly good land and climate—and in cultural development, including modern attitudes conducive to work and progress.

But when looking for the historical roots of the predicament, I learned that my picture of these two separate worlds was quite false. My "two separate worlds" were really just different sides of the same coin. One side was on top largely because the other side was on the bottom. Could this be true? How were these separate worlds related?

Colonialism appeared to me to be the link. Colonialism destroyed the cultural patterns of production and exchange by which traditional societies in "underdeveloped" countries previously had met the needs of the people. Many precolonial social structures, while dominated by exploitative elites, had evolved a system of mutual obligations among the classes that helped to ensure at least a minimal diet for all. A friend of mine once said: "Precolonial village existence in subsistence agriculture was a limited life indeed, but it's certainly not Calcutta." The misery of starvation in the streets of Calcutta can only be understood as the end-point of a long historical process—one that has destroyed a traditional social system.

"Underdeveloped," instead of being an adjective that evokes the picture of a static society, became for me a verb (to "underdevelop") meaning the *process* by which the minority of the world has transformed—indeed often robbed and degraded—the majority.

That was in 1972. I clearly recall my thoughts on my return home. I had stated publicly for the first time a world view that had taken me years of study to grasp. The sense of relief was tremendous. For me the breakthrough lay in realizing that today's "hunger crisis" could not be described in static, descriptive terms. Hunger and underdevelopment must always be thought of as a *process*.

To answer the question "why hunger?" it is counterproductive to simply *describe* the conditions in an underdeveloped country today. For these conditions, whether they be the degree of malnutrition, the levels of agricultural production, or even the country's ecological endowment, are not static factors—they are not "givens." They are rather the *results* of an ongoing historical process. As we dug ever deeper into that historical process for the preparation of this book, we began to discover the existence of scarcity-creating mechanisms that we had only vaguely intuited before.

We have gotten great satisfaction from probing into the past since we recognized it is the only way to approach a solution to hunger today. We have come to see that it is the *force* creating the condition, not the condition itself, that must be the target of change. Otherwise we might change the condition today, only to find tomorrow that it has been recreated—with a vengeance.

Asking the question "Why can't people feed themselves?" carries a sense of bewilderment that there are so many people in the world not able to feed themselves adequately. What astonished us, however, is that there are not *more* people in the world who are hungry—considering the weight of the centuries of effort by the few to undermine the capacity of the majority to feed themselves. No, we are not crying "conspiracy!" If these forces were entirely conspiratorial, they would be easier to detect and many more people would by now have risen up to resist. We are talking about something more subtle and insidious; a heritage of a colonial order in which people with the advantage of considerable power sought their own self-interest, often arrogantly believing they were acting in the interest of the people whose lives they were destroying.

THE COLONIAL MIND

The colonizer viewed agriculture in the subjugated lands as primitive and backward. Yet such a view contrasts sharply with documents from the colonial period now coming to light. For example, A. J. Voelker, a British agricultural scientist assigned to India during the 1890s, wrote:

Nowhere would one find better instances of keeping land scrupulously clean from weeds, of ingenuity in device of water-raising appliances, of knowledge of soils and their capabilities, as well as of the exact time to sow and reap, as one would find in Indian agriculture. It is wonderful, too, how much is known of rotation, the system of "mixed crops" and of fallowing. . . . I, at least, have never seen a more perfect picture of cultivation."[1]

None the less, viewing the agriculture of the vanquished as primitive and backward reinforced the colonizer's rationale for destroying it. To the colonizers of Africa, Asia, and Latin America, agriculture became merely a means to extract wealth—much as gold from a mine—on behalf of the colonizing power. Agriculture was no longer seen as a source of food for the local population, nor even as their livelihood. Indeed the English economist John Stuart Mill reasoned that colonies should not be thought of as civilizations or countries at all but as "agricultural establishments" whose sole purpose was to supply the "larger community to which they belong." The colonized society's agriculture was only a subdivision of the agricultural system of the metropolitan country. As Mill acknowledged, "Our West India colonies, for example, cannot be regarded as countries. . . . The West Indies are the place where England *finds it convenient* to carry on the production of sugar, coffee and a few other tropical commodities."[2]

Prior to European intervention, Africans practiced a diversified agriculture that included the introduction of new food plants of Asian or American origin. But colonial rule simplified this diversified production to single cash crops—often to the exclusion of staple foods—and in the process sowed the seeds of famine.[3] Rice farming once had been common

in Gambia. But with colonial rule so much of the best land was taken over by peanuts (grown for the European market) that rice had to be imported to counter the mounting prospect of famine. Northern Ghana, once famous for its yams and other foodstuffs, was forced to concentrate solely on cocoa. Most of the Gold Coast thus became dependent on cocoa. Liberia was turned into a virtual plantation subsidiary of Firestone Tire and Rubber. Food production in Dahomey and southeast Nigeria was all but abandoned in favor of palm oil; Tanganyika (now Tanzania) was forced to focus on sisal and Uganda on cotton.

The same happened in Indochina. About the time of the American Civil War the French decided that the Mekong Delta in Vietnam would be ideal for producing rice for export. Through a production system based on enriching the large landowners, Vietnam became the world's third largest exporter of rice by the 1930s; yet many landless Vietnamese went hungry.[4]

Rather than helping the peasants, colonialism's public works programs only reinforced export crop production. British irrigation works built in nineteenth-century India did help increase production, but the expansion was for spring export crops at the expense of millets and legumes grown in the fall as the basic local food crops.

Because people living on the land do not easily go against their natural and adaptive drive to grow food for themselves, colonial powers had to force the production of cash crops. The first strategy was to use physical or economic force to get the local population to grow cash crops instead of food on their own plots and then turn them over to the colonizer for export. The second strategy was the direct takeover of the land by large-scale plantations growing crops for export.

FORCED PEASANT PRODUCTION

As Walter Rodney recounts in *How Europe Underdeveloped Africa,* cash crops were often grown literally under threat of guns and whips.[5] One visitor

to the Sahel commented in 1928: "Cotton is an artificial crop and one the value of which is not entirely clear to the natives. . . ." He wryly noted the "enforced enthusiasm with which the natives. . .have thrown themselves into. . .planting cotton."[6] The forced cultivation of cotton was a major grievance leading to the Maji Maji wars in Tanzania (then Tanganyika) and behind the nationalist revolt in Angola as late as 1960.[7]

Although raw force was used, taxation was the preferred colonial technique to force Africans to grow cash crops. The colonial administrations simply levied taxes on cattle, land, houses, and even the people themselves. Since the tax had to be paid in the coin of the realm, the peasants had either to grow crops to sell or to work on the plantations or in the mines of the Europeans.[8] Taxation was both an effective tool to "stimulate" cash cropping and a source of revenue that the colonial bureaucracy needed to enforce the system. To expand their production of export crops to pay the mounting taxes, peasant producers were forced to neglect the farming of food crops. In 1830, the Dutch administration in Java made the peasants an offer they could not refuse; if they would grow government-owned export crops on one fifth of their land, the Dutch would remit their land taxes.[9] If they refused and thus could not pay the taxes, they lost their land.

Marketing boards emerged in Africa in the 1930s as another technique for getting the profit from cash crop production by native producers into the hands of the colonial government and international firms. Purchases by the marketing boards were well below the world market price. Peanuts bought by the boards from peasant cultivators in West Africa were sold in Britain for more than *seven times* what the peasants received.[10]

The marketing board concept was born with the "cocoa hold-up" in the Gold Coast in 1937. Small cocoa farmers refused to sell to the large cocoa concerns like United Africa

Company (a subsidiary of the Anglo-Dutch firm, Unilever—which we know as Lever Brothers) and Cadbury until they got a higher price. When the British government stepped in and agreed to buy the cocoa directly in place of the big business concerns, the smallholders must have thought they had scored at least a minor victory. But had they really? The following year the British formally set up the West African Cocoa Control Board. Theoretically, its purpose was to pay the peasants a reasonable price for their crops. In practice, however, the board, as sole purchaser, was able to hold down the prices paid the peasants for their crops when the world prices were rising. Rodney sums up the real "victory":

None of the benefits went to Africans, but rather to the British government itself and to the private companies. . . Big companies like the United African Company and John Holt were given. . . quotas to fulfill on behalf of the boards. As agents of the government, they were no longer exposed to direct attack, and their profits were secure.[11]

These marketing boards, set up for most export crops, were actually controlled by the companies. The chairman of the Cocoa Board was none other than John Cadbury of Cadbury Brothers (ever had a Cadbury chocolate bar?) who was part of a buying pool exploiting West African cocoa farmers.

The marketing boards funneled part of the profits from the exploitation of peasant producers indirectly into the royal treasury. While the Cocoa Board sold to the British Food Ministry at low prices, the ministry upped the price for British manufacturers, thus netting a profit as high as 11 million pounds in some years.[12]

These marketing boards of Africa were only the institutionalized rendition of what is the essence of colonialism—the extraction of wealth. While profits continued to accrue to foreign interests and local elites, prices received by those actually growing the commodities remained low.

PLANTATIONS

A second approach was direct takeover of the land either by the colonizing government or by private foreign interests. Previously self-provisioning farmers were forced to cultivate the plantation fields through either enslavement or economic coercion.

After the conquest of the Kandyan Kingdom (in present day Sri Lanka), in 1815, the British designated all the vast central part of the island as crown land. When it was determined that coffee, a profitable export crop, could be grown there, the Kandyan lands were sold off to British investors and planters at a mere five shillings per acre, the government even defraying the cost of surveying and road building.[13]

Java is also a prime example of a colonial government seizing territory and then putting it into private foreign hands. In 1870, the Dutch declared all uncultivated land—called waste land—property of the state for lease to Dutch plantation enterprises. In addition, the Agrarian Land Law of 1870 authorized foreign companies to lease village-owned land. The peasants, in chronic need of ready cash for taxes and foreign consumer goods, were only too willing to lease their land to the foreign companies for very modest sums and under terms dictated by the firms. Where land was still held communally, the village headman was tempted by high cash commissions offered by plantation companies. He would lease the village land even more cheaply than would the individual peasant or, as was frequently the case, sell out the entire village to the company.[14]

The introduction of the plantation meant the divorce of agriculture from nourishment, as the notion of food value was lost to the overriding claim of "market value" in international trade. Crops such as sugar, tobacco, and coffee were selected, not on the basis of how well they feed people, but for their high price value relative to their weight and bulk so that profit margins could be maintained even after the costs of shipping to Europe.

SUPPRESSING PEASANT FARMING

The stagnation and impoverishment of the peasant food-producing sector was not the mere by-product of benign neglect, that is, the unintended consequence of an overemphasis on export production. Plantations—just like modern "agro-industrial complexes"—needed an abundant and readily available supply of low-wage agricultural workers. Colonial administrations thus devised a variety of tactics, all to undercut self-provisioning agriculture and thus make rural populations dependent on plantation wages. Government services and even the most minimal infrastructure (access to water, roads, seeds, credit, pest and disease control information, and so on) were systematically denied. Plantations usurped most of the good land, either making much of the rural population landless or pushing them onto marginal soils. (Yet the plantations have often held much of their land idle simply to prevent the peasants from using it—even to this day. Del Monte owns 57,000 acres of Guatemala but plants only 9000. The rest lies idle except for a few thousand head of grazing cattle.)[15]

In some cases a colonial administration would go even further to guarantee itself a labor supply. In at least twelve countries in the eastern and southern parts of Africa the exploitation of mineral wealth (gold, diamonds, and copper) and the establishment of cash-crop plantations demanded a continuous supply of low-cost labor. To assure this labor supply, colonial administrations simply expropriated the land of the African communities by violence and drove the people into small reserves.[16] With neither adequate land for their traditional slash-and-burn methods nor access to the means—tools, water, and fertilizer—to make continuous farming of such limited areas viable, the indigenous population could scarcely meet subsistence needs, much less produce surplus to sell in order to cover the colonial taxes. Hundreds of thousands of Africans were forced to become the cheap labor source so "needed" by the colonial plantations. Only by laboring on plantations and in the mines could they hope to pay the colonial taxes.

The tax scheme to produce reserves of cheap plantation and mining labor was particularly effective when the Great Depression hit and the bottom dropped out of cash crop economies. In 1929 the cotton market collapsed, leaving peasant cotton producers, such as those in Upper Volta, unable to pay their colonial taxes. More and more young people, in some years as many as 80,000, were thus forced to migrate to the Gold Coast to compete with each other for low-wage jobs on cocoa plantations.[17]

The forced migration of Africa's most able-bodied workers—stripping village food farming of needed hands—was a recurring feature of colonialism. As late as 1973 the Portuguese "exported" 400,000 Mozambican peasants to work in South Africa in exchange for gold deposited in the Lisbon treasury.

The many techniques of colonialism to undercut self-provisioning agriculture in order to ensure a cheap labor supply are no better illustrated than by the story of how, in the mid-nineteenth century, sugar plantation owners in British Guiana coped with the double blow of the emancipation of slaves and the crash in the world sugar market. The story is graphically recounted by Alan Adamson in *Sugar without Slaves.*[18]

Would the ex-slaves be allowed to take over the plantation land and grow the food they needed? The planters, many ruined by the sugar slump, were determined they would not. The planter-dominated government devised several schemes for thwarting food self-sufficiency. The price of crown land was kept artificially high, and the purchase of land in parcels smaller than 100 acres was outlawed—two measures guaranteeing that newly organized ex-slave cooperatives could not hope to gain access to much land. The government also prohibited cultivation on as

much as 400,000 acres—on the grounds of "uncertain property titles." Moreover, although many planters held part of their land out of sugar production due to the depressed world price, they would not allow any alternative production on them. They feared that once the ex-slaves started growing food it would be difficult to return them to sugar production when world market prices began to recover. In addition, the government taxed peasant production, then turned around and used the funds to subsidize the immigration of laborers from India and Malaysia to replace the freed slaves, thereby making sugar production again profitable for the planters. Finally, the government neglected the infrastructure for subsistence agriculture and denied credit for small farmers.

Perhaps the most insidious tactic to "lure" the peasant away from food production—and the one with profound historical consequences—was a policy of keeping the price of imported food low through the removal of tariffs and subsidies. The policy was double-edged: first, peasants were told they need not grow food because they could always buy it cheaply with their plantation wages; second, cheap food imports destroyed the market for domestic food and thereby impoverished local food producers.

Adamson relates how both the Governor of British Guiana and the Secretary for the Colonies Earl Grey favored low duties on imports in order to erode local food production and thereby release labor for the plantations. In 1851 the governor rushed through a reduction of the duty on cereals in order to "divert" labor to the sugar estates. As Adamson comments, "Without realizing it, he [the governor] had put his finger on the most mordant feature of monoculture: . . . its convulsive need to destroy any other sector of the economy which might compete for 'its' labor."[19]

Many colonial governments succeeded in establishing dependence on imported foodstuffs. In 1647 an

observer in the West Indies wrote to Governor Winthrop of Massachusetts: "Men are so intent upon planting sugar that they had rather buy foode at very deare rates than produce it by labour, so infinite is the profitt of sugar workes. . . ."[20] By 1770, the West Indies were importing most of the continental colonies' exports of dried fish, grain, beans, and vegetables. A dependence on imported food made the West Indian colonies vulnerable to any disruption in supply. This dependence on imported food stuffs spelled disaster when the thirteen continental colonies gained independence and food exports from the continent to the West Indies were interrupted. With no diversified food system to fall back on, 15,000 plantation workers died of famine between 1780 and 1787 in Jamaica alone.[21] The dependence of the West Indies on imported food persists to this day.

SUPPRESSING PEASANT COMPETITION

We have talked about the techniques by which indigenous populations were forced to cultivate cash crops. In some countries with large plantations, however, colonial governments found it necessary to *prevent* peasants from independently growing cash crops not out of concern for their welfare, but so that they would not compete with colonial interests growing the same crop. For peasant farmers, given a modicum of opportunity, proved themselves capable of outproducing the large plantations not only in terms of output per unit of land but, more important, in terms of capital cost per unit produced.

In the Dutch East Indies (Indonesia and Dutch New Guinea) colonial policy in the middle of the nineteenth century forbade the sugar refineries to buy sugar cane from indigenous growers and imposed a discriminatory tax on rubber produced by native smallholders.[22] A recent unpublished United Nations study of agricultural development in Africa concluded that large-scale agricultural operations owned and controlled by foreign commercial interests (such as the rubber plantations of Liberia, the sisal estates of Tanganyika [Tanzania], and the coffee estates of Angola) only survived the competition of peasant producers because "the authorities actively supported them by suppressing indigenous rural development."[23]

The suppression of indigenous agricultural development served the interests of the colonizing powers in two ways. Not only did it prevent direct competition from more efficient native producers of the same crops, but it also guaranteed a labor force to work on the foreign-owned estates. Planters and foreign investors were not unaware that peasants who could survive economically by their own production would be under less pressure to sell their labor cheaply to the large estates.

The answer to the question, then, "Why can't people feed themselves?" must begin with an understanding of how colonialism actively prevented people from doing just that.

Colonialism

- forced peasants to replace food crops with cash crops that were then expropriated at very low rates;
- took over the best agricultural land for export crop plantations

and then forced the most able-bodied workers to leave the village fields to work as slaves or for very low wages on plantations;

- encouraged a dependence on imported food;
- blocked native peasant cash crop production from competing with cash crops produced by settlers or foreign firms.

These are concrete examples of the development of underdevelopment that we should have perceived as such even as we read our history schoolbooks. Why didn't we? Somehow our schoolbooks always seemed to make the flow of history appear to have its own logic—as if it could not have been any other way. I, Frances, recall, in particular, a grade-school, social studies pamphlet on the idyllic life of Pedro, a nine-year-old boy on a coffee plantation in South America. The drawings of lush vegetation and "exotic" huts made his life seem romantic indeed. Wasn't it natural and proper that South America should have plantations to supply my mother and father with coffee? Isn't that the way it was *meant* to be?

NOTES

[1]Radha Sinha, *Food and Poverty* (New York: Holmes and Meier, 1976), p. 26.

[2]John Stuart Mill, *Political Economy,* Book 3, Chapter 25 (emphasis added).

[3]Peter Feldman and David Lawrence, "Social and Economic Implications of the Large-Scale Introduction of New Varieties of Foodgrains," Africa Report, preliminary draft (Geneva: UNRISD, 1975), pp. 107–108.

[4]Edgar Owens, *The Right Side of History,* unpublished manuscript, 1976.

[5]Walter Rodney, *How Europe Underdeveloped Africa* (London: Bogle-L'Ouverture Publications, 1972), pp. 171–172.

[6]Ferdinand Ossendowski, *Slaves of the Sun* (New York: Dutton, 1928), p. 276.

[7]Rodney, *How Europe Underdeveloped Africa,* pp. 171–172.

[8]Ibid., p. 181.

[9]Clifford Geertz, *Agricultural Involution* (Berkeley and Los Angeles: University of California Press, 1963), pp. 52–53.

[10]Rodney, *How Europe Underdeveloped Africa,* p. 185.

[11]Ibid., p. 184.

[12]Ibid., p. 186.

[13]George L. Beckford, *Persistent Poverty: Underdevelopment in Plantation Economies of the Third World* (New York: Oxford University Press, 1972), p. 99.

[14]Ibid., p. 99, quoting from Erich Jacoby, *Agrarian Unrest in Southeast Asia* (New York: Asia Publishing House, 1961), p. 66.

[15]Pat Flynn and Roger Burbach, North American Congress on Latin America, Berkeley, California, recent investigation.

[16]Feldman and Lawrence, "Social and Economic Implications," p. 103.

[17]Special Sahelian Office Report, Food and Agriculture Organization, March 28, 1974, pp. 88–89.

[18]Alan Adamson, *Sugar Without Slaves: The Political Economy of British Guiana, 1838–1904* (New Haven and London: Yale University Press, 1972).

[19]Ibid., p. 41.

[20]Eric Williams, *Capitalism and Slavery* (New York: Putnam, 1966), p. 110.

[21]Ibid., p. 121.

[22]Gunnar Myrdal, *Asian Drama,* vol. 1 (New York: Pantheon, 1966), pp. 448–449.

[23]Feldman and Lawrence, "Social and Economic Implications," p. 189.

Growing up as a Fore

E. Richard Sorenson

Dr. Sorenson, director of the Smithsonian's National Anthropological Film Center, wrote The Edge of the Forest *on his Fore studies.*

Exploring, two youngsters walk confidently past men's house in hamlet. Smaller women's house is at right.

Untouched by the outside world, they had lived for thousands of years in isolated mountains and valleys deep in the interior of Papua New Guinea. They had no cloth, no metal, no money, no idea that their homeland was an island—or that what surrounded it was salt water. Yet the Fore (for'ay) people had developed remarkable and sophisticated approaches to human relations, and their child-rearing practices gave their young unusual freedom to explore. Successful as hunter-gatherers and as subsistence gardeners, they also had great adaptability, which brought rapid accommodation with the outside world after their lands were opened up.

It was alone that I first visited the Fore in 1963—a day's walk from a recently built airstrip. I stayed six months. Perplexed and fascinated, I returned six times in the next ten years, eventually spending a year and a half living with them in their hamlets.

Theirs was a way of life different from anything I had seen or heard about before. There were no chiefs, patriarchs, priests, medicine men or the like. A striking personal freedom was enjoyed even by the very young, who could move about at will and be where or with whom they liked. Infants rarely cried, and they played confidently with knives, axes, and fire. Conflict between old and young did not arise; there was no "generation gap."

Older children enjoyed deferring to the interests and desires of the younger, and sibling rivalry was virtually undetectable. A responsive sixth sense seemed to attune the Fore hamlet mates to each other's interests and needs. They did not have to directly ask, inveigle, bargain or speak out for what they needed or wanted. Subtle, even fleeting expressions of interest, desire, and discomfort were quickly read and helpfully acted on by one's associates. This spontaneous urge to share food, affection, work, trust, tools and pleasure was the social cement that held the Fore hamlets together. It was a pleasant way of life, for one could always be with those with whom one got along well.

Ranging and planting, sharing and living, the Fore diverged and expanded through high virgin lands in a pioneer region. They hunted out their gardens, tilled them while they lasted, then hunted again. Moving ever away from lands peopled and used they had a self-contained life with its own special ways.

The underlying ecological conditions were like those that must have encompassed the world before agriculture set its imprint so broadly. Abutting the Fore was virtually unlimited virgin land, and they had food plants they could introduce into it. Like hunter-gatherers they sought their sources of sustenance first in one locale and then another, across an extended range, following opportunities provided by a providential nature. But like agriculturalists they concentrated their effort and attention more narrowly on selected sites of production, on their gardens. They were both seekers and producers. A pioneer people in a pioneer land, they ranged freely into a vast territory, but they planted to live.

Cooperative groups formed hamlets and gardened together. When the fertility of a garden declined, they abandoned it. Grass sprung up to cover these abandoned sites of earlier cultivation, and, as the Fore moved on to other parts of the forest, they left uninhabited grasslands to mark their passage.

The traditional hamlets were small, with a rather fluid system of social relations. A single large men's house provided shelter for 10 to 20 men and boys and their visiting friends. The several smaller women's houses each normally sheltered two married women, their unmarried daughters and their sons up to about six years of age. Formal kinship bonds were less important than friendship was. Fraternal "gangs" of youths formed the hamlets; their "clubhouses" were the men's houses.

Learning to be a toddler, a Fore baby takes its first experimental steps. No one urges him on.

During the day the gardens became the center of life. Hamlets were virtually deserted as friends, relatives and children went to one or more garden plots to mingle their social, economic and erotic pursuits in a pleasant and emotionally filled Gestalt of garden life. The boys and unmarried youths preferred to explore and hunt in the outlying lands, but they also passed through and tarried in the gardens.

Daily activities were not scheduled. No one made demands, and the land was bountiful. Not surprisingly the line between work and play was never clear. The transmission of the Fore behavioral pattern to the young began in early infancy during a period of unceasing human physical contact. The effect of being constantly "in touch" with hamlet mates and their daily life seemed to start a process which proceeded by degrees: close rapport, involvement in regular activity, ability to handle seemingly dangerous implements safely, and responsible freedom to pursue individual interests at will without danger.

While very young, infants remained in almost continuous bodily contact with their mother, her house

mates or her gardening associates. At first, mothers' laps were the center of activity, and infants occupied themselves there by nursing, sleeping and playing with their own bodies or those of their caretakers. They were not put aside for the sake of other activities, as when food was being prepared or heavy loads were being carried. Remaining in close, uninterrupted physical contact with those around them, their basic needs such as rest, nourishment, stimulation and security were continuously satisfied without obstacle.

By being physically in touch from their earliest days, Fore youngsters learned to communicate needs, desires and feelings through a body language of touch and response that developed before speech. This opened the door to a much closer rapport with those around them than otherwise would have been possible, and led ultimately to the Fore brand of social cement and the sixth sense that bound groups together through spontaneous, responsive sharing.

As the infant's awareness increased, his interests broadened to the things his mother and other caretakers did and to the objects and materials they used. Then these youngsters began crawling out to explore things that attracted their attention. By the time they were toddling, their interests continually took them on short sorties to nearby objects and persons. As soon as they could walk well, the excursions extended to the entire hamlet and its gardens, and then beyond with other children. Developing without interference or supervision, this personal exploratory learning quest freely touched on whatever was around, even axes, knives, machetes, fire, and the like. When I first went to the Fore, I was aghast.

Eventually I discovered that this capability emerged naturally from Fore infant-handling practices in their milieu of close human physical

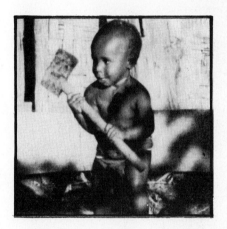

In infancy, Fore children begin experimental play with knives and other lethal objects. Sorenson never saw a child warned away or injured by them.

proximity and tactile interaction. Because touch and bodily contact lend themselves naturally to satisfying the basic needs of young children, an early kind of communicative experience fostered cooperative interaction between infants and their caretakers, also kinesthetic contact with the activities at hand. This made it easy for them to learn the appropriate handling of the tools of life.

The early pattern of exploratory activity included frequent return to one of the "mothers." Serving as home base, the bastion of security, a woman might occasionally give the youngster a nod of encouragement, if he glanced in her direction with un-

certainty. Yet rarely did the women attempt to control or direct, nor did they participate in the child's quests or jaunts.

As a result Fore children did not have to adjust to rule and schedule in order to find their place in life. They could pursue their interests and whims wherever they might lead and still be part of a richly responsive world of human touch which constantly provided sustenance, comfort, diversion and security.

Learning proceeded during the course of pursuing interests and exploring. Constantly "in touch" with people who were busy with daily activities, the Fore young quickly

learned the skills of life from example. Muscle tone, movement and mood were components of this learning process; formal lessons and commands were not. Kinesthetic skills developed so quickly that infants were able to casually handle knives and similar objects before they could walk.

Even after several visits I continued to be surprised that the unsupervised Fore toddlers did not recklessly thrust themselves into unappreciated dangers, the way our own children tend to do. But then, why should they? From their earliest days, they enjoyed a benevolent sanctuary from which the world could be confidently

Babies have free access to the breast and later, like this toddler being helped to kernels of corn by an older girl, can help themselves to whatever food is around—indulged by children and grown-ups.

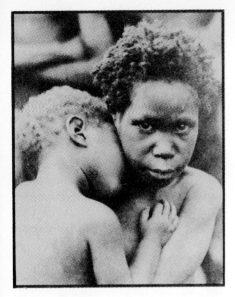

Close, constant body contact, as between this baby and older girl, creates security in Fore children.

viewed, tested and appreciated. This sanctuary remained ever available, but did not demand, restrain or impose. One could go and come at will.

In close harmony with their source of life, the Fore young were able confidently, not furtively, to extend their inquiry. They could widen their understanding as they chose. There was no need to play tricks or deceive in order to pursue life.

Emerging from this early childhood was a freely ranging young child rather in tune with his older and younger hamlet mates, disinclined to act out impulsively, and with a capable appreciation of the properties of potentially dangerous objects. Such children could be permitted to move out on their own, unsupervised and unrestricted. They were safe.

Such a pattern could persist indefinitely, re-creating itself in each new generation. However, hidden within the receptive character it produced was an Achilles heel; it also permitted adoption of new practices, including child-handling practices, which did *not* act to perpetuate the pattern. In only one generation after Western contact, the cycle of Fore life was broken.

Attuned as they were to individual pursuit of economic and social good, it did not take the Fore long to recognize the value of the new materials,

practices and ideas that began to flow in. Indeed, change began almost immediately with efforts to obtain steel axes, salt, medicine and cloth. The Fore were quick to shed indigenous practices in favor of Western example. They rapidly altered their ways to adapt to Western law, government, religion, materials and trade.

Sometimes change was so rapid that many people seemed to be afflicted by a kind of cultural shock. An anomie, even cultural amnesia, seemed to pervade some hamlets for a time. There were individuals who appeared temporarily to have lost memory of recent past events. Some Fore even forgot what type and style of traditional garments they had worn only a few years earlier, or that they had used stone axes and had eaten their dead close relatives.

Remarkably open-minded, the Fore so readily accepted reformulation of identity and practice that suggestion or example by the new government officers, missionaries and scientists could alter tribal affiliation, place names, conduct and hamlet style. When the first Australian patrol officer began to map the region in 1957, an error in communication led him to refer to these people as the "Fore." Actually they had had no name for themselves and the word, Fore, was their name for a quite different group, the Awa, who spoke another language and lived in another valley. They did not correct the patrol officer but adopted his usage. They all now refer to themselves as the Fore. Regional and even personal names changed just as readily.

More than anything else, it was the completion of a steep, rough, always muddy Jeep road into the Fore lands that undermined the traditional life. Almost overnight their isolated region was opened. Hamlets began to move down from their ridgetop sites in order to be nearer the road, consolidating with others.

The power of the road is hard to overestimate. It was a great artery where only restricted capillaries had existed before. And down this artery came a flood of new goods, new ideas

On the way to hunt birds, cuscus (a marsupial) or rats, Fore boys stride through a sweet-potato garden.

and new people. This new road, often impassable even with four-wheel-drive vehicles, was perhaps the single most dramatic stroke wrought by the government. It was to the Fore an opening to a new world. As they began to use the road, they started to shed traditions evolved in the protective insularity of their mountain fastness, to adopt in their stead an emerging market culture.

THE COMING OF THE COFFEE ECONOMY

"Walkabout," nonexistent as an institution before contact, quickly became an accepted way of life. Fore boys began to roam hundreds of miles from their homeland in the quest for new experience, trade goods, jobs and money. Like the classic practice of the Australian aborigine, this "walkabout" took one away from his home for periods of varying length. But unlike the Australian practice, it usually took the boys to jobs and schools rather than to a solitary life in traditional lands. Obviously it sprang from the earlier pattern of individual freedom to pursue personal interests and opportunity wherever it might lead. It was a new expression of the old Fore exploratory pattern.

Some boys did not roam far, whereas others found ways to go to distant cities. The roaming boys often sought places where they might be welcomed as visitors, workers or students for a while. Mission stations and schools, plantation work camps, and the servants' quarters of the European population became way-stations in the lives of the modernizing Fore boys.

Some took jobs on coffee plantations. Impressed by the care and attention lavished on coffee by European planters and by the money they saw paid to coffee growers, these young Fore workers returned home with coffee beans to plant.

Coffee grew well on the Fore hillsides, and in the mid-1960s, when the first sizable crop matured, Fore who previously had felt lucky to earn a few dollars found themselves able to earn a few hundred dollars. A rush to coffee ensued, and when the new gardens became productive a few years later, the Fore income from coffee jumped to a quarter of a million dollars a year. The coffee revolution was established.

At first the coffee was carried on the backs of its growers (sometimes for several days) over steep, rough mountain trails to a place where it could be sold to a buyer with a jeep. However, as more and more coffee was produced, the villagers began to turn with efforts to planning and constructing roads in association with neighboring villages. The newly built roads, in turn, stimulated further economic development and the opening of new trade stores throughout the region.

Following European example, the segregated collective men's and women's houses were abandoned. Family houses were adopted. This changed the social and territorial arena for all the young children, who hitherto had been accustomed to living equally with many members of their hamlet. It gave them a narrower place to belong, and it made them more distinctly someone's children. Uncomfortable in the family houses, boys who had grown up in a freer territory began to gather in "boys' houses," away from the adult men who were now beginning to live in family houses with their wives. Mothers began to wear blouses, altering the early freer access to the breast. Episodes of infant and child frustration, not seen in traditional Fore hamlets, began to take place along with repeated incidents of anger, withdrawal, aggressiveness and stinginess.

So Western technology worked its magic on the Fore, its powerful materials and practices quickly shattering their isolated autonomy and lifestyle. It took only a few years from the time Western intruders built their first grass-thatched patrol station before the Fore way of life they found was gone.

Fortunately, enough of the Fore traditional ways were systematically documented on film to reveal how unique a flower of human creation they were. Like nothing else, film made it possible to see the behavioral patterns of this way of life. The visual record, once made, captured data which was unnoticed and unanticipated at the time of filming and which was simply impossible to study without such records. Difficult-to-spot subtle patterns and fleeting nuances of manner, mood and human relations emerged by use of repeated reexamination of related incidents, sometimes by slow motion and stopped frame. Eventually the characteristic behavioral patterns of Fore life became clear, and an important aspect of human adaptive creation was revealed.

The Fore way of life was only one of the many natural experiments in living that have come into being through thousands of years of independent development in the world. The Fore way is now gone; those which remain are threatened. Under the impact of modern technology and commerce, the entire world is now rapidly becoming one system. By the year 2000 all the independent natural experiments that have come into being during the world's history will be merging into a single world system.

One of the great tragedies of our modern time may be that most of these independent experiments in living are disappearing before we can discover the implication of their special expressions of human possibility. Ironically, the same technology responsible for the worldwide cultural convergence has also provided the means by which we may capture detailed visual records of the yet remaining independent cultures. The question is whether we will be able to seize this never-to-be repeated opportunity. Soon it will be too late. Yet, obviously, increasing our understanding of the behavioral repertoire of humankind would strengthen our ability to improve life in the world.

Hunters & Gatherers!

The Transformation of the Kalahari !Kung

Why after centuries of stability has this society, an apparent relic of ancient hunting and gathering groups, abandoned many of its traditional ways?

John E. Yellen

John E. Yellen, who received a doctorate in anthropology from Harvard University in 1974, is program director for archaeology at the National Science Foundation. Before joining the foundation in 1977, he was a research associate at the National Museum of Natural History of the Smithsonian Institution. Yellen conducted ethnographic and archaeological studies of the !Kung for some 15 years, often in collaboration with his wife, Alison S. Brooks of George Washington University. Today he and his colleagues are excavating sites in Zaire for clues to the emergence of complex hunting and gathering cultures.

We study history to understand the present. Yet sometimes the present can help to clarify the past. So it is with a San-speaking people known as the !Kung—a group of what were once called African Bushmen. (The exclamation point is pronounced as a click.) Dramatic changes now occurring in the !Kung culture are illuminating a major problem in anthropology: Why did most hunting and gathering societies disappear rapidly after coming in contact with societies that kept domesticated animals and plants?

This swift disappearance is puzzling. After all, hunting for animals and gathering wild plants was a robust enough strategy to ensure the survival of anatomically modern human beings from their emergence more than 50,000 years ago until some time after the first animals and plants were domesticated, roughly 10,000 years ago. Conventional wisdom suggests that many traditional societies, recognizing the nutritional advantages of herding and agriculture, simply abandoned their old practices once they learned about newer subsistence strategies. Yet a number of observations indicate that dissatisfaction with foraging is apparently the wrong explanation in many instances.

Archaeologists have shown, for example, that foraging can actually be more beneficial than herding and farming. Detailed analyses of skeletal remains reveal that in parts of North America a shift to agriculture was in fact detrimental to nutrition, health and longevity for certain groups. Similarly, in modern times it has become clear that when droughts strike southern Africa, groups that rely heavily on hunting and gathering tend to be affected less severely than groups that depend primarily on water-hungry herds and crops.

Moreover, foraging probably is not as taxing and unfruitful as it is stereotypically portrayed. Richard B. Lee, when he was a doctoral student at the University of California at Berkeley in the 1960's, found that the !Kung, who at the time were among the few groups in the world still obtaining most of their food by foraging, did not live on the brink of starvation, even though they inhabited the harsh Kalahari Desert. (The !Kung occupy the northwest corner of Botswana and adjacent areas of Namibia and Angola.) Indeed, they spent only several hours each day seeking food.

What, then, accounts for the decline for foraging societies? No one can say definitely, but glimmers of an answer that may have broad application are emerging from studies focusing on the recent changes in the !Kung way of life. Today young boys no longer learn to hunt, and some of the behavioral codes that gave the society cohesion are eroding. One major catalyst of change appears to have been a sudden easy access to goods. Perhaps a similar phenomenon contributed to the demise of past foraging societies.

It is fortunate that a rather detailed portrait of the !Kung's traditional culture was compiled before the onset of dramatic change. Many investigators deserve credit for what is known, including the independent anthropologist Lorna Marshall, who began studying the group in 1951, and Irven DeVore, Lee and other participants in what was called the Harvard Kalahari Project. One aim of the project, which officially ran from the late 1960's into the 1970's (and in which I participated as a doctoral student), was to understand how traditional hunting and gathering societies functioned.

Any description of the !Kung begins most appropriately with a brief history of the peoples in southern Africa. Before the start of the first millennium A.D., Africa south of the Zambezi River was still populated exclusively by foragers who almost certainly were of short stature, had light-brown skin and spoke what are called Khoisan languages (all of which, like those in the San group, include clicks). In the still more distant past, the various groups had apparently shared a common language and culture and then, as they spread out, adapted to the specific conditions of the regions where they settled. Some had adjusted to the seasonal cold of the Drakensberg Mountains, others to the coastal areas (with their wealth of fish), and still others to the drier conditions of the deserts and other inland areas.

The various groups were what archaeologists call late Stone Age peoples; their knife blades and scraping tools were made of stone and specialized for particular tasks. As yet there were none of the hallmarks of so-called Iron Age peoples: domesticated goats, sheep and cattle; cultivated grains such as millet and sorghum; pottery; and smelted and forged iron and copper.

The first Iron Age influences appeared in southern Africa some time early in the first millennium A.D., when, according to the archaeological record, occasional goods and domesticated animals were introduced, presumably by trade with peoples in more northern territories. The items were soon followed by Iron Age settlers themselves. These newcomers from the north spoke mostly Bantu languages and, compared with the foragers, were taller and darker-skinned. Either directly or indirectly, all of the foraging groups were eventually exposed to the new settlers and technologies and, later, to waves of European intruders: the Dutch and the Portuguese beginning in the 15th and 16th centuries and then the English and Germans as well.

Artifacts as well as journals of European settlers indicate that some of the hunting and gathering groups were exterminated by the intruders. In most other instances, according to clues provided by genetic studies, linguistic analyses and other methods, groups broke up (forcibly or otherwise), often merging with their new neighbors through intermarriage.

In certain cases, foragers were able to maintain a distinct genetic and cultural identity. Some of them, changing many practices, became transformed into new cultures. (For example, the first Dutch settlers, arriving at the southern tip of Africa, met "Hotten-

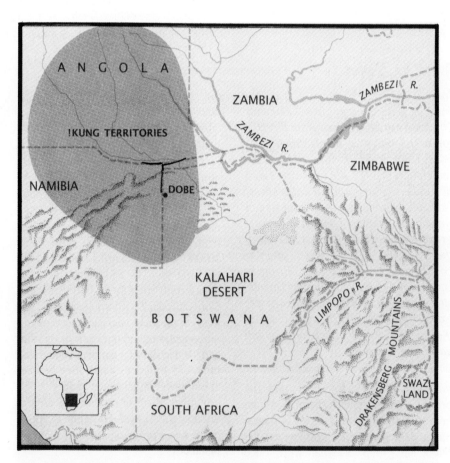

SOUTHERN AFRICA is home to many indigenous groups of San speakers (formerly known as Bushmen), including some who lived essentially as hunters and gatherers, or foragers, well into the 20th century. The !Kung, perhaps the best studied of the San, occupy the Kalahari Desert in parts of Botswana, Namibia and Angola. Much of what is known of the group has been gleaned from anthropological and archaeological studies conducted by a number of investigators in the Dobe region of Botswana.

tots," Khoisan speakers who herded flocks of sheep, goats and cows.) In the Karroo Desert of South Africa and in the northern Kalahari, however, a few hunting and gathering societies—among them, the !Kung—not only stayed intact but also apparently held onto many of their old ways.

Indeed, even as late as 1968, when I first visited the Kalahari as part of the Harvard project, most !Kung men and women in the Dobe region of Botswana still dressed in animal skins and subsisted primarily by hunting and gathering. (Dobe is the site most intensively studied by the project; the people there are, by all indications, quite representative of the !Kung over a broader area.) It is true that iron had long since replaced stone in tools, and plastic and metal containers had supplanted their ceramic counterparts. Yet men still hunted with bows and poisoned arrows, and women set out daily with digging sticks to seek edible plants.

At least it seemed to us that the people we met were behaving much as their ancient ancestors had. Some scholars dissent from that view, contending that the forerunners of 20th-century foragers were probably altered radically by contact with Iron Age peoples. If so, they say, modern foragers, including the !Kung, may reflect but little of the past.

In my view, strong evidence suggests that the !Kung studied in the early years of the Harvard project were very much like their distant forebearers. For example, I have determined that the range of stone tools excavated from what is now !Kung territory remained remarkably constant into the late 19th century (when the grandparents of modern !Kung adults would have been born). This finding means that the region was probably populated continuously by one cultural group and that its foraging and manufacturing practices remained essentially unaffected by Iron Age influences.

What were the traditional ways of the !Kung? Observations made back in the 1950's and 1960's reveal that the group's strategy for obtaining food—and in fact its entire social organization—was exquisitely adapted for survival in the Kalahari. There, rainfall can vary dramatically from year to year and region to region, giving rise to profound shifts in the availability of food.

When it came to securing food, the !Kung followed what I call a generalist strategy. Rather than specializing in the pursuit of a limited number of species, as could be done in more predictable environments, they cast their foraging "net" broadly and so could usually find something to eat even if favored foods were in short supply. Remarkably, Lee found that males hunted more than 60 animal species, ranging in size from hare to buffalo. Females recognized more than 100 edible plant species, collecting perhaps a dozen varieties in a single day.

Certain accepted foraging guidelines minimized competition for the desert's limited resources. For example, groups of people were loosely organized into bands, and each band had the right to seek food in specified areas. During the dry season the members of a single band would congregate, setting up camps near a water hole (a year-round source of drinking water) understood to belong to that band. From the camps, individuals or small clusters of people would fan out each day to forage. During the rest of the year, when rainfall was more frequent and rain collected in shallow depressions in the ground known as pans, bands would disperse; small groups foraged in less trafficked areas, staying for as short as a day (and rarely as long as two months) before moving on.

The band system actually made it easy for people to migrate to more desirable places when the territory allotted to a given band was unproductive or becoming depleted. Band membership was rather fluid, and so a family could readily join a different band having more luck.

Consider the options open to a husband and wife, who would have had few possessions to hamper their travels. They could claim the right to join the bands available to both sets of parents, which means that at least four territories were open to them. Moreover, they could join any band in which their brothers or sisters had rights. If the couple also had married children, they might, alternatively, forage anywhere the children's spouses could; indeed, parents frequently arranged their children's marriages with an eye to the accompanying territorial privileges. Individuals could also claim band memberships on the basis of certain less direct kinship ties and on friendship.

The social values of the !Kung complemented this flexible band system, helping to ensure that food was equitably distributed. Most notably, an ethic of sharing formed the core of the self-described !Kung system of values. Families were expected to welcome relatives who showed up at their camps. Moreover, etiquette dictated that meat from large kills be shared outside the immediate family, which was obviously a sound survival strategy: a hunter who killed a large antelope or the like would be hard pressed, even with the help of his wife and children, to eat all its meat. By distributing his bounty, the hunter ensured that the recipients of his largess would be obliged to return the favor some time in the future.

Similarly, individuals also established formal relationships with non-relatives in which two people gave each other gifts such as knives or iron spears at irregular intervals. Reciprocity was delayed, so that one partner would always be in debt to the other. Pauline Weissner, when she was a graduate student at the University of Michigan at Ann Arbor, analyzed those reciprocity relationships and concluded that individuals purposely selected gift-giving partners from distant territories. Presumably it was hoped that a partner would have something to offer when goods were difficult to obtain locally. Hence, in the traditional !Kung view of the world, security was obtained by giving rather than hoarding, that is, by accumulating obligations that could be claimed in times of need.

7. SOCIOCULTURAL CHANGE

Clearly, mobility was a critical prerequisite for maintaining reciprocity relationships over long distances and for making it possible to move elsewhere when foraging conditions were unfavorable. The !Kung system of justice had the same requirement of ready movement. Like many other traditional foraging groups, the !Kung society was acephalous, or headless: no one was in charge of adjudicating disputes. When disagreements became serious, individuals or groups of disputants simply put distance between themselves, claiming membership in widely separated bands. As long as everyone could carry their few possessions on their backs, and so could relocate with ease, the approach worked well.

The traditional !Kung, then, were well suited to the Kalahari. They were generalists who lived by the ethic of sharing, ensuring that those who were less successful at finding food could usually be fed nonetheless. Because families owned no more than they could carry, they were able to travel at will whenever resources became scarce or disputes too heated.

By 1975, however, the !Kung were undergoing a cultural transition—at least so it seemed by all appearances at Dobe. I left there in 1970 and returned in the middle of the decade. I found that, in the interim, many families had taken on the ways of the neighboring Bantu. A number had planted fields and acquired herds of goats along with an occasional cow. Fewer of the boys were learning to hunt; traditional bows and arrows were still produced but mostly for eventual sale on a worldwide curio market. The people wore mass-produced clothing instead of animal skins, and traditional grass huts were for the most part replaced by more substantial mud-walled structures, which were now inhabited for longer periods than in the past.

An influx of money and supplies had clearly played a part in many of these changes. Botswana became an independent nation in 1966, after having been the British protectorate Bechuanaland. The new government began to encourage the keeping of livestock and the development of agriculture, such as by giving donkeys to the !Kung for pulling simple plows. And it arranged for the routine purchase of traditional handicrafts (for example, bead necklaces), thereby injecting extraordinary sums of money into the community. Later, when the !Kung in Namibia (then a colony of South Africa) were brought into the South African Army, the !Kung in Botswana received more infusions of cash and goods, mainly via interactions with kin.

Yet the exact meaning of such surface changes remained unclear. To what extent did the livestock and fields, the new clothes and the sturdier huts reflect a weakness in the glue that held !Kung society together? Why had the men and women, who had long been successful as foragers and who were not coerced into changing, decided to take on the burdens of herds and crops and to otherwise allow their mobility to be compromised? Archaeological work I undertook at Dobe between 1975 and 1982 (first as a research associate at the Smithsonian Institution and then as an employee of the National Science Foundation), to-

TIME PERIOD	LARGE MAMMALS GREATER KUDU/CATTLE	MEDIUM MAMMALS STEENBOK/GOAT	SMALL MAMMALS SPRINGHARE/ PORCUPINE	REPTILES AND AMPHIBIANS PUFF ADDER/BULLFROG	BIRDS GUINEA FOWL/ CHICKEN
1944–1962	1.40	2.40	1.80	0.80	1.20
1963–1968	2.86	2.86	2.14	1.71	1.86
1970–1971	2.33	3.33	2.33	1.67	1.33
1972–1975	2.00	2.75	2.00	1.25	2.25

AVERAGE NUMBER OF SPECIES

!KUNG DIET remained varied between 1944 and 1975, according to an analysis of animal bones excavated from dry-season camps at Dobe. The author identified and counted the number of bones at each camp to learn the relative numbers of the large, medium and small mammalian species and the reptilian, amphibian and bird species consumed at each camp during four periods. (Selected examples are shown.) The balance across categories changed little, indicating that variety was maintained, as was the !Kung's generalist food-securing strategy. The persistence of a diverse diet even after domesticated animals were acquired in the 1970's indicates that the group had not become dependent on their herds, which apparently were viewed as foraging resources like any others. Hence, the popular notion that dissatisfaction with foraging caused hunting and gathering societies of the past to abandon their old way of life does not seem to hold for the Dobe !Kung.

gether with observations made by other workers during the same period, provides some hints.

To be frank, when I returned in 1975, a methodological question preoccupied me. I hoped to learn about what happened to the bones of hunted animals after the carcasses were discarded and became buried naturally in the ground; such information was important for developing archaeological techniques to determine how people in the past killed, butchered and cooked animals. I thought that by locating the remains of old cooking hearths at Dobe, around which families ate, I might gather a good collection of bones—the remains of meals—on which to test a few ideas. Later I realized the data I had collected in the course of this endeavor might also say something about the transformation of the !Kung.

As part of my studies I identified and mapped the locations of huts and their associated hearths dating back to 1944. I then dug up bones that had been dropped in and around the hearths and identified the species to which they belonged. In visits made after 1975, I no longer collected bones, but I continued to map contemporary camps; in the end, I accumulated almost 40 years of settlement data.

The camps were usually occupied by the same extended family and close relatives, such as in-laws, although the specific mix of individuals changed somewhat from year to year. At the older sites, where all visible traces of occupation had disappeared, the huts and the hearths (which were normally placed outside a hut's entryway) were identified with the help of family members who actually remembered the placements.

My data supported the conclusion that by the mid-1970's long-standing !Kung values, such as the emphasis on intimacy and interdependence, were no longer guiding behavior as effectively as they once did. The data also indicated that, despite appearances to the contrary, the !Kung had retained their foraging "mentality." These generalists had taken up herding as if their

goats and few cows were no different from any other readily accessible foraging resource. This surprising discovery meant that factors other than a failure of the food-securing system were at the root of the !Kung transformation.

My sense that traditional values were losing their influence over behavior came mainly from my analyses of the maps I had drawn (combined with other observations). Traditional !Kung camps, as depicted in the first 25 or so maps, were typically arranged in a circle, and most entrances faced inward. The huts were also set close together, so that from the entrance of one of them it was possible to see into most of the others.

The camp arrangement remained close and intimate until the early 1970's. Then suddenly the distance between huts increased significantly. At the same time, the circular pattern yielded to linear and other arrangements that gave families more privacy; also, in the last two camps I mapped (dating to 1981 and 1982), many of the hearths, which had been central to much social interaction, were located inside the huts instead of in front of them. The changes occurred so abruptly that the pattern of camp design can be said to have been unambiguously transformed from "close" to "distant" within a few years. By implication, such changes in camp design indicate that major changes in social norms for openness and sharing occurred as well in the early to middle 1970's.

This conclusion is consistent with other evidence. In 1976 Diane E. Gelburd, then a graduate student at George Washington University, inventoried the material possessions of individuals at Dobe and compared her data with a survey Lee had conducted in 1963. Whereas Lee found that most people could carry all their worldly belongings with ease, Gelburd found a dramatically different situation.

She showed that many !Kung owned large items, such as plows and cast iron pots, which are difficult to transport. With their newfound cash they had also

purchased such goods as glass beads, clothing and extra blankets, which they hoarded in metal trunks (often locked) in their huts. Many times the items far exceeded the needs of an individual family and could best be viewed as a form of savings or investment. In other words, the !Kung were behaving in ways that were clearly antithetical to the traditional sharing system.

Yet the people still spoke of the need to share and were embarrassed to open their trunks for Gelburd. Clearly, their stated values no longer directed their activity. Although spoken beliefs and observed behavior do not coincide perfectly in any society, at Dobe in 1976 the disjunction had become extreme.

In what way did my other data set— the animal bones—clarify the causes of the social changes apparent by the 1970s? The presence of domesticated animals and cultivated fields at Dobe caused me to wonder if the changes I saw in the !Kung could be traced through some sequence of events to discontent with foraging. If the bones revealed that by the mid-1970's the !Kung derived meat almost exclusively from domesticated animals, the conclusion could then be entertained that a shift in subsistence strategy had preceded other dramatic social changes and, hence, might have somehow given rise to them.

My data confirmed earlier impressions that through the 1950's the !Kung were almost exclusively hunters and gatherers: in sites dating from that period, the bones of domesticated animals are rare. Then, in the 1960s, the consumption of goat and cattle increased markedly; in fact, by 1974 and 1975 these animals were consumed more than any others. The frequency with which chicken was consumed also increased during that period, although the Dobe !Kung never did eat very much of this Western staple. At the same time—from 1944 to 1975—the once great popularity of certain wild animals waned, including the greater kudu (a large antelope regularly hunted in the dry season) and two smaller antelopes (the steenbok and duiker).

A cursory look at these data might

have suggested that the !Kung were indeed abandoning hunting. Yet a closer examination revealed that cattle essentially substituted for kudu, both of which are large animals, and that goats, which approximate steenbok and duiker in size, directly replaced those animals in the diet. It also turns out that the number of species represented at each camp remained essentially the same, as did the mix of small, medium and large species. That is, if the meat diet of the !Kung in the 1940's normally consisted of 10 species, of which 50 percent were small, 30 percent medium and 20 percent large, roughly the same numbers would be found in a 1975 camp, although the species in each category might differ.

These findings show that the !Kung did not reduce the variety in their diet, as would be expected if they had abandoned the traditional, generalist strategy and had committed themselves to becoming herders, who typically are dependent on just a few animal species. Hence, I realized that although anthropologists might view "wild" and "domestic" animals as fundamentally different, the !Kung as late as 1975 did not make such a distinction. From the !Kung perspective, goats were essentially the same as any other medium-size animal (in that they provided a reasonable yield of meat and were relatively easy to carry), and cows were the same as other large creatures. If an animal was easy to obtain, the !Kung ate it, but they apparently did not come to depend on their herd animals to the exclusion of all others.

Anecdotal information supports the assessment that the !Kung of 1975 did not view themselves as herders. For instance, whereas Bantu groups, who depend on their herds for food and prestige, would quickly kill a hyena that preyed on their animals, many !Kung men would not bother to do so. I believe the !Kung would have been less indifferent if they had considered their herds to be all-important sources of meat. Similarly, they seemed to conceive of agriculture and wage labor undertaken for the Bantu and anthropologists—activities they pursued on a

part-time, short-term basis—much as they perceived herding: as foraging resources just like any other.

Thus, well into the 1970's, the !Kung retained their generalist strategy, limiting their reliance on any one type of resource. Obviously that approach was adaptable enough to permit the transition from a foraging to a more mixed economy without disrupting social functioning.

If neither empty bellies nor coercion initiated the !Kung's transformation, what did? The impetus may well have come largely from internal stresses generated by the desire to have the material goods that had become readily accessible. The following scenario—based in part on my map data, Gelburd's work and my interactions with the !Kung over the years—is one plausible sequence of events that may have occurred. The scenario does not attempt to be a comprehensive description of how and why the !Kung culture has changed, but it does describe some of the major processes that seem to be driving the society's transformation.

Once the !Kung had ready access to wealth, they chose to acquire objects that had never before been available to them. Soon they started hoarding instead of depending on others to give them gifts, and they retreated from their past interdependence. At the same time, perhaps in part because they were ashamed of not sharing, they sought privacy. Where once social norms called for intimacy, now there was a disjunction between word and action. Huts faced away from one another and were separated, and some hearths were moved inside, making the whole range of social activities that had occurred around them more private. As the old rules began to lose their relevance, boys became less interested in living as their fathers had. They no longer wished to hunt and so no longer tried to learn the traditional skills; instead they preferred the easier task of herding.

Meanwhile the acquisition of goods limited mobility, a change that came to

be reflected in the erection of semipermanent mud-walled huts. The lack of mobility fueled still more change, in part because the people could no longer resolve serious arguments in the traditional manner, by joining relatives elsewhere in !Kung territories.

With the traditional means of settling disputes now gone, the !Kung turned to local Bantu chiefs for arbitration. In the process they sacrificed autonomy and, like other San groups, increased their reliance on, and incorporation into, Bantu society. In fact, many !Kung families currently have close relationships with individual Bantu and look on them as protectors.

For their part, the Bantu have accepted the role, often speaking of "my Bushmen." Marriage of !Kung women to Bantu men is now fairly common, an ominous sign for the cohesion of !Kung society. The children of these unions obtain full rights within the Bantu system, including the right to inherit livestock, and are more likely to think of themselves as Bantu than as !Kung.

Genetic studies of many Bantu-speaking peoples in southern Africa show that Khoisan speakers have been melding into Bantu societies for centuries. Very possibly some of those Khoisan groups and similar ones elsewhere in the world followed a course something like the modern !Kung at Dobe are following now; that is, the acquisition of goods led to a lack of mobility and to societal stresses fatal to the group's cohesion.

Today the issue of whether the !Kung experience is applicable to foraging societies of the past can best be resolved by comparing the forces acting on the !Kung with those acting on the remnants of other foraging societies in Africa, Asia and South America. These groups merit intense and immediate scrutiny. If they are ignored, an important opportunity to understand more about the ways of past foraging groups and about the forces leading to their demise will soon pass forever.

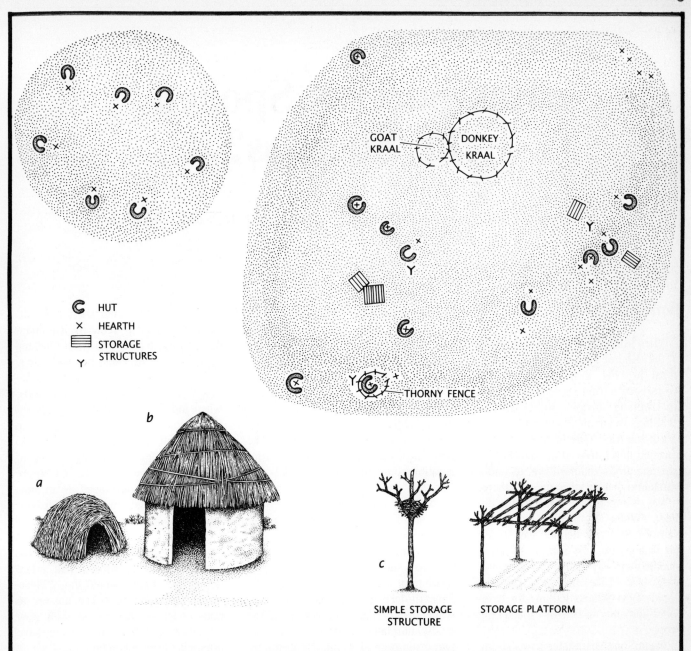

GOAT
KRAAL

DONKEY
KRAAL

C HUT
× HEARTH
▦ STORAGE
Y STRUCTURES

THORNY FENCE

SIMPLE STORAGE
STRUCTURE

STORAGE PLATFORM

ARRANGEMENTS of camps changed markedly between 1944 and 1982. The changes, revealed by a series of maps much like these of dry-season camps, seem to reflect a decline in the cohesion of !Kung society. Until the early 1970's the traditional !Kung camp (*top left*) was intimate: closely spaced huts roughly described a circle, and the entryways faced inward so that from a single vantage one could see into many huts. Then the arrangements changed abruptly (*top right*): the average distance between huts increased, and the circular arrangement yielded to linear and other private arrays. The dwellings—which in the past were made of branches and grass (*a*) and now resembled the semipermanent mud-walled huts of the Bantu (*b*)—were sometimes isolated and fenced. Hearths, formerly the focal point of social exchange, were moved inside many huts. Kraals (pens for animals) gained a central place in camp, and private food-storage structures (*c*) joined the landscape.

FURTHER READING

KALAHARI HUNTER-GATHERERS: STUDIES OF THE !KUNG SAN AND THEIR NEIGHBOURS. Edited by Richard B. Lee and Irven DeVore. Harvard University Press, 1976.

THE !KUNG OF NYAE NYAE. Lorna Marshall. Harvard University Press, 1976.

THE !KUNG SAN: MEN, WOMEN AND WORK IN A FORAGING SOCIETY. Richard B. Lee. Cambridge University Press, 1979.

OPTIMIZATION AND RISK IN HUMAN FORAGING STRATEGIES. John E. Yellen in *Journal of Human Evolution*, Vol. 15, pages 733–750; 1986.

Has Success Spoiled the Sherpas?

A mountain people walk a fine line between business and Buddhism

James F. Fisher

When I first made the two-week trek to the Khumbu region of northeast Nepal in 1964, I hoped, like many Westerners, to find Sherpas, the mountain-dwelling people so skilled in climbing, living in Shangri-La at the end of the trail. One night en route, I dreamed that I arrived in Namche Bazaar, the area's main village, to find a gas station that serviced the cars there. It was a nightmare: Shangri-La defiled. When I finally did reach Namche, I found neither gas station nor Shangri-La, just Sherpas trying to muddle their way through life like anybody else. Like the anthropologist Claude Lévi-Strauss looking for barebones humanity in Brazil, I found only people.

Twenty-one years later I was sitting in a tourist hotel in Namche one evening, immersed in a book, when precisely at 6:00 P.M., the lights suddenly came on. It was a couple of minutes before the extraordinary revelation sank in that over my head there was a light bulb burning, powered by a recently installed hydroelectric turbine in a village that previously had been two weeks away from the nearest source of electricity. Even that did not prepare me for the discovery a little later the same evening that the faint hum I heard during dinner was the portable generator (the turbine had its limits) providing electricity for the video movies (some in English, some in Hindi) being shown at the hotel next door. What were tourist hotels doing in Shangri-La? And what were they doing to the Sherpas? That was what I had come back to Khumbu to find out.

During my first trip, I was a member of an expedition, led by Sir Edmund Hillary, devoted to building schools in Sherpa villages. The Sherpas already had an indigenous institution something like a school—the Buddhist monastery—but the village schools we were installing were very different. For one thing, their curriculum included classes in science, mathematics, and English, instead of purely religious subjects. For another, their medium of instruction was Nepali, the Sanskrit-derived national language, while that of the monastery was the totally unrelated Tibetan. Would the two institutions, I wondered abstractly in 1964, compete as the locus of literacy? Would some kind of social Gresham's law lead to "modernity" at the expense of an eclipsed Sherpa culture and an effaced Buddhism?

When I tried to answer this question more than two decades later, the effects of the schools seemed swamped by a torrent of tourists, for Sir Edmund's expedition had also built a short, dirt airstrip at a deservedly obscure little hamlet called Lukla. At the time neither he nor I imagined that it would soon funnel thousands of trekkers into Khumbu, to see Mount Everest and the other snow and ice fangs that tower over the villages there. We

should have expected such a result, since the airstrip reduced Kathmandu–Namche travel time from fourteen days to forty minutes, but we didn't. Modern mass tourism is a phenomenon dating only from the mid-1960s, when industrial affluence, an expanding middle class, and relatively cheap commercial jet travel combined to make it possible. Following the rise of ecological concerns, its adventure tourism variant developed as an antidote to industrial civilization's discontent.

But all these tourists only raised again, in slightly altered form, the same nagging question I had asked about the schools: would they "Westernize" the Sherpas? The answer to both questions has to do with how education and tourism together have affected life in Khumbu.

Only a handful of Western tourists had visited Khumbu before 1964, but there is nothing new about tourism in India or Nepal. The ancient tradition of pilgrimage (the Nepali term is *tirtha*) is organized and commercialized enough to evoke reverberations of tourism in the modern sense. While the devout derive spiritual satisfaction from pilgrimage to a shrine (the farther the distance, the greater the sanctity), adventure tourists similarly feel relaxed and satisfied the farther they get into the hinterland. In India, most pilgrims are organized by guides who have divided among themselves the whole of India, each one holding a

With permission from *Natural History,* February 1991, pp. 39-44. Copyright © 1991 by the American Museum of Natural History.

monopoly on pilgrims from this area. Western tourists to Khumbu are also often organized by different trekking companies.

What this means for school-going Sherpas is that at some point they will be torn between staying in school and the temptation of signing on to work for a trekking company. On the one hand, the prospect of becoming a sardar (head Sherpa for a mountaineering expedition or tourist group) is much improved if one is literate in English and Nepali; on the other, the lure of handsome wages immediately is hard to resist. The attitude of Sherpa parents toward education is founded on other concerns, but it is equally ambivalent. When my friend Ang Rita wanted to continue beyond elementary school in the mid-1960s, before there were any tourists, his parents wanted him to stay home and help out with the chores—gathering firewood, herding yaks, and so on. Even when he scored the highest grades in the country on the School Leaving Certificate exam (the national high-school graduation exam), his parents tried, unsuccessfully, to discourage him from going to college. Their sentiment was, education is a good thing, but enough is enough.

Although nowadays many students in Ang Rita's village of Khumjung drop out before graduating from high school to work for tourists, the impact of tourism there is not as obvious as it is in Namche, which, videos aside, has been more affected by tourism than any other Sherpa village. Eight-four percent of all Namche households have at least one person working in tourism, many of them among the roughly 200 villagers literate in Nepali (up from virtually none in 1964). Some work as trekking guides, some join mountaineering expeditions as high-altitude porters, some entrepreneurs open shops and hotels (there are roughly twenty-five in Namche alone). Whether shop owners or mountain guides, Sherpas have never in their lives had so much money to spend.

In the mid-1960s, it was easier for Ang Rita to decide to stay in school, because expedition jobs were very scarce and tourist jobs nonexistent. If he could have found a job at all in those days, Ang Rita would have earned fifteen rupees per day, compared to sixty-five rupees now. The similarity in dollar equivalents ($2.00 versus $2.60) masks a critical difference: since any Sherpa who wants a job in today's tight labor market can have one, cash is commonplace rather than, as formerly, rare. Furthermore, Sherpas can now sell potatoes (their main crop) to tourists for twenty-five rupees per kerosene tin as against two rupees before. A significant disadvantage is that the price of rice (a prestigious imported crop that is eaten much more now than it used to be) has climbed from twenty-six to ninety rupees per gallon. Today, with his B.A., Ang Rita's options transcend the normal tourism possibilities.

When asked what they have done with all their substantial earnings, Sherpas reply that they have "eaten" their money—and this usually means that they now eat a more varied and expensive diet than previously. This can mean more fruits and vegetables imported for the weekly bazaar in Namche or even the distribution of candy to children by tourists, which increases dental problems. "Eating" money can also mean, in Kathmandu, spending it not only on more expensive food but also on alcohol, parties, taxis, movies, and so on. Sherpas believe in the Tibetan proverb they quote, "You don't become poor from eating, but from being lazy."

For their part, many tourists to Khumbu are pessimistic about the effects of tourism. For them, the prize trophy caught in the tourist trap is the Sherpas who are its bait. They believe tourism (their own presence exempted) ultimately will dehumanize and destroy the integrity and richness of Sherpa culture because it will transform their way of life into an industry. They also worry about degradation of the environment through deforestation and the polluting effects of their own garbage.

Sherpas also worry about pollution (tip), but their concept of it has nothing to do with the tin cans, plastic, and toilet paper that Westerners leave behind. Tip is something internal, a moral state of mind, and is not generated ultimately from empirical observation of the natural world. Pollution can have religious causes, such as an imbalanced relationship with deities. Or it can be induced socially by contact with low-caste blacksmiths, of whom there are a few families in Namche. Westerners would surely, if they were aware of these social discriminations, moderate their views of Sherpa society as being egalitarian. They would be even more likely to modify their views if they realized that they themselves were a source of tip and that, until recently, many Sherpas returning from expeditions had to be purified before they were allowed back inside their own houses.

Unlike their Western clients, Sherpas do not regard the giant snow peaks that rise out of their villages as lemu, the most general Sherpa term for beautiful. Lemu can describe inanimate objects as well as people. But while a field or forest might be lemu, the mountains are not. Their lack of color (their whiteness) is regarded as boring—not a surprising judgment in view of the Sherpa preference for vivid colors evident in such disparate contexts as religious paintings and women's aprons. As it often does, familiarity has bred indifference rather than awe.

Truth to tell, Sherpas are mystified that Westerners spend so much time and money to see what to them are sometimes sacred but not very interesting mountains. Even the most experienced sardars admit they cannot fathom why Europeans climb, although they have hunches about motives, principal among them fame, money, and science. This does not mean they do not enjoy the camaraderie and the scenic views or the satisfaction of a job well done. It simply means that those reasons alone would never motivate them to go trekking or climbing, because for Sherpas these are not escapes from the workaday world—they are the workaday world.

Despite these mutual misperceptions, a long tradition of mutual admiration has grown up between tourists and Sherpas, based on stereotypes of each other. Westerners see Sherpas as peaceful, honest, hardy, cheerful, brave, and so on. These images are accurate as far as they go, but they capture only one side of Sherpa personality. Only when the trek is over and the tourists have left do the drinking binges and general hell raising, which may last for days, take place. The rare Sherpa who drinks only imported beer (Heineken is a favorite) instead of the traditional homemade *chang* may be using a strategy to avoid mandatory *chang*-drinking responsibilities (Sherpa hospitality is unrelenting) and the alcoholism and ulcers that go with them.

The pre-Lukla airstrip image that Sherpas held of Westerners was one of technologically sophisticated, wealthy, generous, well-intentioned—if not always very physically strong—people. But this image has given way in recent years to a less clearly focused one that has emerged out of the Sherpas' experiences with thousands upon thousands of tourists—from a psychotic Frenchwoman, who had to be straitjacketed and evacuated, to the American who took the vows of a lama. Increasingly self-confident, Sherpas now frequently drop the old "sahib" suffix and address their Western clients on a first-name basis, something no house- or hotel-servant or tour guide in Kathmandu would dream of doing. Foreigners are now as likely to be thought crude as clever, cheap as generous, demanding and arrogant as friendly and unassuming.

The economic shift to tourism has produced an incipient class of "tourist Sherpas," who nevertheless largely remain as culturally rooted in Khumbu as the plain-dirt potato farmer. The new breed of Sherpas no longer wear sheepskin pants, but they know who they are. True, they wear down jackets, drink sugar (instead of salt) tea, and partition their houses into smaller rooms easier to heat, but these are superficial matters in themselves. What is more important is that Sherpas are proud of being Sherpas. No matter how wealthy or famous they have become, through mountaineering accomplishments or university educations, they continue to think of themselves

uncompromisingly as Sherpas and as Buddhists. (When Tengboche monastery burned to the ground in 1989, Sherpas quickly organized an executive committee, chaired by Ang Rita, to oversee the construction of a larger, solar-heated building.) Those with cash—mostly younger Sherpas—have risen in stature and authority at the expense of the traditionally esteemed village elders (but not of the very old, who were traditionally, and still are, concerned with otherworldly matters). Sherpas are so massively reinforced at every point for being Sherpa that there is every reason not only to "stay" Sherpa but even to flaunt one's Sherpahood. One might say that part of the pay they receive from tourists is pay for being Sherpa or at least for performing the role that the popular image of Sherpa demands.

Tourist Sherpas and educated Sherpas, such as Ang Rita, are thus not marginal to their society at all but fully within its fold. Ang Rita has built his own house in a Kathmandu suburb, but he has also, as the youngest son (following the rule of ultimogeniture), kept the house in Khumjung that he inherited from his parents. One Sherpa who has lived in Kathmandu for more than twenty years now holds a high and trusted position in the civil-religious hierarchy in his village, where he returns during the annual *Dumje* festival (a community religious festival with the social atmosphere of a carnival). That he is rarely in his village does not diminish his status there—on the contrary, his success in the travel business in Kathmandu has endorsed and enhanced it.

The transformation of the economy from mixed farming, animal husbandry, and trading to heavy dependence on tourism has already passed from the novel to the traditional. But it is what Sherpas have learned and are learning in the schools that enables them to exploit the change, to control and confront it on their own terms, rather than be exploited and victimized by it. Among other things, education extends their options beyond risking their lives as high-altitude porters (from 1950 through 1988, eighty-three Sherpas died on mountaineering expeditions in

Nepal). Educated Sherpas can excel in the guiding business, and highly educated Sherpas like Ang Rita, who is now executive director of Sir Edmund Hillary's Himalayan Trust, can move beyond it. They can hold front-office jobs, as well as carry loads and set up tents. In 1978 Sherpas had a majority financial interest in only four out of twenty registered trekking companies; in 1988 they owned twenty-six out of fifty-six.

Like the traditional long-distance trade to Tibet in which they used to engage, tourism is a centrifugal force that pulls Sherpas out of their small communities and into a wider world. Thus, tourism fortuitously arose to take up the economic slack created when trade was shut down by the Chinese in Tibet. The Sherpas had a long tradition of dealing with, and profiting from, foreigners; tourists and mountaineers are just the latest variety of foreigner to do business with. For those who are successful in the tourist trade (the more educated are the more successful), it provides substantial wealth without exploiting fellow Sherpas and therefore is evidence of good karma. Sherpas do not admire greed, but they acknowledge it as a universal human trait. Tourism is a novel means to attain a traditional material end.

Employment in tourism means less manpower to farm and herd animals, so the number of yaks has decreased while the number of crossbreeds has increased. These animals are distributed among more, but smaller, herds, which graze, or rather overgraze, closer to the villages. Thus, the highly specialized transhumance of preairstrip days has evolved into a more settled pastoral nomadism.

Because of different grazing and climatic requirements, herders tend to specialize either in crossbreeds or yaks, but some of the rich and successful sardars now own herds of both, which they use for carrying tourist loads but deploy in different ecological zones. They use *zopkio* (the male crossbreed) to carry loads from Lukla as far as Namche (almost 50 percent of Namche's 102 households own *zopkio*, which can carry the loads of two humans), and then switch to yaks for the higher, final leg of the trip to the Everest base camp area, thus capitalizing on the divergent capacities of the animals in different climates and at contrasting altitudes. The investment in a *zopkio* can be recouped in ten round trips between Lukla and Namche, and the only maintenance they require is the hay that the animal itself can carry on top of its load.

Change occurs in the circumventing or shortcutting of tradition, not its elimination. For example, because of the time and trouble and expense involved, some of the stages in the traditional sequence (spread out over several years) of marriage rituals are now frequently omitted. Instead, couples may go directly from *sodhne* (engagement) to *zendi* (final vows) at younger ages, and even more frequently than before on a "love" rather than "arranged" basis. In 1982 the hosts for the annual *Dumje* feast in Khumjung proposed distributing uncooked (rather than cooked) rice to each village house on the grounds that cooking such massive quantities of rice, only to reheat it again later before eating, is a wasteful and inefficient use of energy. The notion was so controversial it was not accepted, but the idea was broached and might be adopted in the future; if it is, the menu will change, but *Dumje* will continue.

My original hypothesis was that the effects of the schools on Sherpa life were minimal compared with the massive restructuring of the economy by tourism. But Sherpas like Ang Rita made me realize that the schools are the crucial link between tradition and modernity: the schools have enabled Sherpas to exploit the forces of change. Having successfully met the modern world on its own ground, these educated Sherpas have the cultural self-confidence to intensify the ethnic identity of all Sherpas. While tourism knocked the Sherpa economy off center, the schools stabilized Sherpa society by giving it the tools to maintain its cultural equilibrium. Coming before tourism, the schools bought the Sherpas time to adjust to the new order.

Trouble in Paradise

*The Matses use scare tactics to keep evil spirits away.
Could our curiosity kill their culture?*

Peter Gorman

The jungle was thick, the path overgrown and close. Around us were signs of Indian hunting: trees notched with a machete and the notches decorated with bits of animal hair and skin—gruesome totems to the spirits of the animals taken nearby. The path led from a natural clearing in the Peruvian Amazon to the small Matses Indian *puebla* of our friend Tumi, an irascible old man hardly touched by the twentieth century. There were easier ways to reach his village, but we never used them. This was the route we had cut when we first visited the *puebla* in 1984, and it had become a sort of ritual to reclear the path whenever we returned. On this trip, however, when we reached the edge of the clearing, we weren't greeted in the customary manner. No bedraggled dogs barked at us; no children shot at us with featherless arrows; none of Tumi's wives ran to welcome us. A few charred posts and some black ash were the only indication that Tumi's longhouse had ever existed. Only the small hut belonging to his eldest son remained. The rest of the village had been abandoned.

Six years ago I had known nothing about the rain forest except that it was being destroyed so quickly that if I wanted to see it I would have to do so soon. I flew to Iquitos, Peru, and spent several weeks on the Ucayali River, traveling by riverboat to isolated fishing villages where the locals regaled me with stories of pink river dolphins that transformed themselves into beautiful women at night; of electric eels that created lightning storms as they danced upon the waters; of black crocodiles so large they could swallow whole canoes; of anacondas that grew so long they lost the ability to move, relying on magical magnetic powers to attract food.

The most spellbinding stories, though, were about the Matses, cannibals with painted faces who lived along the streams deep in the jungle. They moved like the wind, spoke with the animals, and roamed the forest in search of blood, leaving piles of human bones to bleach in the sun.

I didn't believe there could still be tribes that had not yet become tourist attractions or case studies for hordes of anthropologists. Even so, a part of me hoped I was wrong. And when I returned to Iquitos, I asked the local jungle guides about the Matses. Some said missionaries had converted the Matses years ago; others told me they had never existed at all. Only one guide told me what I wanted to hear. A short, thick man in his mid-fifties who had spent 30 years in the Peruvian military as a jungle survival specialist, Moises claimed that the Matses not only existed but many still lived the traditional hunter-gatherer life. "I'll take you into the jungle for four days this time," he said when I asked him to lead me to the Matses. "Maybe next year you will return and meet them."

I didn't know why I needed an introduction to the jungle. But I soon learned that it was like entering a living organism whose defenses all seemed to be geared toward keeping me out. The air was thick and oppressive. The odor of decaying vegetation clung to my clothes and left a sickly aftertaste in my mouth. Stinging insects swarmed by the thousands, their stings festering instantly. I stumbled on the root-covered jungle floor and cut my hands on razor-sharp leaves. Everything I did was wrong, and each time I made a mistake, Moises would explain how the Matses would do it. Afterward I vowed to find the Matses. I wanted to learn everything they knew and find out how they managed to thrive in such an environment.

I took several more short trips into the jungle with Moises. On each occasion we took fewer and fewer provisions, relying more on what we could glean from the forest. The only aspect of our trips that bothered me was the hunting. I tried explaining that I was just a visitor, that we could carry food. I tried to make him understand that he was killing endangered parrots and small game. But even when I carried food, he managed to lose it or give it away. To him the jungle meant killing and being killed.

"*Escuche me, Pedro,*" he said very deliberately. "This isn't Hollywood. The Matses are hunters. They don't know about endangered species. Make a mistake with them and we're finished."

After several weeks Moises got word from a fisherman that he'd seen signs of the Matses' presence, and we set out to find the tribe. We traveled by riverboat for two days on the Ucayali River, until we came to a village where we bartered for a *peque-peque,* an oversize canoe with a small motor. From there we started up the Au-chyako and spent the night in the village of an old man named Esteban, a friend of Moises'. In the morning we started up the Auchyako and paddled for two days until it was too shallow for the dugout. Then we began hiking, using our machetes to slash our way through the thick vines.

I ate only some rice we'd brought with us and whatever we could gather from the forest. I began to get sick and on the fourth day hardly had the strength to get out of my hammock. I finally gave in and stole a bird Moises was roasting on the fire.

"That's the first right thing I have ever seen you do," he said when he found me eating the bird. "Now you're beginning to understand the jungle."

The next day a young Indian silently appeared at our campsite. He was small and dark-skinned, naked except for an old pair of green swim trunks and carrying a long black bow and a handful of feathered arrows. His forehead and eyes were painted with a sort of red dye. His mouth was outlined in blue, and long, whiskerlike splinters stuck out from the flesh of his upper lip.

None of us moved for several seconds. Finally the man spoke in a guttural language, and to my surprise, Moises responded in the same tongue. He handed our shotgun and some shells to the man, who then disappeared into the foliage. "Matses," Moises said, smiling. "I knew they would find us."

Moises, I soon learned, had been in charge of military actions against the Matses after they'd raided river towns in the Seventies. He had learned their language in their camps since then. The Matses' facial markings and the whiskers, he said, imitated those of the jaguar. He had given the man the gun simply because he had asked for it.

When the Matses returned an hour later, he carried two monkeys in a leaf sack on his back and a third, evidently the infant of one of them, atop his head. He rested the gun against a tree, said something, then walked back into the forest. Moises picked up the gun

and turned to me. "Let's go, Pedro."

I grabbed our machetes and we followed the Matses, almost running to keep up with him. An hour later we came upon a small field. Just beyond it lay a stand of trees; beyond that, a small *puebla*. "Don't say anything. Just imitate me," Moises said.

The *puebla* was little more than a clearing along a stream. Around its perimeter, posts were spaced at irregular intervals; on each hung animal skulls. Along the stream's bank children played with small bows and arrows. Smoke issued from an opening cut into the walls of a long, low hut made of leaves. Outside, a second fire burned. And in the center of the clearing stood the framework of a longhouse made of saplings. Nearby, an old man and several women were weaving palm fronds into roof sections. They all bore the jaguar facial markings.

We watched as our guide placed the bloody but still living monkeys by the fire. Nursing a baby, a woman took the monkey infant and placed it against her breast, where it found her free nipple and began to nurse.

A young girl had also joined him and grabbed the arms of one monkey as he took the legs. They held it in the fire, burning off its fur, oblivious to the animal's screams. Carrying a piece of a machete blade, an old woman crawled out of a low opening in the leaf hut and took the now-dead monkey. She walked to the stream, gutted the animal, cut it into pieces, bundled them in some leaves, and returned with the bundle to the hut.

The old man finally stood, picked up a long black spear, and walked menacingly toward us, bellowing as he approached. "Don't act afraid," Moises whispered. He waited until the old man had almost reached us, then raised his shotgun, aimed at the old man's chest, and began to bellow back. The two of them stood toe-to-toe, weapons poised, yelling at each other fearlessly. They abruptly disarmed, and the old man turned and walked toward the hut. "That's how they say hello," Moises said as he began following the old man.

It was dark and smoky inside the hut, where we sat on the bare ground.

An old shotgun and some clothing lay on a raised platform, bows and arrows propped against it. Leaf bags, animal skulls, and other ornaments hung from the ceiling. The rest of the hut was criss-crossed with hammocks, except at the far end, where the fire burned as the old woman roasted the monkey meat.

We sat in silence until the woman took two arms from the fire, placed them on palm leaves, and passed them to the old man, who offered them to us. The meat was sinewy and almost raw, and I had to fight back the urge to vomit. Moises gave me a warning look.

"His name is Tumi, and all of the women are his wives," Moises translated as the old man spoke. "He moved to this place after a jaguar killed one of his sons on the Lubo River. But moving is getting harder because there are so many huts on the rivers. He called for the spirits to tell him if this was a good place. He didn't know because no Matses have lived here for a long time.

"When we first came near," Moises continued, "he thought we were bad spirits and he was going to attack us. But when he saw we were not killing so many of his animals he knew we were good spirits and waited for us. When we didn't come he knew we were lost spirits and he sent his son to bring us here. He knows this is a good place to live if even the spirits cannot find it."

We finished eating and put the bones on the ground. Moises took several shotgun shells from his pockets and gave them to Tumi, who took an animal-tooth necklace from the wall and handed it to me. My hands shook as I held it.

"Put it on. It's a gift," Moises said. "Now give him something in return. Your machete."

Accepting the machete, Tumi turned his back to us.

"Let's go while he still thinks we're spirits, Pedro."

I wanted to ask why but kept silent as I crawled out of the hut behind Moises. Everyone stared at us, the older children holding bows and arrows or spears at the sides, ready.

Moises looked slowly across the camp, then started toward the forest. We'd almost reached the edge of the clearing when Tumi's voice boomed behind us. We froze, Moises holding my arm to keep me from bolting, and turned back to the hut. Tumi gave a bow and arrows to one of his sons, who ran to us. "He says you have nothing to hunt with; he wants you to take them," Moises said.

Trembling, I took the bow and arrows from the boy. Then we turned and stepped back into the forest.

Since then I've returned to the jungle several times, ending each trip with a visit to Tumi. I've visited Matses camps on a dozen rivers with Moises. We've always tried to come and go as spirits, not bringing things they don't need or taking things they don't give.

Not all tour guides in Iquitos, however, share Moises' respect for the Matses. When word of our contact got out, other guides began taking tourists to Tumi's camp. A trail was eventually cut from the Auchyako fishing village to the *puebla,* making access much easier. The tourists took things to trade—watches, calculators, and all kinds of plastic trash the Matses didn't need; they left with arrows, spears, clay cooking utensils. Every year the family seemed more burdened with the objects of "civilization." Every year they seemed less like Matses. I knew I had done the damage with that first visit, but I had no way to undo it. My enthusiasm to see a people in their natural state was now ruining them.

Then we found Tumi's longhouse burned to the ground and the *puebla* deserted except for the young man we'd first encountered in the jungle. He had grown up and built a separate hut, began wearing shoes and long pants, and now went by the name Antonio. We asked what had happened to Tumi.

"My father is crazy," Antonio said in the pidgin Spanish he had learned. "He burned his house and left everything here, all of the things people brought him. He said he wanted to hunt and gather and fish in the jungle, to be a Matses again. He says he now knows you and Moises are bad spirits. You brought the tourists. He should have killed you when he first saw you."

Dark Dreams About the White Man

Thomas Gregor

Thomas Gregor, associate professor of anthropology at Vanderbilt University, is the author of Mehinaku: The Drama of Daily Life in a Brazilian Indian Village, *published by the University of Chicago Press.*

Last night my dream was very bad.
I dreamed of the white man.
            A Mehinaku villager

In 1500 explorer Pedro Cabral landed on the coast of Brazil and claimed its lands and native peoples for the Portuguese empire. Since that time Brazilian Indians have been killed by European diseases and bounty hunters, forced off their land by squatters and speculators, and enslaved by ranchers and mine owners. Today the Indians, numbering less than one-tenth of the precontact population, inhabit the most remote regions of the country.

I have been privileged as an anthropologist to live among the Mehinaku, a tribe of about eighty tropical-forest Indians who have thus far escaped the destruction. The Mehinaku, along with eight other single-village tribes, live in a vast government-protected reservation in the Mato Grosso, at the headwaters of the Xingu River in central Brazil. Collectively called Xinguanos by the outside world, the Mehinaku and their neighbors speak dialects of four unrelated languages. In spite of their cultural differences, they have developed a peaceful system of relationships based on intermarriage, trade, and group rituals. This political achievement persists, thanks largely to the geographic isolation of the Xingu reservation. Even today, the Brazilian presence consists only of an outpost of the Brazilian Indian Agency and a small, dirt-strip air force base. Nearly 200 miles of forest and savanna separate the Xingu villages from Shavantina, the nearest permanent Brazilian settlement of any size.

Despite the remoteness of central Brazil and the traditional character of village life, even a casual visitor to the Mehinaku sees unexpected signs of Brazilian society: battery-operated shortwave radios (usually tuned to backwoods popular favorites), battered aluminum pots for carrying water, and discarded items of Western clothing. But these, and the other flotsam and jetsam of industrial society that drift to the center of Brazil, affect only the appearance of Indian culture. They catch the eye of the visitor, but they do not break the rhythm of traditional subsistence, ritual, and trade that are the heartbeat of Xingu life.

Although geographically and socially distant, urban Brazil peers nonetheless into the world of the Xinguanos. Popular magazines feature articles about their life in a "jungle paradise," and smiling Xingu faces adorn postcards sold at Rio newsstands. Recently, a film shot in the Xingu reservation was woven into a *novela,* an afternoon television soap opera. So heavily exposed are the physically handsome Xingu tribes that in the popular mind they *are* the Brazilian Indian.

Brazilian officials have their own use for the Xinguanos. Faced with charges of neglect and even genocide against its native peoples, the government has used the tribes of the area for public relations. Happy, well-nourished Xinguanos decorate government publications, and when necessary, the Indians themselves can be counted on to amuse visiting dignitaries. High consular officials from the diplomatic corps in Brasília and other international elite have flown out to the Xingu reservation for adventure and entertainment. Almost invariably their visits have been a success and they have returned home with an impression of idyllic relationships between the Brazilian authorities and the Xinguanos. But if such visitors came to know their hosts more intimately, they would learn that contact with the white man has had a profound and bitter impact on the Indians' inner life.

During my work among the Mehinaku I have become increasingly aware of the villagers' anxieties about the white man. The soldiers at the nearby air force base, whom they regard as powerful and unpredictable, are especially frightening to the Mehinaku. On one occasion a rumor swept through the community that a plane from the base was going to bomb the village because one of the Mehinaku had stolen a mosquito net belonging to an air force sergeant. This wild story was believable because it drew on a reservoir of anxiety and confusion about the white man. Recently, I have been studying the villagers' dreams as a way of learning about their unconscious fears.

According to the Mehinaku, dreams are caused by the wandering of the "shadow," or soul, which is conceived of as a tiny replica of the individual living within the eye. As the villagers demonstrate to children or to the inquisitive anthropologist, the soul's image can be seen as a reflection in a pool of water or even in the iris of another person's eye. The soul is said to leave its owner at night to wander about. "Far, far away my soul wandered last night," is the opening phrase that may begin a dream narration. In the dream world of the community and the surrounding forests, the soul meets the wandering souls of animals, spirits, and other villagers. These experiences come into the dreamer's awareness in a way the villagers do not fully understand. "Dreams come up," they say, "as corn comes up from the ground."

The nightly adventures of the soul through the nocturnal village and forest are interpreted with the help of an unwritten dream book, a collection of dream symbols and their deciphered meanings. To the Mehinaku, dream symbols (*patalapiri,* literally "pictures," or "images") represent events to come. Frequently, the predictions resemble the dream symbol in their appearance or activity. For example, since weeds are symbols of hair, a dream of a well-cleared path is symbolic of baldness in later life. Occasionally, the dream symbol is more abstract and poetic. A dream about collecting edible flying ants suggests bereavement, since the rain of ants that descends on the village in the fall of each year is likened to the tears that fall when a kinsman dies.

As the last example suggests, many Mehinaku dream symbols are gloomy forecasts of death or misfortune. The grimmest omens of all, however, are

those that deal with the white man. Any dream about a Brazilian is a bad dream. Even a dream prominently featuring an object associated with Brazilians, such as an airplane, is distressing. Dreams of the white man are, for the Mehinaku, "pictures" of disease. A person who has such a dream is likely to become sick. In support of this interpretation, the villagers point out that many illnesses—measles, colds, influenza—are brought in from the outside. These diseases have had a devastating impact on the community. In the early 1960s, nearly 20 percent of the tribe died in a measles epidemic, and the villagers continue to suffer from imported diseases for which they have neither natural nor acquired immunity. Dreams such as the following one reflect such concerns:

At the post a plane landed. Many, many passengers got off. It seemed as if there was a village in the plane. I was very frightened of them and the things they carried. I was afraid they would bring a disease to the village, the white man's "witchcraft."

The Mehinaku fear of the white man goes beyond the fear of disease, as I learned when I began to make a collection of their dreams. The villagers were willing collaborators in this effort since they regard dreams as significant and make a deliberate effort to recall them when they wake up. In the morning, as I circulated from house to house to harvest the previous night's crop of dreams, I would occasionally be summoned across the plaza ("Tommy, I have a dream for you!") by a villager with a particularly dramatic narrative. Altogether I collected 385 dreams, the majority of which (70 percent) were contributed by the men.

In thirty-one of the sample dreams, Brazilians were cast as the central characters. What is striking about these dreams is their high level of anxiety. While about half of the villagers' dreams show some level of anxiety, fully 90 percent of the dreams of the white man are tinged with fear. Furthermore, when I rated dreams on the basis of their frightening content

and the dreamer's own report of distress, I found that dreams of the white man were charged with more than double the average level of anxiety. This was higher than any other comparable class of dreams, even dreams of malignant spirits and dangerous animals.

Occasionally, the mere sight or sound of an outsider creates anxiety: "I heard them speaking on the radio at the post, but I could not understand. The speech and the language were frightening to me." Within the sample of dreams, however, I found a number of terrifying themes that repeatedly appeared in the villagers' narratives. The most prominent of these are heat and fire. In the dreams, Brazilian soldiers explode incendiary devices in the village, burning houses and people. Fiery planes crash and blow up in the central plaza, covering the villagers with flames. Even when the victims throw themselves in the river, the fire continues to burn their clothes and skin.

We went to the place where the canoe was moored. A plane came overhead and broke in the sky. It crashed in the water and everything caught on fire. The gasoline floated on the water. My mother caught on fire.

Fire and heat are appropriate symbols of terror among the Mehinaku. The villagers live in large thatch houses, often as much as 100 feet long, 30 feet wide, and 20 feet high. Two narrow doors in the middle of the house and a complete lack of windows minimize the intrusion of biting insects, but make the houses firetraps. On occasion, the Mehinaku deliberately burn abandoned houses and the resultant blaze is instructive. While the villagers watch, the house owner sets fire to some of the thatch at the base of the building. Within moments, white smoke pours through the wall, and suddenly an entire side of the house bursts into flame. Seconds later, the convection of air and heat turns the building into a blazing inferno. As the Mehinaku edge back from the wall of heat and flame, they consider what would happen if an occupied house caught on fire. "If the fire begins when the people are asleep," one of the villagers told me, "then everyone burns."

Less dangerous than house fires, but almost as frightening, are fires that are deliberately set to clear the villagers' gardens. The Mehinaku are slash-and-burn agriculturists who clear a plot of land in the forest, allow the vegetation to dry, and then set it on fire. The blaze sends up towers of white smoke that can be seen for miles. Once started, the fire is totally out of control. The villagers say that it is "wildly angry," and they tell myths of how men and spirits have gone to their death, trapped in the burning fields. This danger is more than fictional, since villagers have been badly burned when the wind shifted as they were firing their gardens. Dreams that link the white man to heat and fire thus associate him with one of the most frightening and destructive forces in the Mehinaku environment.

A second recurrent theme in dreams of the white man is assault. Villagers are shot with rifles, strafed from planes, pursued by trucks, and attacked with machetes. At times, as in the following dream of a young man, the assault is sexually motivated:

We were at the air force base, and a soldier wanted to have sex with my sister. He took her arm and tried to pull her away. We shouted at the soldier and at my sister. My aunt and I tried to pull her back. But the soldier was too strong for us. He was very strong. He said "If you don't let me have sex with Mehinaku women I will shoot you." I got a gun and shot at him, many times. But he was hidden and I couldn't see him.

Another dreamer described a similar situation:

A Brazilian doctor tried to take away my sister. . . . "If you don't let me, I will kill you," he said. . . . He shot and killed my two brothers. I cried in my dream, and I cried when I woke up.

Assault, like fire and heat, has an especially potent role in the Mehinaku symbolism of fear. In comparing themselves to other Indians and to whites, the villagers invariably point out that they are a peaceful people. There is no word for war in their language

other than "many flying arrows," nor is there a historical record of the Mehinaku having participated in organized, armed violence. When attacked by the Carib-speaking Txicão tribe in the 1960s, they responded by cowering in their houses as arrows whistled through the thatch walls. After the chief sustained a serious arrow wound in his back, they moved the village closer to the Indian post in the hope that they would not be pursued.

Within the village, strong sanctions bar interpersonal violence. The man who lets his anger get the best of him is slurred as a *japujaitsi* (literally, "angry man," but also a species of nearly inedible hot pepper). There are no *japujaitsi* in the village, and in my year and a half residence in the community, I never saw a fight between men. As one villager put it, "When we are angry, we wrestle, and the anger is gone. When the white men are angry, they shoot each other."

The menace of white society is real to the Mehinaku because of the accounts they have heard at the Indian post about Brazilian atrocities against Indians. They know that in the recent past Indians have been shot, poisoned, and enslaved by bounty hunters and, during one particularly shameful period prior to the establishment of the present Indian agency in 1967, by some government employees working for the former Indian agency. They know, too, that their lands are insecure and that the boundaries of the Xingu reservation can—and do—change according to the whim of bureaucrats in Brasília. A road has already penetrated the far northern end of the reservation and has brought tribes in that area into violent conflict with white ranchers. There is thus good reason to be wary of the Brazilian. As in the case of fire, dreams of assault and aggression link the white man to very real sources of anxiety in waking life.

A final theme of fear that permeates the villagers' dreams is perhaps the most poignant. In many of the narratives, the dreamer expresses a sense of disorientation in dealing with the outsiders. The white men lack

comprehensible motivation and perform capricious acts of malice and violence. They distract mothers from their crying infants, they give presents and demand them back, and they kidnap small children. They lure a man to a distant Brazilian city, cut off his head, and send it back to his horrified kin. Disguised as Mehinaku, they tempt the dreamer to give up his life as an Indian, and urge him to accompany them to distant cities from which he will never return. A mother dreams of losing her young children to the outsider:

My children said they would go to visit the Brazilians. They said they would go to São Paulo and Rio de Janeiro, and Cuiabá. I told them not to go. But they went, far off. We waited a long time, but they did not come back. I went to find them, but I could not. My mother's sister came to help me, and we looked all over. Then I heard them crying from a far way off, but still I could not find them. Then, I awoke.

Some of the dreams border on the Kafkaesque:

A guard pointed a gun at me. He told me to go through a door. I did. The room was filled with a beautiful light. The guard gave me a watch and told me I could come out at a certain time. He locked the door. I looked at the watch, and I realized I did not know how to tell time. There was a wind and a strange smell.

The confused portrayal of the white man stems from the Mehinaku's distorted view of Brazilian life. To the villagers, everyday Brazilian conduct and ordinary material objects are both alluring and strange. Tape recorders, radios, cameras, and other gadgets sported by visitors to the Xingu reservation fascinate the Mehinaku but also perplex them. Even when these objects are dismantled and inspected, they don't give up their secrets. "Are the white men wizards?" I was once asked by one of the Mehinaku.

Those villagers who have visited São Paulo and Rio de Janeiro return home with the same sense of fascinated puzzlement. A young man, the narrator of the dream text above, spent a summer living with a vacationing upper-class family in the beach resort of Guarujá outside of São Paulo.

7. SOCIOCULTURAL CHANGE

He was intrigued and attracted by what he saw, but uncomprehending. The wealth of Guarujá seemed magically produced; certainly members of the family were not making their possessions with their own hands, as do the Xinguanos. On the same trip he saw impoverished beggars on São Paulo's streets, but once he was back in the tribe, most of his stories were about the magic and glitter of the city.

The outsider visiting the Mehinaku senses the gap of understanding in another way. Let a man arrive in the community and he is immediately questioned about his kinsmen. Does he have a wife? parents? sisters? Which of his kinsmen gave him his jacket? Was it his brother-in-law? The Xingu communities are kin based, and the questions are an effort to place the white man in the orbit of understandable social relationships. If he remains within the community, the villagers probe further, often by teasing their guest. His appearance, gait, name, and speech become the object of semihumorous (and often painful) ridicule. This period of hazing has been reported by many researchers in the Xingu, and its predictability persuades me that it is part of the effort to make the powerful outsider knowable. If he has weaknesses and can be hurt, then he is human and understandable.

The many years of friendly but superficial contact with Brazilians have not made the white man more intelligible to the Mehinaku. As of my most recent visit in 1977, none of the villagers was able to explain why the Brazilians had come to the Xingu forests. "The white man is here," the chief told me in all seriousness, "to give us presents." The economic and political forces that led the Brazilian government into the interior of the continent to construct bases such as the Indian post are mysterious to the Mehinaku. The Brazilians and their impersonal society seem nearly as bizarre and disjointed in waking life as they do in the villagers' dreams.

Mehinaku lands and culture remain largely intact, but a part of their inner tranquility has been laid to waste. Neither geographic isolation nor heroic efforts at protection could save it. Contact with Brazilian society has taken a higher toll than we might have anticipated. Certainly the Mehinaku have paid dearly for their steel tools, their cast-off clothes, and the other "gifts of civilization." By day, all appears well. But each night, we outsiders visit the sleeping villagers and haunt them in restless dreams.

Amazon Tragedy

White Man's Malaria and Pollution Imperil Remote Tribe in Brazil
Gold Lures Hordes of Miners Into Yanomami Domains, Despoiling Rain Forest
Erasing Memories of the Dead

Thomas Kamm

Staff Reporter of The Wall Street Journal

PAAPIU, Brazil—Malaria snuffed out Maike, a four-year-old Yanomami Indian child. Then alcohol, another scourge brought by the white man, turned the child's wake into a violent skirmish.

Yanomami funerals are highlighted by mock battles in which warriors of neighboring villages pretend to kill and eat each other by imitating the twang of bows and devouring huge amounts of food. Making a farce out of war, they give evidence of their friendly ties and shared grief over death.

But little Maike's ceremony went awry. Instead of eating their traditional mashed bananas, the Indians gorged themselves on an alcoholic brew laced with disinfectant stolen from a nearby infirmary. Drunken men came to blows, and several youths tried to rape a pre-adolescent girl.

Perverted Rituals

"The whole ritual framework has exploded and been perverted," laments Bruce Albert, a French anthropologist. He has spent more than a dozen years studying the Yanomami, or Yanomamo as they are sometimes called, a 9,000-member tribe that lives on both sides of Brazil's border with Venezuela. Yanomami ceremonies, says Mr. Albert, have become excuses to "express all their anguish and trauma" over the

sudden intrusion of 45,000 prospectors into their once-unspoiled domain.

Considered the last major Stone Age tribe of the Amazon, the Indians were made famous 20 years ago by anthropologist Napoleon Chagnon's best-selling book, "Yanomamo: The Fierce People," which described their fighting skills and culture.

Because of their geographical isolation and their habit of greeting visitors with curare-tipped arrows, the Yanomami were able to escape the outside world's epidemics, alcoholism, and forced assimilation that decimated many other tribes.

But the conquest that began with Columbus's arrival in the Americas has finally overwhelmed them. Lured by huge deposits of gold, diamonds and other minerals in Yanomami lands, the prospectors, called *garimpeiros,* have invaded Indian reserves deep in the rain forest.

Today, the Yanomami are a sick and dying people, victims of disease and ecological damage brought by the garimpeiros.

"We have no hunting because the animals have left, and no fishing because the water is dirty," says Yadusse, a Yanomami in his 20s, sitting in a round, communal hut, called a *maloca.* The village of Paapiu, an hour's flight west by small plane from the city of Boa Vista, is close to a landing strip and an outpost of the Fundacao Nacional do Indio, or Funai, the state agency charged with protecting Indians. But signs of illness and malnutrition abound.

"The situation is catastrophic," says Patrick Aeberhard, who recently led a team from Medecins du Monde, a French medical group, on a tour of Yanomami territory. "Practically every Indian we examined has malaria, some also have tuberculosis, and one of every two children is undernourished. They look like African children: Their hair is turning blond, their stomachs are bloated, their arms and legs are spindly. If nothing is done in the coming month, they're all dead."

Attempts to investigate the full extent of the tragedy run into an unusual cultural barrier: The Yanomami wipe out every trace of their dead.

"A person who dies must be erased from memory," explains Mr. Albert. "Everything he owns is systematically destroyed. His crops are uprooted. They even go deep into the forests to find arrows he may have left behind. It's manic." This zeal extends to the deceased's remains. His body is strung to a tree until dry, then burned to ashes, and the remaining bones are crushed. After a period of mourning, the bone fragments are mixed with bananas and eaten by friends and relatives to preserve his spirit—the only act of cannibalism practiced by the Yanomami.

Another major obstacle to tallying their dead is that the Yanomami can't count. "Anything over two is 'many,' " says Marcos Guimaraes, a Funai doctor in charge of the medical emergency team. If questioned further, a Yanomami holds his hands together with fingers parted, and says *wahoro,* meaning many, placing emphasis on the last syllable to indicate the number is great.

And then there is the Yanomami fear that they will become victims of sorcery if they pronounce the names of dead people from other families. To overcome their phobia, Mr. Albert, the anthropologist, has to take aside a few tribe members he knows well and gently interrogate them about fatalities in their villages.

"I whisper a name, and they whisper back what happened, all the while looking [over their shoulders] to make sure no one is observing them," he recounts. "We have to go through incredible circumlocutions to find out what happened."

But the information he gleans is devastating. In the four villages around Paapiu, 32 of the 233 inhabitants have died since August 1987—a mortality rate of 14%. "It's as if 21 million Brazilians had died," says Mr. Albert,

BRAZIL

YANOMAMI TERRITORY

0   100

Miles

extrapolating the figure to the nation's total population. Worse, only eight infants of less than a year old are left in those Yanomami communities. "That's characteristic of a group on the verge of extinction," says the anthropologist.

In most other villages visited by medical teams, the proportions are similar. About 15% of all Yanomami have died since the gold rush began three years ago. Most of the victims are old people, the custodians of the Yanomami's oral culture, and children, the guardians of the tribe's survival.

A Natural Vulnerability

The Indians have no natural antibodies for the strain of malaria brought by the garimpeiros, because it was unknown to the area before. "Malaria is like AIDS for them," says Ivone Menegola, a doctor who has just returned from Paapiu.

Influenza, dysentery, measles, chicken pox and gonorrhea—other diseases which the Yanomami are encountering for the first time—also wreak havoc, doctors says. With many men lying ill in hammocks, tribes suffer from food shortages. And even able-bodied Indians can no longer find enough fish or game because of the worsening pollution.

Mercury, used by the garimpeiros to amalgamate gold dust and separate it from other particles, seeps into the rivers and contaminates the fish.

The din of the dredging pumps and the noise of the airplanes that service the miners' camps have scared away the wild boars, monkeys, tapirs, armadillos and the birds that the Yanomami traditionally hunt. "I crossed the forest without encountering any animals," says Dr. Aeberhard of Medicins du Monde, in stark contrast to his sojourn among the Yanomami five years ago.

Garimpeiro Protests

The plight of Brazil's Indians has fed charges that the government is intent on ridding the Amazon of its native peoples and opening these frontier lands to mineral exploitation. Faced with this sort of relentless pressure from Indian advocates in Brazil and abroad, the government has finally decided to protect the Yanomami. In the past few months, hundreds of policemen have been flown into the tribal zones to remove garimpeiros.

But the operation is meeting heavy

resistance. When the then Justice Minister Saul Ramos traveled to Boa Vista to survey the withdrawal in February, he was greeted by over 1,000 angry prospectors bearing signs like "Who will feed our families?" and "The Amazon isn't only for the Indians." They occupied Boa Vista's central square—dominated by a monumental statue of a garimpeiro that attests to the city's dependence on gold miners—and refused to leave until assured they would be given another place to work.

"I can't send the garimpeiros to Copacabana Beach," Mr. Ramos said afterwards. "I have to put them where the gold is."

His solution was to close down existing clandestine mines, and move the prospectors to virgin sites. But when the new zones also turned out to be lands claimed by the Yanomami, a top Indian-rights official who was overseeing the operation resigned in protest. A deputy public prosecutor then began legal action against the government for "clear violation" of Yanomami rights.

Meanwhile, with the disappearance of their traditional foodstuffs, many undernourished Indians are trekking to garimpeiro camps where they beg for sardine tins and sacks of rice and flour. This allows the prospectors and their allies to claim that far from rejecting them as the cause of their troubles, the Yanomami view them as friends and benefactors.

Everaldo Martins, a pilot who ferries garimpeiros and their supplies, argues that the Yanomami are being barred from access to "modern civilization" by environmentalists, anthropologists and missionaries. "Indians have a right to evolution, and a lot of ecologists won't admit this," says Mr. Martins. "They want to turn Indians into animals in a game park."

The New Prometheus

Mr. Albert counters that he and other Yanomami defenders "have no intention of preserving them in a glass jar." He adds, "What we want is that they have the means to survive and to choose the changes in their lives."

But protectors of the Indians acknowledge that their task is complicated by the fascination the Yanomami show for the 20th-century trappings brought into the area by the garimpeiros. Wondrous objects like radios and digital watches have transformed the white man into a modern-day Prometheus for many Indians.

According to a new revisionism that has seeped into Yanomami mythology, "the white people are good and [the Indians] want to make contact with them and get things like flashlights, knives and axes," says Father Joao Saffirio, a Catholic missionary and anthropologist who has spent 22 years with the tribe.

The reverence toward the white man's bounty was hammered home to Mr. Albert on a recent walk through the rain forest.

"The young Yanomami who was guiding me looked like a mutant," he recalls. Instead of the traditional skimpy loincloth, "he was wearing shorts, flip-flop [sandals] and diver's goggles. And while in the old days the guide would indicate traces of animals and explain how he hunted, this one was just pointing out white men's objects: 'Here the garimpeiros used to hide their gasoline,' or, 'Look, a pair of sneakers.' "

Bicultural Conflict

Chinese cultural traits conflict with those encountered in America, posing dilemmas for immigrant children

Betty Lee Sung

Betty Lee Sung, professor of Asian studies at City College of New York, is the author of many books and articles on Chinese immigrants in the United States.

The moment a child is born, he begins to absorb the culture of his primary group; these ways are so ingrained they become a second nature to him. Imagine for a moment how wrenching it must be for an immigrant child who finds his cumulative life experiences completely invalidated, and who must learn a whole new set of speech patterns and behaviors when he settles in a new country. The severity of this culture shock is underlined by Teper's definition of culture:

Culture is called a habit system in which "truths" that have been perpetuated by a group over centuries have permeated the unconscious. This basic belief system, from which "rational" conclusions spring, may be so deeply ingrained that it becomes indistinguishable from human perception—the way one sees, feels, believes, knows. It is the continuity of cultural assumptions and patterns that gives order to one's world, reduces an infinite variety of options to a manageable stream of beliefs, gives a person a firm footing in time and space, and binds the lone individual to the communality of a group.

The language barrier was the problem most commonly mentioned by the immigrant Chinese among whom I have conducted field research. Language looms largest because it is the conduit through which people interact with other people. It is the means by which

we think, learn, and express ourselves. Less obvious is the basis upon which we speak or act or think. If there are bicultural conflicts, these may engender problems and psychological difficulties, which may not be immediately apparent but may nevertheless impact on the development of immigrant children.

This article will address some of the cultural conflicts that commonly confront the Chinese child in the home and, particularly, in the schools. Oftentimes, teachers and parents are not aware of these conflicts and ascribe other meanings or other motives to the child's behavior, frequently in a disapproving fashion. Such censure confuses the child and quite often forces him to choose between what he is taught at home and what is commonly accepted by American society. In his desire to be accepted and to be liked, he may want to throw off that which is second nature to him; this may cause anguish and pain not only to himself but also to his parents and family. Teachers and parents should be aware of these differences and try to help the children resolve their conflicts, instead of exacerbating them.

AGGRESSIVENESS AND SEXUALITY

In Chinese culture, the soldier, or the man who resorts to violence, is at the bottom of the social ladder. The sage or gentleman uses his wits, not his fists. The American father will take his son out to the backyard and give him a

few lessons in self-defense at the age of puberty. He teaches his son that the ability to fight is a sign of manhood. The Chinese parent teaches his son the exact opposite: Stay out of fights. Yet, when the Chinese child goes to the school playground, he becomes the victim of bullies who pick on him and call him a sissy. New York's teenagers can be pretty tough and cruel. If the child goes home with bruises and a black eye, his parents will yell at him and chastise him. What is he to do? The unresolved conflict about aggressive behavior is a major problem for Chinese-American males. They feel that their masculinity has been affected by their childhood upbringing.

What do the teachers or monitors do? In most instances, they are derisive of the Chinese boys. "Why don't the Chinese fight back?" they exclaim. "Why do they stand there and just take it?" This derision only shames the Chinese boys, who feel that their courage is questioned. This bicultural conflict may be reflected in the self-hatred of some Asian-American male activists who condemn the passivity of our forefathers in response to the discrimination and oppression they endured. Ignorant about their cultural heritage, the activists want to disassociate themselves from such "weakness," and they search for historical instances in which Asians put up a brave but costly and oftentimes futile fight to prove their manhood. The outbreak of gang violence may be another manifestation of the Chinese male's efforts to prove that he is "macho" also. He may be

From *The World & I*, August 1989, pp. 670-679. Re-edition of Chapter 8, "Bicultural Conflict," from the book *The Experience of Adjustment: Chinese Immigrant Children in New York City.* Center for Migration Studies of New York, Inc.

overcompensating for the derision that he has suffered.

In American schools, sexuality is a very strong and pervasive force. Boys and girls start noticing each other in the junior highs; at the high school level, sexual awareness is very pronounced. School is as much a place for male/female socialization as it is an institution for learning. Not so for the Chinese. Education is highly valued, and it is a serious business. To give their children an opportunity for a better education may be the primary reason why the parents push their children to study, study, study. Interest in the opposite sex is highly distracting and, according to some old-fashioned parents, improper. Dating is an unfamiliar concept and sexual attractiveness is underplayed, not flaunted as it is according to American ways.

This difference in attitudes and customs poses another dilemma for both the Chinese boys and girls. In school, the white, black, or Hispanic girls like to talk about clothes, makeup, and the dates they had over the weekend. They talk about brassiere sizes and tampons. The popular girl is the sexy one who dates the most. She is the envy of the other girls.

For the Chinese girl, the openness with which other girls discuss boys and sex is extremely embarrassing. Chinese girls used to bind their breasts, not show them off in tight sweaters. Their attitude toward the opposite sex is quite ambivalent. They feel that they are missing something very exciting when other girls talk about phone calls from their boyfriends or about their dates over the weekends, yet they will shy away and feel very uncomfortable if a boy shows an interest in them.

Most Chinese parents have had no dating experience. Their marriages were usually arranged by their own parents or through matchmakers. Good girls simply did not go out with boys alone, so the parents are very suspicious and apprehensive about their daughters dating, and they watch them very carefully. Most Chinese girls are not permitted to date, and for the daring girl who tries to go out against her parents' wishes, there will be a price to pay.

It is no easier for Chinese boys. The pressure to succeed in school is even greater than for girls, and parental opposition to dating is even more intense. Naturally, the parents want their children to adhere to the old ways. Some children do not agree with their parents and have to carry on their high school romances on the sly. These children are bombarded by television, advertisements, stories, magazines, and real-life examples of boy-girl attraction. The teenager is undergoing puberty and experiencing the instinctive urges surging within him or her. In this society they are titillated, whereas in China they are kept under wraps until they are married.

The problem is exacerbated when teachers make fun of Chinese customs and the parents. I saw an instance of this at one of the Chinatown schools. A young Chinese girl had been forbidden by her parents to walk to school with a

Many Chinese immigrant parents walk their children to and from school, even as late as the junior high level. Some mothers come to the schools to feed their children lunch.

young Puerto Rican boy who was in the habit of accompanying her every day. To make sure that the parents were being obeyed, the grandmother would walk behind the girl to see that she did not walk with the boy. Grandma even hung around until her granddaughter went into class, and then she would peer through the window to make sure all was proper before she went home.

Naturally, this was embarrassing for the girl, and it must have been noticed by the homeroom teacher. He exploded in anger at the little old lady and made some rather uncomplimentary remarks about this being the United States and that Chinese customs should have been left behind in China. To my mind, this teacher's attitude and remarks could only push the daughter farther away from her parents. What he could have done was explain to the girl, or even to the entire class, the cultural values and traditions of her parents, so that she would understand how they thought and why they behaved in such a fashion. Putting down the parents and their customs is the worst thing he could have done.

SPORTS

The Chinese attitude toward sports is illustrated by an oft-told joke about two Englishmen who were considered somewhat mad. The two lived in Shanghai where they had gone to do business. In the afternoons, they would each take a racquet, go out in the hot sun, and bat a fuzzy ball across the net. As they ran back and forth across the court, sweat would pour from their faces, and they would be exhausted at the end of the game. To the Chinese onlookers standing on the side, this was sheer lunacy. They would shake their heads in disbelief and ask: "Why do these crazy Englishmen work so hard? They can afford to hire coolies to run around and hit the ball for them." The Chinese attitude toward sports has changed considerably, but it still does not assume the importance that it enjoys in American life.

Turn on any news program on radio or television, and you will find one-third of the air time devoted to sports. Who are the school heros? The football quarterback, the track star, the baseball pitcher. What are the big events in school? The games. What is used to rally school spirits? The games.

Yet in the traditional Chinese way of thinking, development of the mental faculties was more important than development of the physique. The image of a scholar was one with a sallow face and long fingernails, indicating that he spent long hours with his books and had not had to do physical labor. Games that required brute strength, such as football and boxing, were not even played in China. Kung fu or other disciplines of the martial arts did not call for physical strength as much as concentration, skill, and agility. In the minds of many Chinese, sports are viewed as frivolous play and a waste of time and energy. Add to this the generally smaller physique of the Chinese immigrant student in comparison to his classmates, and we do not find many of them on any of the school teams.

What does this mean to the Chinese immigrant students, especially the boys? On the one hand, they may think that the heavy emphasis upon sports is a displaced value. They may want to participate, but they are either too small in stature or unable to devote the time necessary for practice to make the school teams. If the "letter men" are the big wheels, the Chinese student will feel that his kind are just the little guys. But most important of all, an entire dimension of American school life is lost to the Chinese immigrant children.

Chinese-American students enjoy a break on the playground at Sun Yat Sen Intermediate School in New York City's Chinatown.

TATTLING

Should one report a wrongdoing? Should one tell the teacher that a schoolmate is cheating on his exam? Should one report to the school authorities that a fellow student is trying to extort money from him? The American values on this score are ambiguous and confusing. For example, in the West Point scandal a few years ago, most of the cadets involved were not cheaters themselves but they knew about the cheating and did not report it to the authorities. Their honor code required that they tell, but the unwritten code among their fellow cadets said that they should not tattle or "fink." If they had reported the cheating of their fellow cadets, they would have been socially ostracized. There is a dilemma for the American here as well.

This bicultural conflict was noted by Denise Kandel and Gerald S. Lesser in the book, *Youth in Two Worlds*, in which their reference groups were

Participation in sports—so heavily emphasized in America—frequently becomes a dilemma for Chinese immigrant students, who experience sharp contrasts in cultures when they come into contact with children from other ethnic groups in public schools.

Danish and American children. The Danish children, like the Chinese, feel duty bound to report wrongdoing. There is no dichotomy of consequences here. Authorities and peers are consistent in their attitude in this respect, and this consistency helps to maintain social control. The teacher cannot be expected to have four pairs of eyes and see everything. The parents cannot be everywhere at once to know what their child is doing during the day. If the siblings or schoolmates will help by reporting wrongdoing, the task of teaching the child is shared and made easier for the adults. But when social ostracism stands in the way of enforcing ethical values, an intense conflict ensues and contributes to the breakdown of social control.

DEMONSTRATION OF AFFECTION

A commonly voiced concern among Chinese children is, "My parents do not love me. They are so cold, distant, and remote." The children long for human warmth and affection because they see it on the movie and television screens, and they read about it in books and magazines. Because their experiences with mother and father and the other members of the family as well are so formal and distant, they come to the conclusion that love is lacking. In China, where such behavior is the norm, children do not question it. But in this country, where expressions of affection are outwardly effusive and commonly exhibited, they feel deprived.

This lack of demonstrative affection extends also to the spouse and friends. To the Chinese, physical intimacy and love are private matters never exhibited in public. Even in handshaking, the traditional Chinese way was to clasp one's own hands in greeting. Kissing and hugging a friend would be most inappropriate, and to kiss one's spouse in public would be considered shameless and ill-mannered.

Nevertheless, Chinese children in this country are attracted to the physical expressions of love and affection. While they crave it for themselves,

they are often unable to reciprocate or be demonstrative in their relations with their own spouses, children, or friends because of their detached emotional upbringing.

In the schools, this contrast in culture is made all the sharper because of the large numbers of Hispanics. In general, the Hispanics are very outgoing and are not the least bit inhibited about embracing, holding hands, or kissing even a casual acquaintance. The Chinese children may interpret these gestures of friendliness as overstepping the bounds of propriety, but more often than not they wish they could shed their reserve and reach out to others in a more informal manner.

On the other hand, the aloofness of the Chinese students is often wrongly interpreted as unfriendliness, standoffishness, as a desire to keep apart. If all the students in the schools were made aware of these cultural differences, they would not misread the intentions and behavior of one another.

EDUCATION

That education is a highly prized cultural value among the Chinese is commonly known, and the fact that Chinese children generally do well scholastically may be due to the hard push parents exert in this direction. None of this means, however, that these children do not experience a bicultural conflict regarding education when they see that the bright student is not the one who is respected and looked up to in American schools. Labels such as "bookworm," "egghead," and "teacher's pet" are applied to the intelligent students, and these terms are not laudatory, but derisive. When parents urge their children to study hard and get good grades, the children know that the payoff will not be social acceptance by their schoolmates. The rewards are not consistent with values taught at home.

Nevertheless, the Chinese immigrant high school students indicated in their survey questionnaire that they prized the opportunity to get an education. In fact, they identified the opportunity to get a free education as one of the most important reasons why they are satisfied with their schoolwork. Of 143 students who said that they were satisfied with their schoolwork, 135 mentioned this one factor. Education is not easily available to everyone in China, Hong Kong, or Taiwan. It is attained at great personal sacrifice on the part of the parents. It is costly and it is earned by diligence and industry on the part of the student. In this country, school is free through high school. Everyone has to go to school until sixteen years of age in New York, for example. It is not a matter of students trying to gain admittance by passing rigorous entrance exams, but a matter of the authorities trying to keep the dropout rates low that characterizes the educational system here.

This is ground also for conflict, however, since what is free and easy to get is often taken lightly. New York State's academic standards are lower than those in Hong Kong or Taiwan, and the schoolwork is easier to keep up with. As a result, there is less distinction attached to being able to stay in school or graduate. What the Chinese immigrant students prize highly has less value in the larger society, and again the newcomers to this country start to have doubts about the goals that they are striving for.

THRIFT

Twelve, perhaps thirteen, banks can be found within the small core area of New York's Chinatown. When the Manhattan Savings Bank opened a new branch in October 1977 it attracted to its coffers $3 million within a few months' time. Most of the large banks are aware that Chinatown is fertile ground for the accumulation of capital because the Chinese tend to save more of what they earn than other ethnic groups in America, in spite of the fact that their earnings are small.

Two major factors encourage the growth of savings among Chinese immigrants. One is the sense of insecurity common to all immigrants, who need a cushion for the uncertainties that they feel acutely. The other is the esteem with which thrift is regarded by the Chinese. A person who is frugal is thought of more highly than is one who can sport material symbols of success.

I was once sent on an assignment to cover the story of a very wealthy Chinese man from Bangkok who was reputed to own shipping lines, rice mills, and many other industries. He was a special guest of the United States Department of State, and that evening he was to be honored at the Waldorf-Astoria. I found this gentleman in a very modestly-priced midtown hotel. When he extended his hand to shake mine, I saw that his suit sleeves were frayed.

The value placed upon thrift poses acute bicultural conflict for Chinese immigrant children who see all about them evidence of an economic system that encourages the accumulation and conspicuous consumption of material possessions. A very important segment of the consumer market is now the teenage population. The urge to have stylish clothes, a stereo, a camera, a hi-fi radio, sports equipment, and even a car creates a painful conflict in the child who is enticed by television and other advertising media, but whose parents reserve a large percentage of their meager earnings for stashing away in the banks.

In school, the girl who gets money to spend on fashionable dresses and the latest rock record feels more poised and confident about herself than do her less materially fortunate classmates. She is also admired, complimented, and envied. In the Chinese community, on the other hand, a Chinese girl who spent a lot of money on clothes and frivolities would soon be the object of grapevine gossip, stigmatized as a less-than-desirable prospective wife or daughter-in-law, whereas praises would be sung for the more modestly dressed girl who saved her money.

From my students I hear a commonly voiced complaint about their parents as "money-hungry." They give their children very little spending money. They do not buy fashionable clothing; rather, they buy only serviceable garments in which the children are ashamed to be seen. The Chinese home is generally not furnished for comfort or aesthetics, so when Chinese children visit the homes of their non-Chinese friends and compare them with their own living quarters, they feel deprived and ashamed of their parents and their family. They certainly do not want to bring their friends home to play, and the teenagers may themselves stay away from home as much as possible, feeling more comfortable with their peers in clubhouses or on the streets.

The contrast in spending attitudes between the underdeveloped economy from which many Chinese immigrants have come and the American economy, which emphasizes mass and even wasteful consumption, is very sharp, and it creates many an unresolved conflict in the children, who do not realize that cultural differences lie behind it. They think that their parents value money more than they care for their children, and exhibit this by denying material possessions that give them pleasure and status in the eyes of their peers.

Credit is another concept foreign to immigrants from the Far East. If one does not have the money, one should not be tempted to buy. Credit is borrowing money, and borrowing should be resorted to only in extreme emergencies. The buy now, pay later idea goes against the Chinese grain. So the Chinese families postpone buying until they have saved up enough to cover the entire purchase price. This attitude is fairly common even when it comes to the purchase of a home. The family will scrimp and economize, putting aside a large portion of its income for this goal, denying itself small pleasures along the way for many, many years until the large sum is accumulated. To the Chinese way of thinking, this singleness of purpose shows character, but to the more hedonistic American mind, this habit of thrift may appear asinine and unnecessary.

DEPENDENCY

In her study, "Socialization Patterns among the Chinese in Hawaii," Nancy F. Young noted the prolonged period of dependency of the children commonly found in the child-rearing practices of the Chinese in Hawaii. She wrote:

Observations of Chinese families in Hawaii indicate that both immigrant and local parents utilize child-rearing techniques that result in parent-oriented, as opposed to peer-oriented, behavior. . . . Chinese parents maximize their control over their children by limiting their experiences with models exhibiting nonsanctioned behavior.

Analyzing and comparing the results of the Chance Independence Training Questionnaire that she administered to six ethnic groups and local (American-born) Chinese as well as immigrant Chinese, she found the mean age of independence training for American-born Chinese to be the lowest (6.78 years), while that for immigrant Chinese to be the highest (8.85 years). Among other ethnic groups in Young's study, the mean age of independence training ranged as follows: Jewish, 6.83; Protestant, 6.87 years; Negro, 7.23 years; Greek, 7.67 years; French-Canadian, 7.99 years; and Italian, 8.03 years.

Immigrant mothers exercise constant and strict supervision over their children. They take the children wherever they go, and babysitters are unheard of. They prefer their children to say home rather than go out to play with their friends. Friends are carefully screened by the mother, and the child is not expected to do things for himself until about two years beyond the mean age that a Jewish mother would expect her child to do for himself.

On the other hand, American-born Chinese parents expect their children to cut the apron strings sooner than any of the other ethnic groups surveyed. Young did not elaborate and explain why, but it seems that Chinese parents who are American-born have assimilated the American values of independence at an early age and may even have gone overboard in rearing their own children. There are areas of dependence and independence in which Young found divergence. The immigrant Chinese child is expected to be able to take care of himself at an earlier age, but he is discouraged from socializing with people outside the family until a much later age.

The extremes exhibited between the American-born and immigrant Chinese may be indicative of the bicultural conflict that the Chinese in this country feel. As children, they may have felt that their parents were overprotective; this was frequently mentioned by the teachers to whom we talked. We saw evidence of this in the elementary schools—the previously mentioned practice of mothers coming to the school from the garment factories during their own lunch hours to feed their children lunch. Many walked their children to and from school, even as late as the junior high level, but it was not clear to us whether the parents were justifiably afraid for their children's safety from the gangs or whether they were being overprotective. The teachers thought the mothers were smothering the children and restricting their freedom of action. By adolescence, the children must have felt the same. They were chafing against parental control over what they presumed to be their own business, while the parents thought they were merely doing their parental duty.

Teachers and parents do not agree on this score, with the result that parental authority is often undermined by a teacher's scoffing attitude. A personal experience of my own reveals how damaging this can be to a parent's ability to maintain some kind of control over the growing teenager.

My seventeen-year-old son was

Many adolescents in Chinese immigrant families chafe under parental control, considering their parents overprotective. Stylish dress and dating are two issues indicative of the bicultural conflict Chinese immigrant families experience.

Chinese immigrant mothers exercise constant and strict supervision over their children and do not expect a child to do things for himself until he is nearly nine years old—the highest mean age for independence training among all ethnic groups in America.

coming home late at night, and I found it hard to fall asleep until he was home. I did not feel that he should be up so late, nor did I wish my sleep to be disturbed. My son objected strenuously to a curfew of midnight during the week and 1 A.M. on the weekends. His objection was based on the fact that no other teenagers he knew had such restrictions, that most get-togethers did not get going until 11 P.M., and that he would be the "wet blanket" if he left early. I understood his concerns and tried to get the parents of his friends to agree to a uniform time when the group should break up and go home to bed. I felt that if everybody had to go, my son would not mind leaving.

To my utter surprise, not one of the parents felt that boys or girls of seventeen years of age should have a curfew. They felt that I was being too strict and overprotective and that it was time for me to cut the apron strings. The worst part of it was that my conversation with the parents got back to my son, who immediately and gleefully confronted me with, "See, none of the other parents agree with you. You are the only old-fashioned, strict one." This lack of understanding on the part of the other parents in telling my son about our conversation undermined my authority. From that day, I was unable to set hours for him anymore.

The Chinese value of respect for one's elders and for authority is common knowledge and needs no further elaboration here. We have already mentioned that the Chinese immigrant children encountering the disrespect accorded teachers and school authorities for the first time in American classrooms find themselves extremely upset and dismayed. In our interviews with the students, this concern was voiced frequently.

Challenging established authority has been a notable feature of youth culture over the past two decades. The parents, the teachers, the police, the government, the church—all authority figures in the past—have been knocked down and even reviled. Violence against teachers is the leading problem in schools across the nation. If students do not have respect for the teacher, neither will they have respect for the knowledge that the teacher tries to impart. The issue is a disturbing one, not only for the immigrant children but for the entire American society as well.

HEROES, HEROINES, AND INDIVIDUALISM

Who are the people who are praised, admired, looked up to, and revered? The idols of different cultures are themselves different types of people, and the values of a society may be deduced from the type of people who are respected and emulated in that culture. In the United States, the most popular figures are movie, television, and stage stars, sports figures, politicians, successful authors, inventors, and scientists; probably in that order. Who are the heroes and heroines of China? If we use literature as a guide, they are the filial sons or daughters, the sacrificing mother, the loyal minister, the patriot or war hero who saves his country, and revolutionaries who overthrow despotic rulers and set up their own dynasties. Even in modern China, the persons honored and emulated are the self-sacrificing workers who put nation above self.

Priests, ministers, and rabbis once commanded prestige in this country, but the status of these men of God has declined. In China, monks or priests have always occupied lowly positions. In contrast to the United States, in China actors were riffraff. Women did not act in the theater, so men had to play the female roles. Western influence has brought about changes in the pseudo-Chinese cultures of Hong Kong and Singapore and stage performers and movie stars are now popular and emulated, but this was not always so.

As a rule, Chinese heroes and heroines were people of high moral virtues, and they set the standards of conduct for others. In this country, the more sensational the exposé of the private lives of our national leaders or entertainment figures, the more our curiosity is aroused. How movie stars retain their popularity in spite of the relentless campaigns to strip them naked is very difficult for someone not brought up in the United States to comprehend. An old adage says, "No man is a hero to his valet." Yet, the very fact that American heroes and heroines survive and thrive on notoriety and self-confession can only mean that the American people admire such behavior. One might say, Chinese heroes are saints; American heroes are sinners.

Noted anthropologist Francis L. K. Hsu has written extensively about individualism as a prominent characteristic of American life. According to Hsu, the basic ingredient of rugged individualism is self-reliance. The individual constantly tells himself and others that he controls his own destiny and that he does not need help from others. The individual-centered person enjoins himself to find means of fulfilling his own desires and ambitions.

Individualism is the driving force behind the competitiveness and creativity that has pushed this nation forward. Loose family ties, superficial human relationships, little community control, and weak traditions have given the individual leeway to strike out on his own without being hindered by sentimentality, convention, and tradition. Self-interest has been a powerful incentive.

In contrast, Dr. Hsu contends, the Chinese are situation-centered. Their way of life encourages the individual to find a satisfactory adjustment with the external environment of men and things. The Chinese individual sees the world in relativistic terms. He is dependent upon others and others are dependent upon him. Like bricks in a wall, one lends support to the other and they all hold up the society as a whole. If even one brick becomes loose, the wall is considerably weakened; interlocked, the wall is strong. The wall is the network of human relations. The individual subordinates his own wishes and ambitions for the common good.

Dr. Kenneth Abbott, in his book *Harmony and Individualism*, also points out that the Western ideas of creativity and individualism are not accented in Chinese and must be held within accepted norms. One of the reasons for this is the importance ascribed to maintenance of harmony. Harmony is the key concept in all relationships between god(s) and man and between man and man. It is the highest good.

To the Chinese, the sense of duty and obligation takes precedence over self-gratification. It is not uncommon to find Chinese teenagers handing over their entire paychecks to their parents for family use or for young Chinese males to pursue a course of study chosen for them by their parents rather than one of their own choosing. Responsibility toward distant kin is more keenly felt by the Chinese than by other Americans. Honor and glory accrue not only to the individual but to all those who helped him climb the ladder. This sense of being part of something

greater than oneself gives the Chinese a feeling of belonging and security in the knowledge that they do not stand alone. On the other hand, individual freedom of action is very much restricted.

Some of the better known problems that confront a Chinese immigrant to these shores, such as respect for elders, modesty and humility, and male superiority, were omitted here because they have been dealt with at length elsewhere. The foregoing examples—aggressiveness, sexuality, sports, tattling, demonstration of affection, education, thrift, independence training, respect for authority, heros and heroines, and individualism—represent other important areas of bicultural conflict that confront Chinese newcomers to these shores.

ADDITIONAL READING

Francis L. K. Hsu, "Rugged Individualism Reconsidered," *The Colorado Quarterly*, vol. 9, no. 2, Autumn 1960.

_____ *Americans and Chinese: Reflections on Two Cultures and Their People*, American Museum of Science Books, New York, 1972.

_____ "Culture Change and the Persistence of the Chinese Personality," in George DeVos, ed., *In Response to Change*, D. Van Nostrand, New York, 1976.

Denise Kandel and Gerald S. Lesser, *Youth in Two Worlds*, Jossey-Bass, Inc., San Francisco, 1972.

Richard Sollenger, "Chinese-American Child Rearing Practices and Juvenile Delinquency," *Journal of Social Psychology*, vol. 74, 1968.

Shirley Teper, "Ethnicity, Race and Human Development," N.Y. Institute on Pluralism and Group Identity of the American Jewish Committee, 1977.

Nancy F. Young, "Socialization Patterns among the Chinese in Hawaii," in *Amerasia Journal*, vol. 1, no. 4, February 1972.

Inuit Youth in a Changing World

Richard G. Condon

Richard G. Condon is an assistant professor in the anthropology department at the University of Arkansas and a research fellow of the Center for Northern Studies in Wolcott, Vermont. He is researching a follow-up study of Inuit adolescent development in Holman Island in the Northwest Territories of Canada.

The rapid social changes that have taken place in the Canadian Arctic over the past 20 to 30 years have created a host of challenges and dilemmas for young Inuit. The members of this younger generation are coming of age during a period of fundamental change in northern society. A previously nomadic population has been concentrated into centralized settlements and towns, resulting in population growth and increased economic security. More Inuit are exposed to southern values through travel, schooling, television and radio. Because of all these changes, young people have grown not only more autonomous but have been able to delay the acceptance of adult roles and responsibilities. As a result the patterning and sequencing of traditional Inuit life stages has altered significantly, creating a prolonged adolescent life stage that has up until now been absent in Inuit tradition.

Few regions of the world have experienced such a rapid pace of development and change as the Canadian Arctic. Recognition of the strategic significance and resource potential of Canada's arctic regions has led to an increase in government and corporate involvement with the North and its residents. Such involvement has had both positive and negative consequences for young Inuit. On the positive side, the economy is more secure and schooling and advanced vocational training are more available, creating opportunities for young people that did not exist just 10 to 20 years ago. On the negative side, however, young people face the significant social and psychological stresses incurred by rapid social change, as they strive to find a place in this newly emerging social order. Many young people lack sufficient employment opportunities, are inadequately prepared for advanced high schooling and are unwilling or unable to relocate to larger northern communities where jobs are more available. These adjustment dilemmas have contributed, in part, to the high rates of alcohol and drug abuse, suicide and juvenile delinquency which are characteristic of Inuit teenagers and young adults throughout the North (*Report on Health Conditions in the N.W.T.* 1983:35).

INUIT YOUTH: PAST AND PRESENT

The world of today's Copper Inuit youth is markedly different from that of their parents and grandparents. In the past, young people not only made a rapid transition into adulthood, but faced predetermined roles and responsibilities imposed by the demands of a harsh and unproductive habitat. The Copper Inuit of the Holman region occupied one of the most marginal environments within Canada's Arctic. Gender roles were narrowly defined, and options were extremely limited. A young man could aspire only to be a skilled hunter and provider for his family; a woman could strive to acquire the skills necessary to be an expert seamstress and household manager. Gender roles were learned through observation of and intense interaction with parents and other adult relatives. Because residential units were small and infant mortality rates high, young people had no peers to draw them away from the socializing influence of their parents (Jenness 1922:163–164).

In the past, parents made marriage arrangements, especially for young women, when the child was an infant, and in some cases even before a child's birth (Damas 1975:409).[1] Parentally

From *Cultural Survival Quarterly*, 1988, Vol. 12, No. 2, pp. 63-66. Cultural Survival Inc., 11 Divinity Avenue, Cambridge, MA 02138. Reprinted by permission.

arranged marriage and child betrothal were most adaptive in a society in which prospective spouses were few and far between and in which female infanticide reduced the number of marriageable females (Balikci 1967:616; Damas 1969:53; Riches 1974:358). As a result, parents sought marriage partners for their offspring through kinship and alliance networks. Most young women married at or just before their first menstrual period, and began bearing children three to four years later.

Young men, however, faced a different set of requirements. They were not considered old enough for marriage until they had proven themselves capable as hunters and providers. Until a man could develop the skills and strength necessary to build a snowhouse or hunt large game unassisted, he was not considered mature enough to take on and support a wife. In chronological terms, he would not reach marriageability until around 17 or 18 years of age. He then went through a period of bride service, during which he joined his future father-in-law's household, often while his betrothed was still pubescent. During this trial marriage period, the young man worked with his father-in-law for three to four years until the young couple was considered mature enough to establish a separate household (Damas 1972:42, 1975:409).

The rather rapid transition from childhood to adulthood in traditional Copper Inuit society stands in marked contrast to the situation today. In the past, Inuit teenagers were raised exclusively within the context of small family groups and spent much of the year in isolated hunting/fishing/trapping camps where there were few, if any, activities to distract them from participating fully in assigned chores. Today, a large adolescent peer group dominates the recreational activities of teens. Young people now have a great deal more autonomy than they ever had in the presettlement era. When they are not in school, they pass much of their time with their peers, more often than not engaged in social rather than work activities. The increased economic security of contemporary settlement life now makes it possible for teenagers to delay taking on the roles and responsibilities of adulthood. As a result, young people now make their own decisions concerning when and who to marry, often only consulting minimally with their parents.

DEMOGRAPHIC CHANGES

As of the early 1960s, the Canadian government sponsored population concentration in the Holman region, which significantly altered the demographic profile and social/physical context of contemporary Inuit society. Prior to this program, the regional population resided in isolated, scattered hunting and trapping camps. Through the construction of government-subsidized housing and a school, the government created a regional center from which it could more effectively deliver health care and social services.

Most importantly, the creation of settlements contributed to the unprecedented population growth of Holman and other northern communities. In 1963, for example, the population of the Holman region was 135 (Usher 1965:72). Since then, the Holman population has increased to its present size of more than 350. At present, children and teenagers comprise more than 52 percent of the population. Several factors have contributed to the rapid population growth since the early 1960s: (1) the introduction of bottle feeding, which has shortened birth intervals between offspring;[2] (2) improvements in prenatal and postnatal health programs, which have lowered the Inuit infant mortality rate; (3) improvements in nutrition, which have probably increased fertility by eliminating periods of nutritional stress; and (4) increased economic security, which now makes it possible for parents to support larger numbers of offspring.

One result of these demographic changes is that the teenage sector is much larger today than it ever was in the past; settlement existence has provided the social context for a large, active adolescent peer group.

ECONOMIC CHANGES

Since the creation of the settlement, residents of Holman and other Inuit communities have experienced a degree of economic security unheard of in either the traditional period or in the immediate post-contact period. Many of the uncertainties associated with a subsistence level of existence have been eliminated by the availability of wage employment, social assistance payments and government-subsidized housing. The introduction of firearms (in the 1920s) and snowmobiles (in the 1970s) has allowed the Inuit to hunt game more efficiently and over a wider area. Most wage-generating and subsistence-hunting activities have become highly individualized, thus diminishing the amount of cooperation and sharing between households. Today's young generation of Inuit is no longer socialized within a value system that emphasizes the importance of mutual cooperation and sharing.

The shift from a predominantly hunting-oriented economy to one based upon wage employment and government subsidy is not without some complications. Although the available wage employment increases economic security, the relative shortage of local employment opportunities limits the income prospects for Inuit teenagers and young adults. The little employment that is available tends to be only temporary or part time. As a result, even older youths who would prefer to be working end up with a lot of free time. Even though young men could go out trapping or subsistence hunting, most display little interest in these activities because the high investment in time and energy far outweighs the return. The anti-trapping and anti-sealing campaigns waged by southern-based animal welfare groups also have undermined the economic viability of such pursuits in Holman and other Inuit communities (Wenzel 1985). Many of the young people interviewed indicated that they preferred high-paying and highly skilled occupations such as carpentry, heavy duty equipment operation, mechanics, welding, teaching and nursing.

SOCIAL AND ATTITUDINAL CHANGES

As Holman integrates with the outside world, its residents are exposed to southern lifestyles and behavioral standards. Much of this "attitudinal assimilation" is due to the introduction of formal schooling. The local school in Holman has been operating since the early 1960s and is staffed by southern teachers who use a predominantly southern Canadian curriculum. Since schooling is compulsory until age 16 (although, in fact, many students quit well before their sixteenth birthdays), children spend much of the day isolated from the socializing influence of parents and other adults. Thus, as expected, children learn more about the southern way of life than about their own cultural traditions. In addition, the Holman school has done much to create a whole category of individuals who, although physically mature, are chronologically labeled as teenagers (or schoolchildren) rather than adults.

In the fall of 1980, television was introduced in Holman and yearly school exchange trips to southern Canada were instituted. Both of these acculturation agents have increased young people's exposure to southern standards of teenage behavior, attitudes and expectations. Television is the most important source of increased knowledge and awareness of current events happening in the outside world. On the negative side, however, Graburn (1982) has gone so far as to suggest that television is a form of cultural genocide: it has reinforced use of the English language, disrupted social visiting patterns and contributed to a generation gap. Young people in northern communities have been profoundly affected by the assimilationist qualities of television programming; it has helped to alter their behavior, their outlook on life and even their language. The word *teenager*, in fact, was not used widely until *after* television was introduced in the community. Television not only is a window to the outside world; it is a window to the adolescent subculture of the US and southern Canada!

As a result of these demographic, economic and social changes in settlement life, parents and children interact much less than in the past. When children and teenagers are not attending school, they spend time with their peers. Many parents complain about this dramatic increase in adolescent autonomy, saying that they rarely see their teenage sons and daughters.

ASPIRATIONAL DILEMMAS

As Holman teenagers struggle to acquire the customs and values of Inuit society, they are also mercilessly inundated with the values, social expectations and behavioral norms of southern society. Exposure to southern value systems has raised young people's aspirations at a time when the northern economy is changing, but not expanding sufficiently to accommodate the employment needs of the new generation. Lack of local employment opportunities may partially explain the delay in social maturity among Inuit adolescents.

In school, young people learn within a value system that promises high-paying and challenging careers after high school. High schooling, however, is not provided on the local level; students must be prepared to spend three years attending the regional high school in the territorial capital of Yellowknife. Although an increasing number of young people in Holman recognize the importance of a formal high school degree, few have the skills to complete the required course of study. (It is not unusual for a ninth-grade student in Holman to discover, after taking the high school entrance exam, that he or she is operating at a fifth- or sixth-grade level of academic achievement.) In addition, the stress of being separated from family and friends, combined with the regimented life in the school's residence hall, simply adds to the students' sense of frustration and helplessness. As a result, many drop out after several months or even weeks. Many of those who remain cut classes or turn to drugs and alcohol, which are more readily available in Yellowknife than in Holman. As of the fall of 1987, only five

students from Holman had remained in Yellowknife long enough to complete their high school educations. The rest either did not try to attend or dropped out early, passing their time in Holman with casual work and hanging out with friends and peers.

Those Holman teens who are fortunate enough to receive either a high school diploma or vocational training often have to move to another community to find suitable employment, separating them from a close and supportive network of friends and relatives. As a small community, Holman does not have the employment base to support even a moderately sized work force; the young people who choose to stay in Holman have to settle for a combination of low-paying jobs and social assistance. The recent economic depression in the western Canadian Arctic, a result of the abandonment of oil and mineral exploration in the Beaufort Sea region, has made matters worse. With the promise of material wealth and job satisfaction unfulfilled, an increasing number of Holman's youth will turn to alcohol abuse, drug addiction and even suicide as a means of coping with their frustration. In addition, the lack of parental control and parental role models may further aggravate many youths' sense of alienation from the emerging social and economic order.

There is no doubt that further research, preferably of a longitudinal nature in a number of northern communities, is required to develop a full understanding of the wide-ranging impacts that rapid social change has had upon this new generation of Inuit. For example, many of the Holman youths studied in 1982–1983 have begun to raise families and assume important leadership and political positions within the community. How has their collective experience as a transitional generation affected their abilities to operate in a social environment increasingly oriented to the local control of political processes? Will recent settlement of land claims in the western Canadian Arctic and the subsequent creation of regional and village corporations increase local economic opportunities for young people in Holman and other small communities? Hopefully, as such economic and political opportunities become increasingly available, this transitional generation will find it possible to control the direction of their own lives and home communities.

ACKNOWLEDGMENTS

This research was conducted under the auspices of the Harvard Adolescence Project, directed by Professors John Whiting, Beatrice Whiting and Irven DeVore of Harvard's Department of Anthropology. Holman Island was but one field site in a larger cross-cultural study of adolescent development, which sent other post-doctoral researchers to Nigeria, Kenya, Romania, Morocco, Thailand and Arnhemland, Australia. The goal of the Harvard Adolescence Project was to collect comparable data on adolescent development from a sample of non-Western societies and, in so doing, assess the social and psychological impacts of modernization upon young people in these societies. These data are being published in a series of books by Rutgers University Press called "Adolescents in a Changing World." The first of these books, *Inuit Youth: Growth and Change in the Canadian Arctic* (Con-

don 1987), discusses adolescent behavior and socialization in the isolated Copper Inuit community of Holman Island.

NOTES

1. In traditional Copper Inuit society, as in most other Inuit societies, marriage did not imply the same legal, ceremonial or religious obligations as it does in Western culture. The term *marriage* is used here in a rather loose sense, for lack of a better word. A man and woman were married only after they had established a separate household and were recognized as husband and wife by members of the community. Even today, Inuit consider a young couple living together in a separate household married, even if they have not had a formal marriage ceremony.

2. Prior to the introduction of bottle feeding, Inuit mothers breastfed their offspring for three to four years, and sometimes up to five years (Jenness 1922:165; Graburn 1969:61). Recent studies have established that frequent and unrestricted suckling contributes to postpartum infertility (Kippley and Kippley 1977). For the Inuit, such prolonged suckling provided an ideal system of population equilibrium, whereby prolonged birth intervals maximized each child's chances of survival. With the introduction of bottle feeding in the 1960s, however, traditional birth spacing altered significantly, resulting in both a shortening of birth intervals and an acceleration in the livebirth rate (Schaefer 1959, 1973; McAlpine and Simpson 1975).

REFERENCES

Balikci, A. 1967. Female Infanticide on the Arctic Coast. *MAN* 2(4):615–625.

Condon, R. 1987. *Inuit Youth: Growth and Change in the Canadian Arctic.* New Brunswick, NJ: Rutgers University Press.

Damas, D. 1969. History, Environment, and Central Eskimo Society. In D. Damas, ed. *Ecological Essays.* National Museum of Canada, Bulletin 230:40–64.

——— 1972. The Structure of Central Eskimo Associations. In L. Guemple, ed. *Alliance in Eskimo Society.* Seattle: University of Washington Press.

——— 1975. Demographic Aspects of Central Eskimo Marriage Practices. *American Ethnologist* 2:409–418.

Graburn, N. 1969. *Eskimos Without Igloos.* Boston: Little, Brown.

——— 1982. Television and the Canadian Inuit. *Etudes/Inuit Studies* 6:7–17.

Jenness, D. 1922. *The life of the Copper Eskimos.* Report of the Canadian Arctic Expedition, 1913–1918, Vol. XII, Part A, Ottawa.

Kippley, S. K. and J. F. Kippley 1977. The Relation Between Breastfeeding and Amenorrhea: A Report of a Survey. *Journal of Tropical Pediatrics* 23:239–245.

McAlpine, P. J. and N. E. Simpson 1975. Fertility and Other Demographic Aspects of the Canadian Eskimo Communities of Igloolik and Hall Beach. *Human Biology* 48:113–138.

Report on Health Conditions in the N.W.T. 1983. Yellowknife, N.W.T.: Chief Medical and Health Officer, Government of the N.W.T.

Riches, D. 1974. The Netsilik Eskimo: A Special Case of Selective Female Infanticide, *Ethnology* 13:351–362.

Schaefer, O. 1959. Medical Observations and Problems in Canadian Eskimos, Part II. *Canadian Medical Association Journal* 81: 386–393.

——— 1973. The Changing Health Picture in the Canadian Arctic. *Canadian Journal of Opthalmology* 8:196–204.

Usher, P. 1965. *Economic Basis and Resource Use of the Coppermine/Holman Region, Northwest Territories.* Ottawa: Department of Northern Affairs and National Resources.

Wenzel, G. 1985. Marooned in a Blizzard of Contradictions: Inuit and the Anti-Sealing Movement. *Etudes/Inuit/Studies* 9: 77–91.

Back on the Land

Rejecting the comfort and security of settlement life, many of Canada's Inuit have chosen to return to the traditional hunting-and-gathering life-style of the Arctic

Bryan and Cherry Alexander

Bryan and Cherry Alexander are free-lance photojournalists based in England.

The five caribou seemed to sense the danger. They stopped grazing, raised their heads, and scented the air uneasily. Lying prostrate on a ridge of snow two hundred yards away, Augustine Taqqaugaq squeezed the trigger of his old and battered rifle. A shot rang out; the caribou began to run. One faltered, and then fell dead onto the ground. Taqqaugaq stood up and, brushing the snow from his caribou-fur clothing, walked back to his snowmobile, a smile of satisfaction on his face. He started the machine, revving the engine before setting off toward his fallen prey. By the time we reached it, what little blood that had spilled onto the snow had frozen, for this was early March and the temperature was minus thirty-six degrees Centigrade.

Taqqaugaq produced a pocketknife and set about skinning the caribou, a task he performed with remarkable speed. Within fifteen minutes, he had folded the skin and loaded the carcass onto a sled. The wind had picked up, and blown snow was snaking across the tundra. Taqqaugaq pointed to some

A group of hunters from the Iglurjuat winter camp take a tea break while out hunting.

small, narrow clouds near the horizon. "Maybe later there will be a storm," he said, as he pulled the starter cord of his snowmobile. After checking that I was firmly seated on the sled, he set off for camp.

"Camp" was at Iglurjuat on the west side of Steensby Inlet, Baffin Island. In March it didn't look like much, for the large wooden hut that Taqqaugaq had built was completely covered by snow. If not for some oil drums, a dog team, and a couple of snowmobiles, one would hardly have known it was there.

To describe the camp as remote would be an understatement. The nearest shop is the Hudson Bay Company store at Igloolik, more than a hundred miles away. That does not worry Taqqaugaq or the thirteen members of his family. Iglurjuat is their winter home, and has been since 1983 when, disillusioned with settlement life in Igloolik, Taqqaugaq and his wife took their kids out of school and returned to a life on the land.

The sound of our return brought Taqqaugaq's wife, Theresia, and several children out of the hut, all eager to see how we had fared on the hunt. The caribou carcass was unlashed from the sled and put up on a meat rack, while Theresia cast a critical eye over the skin. Keeping a large family in fur clothes means that she spends much of her time sewing skins. Back inside the warm hut, we removed our caribou-fur parkas and gradually thawed out over a mug of hot coffee. Theresia prepared a meal, putting walrus meat, a caribou haunch, and an arctic char, all raw, on a plastic sheet in the center of the floor. I joined the family as they gathered round to eat in traditional fashion, hacking off pieces of meat and fat with a knife and licking off any blood and fat that ran down their hands. Theresia's homemade bannock was one of the few concessions to white man's food.

Taqqaugaq's prediction of bad weather proved correct. We had barely finished eating when the plastic sheeting stretched across the hut's small window began to flap violently as the wind increased. Within minutes, blowing snow reduced the visibility to twenty-five yards. As darkness fell, Taqqaugaq called Igloolik and another outpost camp on his shortwave radio, his only link with the outside world. They too had wind—it seemed as though the bad weather was widespread. The evening was spent chatting and playing cards for matches by the light of a kerosene lamp. Luke, Taqqaugaq's son, won enough matches to keep his Coleman stove lit for the next year. It got late, and one by one the family stretched out to sleep on the communal sleeping platform that ran the width of the hut. As we settled down for the night, and the hut became quiet, I became very aware of the howling wind outside and was grateful for the snugness of the hut. "Maybe there will be fine weather tomorrow," said Taqqaugaq as he turned off the kerosene lamp.

This time his weather prediction proved optimistic. The storm raged for another two days, confining us to the hut, with odd brief excursions outside to collect ice. The hut was transformed into a busy workshop. Luke stripped

down one of the snowmobile engines on the floor; Theresia cut pieces of sealskin for a pair of *kamik* (boots) for her grandson; and the two teenage daughters spent most of the time entertaining the younger children or thumbing through magazines while listening to Dire Straits on a Walkman. Taqqaugaq began work on a soapstone carving of a walrus, first chipping away at the stone with a grub axe, and later using a file and a pocketknife for the finer details. The carving would eventually be sold to the cooperative in Igloolik on a trip to buy more supplies.

Apart from Taqqaugaq and Theresia, the only other adults at the camp were a son and daughter with their respective partners. The nine children ranged from their sixteen-year-old son Marc to a two-year-old grandson. Only one son, who works in a mine at Nanisivik, was not with them. Theresia has no regrets about taking the children out of school. "They learn more useful things with us out on the land," she explained. She plays many roles herself, including hunter's wife, mother, teacher, and priest, for the family are Catholics and she holds a service at the camp each Sunday. She also acts as camp midwife and delivered her two grandchildren, who were both born at the camp.

Though they spend most of the year at Iglurjuat, in the spring they move to another camp at Ikpik Bay to hunt seal. Later in the summer they move again to a camp where they fish for arctic char. Cash for their everyday needs is raised by selling skins—mainly wolf, arctic fox, and seal—either to the Hudson Bay Company or to the cooperative store in Igloolik where they buy their supplies.

When the hunting is lean, and in periods of bad weather, Taqqaugaq carves soapstone figures to raise cash. He is an extremely talented carver. From the sale of three carvings to the cooperative the previous summer, he was able to buy a new outboard motor for his boat.

DISINTEGRATION OF INUIT CULTURE IN SETTLEMENTS

Some of the sites of camps like

Iglurjuat have been used by the Inuit for four thousand years or more. Before the days of settlement living, camps were scattered right across the Arctic. Each northern community evolved its own seasonal cycle of life, following the movements of the animals they hunted from one area to another. Camps were formed at strategic points in good hunting areas.

Many of today's settlements in the Canadian north began with a trading post back in the pioneering days of the world-famous Hudson Bay Company. It was its role as the first trading company to establish itself in arctic Canada that gave rise to the joke that the company's initials stood for "Here Before Christ." In those days, it was acceptable to kill animals for their fur. Traders were anxious for every skin that the Inuit could provide.

The influence of the traders had a pronounced effect on the Inuit, who became no longer purely subsistence hunters, but came to be dependent on trading pelts. Missionaries followed hot on the heels of the traders, and after them came the administrators. Settlements began to be established, though many Inuit stayed at hunting camps. Hunger and starvation traditionally were always close at hand in Inuit life. Even as late as the 1950s, researchers found groups of Inuit starving in the Canadian north. Canada would not tolerate any of her people starving, and so the government began to pour vast sums of money into the north. Many Inuit were "persuaded"— and in some cases even forced—to abandon their traditional life at hunting camps for a more sedentary existence at newly formed settlements, housed in prefabricated bungalows. Many of these settlements were closer to a Hudson Bay Company store and a church than to good hunting grounds.

To begin with, all this seemed too good to be true to the Inuit: no more starvation, houses where heat and light came with the flick of a switch, medical facilities, and schooling for their children. None predicted the considerable problems to come. Large boarding schools were built in the main settlements like Iqaluit (formerly Frobisher Bay), and children from camps and small villages were sent to them to be educated and prepared for life in the modern Arctic. But insufficient jobs had been provided for the Inuit, and unemployment among the Inuit communities throughout the Arctic was high (in Igloolik, it is currently over 50 percent). The young Inuit found themselves caught between two cultures. Because they were away from their families so much during their formative years, they lacked the knowledge and skill necessary to become hunters. But the modern world had no work to offer most of them. They were faced with having to live on government handouts. In their frustration, many turned to alcohol, and later, to drugs.

By the late sixties, the Inuit culture seemed to be facing an inevitable disintegration. Some Inuit realized that living on government handouts in government settlements, with televisions and stores full of consumer goods and junk food, was doing more harm than good to many communities. An increasing number of families, disillusioned with modern settlements, gave up their homes and moved back to the old hunting camps, in what became known as the back-to-the-land movement.

THE OUTPOST CAMP PROGRAMME

To its credit, the government of the Northwest Territories decided to assist those Inuit who wanted to return to a life on the land, and in 1975, it introduced the Outpost Camp Programme. Operated by the government's Department of Renewable Resources, it provides families who want to return to the land with both financial and material help. Each camp is provided with a grant for materials to construct a small single-room wooden hut, gas for snowmobiles and outboard motors, and four gallons of heating fuel a day between September and May. Inuit can borrow a two-way radio and are provided with a basic medical kit. Loans are available to enable them to buy things like ammunition, tools, and other essentials to get started: after that, they are on their own.

Today, the Outpost Camp Programme operates in three regions of the Canadian Arctic: Inuvik in the west, Kiktikmeot in the central Arctic, and the Baffin region in the east. Some sites of traditional camps were never vacated, but many new camps formed as the back-to-the-land movement gathered momentum.

There is, of course, a certain irony in that the Canadian government, having spent millions of dollars over two decades to get the Inuit to move off the land and into settlements, is now paying for them to move back again. Critics of the Outpost Camp Programme initially saw it as throwing away money in an attempt by some nostalgic members of the Inuit commu-

The Taqqaugaqs make a journey of over a hundred miles to purchase supplies at the Hudson Bay Company store at Igloolik.

nity to turn back the clock. They have been proved wrong, even though some Inuit, mainly the young, did not take to camp life. After their initial enthusiasm waned, many young Inuit returned to the rock music, videos, and coffee bars of the modern Arctic settlements. Many, however, did stay, and new camps were formed as interest in the program grew. In the early 1970s, before the start of the program, there were only three camps left on Baffin Island. By 1986 that figure had grown to twenty-nine, and there were a total of seventy-three camps in the three regions of the Arctic where the Outpost Camp Programme was in operation.

The program peaked in the early 1980s. Now, although there are more camps, there are fewer Inuit out on the land. In the early days of the program, there were a number of what Bob Decker of the Northwest Territories' Wildlife Management Department describes as megacamps, which had up to sixty Inuit at any one time. Now camps tend to comprise smaller family groups, and usually contain no more than twenty people. One reason for this decline is that in the last five years, it has become much harder to live as a hunter, though not because of any change in the Arctic.

The biggest threat to the Inuit and their culture in recent years has come from the emotional outcry over Canada's annual harp seal cull. A campaign mounted by Greenpeace and other conservation groups, illustrated with gruesome pictures of baby seals being clubbed to death on the ice, brought such a public outcry that the U.S. government

banned all sea mammal products from its markets. Meanwhile, the European Economic Community took similar action, banning the import of all seal products. Inevitably, the market for sealskins collapsed.

During the 1970s, a good-quality sealskin might have fetched sixty dollars or more at a fur auction. In the spring of 1985, the average price of sealskins at one European auction was $3.68. The collapse of the sealskin market meant that hunting communities throughout the Arctic faced economic disaster. Welfare officers throughout the north believe that the result of the "Save the Seals" campaign was that many more native people were thrown onto the dole. The Inuit are understandably bitter, for they had nothing whatsoever to do with the commercial seal cull. They mainly hunt adult ringed seals, the most common seal found in the Arctic. They take relatively few harp seals, and they certainly do not club baby "whitecoats" to death. Understandably, the Inuit feel aggrieved that self-righteous people did not consider the north's native people and the important part seal hunting plays in their existence.

The Inuit have a tradition of looking after their environment. They point out that it was not the Inuit who decimated the Arctic's great whale population. Neither are they responsible for polluting the arctic seas. They have always been concerned with preserving the wildlife they depend on. They have agreed with government ecologists on quotas for hunting polar bears and musk-oxen. They also have agreed with the government to vacate outpost

camps if wildlife in the area is at all threatened—though this has yet to occur in the program's thirteen years of operation.

It is not surprising that Greenpeace is loathed throughout the Arctic, even though it halted its campaign against the fur trade (because, as one of its London spokesmen put it, "European cultures were again dictating to older cultures how they should live their lives"). Few people know that its campaign has ended; irreversible damage has already been done. In the north, memories die hard. In the Arctic, employment possibilities for native people are few. For most Inuit, the only real alternative to hunting is a life on the dole.

One of the most important things about the Outpost Camp Programme is that it gives the Inuit a choice. They no longer have to be part of the wage-earning community, and they can get away from the social problems of the settlements. Outpost camps also have the advantage of being in better locations for hunting and gathering food. Everyone contributes to the running of a camp, and by and large camps are relaxed and happy places. Above all, the Outpost Camp Programme is helping to preserve the Inuit culture. The children are able to travel with their parents and learn how to hunt and survive in the harsh Arctic environment. Camp life also cements the strong bond that exists between the Inuit and the land, and helps them retain their cultural identity. As one of Taqqaugaq's sons at the outpost camp at Iglurjuat told me, "When I am here, I feel like an Inuk; at Igloolik, I don't.

Easter Island: Scary Parable

The decline of a mysterious culture contains a stunning lesson for mankind. Its people nearly destroyed their habitat and themselves. Now their island's accidental name may be prophetic.

Louise B. Young

Louise B. Young has written about Earth's environment for more than 20 years. She holds a master's degree in geophysical sciences from the University of Chicago. Her latest book is "Sowing the Wind: Reflections on the Earth's Atmosphere." Two earlier books, "Earth's Aura" and "The Blue Planet," also dealt with Earth and its halo of vital gases.

Easter Island is a little mote of land set in the middle of the widest marine solitude, the emptiest extent of ocean there is in the world. It carries the ruins of a unique Stone Age culture that flourished here four or five hundred years ago. If we could have visited the island during the classic period of this civilization we would have seen a strange, dramatic sight. Along the forbidding coast line, crowning the steep wave-lashed cliffs, great stone platforms were erected, and on these ceremonial altars the inhabitants raised giant statues, carved from brown tuff, the porous rock formed of compacted volcanic ash. Many were capped with red stone topknots. Several hundred of these effigies dominated the scant 35 miles of shoreline. They stood 35 to 60 feet tall, each one weighing at least a hundred tons. Facing inward with their backs to the sea, the austere faces with pursed lips and hypnotic eyes made of white coral and black obsidian looked out with stern and melancholy gaze at

this tiny piece of the earth's surface, this triangular island pockmarked with the craters of great volcanoes.

The statues seem to be guarding the land—but from what? From demons or the ravages of storms sweeping in from the sea? Or perhaps from the awesome forces that lie hidden deep within the earth itself and erupt in sudden violence, spreading incandescent lava across the land? If so, they failed to guard it against a less expected danger: man himself.

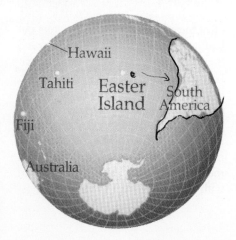

In Easter Island's tragic saga we can see many analogies to the problems faced by modern man. The whole earth is like a little island isolated in the vast seas of space. Its resources, though rich and various, are limited. And the increasing population of human beings is beginning to press hard upon these limits.

The identity of the people that settled Easter Island, and the meaning of

their great stone effigies, which are called *moai* in the native language, is still a mystery. The skill used in carving them and the building of the great ceremonial platforms (called *ahus*) suggests a higher cultural heritage than has been evidenced in any other island of the South Pacific. The people responsible for this work also had some knowledge of astronomy. Several of the *ahus* are so oriented that their façades face the rising or setting sun at the equinox or the summer or winter solstices.

A form of writing was also known, but the hieroglyphics carved on pieces of wood ("talking sticks" or *rongo-rongo* tablets) have never been translated. No other form of ancient writing has been found in Polynesia.

These are a few of the facts that suggest an origin different from the peoples who settled the islands farther west. There are some similarities to Inca culture, as Thor Heyerdahl pointed out. The precisely fitted stonework of the *ahus* is reminiscent of examples of ancient stone walls in Cuzco, Peru. Several forms of vegetation, such as the bottle gourd and sweet potato, are typical South American plants. Totora reeds like those that grow on Lake Titicaca on the Bolivia-Peru border, and which are used there to build reed boats, are also found on Easter Island. But the language and the physical characteristics of the natives are Polynesian.

Scientists have recently unearthed facts that only deepen the mystery.

From *World Monitor*, August 1991, pp. 40–45. Copyright © 1991 by Louise B. Young.

Several hundred of the many skeletons found on the island have been measured, X-rayed, and classified by anthropologists. They found distinct variations in the shape of kneecaps and pelvic girdles. These findings were interpreted as suggesting that at least two separate groups settled on Easter Island. That assumption has been challenged by other anthropologists and the question remains unresolved.

Another very interesting fact was discovered by scientists examining blood samples of the living Easter Islanders. An unusual characteristic showed up in these samples—a characteristic that is found in the blood of only one other population group in the world, the Basque people whose homeland is the northwest corner of the Iberian peninsula. It is hard to imagine how there could have been any connection between the Basques and Easter Island. But one possibility has been suggested. In the early 16th century a Spanish galleon carrying a large crew of Basque sailors was lost in these waters. Could some of these shipwrecked men have found their way to Easter Island? Science may soon have the tools to provide a definitive answer to these questions. DNA taken from samples of ancient human bones on the island could reveal the genetic origin of these peoples.

There is abundant evidence that in its original state Easter Island was heavily forested. Cores taken from the volcanic craters have revealed the presence of pollen from as many as 20 species of trees.

While many questions still remain concerning the origin of this culture, the circumstances that led to its destruction are now quite well understood. The sequence of events has been pieced together from stories handed down from generation to generation and confirmed by laboratory testing.

The story is of great human interest. It shows what can happen to a promising culture when population growth puts great stress on limited natural resources and fighting breaks out over the remaining supplies of food and fuel and water. Isolated from all other land masses, the inhabitants of Easter Island were entirely dependent on its own internal resources just as the environment of Earth itself, as it travels alone in space, is confined and limited to the natural wealth that exists here.

Easter Island is totally volcanic in origin. Like the Galapagos Islands or Surtsey off the coast of Iceland, it erupted in a cloud of smoke and fire from the bottom of the sea sometime in the last 50,000 years. And in subsequent years eruptions continued, altering the shape of the land. Geologists believe that the most recent one may have occurred within the last one or two thousand years. This volcano is known as Rano Raraku and it is from the rock at the heart of this volcanic cone that the great stone figures were carved.

The eruptions that created Easter Island were very violent in nature; the lava emerged with great explosive force, ejecting showers of "volcanic bombs" which lie in profusion across the rolling countryside. These bombs are made of porous black rocks, about the size of coconuts. They obstruct travel and are a disadvantage for agricultural development.

It is not surprising that this island bears so many marks of its volcanic origin. It sits squarely on one of the most active rift zones in the world—the East Pacific Rise. Here the earth's crust is moving at a faster rate than anywhere else on the planet. Two plates are separating from each other and new earth crust is being formed in the rift between them. At the same time the plate on which Easter Island rides is being subducted beneath the west coast of South America.

Easter Island is bathed by the cool Humboldt Current. The waters here are not warm enough to provide ideal conditions for coral growth; so there is no fringing reef like those that surround the shores of many South Pacific islands, no sheltered lagoon, no protected anchorage. The island, however, enjoys a favorable climate. Average temperatures lie in the ideal range between the high 50s and the mid 70s. And they vary only a few degrees between winter and summer. Rainfall is abundant, averaging 56 inches a year—almost twice as much as that which falls on the rich corn belt of the United States.

Given the physical characteristics of the island, one would expect to find a pleasant landscape with varied vegetation—many trees, pasture lands, perhaps fields of sugar cane, and blooming plants like those on similarly sited, volcanic Mauritius Island in the Indian Ocean. So it is surprising to find a desolate landscape covered with parched grasses. No streams, no lakes, no trees break the stark outline of the brown hills against the sky. It is a scene that bears the scars of the impact of man.

There is abundant evidence that in its original state Easter Island was heavily forested. Cores taken from the volcanic craters have revealed the presence of pollen from as many as 10 species of trees, including large deciduous trees, palms, and conifers. Many of these were useful to man: mahogany and the indigenous toromiro were both used for building purposes and for sculpture. The bark of the paper mulberry was used to make tapa cloth. Another tree, perhaps the coconut palm, yielded fiber for ropes and fishing nets. The nuts of the sandalwood tree were a staple of the early Easter Island diet, and its light-colored wood was much prized for its sweet fragrance.

But early inhabitants were so prodigal in the use of these resources that the island was gradually stripped of its forest growth at a time when the population was large and increasing. These factors are closely related not only on Easter Island but everywhere in the world. As more people must be supported, more land must be cleared to grow crops and more wood is needed as fuel to cook the food. The forests are cut down, erosion occurs, and the land becomes less able to yield abundant crops.

The soil of Easter Island, being of volcanic origin, originally contained important nutrients—lime, potash, phosphates. But this soil lies in a thin layer over very porous lava formations like a giant pumice stone. The abundant rain, falling on land without forest cover runs swiftly through the thin layer of soil, leaching out some of the essential ingredients and flowing down through the porous rock formation to the sea.

Tree roots in forested areas strike deep and are strong enough to crack the rock formations, gradually turning them into soil. The leaves of the trees break the impact of every shower. They hold the drops and little puddles, allowing it to drip softly down to the forest floor, so the soil can absorb it slowly. Trees shade the soil from the direct rays of sunlight, reducing the rate of evaporation and the land remains moist for a long period of time. As fallen leaves decay they become a soft, nutrient-rich mulch that slowly builds up into more soil. And the trees break strong winds that destroy tender young growth and further desiccate the land.

When Easter Island became stripped of forest growth it began to suffer from chronic drought, raked by the winds that sweep unimpeded over thousands of miles of open sea. Now less than an hour after every heavy shower the land is dry but the ocean all around the island is stained dark brown with the soil that has been carried with the rain out to sea. This influx of fresh water contaminated with eroded soil is a very unfavorable environment for fish and drives them away from shore.

The destruction of the forests on Easter Island, of course, did not take place all at once. It must have occurred gradually over several centuries. And this period of time seems to have coincided with the period when most of the great *moai* were carved, between the 14th and the 17th centuries. At that time the population must have been large to provide the manpower for carving and moving these enormous stone effigies. There are at least 500 of them on the island and it has been

estimated that a crew of 20 men would take almost a year to create each one. The manpower required to move one of these statues is estimated to have taken another crew of about the same size many months. The people of Easter Island did not have the wheel. They had no metal tools. For carving they used the basalt rock and obsidian, a volcanic glass that can be flaked into razor-sharp cutting edges. Although quite rare around the world, obsidian is found in abundance on Easter Island.

All of this work must have taken place in a highly disciplined and organized society. Since the island's food resources were not great even in times when it enjoyed a stand of forest growth, the work of planting, cultivating, and harvesting crops to feed a large population must also have been carefully planned and strictly carried out. It seems likely that a repressive society had evolved, with a small group of overlords and a large laboring class.

ANCIENT CLASS SYSTEM

These assumptions are supported by the stories that have been passed down from generation to generation of Easter Islanders. There were, according to these tales, two distinct classes of people: the Long-ears, the Hanau Eepe, who hung heavy ornaments in their earlobes stretching them almost to the shoulders; and the Short-ears, the Hanau Momoko, who did not engage in this practice. The Hanau Momoko were much more numerous than the Hanau Eepe, who represented a small privileged autocracy. The system, although dictatorial, worked well enough to provide sustenance for many people and countless hours of labor for carving and transporting the great stone *moai*. But as the population continued to grow, more trees were cut down to clear more land for agriculture. The moving of the *moai* required the use of long wooden poles to lever the heavy statues and to slide them over the rough terrain. Wood was also needed to build boats for fishing and for fuel to cook the food. More trees were harvested and all this time the land became less

fertile, more susceptible to periods of drought, less able to yield good crops.

At this time—about 1678, according to oral history—the ruling Long-ears ordered the Hanau Momoko to pick up all the volcanic bombs that lay strewn throughout the island and throw them into the sea. This new demand on their labor was the spark that fired the rebellion of the Hanau Momoko. All work suddenly ceased on the *moai*. Hundreds of them were left unfinished at the quarry and along the slopes of Rano Raraku. Stone tools were cast aside and still lie scattered there.

Then a terrible battle was fought on the hillside known as Poike Point. Excavations and carbon dating have verified the oral history of this brutal conflict. The Long-ears assembled on the promontory, which was surrounded on three sides by water. At the land side, at the base of the hill, they dug a series of trenches to protect themselves from invasion—a primitive Maginot Line. They filled the trenches with brush and logs, thus further stripping the forests. Their plan was to conceal themselves behind the piles of dirt thrown up by the excavations and to set the brush on fire in the event of an attack. But the plan backfired as such plans are apt to do.

A Hanau Eepe man who lived on Poike Hill had a Hanau Momoko woman working for him as a cook. She was loyal to her own people and sent them a signal when all the Eepe men were asleep. She led two bands of Momoko warriors along the shore around both ends of the line of trenches. A considerable force remained in front of the line, and at dawn they launched a frontal attack. The brush was set on fire. But Momoko warriors who had penetrated behind the lines attacked from the rear and drove the Eepe warriors into their own flaming trenches. Only one Eepe man survived. Allowed to live, he married a Momoko woman and had many descendants.

Recent excavations have found charred remains in the ditch. Carbon dating has verified a date of 1678, plus or minus a hundred years.

When the repressive regime was

wiped out the whole fabric of the society was destroyed and anarchy prevailed. The victorious Momokos broke up into tribal groups that turned on each other, fomenting almost continuous warfare. Families hid in the many caves that honeycombed the island or barricaded themselves in stone houses with doors so small that to enter them one must crawl on all fours.

Labor in the fields and gardens was dangerous and was considered degrading because all organized labor was associated with the time of autocratic rule. The food supply dwindled until it was insufficient to feed the considerable population that had survived. Cannibalism became widespread. Gnawed human bones found heaped in the caves of Easter Island bear witness to the scale of this practice.

For almost two centuries the conflict continued, becoming ever more violent as the food supply dwindled. During this time all the objects that had been held sacred were desecrated. One by one the great statues were toppled onto their faces and the ceremonial *ahus* were destroyed.

SOURCE OF SLAVES

The final tragedy occurred about 1860. During a three-year period Peruvian ships came repeatedly to Easter Island to capture and carry off slaves. They seized all the leaders of the community—the strongest men as well as those who could read and write the hieroglyphics on the *rongo-rongo* tablets. These were the guardians of whatever written knowledge remained concerning the origin and evolution of this culture.

Years later a pitiful little remnant—only 15 men—were returned to Easter Island. They carried with them small pox and tuberculosis. Epidemics swept through the remaining population, reducing it to only a few hundred. This was all that remained of a population of approximately 8,000 believed to have lived on the island during the height of the culture.

It was during these centuries of internal conflict that the first contacts with Europeans were made. In 1722 a Dutch fleet captained by Jacob Roggeveen visited the island on Easter Day and named it in honor of that occasion. An account written by Carl Friedrick Behrens, who was a member of the expedition, reported that the outward appearance of the island was not inviting: "parched-up grass and charred brushwood." A party of crewmen that went ashore were disappointed to find no sign of running streams or ponds to replenish the ship's supply. When asked for food, the natives produced sandalwood nuts, sugar cane, chickens, yams, and bananas.

CAPTAIN COOK'S ASSESSMENT

Half a century later Captain James Cook on his second voyage around the world found an even less inviting scene. Only three or four canoes could be seen on the whole island. "These were very narrow, built of many pieces sewed together with fine line . . . as small and mean as these canoes were, it was a matter of wonder to us where they got the wood to build them with; for in one of them was a board six or eight feet long, fourteen inches broad at one end and eight at the other; where I did not see a stick on the island which would have made a board half this size. . . ." The account of Captain Cook's visit gives the impression that the island had just suffered a serious major conflict. Straw houses had recently been burned and many fires lighted the skies at night.

A few years later a French mariner, Jean François de la Pérouse spent just eight to ten hours on the island, but in this short time he identified the reason for its poverty of natural resources. The inhabitants, he said, had been so imprudent as to cut down all the trees that had grown there in former times, leaving it fully exposed to the rays of the sun and the sweep of the winds. Trees do not grow again in such a situation, he observed, unless they are sheltered from the sea winds, either by other trees or an enclosure of walls. La Pérouse attempted to help the islanders amplify their small food supply. He gave them lambs, hogs, and goats as well as many seeds and tubers to start gardening. But the people were so improvident that they ate the animals before there was a chance for them to bear progeny. They were not willing to work at building protective walls for the young trees or cultivating vegetables.

In 1872 the young Frenchman, Pierre Loti, came as a crew member on a frigate that stopped at Easter Island. He was deeply moved by the tragic character of this tiny spit of land with its dying remnant of humanity. Loti, who became a prominent writer, felt instinctively that there was something sinister about the island. "The country seems an immense ossuary," he said. "Skulls and jawbones we find everywhere. It seems impossible to scratch the ground without stirring those human remains."

By the time of Loti's visit all the completed statues had been toppled. They lay on their faces where once they had stood proudly dominating the landscape. Only the unfinished *moai* where the carvers had thrown down their tools two centuries earlier still looked up at the sky with sightless eyes.

MORAL OF THE MOAI

Today forests all over the world are being cut down to make space for growing more food and to provide fuel to cook the food. In today's complex civilization trees are cut down for many special purposes in addition to the essential ones of food and fuel. To take just one example, a single Sunday edition of a newspaper with a circulation of 1 million requires the destruction of 15,000 trees. Around the world tropical forests are being destroyed at the rate of approximately 100 acres per minute. As resources become scarce wars are fought over the division of those remaining, and in the conflict more of the scarce resources are squandered.

An interesting analogy exists between the fire ditch at Poike Point and a defense plan used by Saddam Hussein. Trenches were dug along the border of Kuwait and oil was piped into them. The plan was to set the oil on fire at the time of an attack, thus providing an impenetrable barrier against the invading ground force. But as on Easter Island the plan failed. The Allied Forces set the trenches afire with napalm bombs well before the invasion. Alternative measures used by the Iraqis were more devastating but equally futile. They set on fire more than 500 oil wells in Kuwait in order to cloud the atmosphere with heavy smoke and ash, making aerial bombardment more difficult. More oil was pumped into the sea to foul the desalination plants of the Gulf states and cut off this source of fresh water. The almost incredible wanton waste of oil—this most valuable resource of the modern world—is comparable to the burning of trees (perhaps the last forest stand) in Poike Ditch. And the long-term effect on the environment, the climate, and the health of the earth casts its shadow far into the future.

But the most alarming part of the message that comes down to us from Easter Island is the way violence breeds more violence. Acts of cruelty become progressively easier to commit when they are reinforced by example and supported by tradition. On the other hand, acts of kindness and compassion can be reinforced in a civilized society. Human nature is complex, volatile, and impressionable. Capable of both good and evil, it can be influenced by life experiences. An education in violence uncovers the beast in the nature of humans.

There is, however, light at this end of the Easter Island story. The name Easter Island may have been prophetic.

A rebirth of life and a resurrection of the environment is beginning to occur here. Motivated by the lure of a tourist industry, the islanders and the Chilean government, aided by the United States, have gone to work. An airstrip has been built and several times a week commercial airlines bring in tourists. A number of small hotels have sprung up along the southwest shore. Plantings of trees and flowers around the hotels relieve the older stark landscape. Magnolia and hibiscus are thriving. Nasturtiums and tropical lilies in many bright colors grace the garden beds. Wild guava has been introduced and has taken over some of the open countryside. The fruit is eaten by birds who pass the seeds through their digestive systems and distribute them over a wide area.

Government agencies have undertaken the planting of trees along the mountain slopes. These are mostly eucalyptus, a fast-growing tree which is tolerant of dry conditions. But, unfortunately, it is not a favorable species for soil-building. Eucalyptus leaves do not rot; they lie in a smothering layer on the ground and discourage new growth.

There are also, however, several small groves of mahogany and coconut palms. The fact that they are doing well suggests that eventually the whole island may be restored.

In fact, Easter Island may serve as an example of how land that has been decimated can be returned to health and fertility. Conventional wisdom has held that once the forest has been stripped from the land a vicious circle of erosion and loss of fertility occurs and cannot be broken.

EASTER ISLAND'S HOPE

Recently, however, there is some indication that restoration can be achieved by hard work and intelligent land management. The first steps are the hardest because most seedling trees exposed to wind and direct sunlight all day cannot survive. They need some protection, such as a small stone wall, to provide some shade and to break the wind. These saplings need regular watering, cultivation, and weeding to prevent competition with other species. But as soon as the first trees attain a reasonable size, other species can take hold in their shadows. As the grove increases in size it begins to make its own environment. Litter builds up on the ground, acting as a giant sponge to hold the water and retard evaporation. The earth remains cooler beneath this litter, and the decaying leaves provide additional nutrients and soil conditioning for the young plants. Trees that bear fruit and blossoms attract birds that help to disseminate the seeds. Thus a positive cycle of cause and effect promotes the rebuilding of the environment.

Our understanding of these processes gives hope that the terrible last phases of the tragedy of Easter Island need not be repeated on Planet Earth. But the achievement of a proper balance between the natural resources and the population of mankind is a challenge that must be met soon in order to break the downward spiral leading to the depths of human degradation, and to speed the resurrection of the variety and beauty of the whole web of life on Earth.

Index

Credits/ Acknowledgments

Cover design by Charles Vitelli

1. Anthropological Perspectives
Facing overview—United Nations photo.

2. Culture and Communication
Facing overview—United Nations photo.

42, 43, 45, 46—Illustrations by Richard Gage.

3. Organization of Society and Culture
Facing overview—United Nations photo by S. Jackson.

84—Photos by Jason Laure. 94, 96—Photos by Christi Ann Merrill.

4. Other Families, Other Ways
Facing overview—United Nations photo by John Isaac.

115—Photo by Enid Schildkrout. 119—United Nations photo.

5. Sex Roles and Statuses
Facing overview—United Nations photo.

131, 133, 134—Photos by Longina Jakubowska.

6. Religion, Belief, and Ritual
Facing overview—United Nations photo by S. Stokes.

7. Sociocultural Change
Facing overview—United Nations photo.

194-197—Photos by Dr. E. Richard Sorenson. 221-223, 225—Photo by Paolo Galli/The World & I. 232, 234—Photos courtesy of Bryan and Cherry Alexander. 236—Map by Dave Herring.

ANNUAL EDITIONS ARTICLE REVIEW FORM

■ NAME: _____ DATE: _____

■ TITLE AND NUMBER OF ARTICLE: _____

■ BRIEFLY STATE THE MAIN IDEA OF THIS ARTICLE: _____

_____

_____

_____

_____

■ LIST THREE IMPORTANT FACTS THAT THE AUTHOR USES TO SUPPORT THE MAIN IDEA:

_____

_____

_____

_____

_____

_____

■ WHAT INFORMATION OR IDEAS DISCUSSED IN THIS ARTICLE ARE ALSO DISCUSSED IN YOUR TEXTBOOK OR OTHER READING YOU HAVE DONE? LIST THE TEXTBOOK CHAPTERS AND PAGE NUMBERS:

_____

_____

_____

_____

_____

_____

■ LIST ANY EXAMPLES OF BIAS OR FAULTY REASONING THAT YOU FOUND IN THE ARTICLE:

_____

_____

_____

_____

_____

■ LIST ANY NEW TERMS/CONCEPTS THAT WERE DISCUSSED IN THE ARTICLE AND WRITE A SHORT DEFINITION:

_____

_____

_____

_____

_____

*Your instructor may require you to use this Annual Editions Article Review Form in any number of ways:
for articles that are assigned, for extra credit, as a tool to assist in developing assigned papers, or simply
for your own reference. Even if it is not required, we encourage you to photocopy and use this page;
you'll find that reflecting on the articles will greatly enhance the information from your text.

ANNUAL EDITIONS:
ANTHROPOLOGY 92/93
Article Rating Form

Here is an opportunity for you to have direct input into the next revision of this volume. We would like you to rate each of the 45 articles listed below, using the following scale:

1. **Excellent: should definitely be retained**
2. **Above average: should probably be retained**
3. **Below average: should probably be deleted**
4. **Poor: should definitely be deleted**

Your ratings will play a vital part in the next revision. So please mail this prepaid form to us just as soon as you complete it.
Thanks for your help!

Article	Rating	Article	Rating
	1. Doing Fieldwork Among the Yąnomamö		23. The Global War Against Women
	2. Doctor, Lawyer, Indian Chief		24. Blaming the Victim: Ideology and Sexual Discrimination in the Contemporary United States
	3. Amazon Journey		
	4. Eating Christmas in the Kalahari		
	5. Are the Horrors of Cannibalism Fact—or Fiction?		25. A Primitive Prescription for Equality
	6. The Mother Tongue		26. Psychotherapy in Africa
	7. The World's Language		27. The Mbuti Pygmies: Change and Adaptation
	8. Language, Appearance, and Reality: Doublespeak in 1984		28. The Initiation of a Maasai Warrior
	9. Who's Interrupting? Issues of Dominance and Control		29. The Secrets of Haiti's Living Dead
			30. Dark Side of the Shaman
	10. The Blood in Their Veins		31. The Real Vampire
	11. Trading With the Eskimos		32. Rituals of Death
	12. The Yąnomamis: Portrait of a People in Crisis		33. Body Ritual Among the Nacirema
			34. Death and Taxes
	13. Mystique of the Masai		35. Why Can't People Feed Themselves?
	14. Life Without Chiefs		36. Growing Up as a Fore
	15. Symbolism of the Turban		37. The Transformation of the Kalahari !Kung
	16. Gauging the Winds of War		38. Has Success Spoiled the Sherpas?
	17. Memories of a !Kung Girlhood		39. Trouble in Paradise
	18. When Brothers Share a Wife		40. Dark Dreams About the White Man
	19. Young Traders of Northern Nigeria		41. Amazon Tragedy
	20. Child Care in China		42. Bicultural Conflict
	21. Society and Sex Roles		43. Inuit Youth in a Changing World
	22. A Matter of Honor		44. Back on the Land
			45. Easter Island: Scary Parable

(Continued on next page)

ABOUT YOU

Name_____ Date_____

Are you a teacher? ☐ Or student? ☐

Your School Name _____

Department _____

Address _____

City_____ State _____ Zip _____

School Telephone # _____

YOUR COMMENTS ARE IMPORTANT TO US!

Please fill in the following information:

For which course did you use this book? _____

Did you use a text with this Annual Edition? ☐ yes ☐ no

The title of the text? _____

What are your general reactions to the Annual Editions concept?

Have you read any particular articles recently that you think should be included in the next edition?

Are there any articles you feel should be replaced in the next edition? Why?

Are there other areas that you feel would utilize an Annual Edition?

May we contact you for editorial input?

May we quote you from above?

ANNUAL EDITIONS: ANTHROPOLOGY 92/93

BUSINESS REPLY MAIL

First Class   Permit No. 84   Guilford, CT

Postage will be paid by addressee

The Dushkin Publishing Group, Inc.
Sluice Dock
DPG **Guilford, Connecticut 06437**

No Postage
Necessary
if Mailed
in the
United States